SHITTY to HAPPY in 21 MINUTES

THE SECRET KINGDOM

SHITTY to HAPPY in 21 MINUTES

THE SECRET KINGDOM

Steve Hanks

Paperback ISBN: 979-8-9878999-3-9
Hardback ISBN: 979-8-9878999-4-6
Audiobook ISBN: 979-8-9878999-2-2
E-book ISBN: 979-8-9878999-1-5

Library of Congress Number: 2023904882

First paperback edition April 2023

Cover photo and cover design by Jim Jordan Photography
JimJordanPhotography.com

Graphic arts by Gabriel Campisi
GabrielCampisi.com

This book is dedicated to the young girl who asked me, "What is my purpose in life?"

STORYLINE

VOLUME ONE: *The Secret Kingdom*

Shitty to Happy in 21 Minutes: THE SECRET KINGDOM

INTERMISSION

ACT 10: Emotions Control Your World

INTERMISSION

ACT 11: Problems Are Golden

INTERMISSION

INTERMISSION

INTERMISSION

INTERMISSION

Prologue

A young girl asked me, "What is my purpose in life?"

I said to her, "Your purpose in life is…" I thought about it for a moment… "Your purpose in life is to be happy."

"That's it?" She was dumbfounded. *"That's my purpose in life? To be happy?!?"*

I hesitated for a moment. "Yes." And then I said it again, as if to convince myself, "YES." And then I triumphantly declared it one more time as if it was a spark of genius, *"YES!"*

****

Think of all the things you want…money, love, family… Why do you want them? *You want them so you can be happy.* You want money so you can be happy. You want a job, a career, a business so you can be happy. You want friends so you can be happy. You want a family so you can be happy. You want this, you want that…everything in life you want so you can be happy, is that right?

But what if you could be on a forever happy high even if you don't have those things? What if you could have an otherworldly peace that's beyond the ability of the human mind to understand, a peace that transcends this natural world, a peace that is not dependent on money, love, and family?

What if you could learn how to be happy, no matter what your past, no matter what your present, no matter what your future? What if there is a power that's simpler than anything you can imagine, a power that coerces you to live happily for the rest of your life, with no more worry and no more stress? Could it be that such a world power exists, and if so, wouldn't it be the greatest revelation ever known to man? Wouldn't it be the hidden secret of the ages?

Do you think if such a power exists, that it would be the most sought-after, priceless treasure more valuable than diamonds, emeralds, rubies, and fine gold? If there is such a treasure, then it has certainly eluded man's clutches since the beginning of time.

Oh but listen to me, I have GOOD NEWS—

I accidentally stumbled upon this power…I wasn't even looking for it, yet I ran headlong into it on a sunny summer California afternoon back in 1983.

Forty years ago I discovered this power that has eluded man since the beginning of time.

Forty years ago I discovered the most radical, prolific, powerful…dominant and supreme power that *force-feeds* peace and happiness into your heart. Yes, I said it *forces* you to be happy—even if for some strange reason you didn't want to be happy—*it's that powerful.*

Come with me on an adventure that very few folks dare to set off where you'll feel more peace and happiness than you ever dreamed possible, a world absent of worry and stress, a world where you'll learn how to heal a broken heart, a world where you'll have peace of mind in the midst of a thunderstorm, and best of all you'll see that you can live eternally happy, worry-free, and stress-free, and it's easier than catching herpes from a hillbilly hooker.

Why Are We So Messed Up?

Why do you feel anger instead of calm? Why do you lash out at people instead of loving them? Why do you feel brokenhearted instead of peaceful and happy? And what about worry and stress…how the heck do they magically overtake you so easily and effortlessly? Why are we such a whacked-out mess, and why is it so friggin' hard to fix it?

Over seven billion of us have mastered the art of *unhappiness, worry, and stress*. We're so good at it that we teach our kids how to do it, and they teach their kids how to do it, and so on. If we got paid $50 an hour for unhappiness, worry, and stress we could all retire and live *unhappily ever after.*

How would you like to turn that giant ship around? On this exhilarating adventure you'll take a wild ride from the village called *Hellsville* to the paradise called *Happydale.* You'll learn the ins, the outs, the ups, the downs, the sideways and front ways of this power that *force-feeds* happiness into your heart, and I'm talking about *forcefully…*yes, it *forcibly ramrods* happiness and peace into your heart, no matter how much you resist, no matter that your life is so shitty that when you play in a sandbox the cat tries to bury you.

Are you ready?

Let's start with how *not* to be happy. Here's some common advice from your friends when you're angry, worried, and stressed…advice that does *nothing at all* to fix your broken heart or that dreadful monster called *depression.*

Your Friend's Worthless Advice

How many times have you been depressed or upset when a friend says, "Just be happy!" Does that make you happy, or does it make you want to punch their teeth out? Or how about this one, "Just forgive your husband even though he's a douchebag." Nails on a chalkboard, that's what that sounds like. And how about this one, you've heard it, "Happiness is a *choice.* All you gotta do is *choose* to get over your mean boss and tiny paycheck and move on…it's easy!"

It's easy? Yeah, right, so is hopping on a pogo stick in quicksand.

Their hollow advice is true—yes, it's *unmistakably* true, but have you ever tried to "Just be happy!" when you're depressed? Can you honestly—don't lie to me—can you unwaveringly tell me you know *how* to "Just be happy!" no matter that your world crashes around you? Can you tell me you're strong enough to "Just be happy!" when you've lost your job, the dog died, your husband cheated on you, and Garth Brooks called to get the lowdown on your honky-tonk life so he can write his next hit song?

Listen to me, you know you *should* be happy no matter what goes on around you. You know you *want* to be happy even when the walls come crashing down, but be honest with me: Do you know *how to be happy* in the middle of a horrific situation that scares you half to death that makes you want to lay in bed all day and makes you so despondent there's no way out?

Your friend's advice is darn near *impossible* because when they say, "Just be happy!" or "Don't let it get to you"—it's good advice, it really is, but so is "Eat more veggies" to a 491-pound fat man at the donut shop as he drools over a box of double-dip cupcakes covered with sprinkles and honey glaze. It's excellent advice, it really is…*but how does a weakling such as I do it?*

Here's how *not* to do it—are you ready Twizzle Toes?

Willpower.

Willpower Doesn't Work

Your friend's advice is downright annoying because it depends on a strong *willpower* which most of us don't have. If you're anything like me your willpower is weak. If yours is strong great, but mine isn't. My willpower *has never* been able to make me happy. How about yours? Have you ever tried to *muscle your way* through depression, and anger, or anxiety? I have. It's as worthless as taking a leak on the Great Chicago Fire of 1871.

You Have a Secret Weapon

I have fantastic news for you. You have a secret weapon—a mighty weapon—a weapon that's exceedingly *more powerful than your wimpy little willpower*. It's simple. It's easy. It's dependable, it dominates you, and yet it works separately and independently from you.

This weapon *forcibly controls your thoughts*. That's great, but that's only half the battle. This power is even more electrifying than just to control your thoughts. *It forcibly controls your feelings*—your EMOTIONS.

****

Listen, your emotions are like vultures that sink their claws deep into your thoughts, and once they latch on, they've got you by the balls. You've tried to get rid of them, but you can't. You're too weak. They circle overhead menacingly before they swoop down and devour you like a dead carcass on a deserted highway in a hot Arizona desert.

Wouldn't it be nice if your emotions did what you told them to do? Well, get ready because this weapon does just that. It annihilates not only your thoughts, but *it controls and calms your awful feelings and painful emotions that sink their claws deep into your thoughts.* This powerful weapon obliterates and thoroughly destroys the bloodthirsty vultures of worry and stress, anger and despair, depression, and sadness.

I make a promise to you—I promise you that your anger, and worry, and stress…depression, anxiety, loneliness…unforgiveness, a crushed spirit, and a broken heart…*they will never again control you, nor hurt you, nor harm you* ever again.

I promise you that over the next few hours you'll learn how to annihilate worry, and stress, and anger, and your heartache that torments you and paralyzes you. I promise you—these evils will never plague you again for as long as you live.

"How" Is the Most Critical Word

I'll show you the power *how* to be happy. You heard me right, I said *how*. Not just that you CAN be happy and SHOULD be happy, but HOW to be happy.

You'll learn how to skillfully use this infallible, reliable, and simple weapon like a surgeon uses a scalpel, and when you set this laser-like precision power in motion, you'll trigger the force of peace so much so that you will never again fall prey to the misery of hopelessness that you can't pay your bills and your business dreams seem to take forever, or you helplessly suffer that agonizing feeling of desperation that you're trapped in a world of despair with no hope, or that empty feeling of loneliness that you're doomed to struggle with sadness and a broken heart with no end in sight.

I'll give you the cure. I'll give you the secret HOW *to be happy and live worry-free and stress-free every day of your life for the rest of your life!*

And not only will you learn HOW *to be happy,* but you'll also learn *why* it works and *how* it works. And you'll learn how *easily* it works. You'll see how simple this really is. This is all in volume one of this three-part trilogy *Shitty to Happy in 21 Minutes: THE SECRET KINGDOM.*

****

In volume two of this trilogy *THE EVIL QUEEN* I'll share with you the struggles and trials I went through as I evaluated the authenticity of this powerful secret weapon. I ran it through every obstacle course imaginable to test its veracity, and to make certain that it works in every situation so that I can fully trust its power; and to make sure that you can trust it too, so that you can be certain that it'll give you happiness and peace whenever you want.

You'll meet the person that taught me this unfailing power.

You'll learn how you can harness this power in your everyday life so that you can have more peace, happiness, and love than you could ever imagine.

And finally, you'll learn this peace and happiness open doors into everything you need, want, dream, and desire.

****

And I've saved the best for last. In volume three of this trilogy *THE GREAT INVASION* you'll learn how to salvage your broken relationships, your wayward kids, your nosy neighbors, the wild and wooly streets of your city, and how to mend the broken hearts of every man, woman, and child so that we can ALL live together in peace and harmony.

And finally, you'll learn how you can have the marriage that you've always dreamed of; a marriage so intimate, so overflowing with love that the two of you will feel like you have starring roles in the greatest love story ever told.

Oh…and one more thing I told the young girl. I said to her, "Once you've reached your purpose in life—to be happy—then your purpose grows. Your purpose expands for more than just for *you* to be happy."

I said to her, "Your purpose expands for you to share this glorious weapon with others so that they too, can be happy. And when everybody's happy…we have a huge-ass party."

Amen.

The secret to happiness all started with an accidental discovery that I stumbled upon on a sunny summer California afternoon in the summer of 1983.

****

BOOK ONE *The Secret Kingdom*

ACT 1: How it Began

Scene 1

Sucky Happiness Solutions

Throughout history men and women have searched endlessly for peace of mind and happiness. Men and women have written thousands of books and internet articles about happiness, peace, and joy.

Here's a rundown of a typical "How to be Happy" book. First, they describe in vivid detail how awful it is to be depressed, angry, and sad. Thank you, Captain Obvious!

Secondly, they tell us to dig deep to find the root cause of the problem. Find the root cause of the problem? You mean, like blame my mom and dad? Or blame society for my shitty life? *I don't care who caused it*—I don't care *what* caused it—*please just show me how to fix it!*

Thirdly, they tell us how wonderful and rewarding it is to be happy. They motivate us and inspire us to be happy. They tell us how vitally important it is to be happy…they tell us how beneficial it is to be happy…they describe the beauty of happiness without ever telling us *how to be happy* until finally—*at long last*—they get to the part on *HOW TO BE HAPPY*…ready for it? It's earth-shattering. It's mind-blowing. Get ready for it. Here it comes— "Just choose to be happy."

That's it?

That's IT? *Just choose to be happy?!?* Well, DUH on my part. Why the Sam Hill hell didn't I think of that!

They Leave Out the Most Important Part

Their emaciating advice makes me want to high five them in the jaw with a rickety wooden chair. Why? Because they leave out the tiniest of details. In fact, it's the most *important* detail. What is it? Think about it…

They never tell us HOW to "Just choose to be happy."

Nobody tells us HOW *to be happy*

****

Yes, the two Bobby's, McFerrin and Marley sang in the key of C, "Don't Worry, Be Happy." Thank you for singing the uplifting platitudes, but I don't know HOW to *Don't Worry, Be Happy.*

Yes, folks tell us we *should,* and they're right, we *should be happy.* But HOW?

And they tell us how great life will be if we're happy. Right again, our life will be terrific if we're happy. But *how* do we do it? How do we get there? HOW do we be happy?

Motivational speakers bellow, "You can be happy, you *must* be happy, *happiness is the key to life!"* They whip us into a frenzy. We burst with excitement as we drink in their stirring oratory, but the excitement is short-lived, like an orgasm that you soar, then you snore. Why? *Because they never explain to us HOW!!*

Make it clear to me. Explain to me HOW. Gimme the details.

Listen, I need a heckuva lot more than pep talks to make me happy. I need more than inspirational platitudes to make me happy. I need more than rah-rah motivational speeches to make me happy.

I need to know *how to execute that choice.*

****

I once heard of a happiness solution that I'm sure you've read something like it. Here it is. "Write your worries down on a piece of paper. Look them over carefully. Now, imagine that the pain leaves your mind as you crumple up the sheet of paper. Crumple it tightly into a little ball. Light it with a match and toss it in the trash can. As you watch it burn, slowly inhale *three deep breaths.* As you gently exhale, imagine your pain turns to ashes that blow harmlessly away."

Are you kidding me?? *Three deep breaths and watch the pain blow away?* That touchy-feely bullshit is as useless as sucking on a titty through a sweatshirt.

Why Can't ANYBODY Give Me the Answer *HOW to be Happy?*

"Three deep breaths" works if you're upset because you burned the dinner.

"Three deep breaths" works if the kids are late for school.

"Three deep breaths" works if the shower water turns cold.

But *"three deep breaths"* doesn't work for the mom who just got the news that she has cancer with only weeks to live.

"Three deep breaths" doesn't work when your gut is so twisted that you wanna throw up because you are worried sick about your life…or your heart is ripped wide open because your marriage just ended…or you want to die because you feel there's no hope left in the world.

"Three deep breaths" doesn't work for the soldier who comes home from the battlefield, his mind ravaged with the horrors of war and memories of his friends' mangled bodies with arms and legs blown off, even his own.

"Three deep breaths" doesn't work for the little girl left all alone in the world whose mom died when she was five, her father abandoned her, and she cries herself to sleep every night in the orphanage as she prays, "Please God, why doesn't anybody want me?"

I would push a peanut with my nose from Los Angeles to San Francisco if somebody could tell me in *those* times HOW to be happy and peaceful.

Somebody Please…Just Tell Us HOW to be Happy

Why do you read countless books and endless internet articles on happiness, but you still don't know how to be happy? Why do you visit a psychotherapist's office and use up a box of Kleenex, but he doesn't tell you *how to be happy?* Or sit in a Sunday morning church service, and after a rousing sermon here comes Monday morning and you *still* don't know *how* to be happy.

The fact is they emphatically tell us to *BE* happy, yes. *Everybody* tells us to be happy—but nobody tells us *how to do it*. Why not? Is it because they don't have the answer? Is it because they don't know how to articulate it? Why don't they give us the answer?

If you ask any of these folks *HOW to be happy* their explanations are often long and drawn out, convoluted, confusing, even perplexing. Even the experts offer up nothing more than languid platitudes and lazy clichés like "Just *choose* to be happy." After you muddle through all their twaddle, you're as frustrated as a blind lesbian in a fish market.

****

Somebody, anybody out there on the world stage…please tell us more than *how vitally imperative it is* to be strong, and happy. We *know* that already and thank you but tell us HOW!

And that we must *do everything within our power* to be happy and peaceful. I agree wholeheartedly but tell us HOW!

And that we must *decide to take control of our mind.* I agree with that too, but the same question is HOW?! *How* do we take control of our mind?

The church people tell us we need to "Trust God" to be happy. I wholeheartedly agree, but HOW? How do you trust God?

The choir sings, "Give it all to Jesus." I agree, but HOW do you give it all to Jesus?

It's all excellent advice, it truly is, and I don't dispute it. As a preacher's kid I heard my whole life to "Give it all to Jesus," but as hard as I tried to trust God and give it all to Jesus, I struggled like a constipated pregnant wife trying to poop, because *nobody ever told me how to give it all to Jesus!*…and all I got was an advanced case of hemorrhoids.

Please somebody…I'm begging you! *Please* give us a surefire practical solution HOW to be happy. HOW to have peace. HOW to get rid of stress and worry. Not just that we *should*...and *can*...but *how!*

****

If you're one of the lucky ones that already knows how to live life happily, with no worry and stress, then *keep doing what you're doing.*

But if you're tired of the struggle…if you're sick of the vice grip of worry and stress…if you simply want peace…then why not try this whacked-out, half-crazed, accidental discovery unearthed forty years ago by a demented young actor as he viciously screamed at God Almighty like a scathing sociopath on the sidewalks of Olympic Boulevard in West Los Angeles in 1983.

That afternoon as I freakishly disrespected and metaphorically pissed on God (and risked getting struck by lightning) that's the day I accidentally stumbled upon the simplicity and effectiveness of a mighty river of power.

I've no idea how it feels to get struck by lightning but I'm sure it's not a Swedish massage.

In this three-volume *Shitty to Happy in 21 Minutes* series—the first book is *THE SECRET KINGDOM,* the second is *THE EVIL QUEEN,* and the third is *THE GREAT INVASION.* In these three volumes you'll learn how to exploit that accidental discovery that I stumbled upon that sunny summer California afternoon in 1983 to skillfully dominate your emotions, and you will learn your breathtaking journey from *Shitty to Happy* takes *21 minutes!*

****

Now, let me explain something to you before you pee all over yourself that you get happy in 21 minutes. When you eat dinner, you're full. It takes about twenty minutes. You eat, get full, and feel satisfied, but then the craziest thing happens. You get hungry again a couple hours later, right? So, what do you do? Eat again. You don't just eat on Mondays and Fridays.

Ladies and gentlemen, you WILL get happy, peaceful, and calm in 21 minutes. *Every single time*. But then the craziest thing happens. You get hungry again in a few hours.

So, what happens? You eat. You get full of happiness and peace. But you get hungry *again*. So…what's the cure? The cure is the same as hunger: *When you get hungry you eat again.* Is that right? *You eat again. And then again. And tomorrow, and the next day. And again, and again, day after day, week after week, month after month.*

How often do you eat? How many times a day? How much food? That's up to you, but every time you eat, you're not hungry anymore, isn't that right? The same is true when you get happy in 21 minutes. You get full, but sure as shiggity you get hungry again. In fact, I promise you that the worry or anxiety, or whatever it is…it *will* come back.

How many times do you gotta fight it? *Every time you feel it.*

There're times I've had to fight it *seven times a day* if the storm is huge because it keeps coming back. There're other times I've only had to do morning and evening 21-minute sessions when things are going smoothly. There have been times in my life where I've felt so horrific that I've had to fight all day and into the night because the storm was relentless.

Peace and Happiness ALWAYS Show Up at Your Door

The good news is—no matter how relentless the storm, no matter how painful your emotions, no matter how often they return—you dominate them in 21 minutes. You will get relief from your thoughts and emotions in 21 minutes even if every voice within you screams (as it often does for me) … "This is stupid. It won't work. I don't want to do it." Just like you don't wanna brush your teeth, but you do it anyway.

You'll feel this remarkable power *forcibly pound peace into you* while every religious leader within three counties clamors vociferously that this book is heresy and will send you to hell. Oh yes, religious judgmental people will criticize you.

And best of all you'll learn how unbelievably *easy* it is. Yes, I said *easy,* as in *uncomplicated, effortless, and painless.*

You'll get such a wealth of knowledge about how *easy* it is to be peaceful and calm that by the time you finish this trilogy you'll be happier than a cucumber in a convent.

****

Scene 2

Secrets to Happiness

The secret to happiness all started with an accidental discovery that I stumbled upon on a sunny summer California afternoon back in the summer of 1983. My British racing green convertible was the ideal ride for Southern California. My younger brother gave me the keys and said, "Take over the payments." That seemed simple enough. How would I know that seven months later the bank would repossess it! (Banks do that when you don't make the payments.)

Several years earlier my acting career was on fire when Aaron Spelling cast me as a series regular in the starring role of the television series *B.A.D. Cats* with the beautiful Michelle Pfeiffer on ABC television on Friday nights at 8:00 p.m. The show aired at the same time as *The Incredible Hulk* on CBS, so if you never saw our show, you were watching the green giant, or you weren't even born yet because the year was 1980.

Soon after ABC canceled the series, I flew to Miami to play the starring role in a film about a giant crab that ate Key Biscayne. Over the next several months I appeared on all the Aaron Spelling shows that were on television at the time: *Charlie's Angels, T. J. Hooker,* and *Fantasy Island.* I was Daisy Duke's boyfriend on *The Dukes of Hazzard,* so I'm one of the lucky guys in the world that can claim to have kissed Daisy Duke.

Work was so steady that I didn't have time to spend the money.

Life was good.

But a couple years later, after no work in television and film, my local hangout was the Santa Monica unemployment office where I'd pick up my biweekly unemployment checks. What a demotion from starring in my own television series! I was dead broke, sleeping on friends' couches, couldn't get a job, no money to pay bills, and no money to make a car payment.

I felt angry, depressed, and discouraged, and to top it off, the battery in my green convertible had just died. It was so dead I couldn't start it even with jumper cables.

I had no money for a new battery, and certainly didn't have money for a tow truck. And on top of all that—I was still broken-hearted over my girlfriend that dumped me. I was devastated. My heart ached. I was discouraged. I was broken.

Life had gone from Happy to Shitty.

I slouched against the passenger side of my car and managed a limp-wristed wave bye-bye to the Good Samaritans, two adorable little old ladies with blue hair who were kind enough to loan me their jumper cables.

Anger at my lot in life started at the bottom of my feet and rapidly climbed up my body till it flew out my ears. Motorists and passers-by could see the escaping steam. I was not a pretty sight. My anger had hit climactic proportions…no, that's too mild. My anger was at critical mass, enough to sustain a nuclear explosion.

A friend and his wife were kind enough to let me sleep on their living room floor on a skanky throw rug underneath their rented piano in their tiny one-bedroom apartment in West Los Angeles, so in a huff I trudged back to the apartment.

During that four-mile trek I wanted to scream how mad I was that I was food-stamps-broke. I wanted to scream obscenities at the television industry. I wanted to scream how stressed I felt that I couldn't pay my car payments and couldn't shake the despair over my girlfriend. And you wanna know who I *really* wanted to blame? God. That's right. That's easy to do, ain't that so? He never argues. (You've *never* wanted to do this, right? Shut up, you know you have!)

Every Holy Book Instructs Us to Control the Tongue

Now, here's where this story gets interesting. Every holy book of every religion says to control your tongue when you're pissed off and angry. All the holy books—every one of them agrees: *Control your tongue.*

But who wants to control their tongue when they're imperially pissed and broken-hearted? I sure don't. That's the last thing—the very *last* thing you want to do. It's a whole lot easier to sling snotty and venomous cuss words, and whine and complain about 'woe is me' and 'my life sucks.'

But slow down Cowboy. Many of these holy books say that no matter how lousy you feel…no matter how bad your life is…no matter how discouraged you are…*still* you should control your tongue and speak how great and good God is. It's called *praise.*

I thought to myself, "If the Bible, the Torah, and other holy books say to speak praises when I'm madder than a wildcat with his ass hairs on fire then fine, that's what I'll do, but I'll speak those praises *with the anger that I feel!"*

****

This brings up a thought-provoking question. What words do you shout when you are angry? Do you scream profanities like "dammit" and "holy shit"? If you don't cuss, you might say "Oh NUTS." Or as my saintly mother used to say, "Oh fiddlesticks!" Fiddlesticks? Nuts? What do fiddlesticks, nuts, and "holy shit" have to do with anger? Really? Feces? —*Excrement?* Are you kidding me?!? What logic is it to shout, "Holy feces-excrement!" They're irrelevant words. You might as well shout, "Holy Czechoslovakia!"

And anybody that's acquainted with curse words, the F-bomb is their favorite. The word means "be fruitful and multiply." How does "Be fruitful and multiply" calm your anger? It makes no sense. It makes even *less* sense when you precede the F-bomb with "mother" …or follow it up with "off," right? (But it feels momentarily good, can I get an "Amen!")

Anyway, the question is…how is it relevant to scream profanities when you're angry? But you wanna scream *something* because when you're angry, fuming, and furious you *never* just sit quietly in a corner and don't say a word. Not unless you're trained to be stoically quiet by a bunch of stoners on a mountaintop in Tibet.

Be honest—you wanna scream cuss words! And you most probably have. (Don't look at me with that tone of voice like, "Who, me?")

Why Not Cuss with God's Words?

So, what could it hurt if I—rather than scream a *thousand irrelevant and meaningless cuss words*—instead, scream a *thousand power-packed praise words?* I wanted to cuss like Robert De Niro in *Midnight Run,* but on the other hand many of the holy books say to praise God, so I thought, "Here's what I'll do. I'll combine the two. I'll 'cuss' with praise words."

Brilliant idea. "Praise cuss words."

Every religion says control your tongue when you wanna smash the windshield of your broken-down green convertible with a sledgehammer, so here's what I'll do… I'll control my tongue, but I'll do it like this: I'll "cuss" like De Niro, but instead of F-bombs, holy feces-excrement, and fiddlesticks, I'll "cuss" with praise words.

PRAISE Words with a THUG Attitude

And so it was. On this sunny summer California afternoon in 1983 during the agonizing walk home I cut loose a ballyhoo of praise words…a barrage of heavenly braggadocios. However, I ripped through those words with the same fervor as if I was dropping F-bombs. Yeah, that's what I did.

Now listen, I've got to make sure you get this. I was furious. I was livid, yet the words I spoke were straight out of the writings of some of the greatest prophets ever known, like Moses, Solomon, and King David. You got that? I indeed spoke the words of these world-renowned prophets, but since I was angry enough to poke a hole in an elephant, I saddled their words with rancid insincerity and putrid cynicism. Consequently my words were not heartfelt. I was not sincere. In fact, I felt deeply *insincere.* I hissed those praise words with the venom of a viper. I drenched every word with my bottled-up poison and sarcasm, and I saturated them with all the bitterness and anxiety that I felt.

"Go to Heaven" Words with a "Go to Hell" Attitude

Let me give you a comparison of what I did. Let's say you're angry at your friend. Let's call him "Bob." You want to scream, "Go to hell Bob you sonofabitch!" Really? You called Bob a *male puppy of a female dog*. What the hell does that mean? Are they not irrelevant meaningless cuss words, like nuts, fiddlesticks, and F—you?

However, instead of "Go to hell you sonofabitch!"—you stop yourself dead in your tracks. Instead, suddenly…you scream at the top of your lungs, "Go to heaven you son of the living God!" Have you ever done that? I'll bet not.

It sounds crazy, right? To shout at Bob "Go to heaven," but say it meaner than a one-legged man in a butt-kicking contest…that's silly!

In the story of *The Strange Case of Jekyll and Hyde* all the townsfolk think Jekyll and Hyde are two persons—one generously good, the other hideously evil, but ironically they are *the same person* with two strangely different personalities. So when I scream, "Go to heaven, Bob!" with a scathing "go to hell" anger then I'm Jekyll and Hyde—one person with two strangely different personalities. My "Go to heaven" words are my *good personality*... My "Go to hell" anger is my *hideous personality*.

****

In your quest to achieve happiness, you gotta understand that you have two natures: two personalities. They both live inside you. You have a bad one and you have a good one. Johnny Cash quips, "Sometimes I'm two people. Johnny is the nice one. Cash causes all the trouble. They fight."

How about you? Have you ever noticed that your "Cash" tends to be stronger than your "Johnny"? —And every minute of every day, the two fight against each other to control you. So in exasperation you visit your psychotherapist, and you say to him, "Doc, quick, you gotta give me something, I hear voices arguing in my head." Dr. McQuack says, "Here, gulp down three Dirty Martinis for *crowd control.*"

After you finish your martinis, I'm gonna teach you a game.

****

This game that you're about to watch illustrates the tension that afternoon between my *evil personality* and my *good personality.* There are two players in the game: an angry husband and his livid wife. They're in a knock-down drag-out argument.

There are two rules of this game.

Rule number one: They must NOT say what they want to say. They must say the *opposite* of what they want to say. The angry husband *must give COMPLIMENTS* to his livid wife. In return, his livid wife *must give COMPLIMENTS* back to her angry husband. Even though they don't want to, they do it anyway. That's rule number one.

Rule number two: They must speak those compliments—listen carefully—they must speak those compliments *with the torrid anger and vicious attitude that they feel toward each other*. In other words, the rules of the game do not allow them to speak *kindly* or *sincerely* to one another. Not at all. The rules state that THEY ARE **REQUIRED** to speak the compliments to each other *with rabid bitterness and vitriolic hatred.*

To reiterate the rules of the game, this couple must not say what they feel like saying, but instead must speak compliments. And most importantly they must speak those compliments *with the rabid bitterness and vicious anger that they feel toward one another.* Got it? So here we go…and remember: *Vicious compliments!*

The Husband-and-Wife Scream Game

WIFE: "You are a son of a…" [STOP. The rules of the game do not allow her to finish her sentence with 'son of a bitch,' so instead she hisses in her most seething, angry tone of voice…] "You are a son of a most amazing father and mother any son has ever been raised by!" [**Round 1**]

HUSBAND: "You make me so…" [Remember the rules Ladies, he can't speak what he wants to, which is 'You make me so angry that I want to strangle you.' So instead, in his wild rage, he changes it to] … "You make me so happy to be married to you that I want to hug you and hold you tight!"

He winces at what he just said. [**Round 2**]

WIFE: "You are nothing but a…" [She can't say 'low-life, scumbag, loser of a husband,' although she would love to. So instead, she viciously retorts] "You are nothing but a successful, amazing, and perfect husband who takes care of me and is crazy in love with me, and you treasure me and treat me like a queen!"

She can't believe what she just said, but she wants to win the game. [**Round 3**]

HUSBAND: [He's stumped. What does he do next? He blurts out every man's dying wish…] "Make-up sex!"

WIFE: [Without hesitation] "Fine, I get top this time!" [**Game over, they score**.]

I'd say this couple just put the F-U in *fun.*

****

Is this a crazy game, or what? The man and his wife are pissed at each other. They're furious. Even so, in their quantum rage they force themselves to *speak loving words* to each other, but their loving words overflow with effusive hatred. There's a tug-of-war inside their head between their *complimentary words* and their *vile anger.* It's like the "Fight of the Century" in Las Vegas between two world-class fighters, except for the fight is *inside their head.* That's why Dr. McQuack prescribes three Dirty Martinis.

And then they have *drunk* make-up sex.

This was an actual fight my wife and I had soon after we got married. The results will *shock you!* I'll give you the details when you travers the raging waters of "How to Create a Perfect Marriage" in volume three *THE GREAT INVASION*. The episode with Bob was also an actual event I'll tell you about in volume three. The results of both episodes will shock you like you can't imagine, in a GOOD way.

Meanwhile Back at the Green Convertible…

Let's get back to my story. On that sunny summer California afternoon in 1983, I too had the "Fight of the Century" inside my head between two world-class fighters: my *good man* and my *evil man*. Listen to how it went down.

I *forced* myself to speak encouraging and inspirational words, just like the husband and wife. That's my *good man* Dr. Jekyll. And I spoke with an attitude that was *just like theirs*—nasty…putrid…and *sinister*. That's my *evil man* Mr. Hyde. Folks, my attitude was despicable, contemptible, and a hundred times angrier than Elton John at an anti-gay rally.

So, check this out. Rather than a litany of worthless cuss words like "shit" or "nuts" …and don't forget my mom's favorite, "Oh fiddlesticks!" …instead, I bellowed *God's words at him*.

BUT…

…I shouted the words at God with the same venom and nastiness as if I dropped a burst of F-bombs.

****

Here's the golden nugget I want you to grasp.

In the next few paragraphs, you'll read the praise words I screamed at God that day, but you'll notice that nothing in them sounds *genuine*. Nothing in me is *sincere*. To put it bluntly, I didn't "mean it"—I didn't *try* to mean it—and I didn't care that I didn't mean it.

*Nevertheless I determined to control my tongue with the words of the prophets…*so get ready, because what you're about to hear is the shouting match I had with God that sunny summer California afternoon in 1983, just like the shouting match between the husband and the wife that was so filled with venom and sarcasm, and just like nasty shouts at my friend Bob.

Brace yourselves, here we go.

My Screaming Match at God

With full-on bitterness I screamed at God, "Praise the Lord! Oh yessss, you are a mighty God, a powerful God, a wonderful God. You, oh great and mighty king, deliver the needy out of the dunghill." *So much sarcasm!* Like the husband to his wife.

I love that word *dunghill.* It's a funny word to me. It means "cow manure." And my pile was huge…I was in deep doo-doo. These praise words are a quote from King David, "God will deliver us from the massive pile of doo-doo," a paraphrase of Psalm 113:7.

God didn't say anything to me, so since he didn't reply, I charged full speed ahead with my recalcitrant rant.

I fumed just like the husband and wife as I mimicked their *nasty tone of voice* to shout at God about my car. Cover your ears kids, because here's what I *wanted* to say, "I hate my car. It's a worthless piece of shit." That's what I *wanted* to say. But instead, I fumed—just as nastily—the complete opposite, filled with bitterness and vitriol, "Thank you God, that my green convertible has a strong battery and runs perfectly, like a well-oiled machine." Moses heard promissory words like these in Genesis 17:5.

And then instead of "I'm so dead broke and can't pay my stupid bills," I seethed with a fake smile, "The blessings of God have come on me and overtaken me." That's a quote from that same Moses fellow in Deuteronomy 28:2.

God still didn't say anything to me, but undeterred I forged ahead.

****

As you can see, all these words are passages from the prophets in the Bible and other holy books; each one of them instruction manuals on *peace and happiness.*

I *forced* myself to speak praises even though they were the *opposite* of what I wanted to say, as did the husband and wife. Can you see that? My words were those of King David and Moses, that's for sure, but I drenched them in toxic acid, like the battery acid in my dead car battery. My attitude was angrified on steroids. I pierced those beautiful words with rancor and sarcasm.

It might not be a clever idea to have a *go to hell* attitude with God, is it? But I did it anyway cuz I was angrier than a soaking wet mule gnawing on a downed high-tension power line.

****

But I wasn't through, not at all. I walked a little faster and speeded up my words. By now I'm working up a sweat and having some psycho fun because I must admit that strangely, this feels as good as cussin'.

I reached into my back pocket and yanked out a cheap money clip that I bought from a Salvation Army store for $.89 plus tax; had scratches all over it and four sweaty one-dollar bills. I waved that tiny wad of cash wildly in the air and pierced the smoggy heavens of Los Angeles with these ugly sardonic shouts at God, "What a mighty God I serve. Oh, hell yeah…yeah, yeah, yeah…you're a God of abundance. Whoopee God…let it flow! Don't ever let it be said of my God, 'He doesn't supply all my need according to his riches in glory by Christ Jesus.'" The Apostle Paul declared that promise in Philippians 4:19.

Now remember, every holy book of every major religion teaches you the same self-discipline—*control your tongue*.

Can you see that's exactly what I did? *I controlled my tongue.*

But most people regardless of their religion—even though I controlled my tongue they're *horrified* at my despicable attitude. Some have even warned me, "Dude, you'll go to hell if you disrespect God like that." (*Atheists* said that to me…just kidding.)

But I was on a rollercoaster. My feeble acting career was next. Instead of "I'm so sick and tired of being out of work," I spoke the complete opposite as I mockingly wheedled him, "Hey God, anybody can see I'm the actor you've made me to be. Wheeeeee…look at all this work coming my way. Oh, how great you take care of me, O Great and Mighty One." These are King David's praise words found in the 23rd Psalm.

By this time I feel like Anton LaVey at a church picnic. My goodness, he's the founder of *The Church of Satan.* Geez, it sucks to have to explain a joke to you youngins.

God *still* didn't answer me.

Anyway, I've been striding lickety-split down Olympic Boulevard in West Los Angeles for about twenty minutes. I'm irreverently spewing bible words like a drunk frat boy on spring break in South Beach, but something strange…something *very strange* was happening inside of me.

You'd think lightning would strike me for my blasphemous and disrespectful rant, so I didn't expect to happen next what did happen to ever happen. Not in a million years. And to this day—forty years later—is the most crazy, ludicrous, miraculous, life-changing, divine intervention I have ever experienced.

That afternoon I accidentally unearthed THE authentic, transformational *happy force.*

This *happy force* revealed itself to me that day—this *happy force* appeared to me in full grandeur that sunny summer California afternoon in 1983 the day my green convertible died.

****

Scene 3

The Great Invasion

My praise cuss words were godawful venomous—my anger raged wildly out of control. I was a hot-ass mess. Consequently, I was oblivious to the unseen wonder that lurked in the shadows of my heart. I was blinded to the unfathomable presence that stirred deep inside me—a radical, upending force that would soon envelop me with the incapacitating strength of a mighty army. I barely felt this subtle power wind its way up from deep within my soul. I hardly even noticed it because of how crazed I felt from the anger.

Nevertheless, out from the depths of my fiery torrential rage there appeared a powerful energy. This energy moved with the ominous silence of a highly skilled Navy SEAL team that sweeps the beaches of enemy territory in the middle of the night. *This lethal force stealthily sneaked up on me.*

And just like the Navy SEALs without warning unleash their massive firepower on the sleeping enemy, this stealth force sneaked up on me and unleashed a massive firepower of *peace that passes all understanding* that completely caught me off-guard.

Peace engulfed me.

Peace flooded me.

This peace swept through me with the force of a tsunami and thoroughly annihilated my anger.

Within twenty minutes from the moment that I launched my savage attack with a deluge of rancid angry words, my enraged heart was conquered by a mysterious yet comfortable joy...a supernatural yet soothing peace…and an astounding and indescribable calm. My pissed-off anger was gone and nowhere to be found.

I thought to myself, "What the fuck just happened?!"

Scene 4

Revolutionary Transcendent Peace

Yeah, I know, I know, I could just as easily spell it f*ck, but when you spell it that way Jesus still knows what you're saying, and he thinks you're a pussy.

Anyway, let's do a play-by-play recap of what just happened.

I fan the flames of my anger with praise words that I speak viciously and venomously. Full of pure spite. And for a few wild and wooly minutes my infantile tirade tastes delicious as it feeds the ravenous beast of anger.

But the high-octane-fueled words do nothing to further infuriate the savage beast. On the contrary they do the complete opposite. Those biblical words, bristling with lethal anger, suddenly and unexpectedly—like a narc at a drug bust—whirl around and aim their firestorm of power *against me.* They arrest my anger in a cataclysmic blaze of destruction. After the smoke clears…*I feel peaceful*…and *calm*...and *happy.*

How could those angry words give me peace when I didn't mean them?

How could they make me feel calm when I shouted the words like a raging maniac?

How could they make me feel happy?

What is going on here? I was shocked to the core. Is this a cruel joke? Everything in me recoiled at what just happened. I was dumbfounded at how perfectly peaceful I felt when only twenty minutes earlier I was an egomaniacal jackass with a stinging rage that burned deep down in my soul.

I was shocked at how radically those words made me peaceful *despite my demonic attitude.*

I never expected the anger to disappear. It was an accident.

Yet this monumental force torpedoed my anger out of the water.

It was *unintentional.* It was *accidental.* Yet it *happened.*

My head was spinning…what is going on here? What just happened? Is this an abnormality? Is this an invasion from outside the space-time continuum? Is this a freak accident that peace invaded my heart even though my words were caustic, and my attitude was vicious?

But what if it's something else? Did I just tap into the supernatural? Did I just awaken a sleeping giant? *Did I just unlock a force powerful enough to overcome my anger to make me strangely peaceful anytime, anywhere, anyhow?*

My Discovery Was an Accident

You see, I had always believed that the words of Moses and King David have a preeminent requirement for them to make me happy. And peaceful.

What is that preeminent and universal requirement?

That requirement is that I must speak the words of these great prophets genuinely, and with heartfelt sincerity. I gotta *mean those words from the bottom of my heart.* That's what I believed…that *I must feel sincere.*

But that afternoon when I felt so angry over my messed-up life, my praise words were *not* sincere. They were not heartfelt. Not at all. Are you kidding me? How can you *mean it* and *feel sincere* when you're so angry and pissed off?

I didn't mean those words *at all.* I spoke those praise words with rabid bitterness and vicious contempt, just like the angry husband and his livid wife. I spoke those words with evil disrespect—*without a smidgeon of sincerity.*

Sincerity was the furthest thing from my mind.

Instead, do you know what scandalously ruled my mind? *Insincerity!* That's right. Pure disrespectful insincerity. Anger and wrath ruled my heart. *Anti-sincerity* ruled my heart. My only *sincerity* was that I felt *sincerely angry.*

And yet this strange and beautiful calm thoroughly engulfed me.

This strange and beautiful calm—dare I say—*forced* itself…yes, it *forced itself* into me.

****

Scene 5

Sincerity Is Twaddle

Let's think about this for just a moment. If sincerity (which you'll *never* feel when you're angry, hurt, and frustrated) is so vitally important for you to get peaceful and happy, then isn't it true that my irate, hot-blooded, poisonous praises were nothing more than empty words with no more power than a braying mule?

Well then, I have a question for you. If sincerity is so high-and-mighty special, how could my *insincere* words give me peace?

Great question, huh?

Here's the fantastical, amazeballs discovery—I had no sincerity to offer to the words. *Not a bit.* I offered no sincerity…no genuine feelings. *Nothing.*

But did it matter?

NO. Why?

Because…those *insincere words* gave their power to me.

Whaaat?!?

Yes, those insincere, nasty, putrefied words that I spewed so venomously into the smoggy heavens of Los Angeles surgically infused their life-giving power into me. The words gave their magnificent power to an angry and unemployed, broke, and discouraged young actor with a dead battery and a broken heart.

I didn't have power to give to the words. None. Not one teensy weeny little bit.

Now, listen to me carefully, and let this truth sink in deeper than a Jacques Cousteau underwater expedition.

I did NOT *need* to give power to the words. Why? Because…

The words…gave THEIR power…to me.

Pause for a moment…let that sink in.

My insincere words…gave THEIR power…to me

Could it be that even insincere, wickedly spoken praise words—in fact, let's give them a name—I'll call them *biblical cuss words.* Could it be that "biblical cuss words"—that is *praise words spoken with anger, bitterness, and contempt*—is it possible they have mystical powers to assault our evil nature, and thus, crush our sickening, gut-wrenching worry, stress, and anger?

Could it be that those words *intrude into our evil heart* so powerfully that they autonomously *force* us to have peace of mind?

Could it be that those insincere words *force* themselves upon us *even against our will?* They surely did to me.

Think about it. If those words *force* themselves into us so easily and effortlessly, if those words *force-feed* peace into our heart—even against our will, even in the middle of a shitstorm—then you and I…we have a genuine earth-shattering weapon to radically alter our emotions of anger, hurt, loneliness, and pain…a weapon that brings us peace of mind and happiness to our fragile and broken hearts no matter how worried, anxiety-ridden, or angry we feel! *And no matter how weak our namby-pamby willpower…!!!*

****

Thus began my dizzying forty-year quest through the horrendous depths of an earthly hell to the bewildering adventurous heights of an earthly heaven. Throughout these last forty years I have studied, tested, and evaluated what turned out to be the greatest gift I could ever give you, and it's this…

Your insincere praise words FORCE-FEED peace into your heart

Listen, for forty years I have rested my weary soul upon these insincere, yet mighty words. For four decades these insincere words have forced peace into me. They've never failed me. They have never…not even once…failed to *force-feed* peace into me.

Whenever I have spoken these words, every time, without fail, my heart goes from *Shitty to Happy in 21 Minutes.* But hold on, before you get too excited. *There is a thief that lurks in the shadows.*

Scene 6

World's Hoariest Cockblock

There's a menacing threat to this discovery that's been around for thousands of years. It has indiscriminately wrecked people's lives since the beginning of time.

Let me explain. People in every religion on every continent agree that if you speak these mighty words to fight your anger, you do well. You'll get peace. We see that *many holy books of many religions* agree that you should speak words of praise to control your pissed-off emotions because when you do, they force your body to do a turnaround and get peaceful and happy.

The Bible, the Torah, the Bhagavad Gita, the Quran, and others....listen to what each one proclaims: *Bhagavad Gita* means "Song of the Lord." *Quran* is "a book to be recited." Buddhism is about *Right Speech.* Each of these talks about *right words. Torah* is "a set of instructions from a father to his children." The Bible and the Torah both agree to "control your tongue." What do all these books have in common? —*Control your tongue with the words written therein.*

However, people in every religion attach an onerous restriction. It's like the fine print in a contract. That restriction is: *You must speak the words with a sincere heart.*

Have you ever heard that? Of course you have! Yes indeed, you must "mean" those words. You must speak them with heartfelt sincerity. You gotta *feel* it. You gotta "mean those words from the bottom of your heart."

But...What If You *Don't* "Mean It"?

What happens if you don't "mean those words from the bottom of your heart"? What if you're *not sincere?* What then? Well, according to religious folks the world over, the words are meaningless. They won't do you any good. They're the empty words of a cackling cockatoo.

But let's take it a step further. What happens when a crazed young man like me comes along and spews those words with a scathing, gangsterific attitude…like cuss words…like the husband and wife— "go to heaven" words with a "go to hell" attitude…what then?

Look out Jack!! Every religious person on seven continents unanimously agrees—*that* kid has gone beyond the pale. They unreservedly say, "The boy's hostile words are blasphemous! He mocks the Lord God Almighty! *How dare he mock the Lord God Almighty!"*

Well-meaning religious people and even non-religious people sincerely believe this. But what if their belief is *sincerely wrong?*

What if they're wrong!

You decide for yourself. You just heard the story…take a deep breath…you just heard the story of an angry young man with a nasty-ass attitude who dared to mock the Lord God Almighty with "cussin' praise words" …yet, despite the young man's devilish brashness and poisonous tongue there appears to him in full grandeur from out of nowhere *an invasion by the* ***Prince of Peace*** to comfort the young man's broken heart, and to bathe his angry soul with peace, calm, and tranquility.

The boy's hostile words comforted him and made him happy.

****

In the movie *Butch Cassidy and the Sundance Kid* the pack of skilled trackers aggressively pursue Butch and Sundance. The trackers don't give up. They are relentless and they just keep coming after Butch and Sundance. Robert Redford turns to Paul Newman, and exasperatedly asks, *"Who are those guys?!?"*

Well, let me ask the same question about those insincere words.

Who are those words?!?

I'll put it bluntly: *Those words* are like the skilled trackers that hunted Butch and Sundance. *Those words* didn't give up. They were unyielding. They kept coming after me and coming after me until they trapped my anger. They were persistent. They were relentless, and within twenty minutes *those words* performed a miraculous feat. They unleashed the fiery power of the **Prince of Peace**. The *Prince* appeared to me that afternoon, and even though I was a snot-nosed little kid with a rebellious pissy punk attitude he calmed my anger, quietened my stress, and gave me comfort.

The Prince of Peace relentlessly tracked me down and FORCED peace into my heart!

****

Oh…and another thing. God didn't shake his bony finger at me and strike me with a bolt of lightning any more than a mother would if her three-year old sticks his tongue out at her and screams, "I hate you Mommy!" A loving mother would never do that to her young child.

And neither did God do that to me. He didn't gobsmack me with a left hook to the nose for my insolent childish attitude. Not even.

Instead, as I spoke those words chock full of anger and frustration, he lovingly picked me up, carried me in his arms and laid me down in the shade underneath the coconut palms on the beaches of Bora Bora. He bathed my ugly soul with the soothing tropical waters of the French Polynesia, and in response my exhausted heart, my weary and broken heart cries out, "Thank you Lord, I love you."

A still small voice whispers, "You're welcome Steve, I love you."

Well holy cannoli with mashed guacamole…*God finally answered me!*

****

Scene 7

Ugliest Birthday Gift

That afternoon my words were not pretty. They were ugly, putrefied, and sinister.

But they were all I could offer. They were the best I had to give.

I had no sincerity to offer.

****

I remember back when I was a little kid when a cute little girl invited me to her birthday party. My mom took me to the store so that I could pick out a gift. We didn't have much money, but I was so excited I didn't care. I spent all night long wrapping my cheap gift.

The next afternoon my mom drops me off at the birthday party. The kids are eating cake and ice cream. They're playing games, and everybody is having fun.

Then it's time to open the gifts. All the kids gather excitedly around. The birthday girl carefully unwraps each present. I see all her lovely gifts, how pretty they are.

But I quickly notice something, and my heart drops.

My gift isn't as nice as all the others. Not even close.

I glance around at all the other kids, how they squeal with excitement as she opens each gift. I cringe with embarrassment as she gets closer and closer to opening my gift. I figure now would be a perfect time to go to the bathroom.

The moment finally arrives, and she opens my gift. All the other kids watch as she opens it. She tears off the wrapping paper that I worked on for so long. It feels like slow motion as my wrapping paper and red bow float to the ground. I have a pit in my tummy.

Then she does the unthinkable. She holds up my cheap gift for everybody to see! I hear the other kids snicker. My heart pounds. I look the other way. I'd rather be in hell with a broken back and colon cancer.

My inexpensive gift was all my family could afford.

But suddenly, with her vivacious smile and Disneyesque voice, she exclaims at the top of her lungs, "This is the most beautiful gift EVER…I LOVE this gift…it's *perfect* for me."

She runs over to me with her blonde curls bouncing, smiles, and gives me a huge hug and says, "Thank you Stevie Hanks for my wonderful gift." As she walks back to the table to continue to unwrap gifts, she turns around to me and mouths the words, *"Thank you for coming to my party."*

Whoa. Now I'm an excited seven-year-old, grinning from ear-to-ear! There is no way I expected the cute little birthday girl to appreciate my gift after I saw how beautiful all her other gifts were. I high-five the short kid standing next to me even though we didn't do 'high-fives' in 1960.

I wanted to run and hide that day at the little girl's birthday party, but she made me feel special and loved the moment she graciously accepted my cheap gift.

God Graciously Accepts My Cheap Gift

People bring their lovely gifts to God's party. The girls come dressed in their exemplary white dresses, the boys in their spit-shined shoes, and everyone's hair is perfectly combed. *Their gifts are beautiful.*

Me? I come to the party in a tattered flannel shirt, my pants have holes in them, and I smell like the corner of 5th and Main where the homeless guys piss behind the dumpster—which is where I wanted to toss my cheap gift when the other kids laughed at me. I'm ugly. I'm a mess. My gift is ugly. It isn't pretty like everybody else's, but it's the best I can do. It's all I can afford.

My words that sunny summer California afternoon in 1983 were my ugly gift to God. They weren't pretty like all the others who bring their "sincere" words to God. It's true that I controlled my tongue, but my words were *not* "sincere." My words were ugly. They were putrid. They were sinister.

But they were all I could afford. They were all I had to give.

And just like I never imagined the little girl would graciously accept my birthday gift the way she did, I never imagined God would graciously accept my ugly gift the way he did that sunny summer California afternoon.

That was many decades ago back in 1983.

Since that sunny summer California afternoon I have brought my ugly gift of putrid, sinister, and even hostile words to God thousands of times over the last four decades, and every time I bring my ugly gift to him, he graciously accepts it, *and my ugly gift executes the same lethal effect on my rancorous, angry, despicable emotions.* These nefariously spoken words *force* me to feel peace in a thunderstorm. They calm me, no matter how dreadful I feel. They *force-feed* peace into me no matter how worried and stressed I am, and they savagely pound happiness into me no matter how broken my heart.

And I unabashedly thank God that he accepts my ugly gift because I am a *weakling*. I can never be strong enough, or make myself sincere enough to get his peace, and joy, and happiness. I can't do it.

And yet every time, just like the cute little girl at her birthday party, God holds up my ugly gift for everybody to see! When the other party guests start to snicker, and when I want to run and hide, he turns to me and exclaims, "This is the most beautiful gift EVER…I LOVE this gift…it's *perfect* for me. Thank you, Stevie Hanks" …and then he turns to me and mouths the words, *"Thank you for coming to my party."*

****

The birthday girl's triple chocolate cake and vanilla ice-cream slathered with loads of hot fudge and mounds of whipped cream tastes especially delicious when she appreciates your gift. That's why I ate four…no, I ate five *huge* helpings.

Later that afternoon my mom picks me up from the little girl's house. I jump in the front seat of the Buick, and my mom asks me, "How did she like your gift?" My tummy feels queasy from all the birthday cake and ice cream, but I grinned big enough to show my two missing front teeth, and said, "She liked it."

My stomach felt like a meat grinder at high speed. I couldn't hold it any longer. I leaned out the car window and threw up chocolate cake and ice cream all over the little girl's driveway. It was more embarrassing than if I'd farted at her party.

"Are you okay, Honey?"

I screamed, "Drive Mom, DRIVE, let's get out of here before she sees me!"

THE ADVENTURE BEGINS…

Come along with me on a journey—an adventure—into a world of freedom. A world of emotional liberation where joy and peace are the norm, even in a crisis. Let's venture into a world of peace and happiness where fretting, anxiety, worry, and stress are weird, unnatural, and foreign behaviors, outlaw invaders that intrude into your heart.

When you enter this exhilarating world of happiness and peace, then your worry, stress, painful emotions, and broken heart become a relic of a long-ago past.

On that sunny summer California afternoon in 1983 I accidentally discovered the force that liberates you in your colossal struggle against the emotions of sadness, anxiety, worry, stress, and a broken heart.

I accidentally discovered HOW to be happy.

Come explore with me the depths of this accidental encounter, this colossal breakthrough, this remarkably simple discovery of a powerful weapon that awaits you to grant you peace and happiness whenever you want, even if you're like me—a snot-nosed little kid with an angry soul and a broken heart.

****

The young girl asked me, "What is my purpose in life?"

I answered her, "Your purpose in life is to be happy," and then added, "But remember, once you accomplish your purpose in life to be happy, then your mission grows. It *expands* for you to share this with others so that they can be happy too."

I found the power to be happy that sunny summer California afternoon in 1983 the day my green convertible died.

And now—forty years later—my mission expands to share with *you* how to be happy, live worry-free, and stress-free, and then to get all your beautiful dreams, goals, and wishes, and all the desires of your heart in this earthly life.

****

TAKE A BREATHER

Broadway plays have intermissions to give the audience a little break during the show. This trilogy is a monstrous undertaking to read from start to finish, which is why I strategically place intermissions throughout. It's important that you take the breaks that I've planned for you.

Here's your first one, so I suggest you take a little breather here. Not a long one, but take a quick walk, relax at your kitchen table, or run an errand before you dive into the next act. This trilogy gets more complex the deeper you dig, so take my advice: Take a break. I'll see you in a few minutes.

****

ACT 2: Why We're So Messed Up...And What's the Cure

Scene 8

The Evil Queen

Let's go back to the beginning, long before my wild and wooly discovery that sunny summer California afternoon in 1983 the day my green convertible died to see where anger, sadness, despair, worry, and stress originate from.

I was born in August of 1953 when Dwight D. Eisenhower was president of the United States. For the first thirty years of my life nobody taught me how to be happy, not even Dwight. I was a hapless victim held prisoner in the shackles of my excruciating emotions.

I've always known that stress, worry, fear of failure, and unforgiveness are poisonous emotions that damage you, they're unhealthy, and can even kill you, but how do we get rid of them? How do we replace them with peace? How do we get joy? *How do we be happy?*

And why is it that worry, stress, unhappiness, bitterness, resentment, anger, fear of failure, and a broken heart happen so *naturally*...and why is it that happiness, joy, and peace are so *elusive* even though they're immensely more attractive and pleasurable?

For centuries, people the world over have searched for *how to be happy.* They've sought the answers to *why is my life so miserable.* What causes it? Where does it come from?

WHO causes it?

The answer is quite simple...*The Evil Queen* causes it, that's who. Remember her? Yep, even Snow White had to deal with this dastardly damsel.

Stay with me here because this is where this movie plot thickens.

The Evil Queen appears to Snow White and offers her the poison apple, but she must first disguise herself, because if Snow White recognizes the evil temptress she'll never fall for the Queen's wily deception.

The Evil Queen's poison apple…it's mouthwatering. It's tempting. It looks delicious. Snow White slowly raises it to her lips. All the kids in the movie theater gasp, "Don't eat the apple, Snow White! Don't eat it! It's full of deadly poison!"

But alas, Miss White takes the fatal bite.

Snow White is deceived.

And so are you…and so am I.

Who Is This Evil Queen?

The Evil Queen appears to you and me and offers us the delectable apple. She is that wicked temptress who comes to us dressed in disguise, like the Evil Queen clothed herself in disguise before she approached Snow White. She must hide herself behind a cloak of deception, because if we recognize her, we'll never fall for her clever deceit, so she comes to us disguised as our *thoughts.* They seem innocent. They seem harmless. They're tantalizing. However, unbeknownst to us they are the full-blown madness of the Evil Queen with her forbidden fruit filled with deadly poison.

The apple is mouthwatering…sooo tempting. It looks delightful, but inside her poison apple awaits a towering array of demons: worry, anger, fear of failure, and stress. We admire the apple. We touch it. We flirt with it. It's irresistible, so we give in to its temptation. We take a big juicy bite, and suddenly with a sickening thud, the prison doors slam shut, and the Evil Queen's hideous screams pierce the air. She wraps her tentacles around our neck. We're trapped! Our thoughts are invigorated and energized by her vulturous emotions, and now they run rampant and there's *nothing we can do to stop their relentless attack.*

And then the unthinkable happens. Our poisonous emotions of anger, fear, worry, and stress release cortisol that seeps into our body—cortisol is known as *the death hormone*—it triggers sickness, disease, high blood pressure, aging, and an early death. The audience gasps, "Don't eat it!! Don't eat the apple! It's filled with deadly poison!"

But alas, we take the fatal bite, and suddenly the Evil Queen unleashes her forces of anger, fear, worry and stress…and *she traps us.* Anger, fear, worry, and stress *hold us captive by their evil power.*

As the story goes, the poison apple hurtles Snow White into a death-like sleep. It seems like all is lost. She has no hope.

But all is *not* lost. She *does* have hope.

What is Snow White's hope? A kiss. A kiss from the prince. That's what wakes her up. You remember that, right?

And likewise, you and I…we fall into a death-like trap filled with fear, worry, anxiety, and anger where all seems lost, and we have no hope.

But all is *not* lost. We *do* have hope. Our hope is a kiss that wakes us up…a kiss from the prince—*The Prince of Peace.*

Who's This Mysterious Prince of Peace?

He's that inexplicable force that appeared to me that sunny summer California afternoon in 1983 the day my green convertible died. He's the one who miraculously calmed my anger and gave me peace. He's the one who *force-fed his happiness into me.*

The *Prince of Peace* gave me the kiss that resurrected me from the Evil Queen's death-grip of anger, worry, stress, and a broken heart, fear of failure, and hopelessness.

The prince unfurled his mighty peace into me by means of my very own angry insidious words.

I accidentally and unwittingly stirred up his mystifying power by my scriptural cuss words. He then lifted me up from the deathbed of pain and hopelessness, anger, and a broken heart, and he forced me—yes, he *forced* me to be filled with his peace that passes all understanding and joy unspeakable and full of glory.

The prince kissed me and woke me up from my deathbed of anger when he force-fed his peace into me.

A Curiously Simple Power

I devoted—this is no exaggeration—I devoted ten hours a day, seven days a week for *the next seven years* after that sunny summer California afternoon in 1983 to plumb the depths of this curiously simple power, and that which remarkably began as a chance accident has grown to an indefatigable power that forces us to be happy, and kicks worry and stress out of our life *whenever we want.* This power *forcibly fills us* with indescribable peace and happiness.

What is this curiously simple, yet unpretentiously powerful force?

****

Scene 9

Strange Ball-Busting Force

This force, in all its simplicity, is *words*—not just words on a page, but words that you SPEAK, like I did those wild and wooly words that sunny summer California afternoon in 1983 the day my green convertible died. My crazy angry audible words *overpowered* my tormented thoughts and vulturous emotions, and in so doing they forced peace into my exhausted heart. Yes, they *force-fed* themselves into me—like a sperm forces itself to penetrate the egg to spark a human life, they *FORCED THEMSELVES* into me to penetrate my weary heart and thus spark a blast of peace that was beyond my comprehension.

Sundance exasperatedly asked Butch, *"Who ARE those words?!"*

I'll tell you who they are. They are non-sincere, triumphant "biblical cuss words," also known as "praise cuss words." There are twelve hundred and twenty-five of them that I recorded for you in volume three of this trilogy THE GREAT INVASION, but you can download them for free, and I'll tell you how in a few minutes.

They're the same 1225 words I've used tens of thousands of times since that sunny summer California afternoon in 1983 the day my green convertible died. These 1225 words, even packed with insincerity—like mine were—*force* your heart to feel peaceful and happy during any trial, no matter how worried and stressed you are, no matter how nasty and impossible your situation seems.

****

When you face a mountain—yes, a dunghill—a big pile of poo-poo…

When your thoughts run rampant, and you can't control your mind…

If you think you're gonna go crazy because all seems hopeless…

When you wanna give up…

When the worry and stress overwhelm you…

I have great news for you!

You can pulverize—*pulverize* means "smash to dust" like you'd *smash a rock to powder*—you can *smash to powder* your gigantic mountain of mental anguish with the explosive power of your 1225 words.

These 1225 words supernaturally unshackle the power triplets of peace, joy, and happiness, a mighty army of emotions that arise from the ashes of your broken heart by the ever so simple, yet ever so powerful energy of your 1225 scriptural cuss words.

These 1225 words readily smash to dust your torrid thoughts, your raging confusion, your heart-wrenching pain, worry, and anxiety as they *force-feed* peace into your mind.

This Gets Even More Eccentric

When you unleash those 1225 words into the skies—even nastily and vitriolically like I did that sunny summer California afternoon in 1983 the day my green convertible died when I accidentally discovered their overwhelming awe-inspiring power…well, that's at once gangsterific.

However, and I want you to listen carefully, because what you're about to hear is a total and complete roundhouse mindfuckification.

Yes, it's true that the words work *even if you shout them with anger, frustration, and despair* but this gets even better…

Here it comes…I'll bet you've never heard anything like this ever before…

The words work* QUICKER…*the more* ANGRILY *you speak them.

Whaaat?!?

I know. This sounds crazy. It borders on ridiculous. Even silly.

It goes contrary to everything I've ever heard, read, or studied.

It's highly absurd—even controversial. Some say *sacrilegious.*

I stumbled onto this by accident but listen…when your anger owns you to such a degree that you'd kill if it was legal, then it's not just an *indulgence* for you to cram your words full of that hatred and anger…

It's more than an indulgence…

It's more than a luxury…

It's an outright necessity!

It's how this system fires on all twelve cylinders.

Have you ever heard anything like this before?

The ANGRIER you speak, the quicker and more efficiently the words pulverize your anger.

The angrier you speak the quicker the words punish and pulverize your anger

Steve, this is the craziest, whackiest, marvelously intriguing crock of mind-soup I've ever heard. I'm gonna be honest with you Steve, I have NEVER heard anything quite like this ever before in my whole life.

Yep, I agree. Neither had I ever heard a single person ever tell me that my words work quicker the angrier I speak. It wasn't until that sunny summer California afternoon in 1983 that I accidentally discovered, indeed, that your anger forces those 1225 words to burrow deep into the nuclear reactor core of your heart. In case you didn't know it, a reactor core contains nuclear fuel and all the nuclear fuel assemblies that generate massive amounts of white-hot energy.

Anger is the white-hot atomic fuel that drives the nuclear reactor to generate massive pent-up energy that generates inexplicable PEACE

Do you need a mental break? I sure do. You've heard of Murphy's Law, right? But have you ever heard of Cole's Law? *What's Cole's Law?* It is thinly sliced cabbage mixed with vinaigrette or mayonnaise. [Rim shot "ba-dum-ching"] Okay, mental break is over. Back to *What is Anger...*

What is Anger? What IS it?

What is anger? It's a simple question with a simple answer: Anger is *your passion.* That's all it is. The same with frustration and anxiety. And worry. And fear. All these are your *passions.*

What is passion? The dictionary defines *passion* as "strong and barely controllable emotion."

Passion is your strong and barely controllable emotion that is the atomic fuel that generates massive energy

Anger is a fitting example of a strong and barely controllable emotion, just like my anger the day my green convertible died. Just like *your* anger is the *strong and barely controllable emotion* that you feel when you're so frustrated you want to punch a wall, or when you're so worried and stressed that your stomach ties up in knots, or you have that instinctive urge to smack your husband in the face with a pitchfork.

Such are these *strong and barely controllable emotions* that work AGAINST you.

But…

These same strong and barely controllable emotions can work FOR you.

Rageful Emotions Can be a *Dangerous Master*…BUT…
Those Same Raging Emotions Can Also be a *Beautiful Servant*

Rageful anger is your *strong and barely controllable emotion* that torments you with the poisons of misery, sadness, pain, depression, worry, stress, hatred, and even sickness and disease. Rageful anger, left unchecked, is a **dangerous master**.

However, when you harness your rageful anger to work FOR you—like what I accidently encountered that sunny summer California afternoon in 1983 the day my green convertible died—then your rageful anger is a **beautiful servant**.

Anger is a beautiful servant that *defeats itself*. How ironic is that?! Anger is a force that crushes its own damn self!

This defies all human logic.

Your strong and barely controllable emotion has many assorted colors. At times it's rageful anger, like what I felt when my green convertible died.

At other times it's ebullient excitement, like what you feel when you cheer wildly at a football game, or the excitement you feel when you have a hot date this weekend. Whether rageful anger or ebullient excitement—they are two sides of the same coin. They are both *barely controllable emotions* that are fueled by the same power source—**passion**.

Whether it's the *barely controllable* passion of ANGER, or whether it's the *barely controllable* passion of EXCITEMENT—these both are *barely controllable emotions.*

Rageful anger and ebullient excitement—both are *barely controllable emotions* that when you harness either of them, they make the words work more quickly, powerfully, and efficiently.

****

I certainly had no ebullient *excitement* the day the battery in my green convertible died, but I surely had a metric shitload of *rageful anger*.

Therefore, when you're full of rageful anger, be the wise man that harnesses that rageful anger, because the more angrily you speak—in other words the more *passionately* and with *barely controllable emotion* that you discharge the 1225 words of Moses and King David, Isaiah, Jeremiah, and others…yes, the more *aggressively, fiercely, and passionately* you speak the 1225 words such as I did that sunny summer California afternoon in 1983 the day my green convertible died as spit flew out of my mouth, well then the quicker and more powerfully they drive anger, worry, and stress into the abyss while *at the same time* they thrust happiness, peace, and joy onto the throne of your heart.

The ANGRIER you speak… the QUICKER your 1225 words generate peace

This might sound crazy to speak the 1225 words angrily to force peace more quickly into your heart, which prompts some people to say I'm eccentric, and they're right. Others say I put the ***fun*** in *dys**fun**ctional.* They're right too, but here's the beauty of eccentricity: If I had never acted so strangely, so neurotically odd like I did that sunny summer California afternoon in 1983 the day my green convertible died, then I wouldn't have discovered what I did that day.

I wouldn't have discovered that we can sling some cranky words out into the heavens, and lo and behold those crassly spoken words conquer our wicked anger as they *force-feed* peace into us. Yes, they *force* peace, happiness, and joy to explode in our hearts.

You gotta be a freeze-dried whackaloon to stumble onto something so bizarre, but that sunny summer California afternoon when I gave it my best shot to traverse the highway to hell, instead I stumbled into a detour that led me onto the highway to heaven. This detour uncovered the most magical supernatural gift I've ever known.

****

Why had nobody ever told me this before? Why had nobody ever taught me that I could harness my anger? *Who would've ever thought that my anger that was meant to destroy me would instead destroy itself?!?*

And the crazy part is…this discovery was an accident! A fricking *accident!*

****

Scene 10

Accidental Medical Discoveries

Some of the most prolific medical miracles were discovered by accident. Penicillin, the pacemaker, and Viagra…these were all discovered purely by accident.

A lab technician returned after a two-week vacation to discover the petri dish with staph bacteria that he'd carelessly left uncovered grew mold. He went to throw it away but discovered the mold had dissolved the deadly bacteria.

Voila— **Penicillin!**

An inventor was tinkering around when he accidentally installed the wrong resistor in his oscilloscope, and realized his device behaved just like a heartbeat.

Poof— **The pacemaker!**

And who can forget when scientists at Pfizer accidentally discovered the powers of Viagra during trials in the early nineties of a drug to treat angina. They hoped that the drug would dilate the blood vessels of the heart but instead it dilated the blood vessels of their penises.

Holy hallelujah— **The hard-on!**

****

My breakthrough on that sunny summer California afternoon back in 1983 was also an accidental discovery. I didn't expect my angry words to make me happy any more than I'd expect to catch a fish in the desert. I was just messin' around. Happiness was the furthest thing from my mind. I didn't expect my angry words to make me happy any more than the scientists at Pfizer expected their angina drug to make "Mr. Happy" happy.

My breakthrough discovery was like Viagra: Pack the **vagina** though meant for **angina** and gives *wowful pleasure beyond measure.*

I discovered the same about my fussin' and cussin' "biblical cuss words." They shoved me headlong into a speeding passenger train that turned out to be "The Prince of Peace." *Wowful pleasure beyond measure.*

The Day I Figured Out to *Intentionally* Speak Angrily

Fast forward from 1983 to thirty-five years later...April 2018. I was going through a hellhole of an emotional mess. My heart felt completely sick over a new girlfriend I was dating. I had only felt that broken-hearted (and *jealous*) a handful of times in my life. So, I began to speak praises. Just in a normal voice, which I had done for years. However, they didn't work as well. I got peace, yes, but it took me four hours.

I got so irritated that I was ready to trash this book altogether, or at least change the title to *Shitty to Happy in FOUR Hours.* Hey, four hours is better than never, right? But the title of the book is *Shitty to Happy in 21 Minutes.* NOT four hours.

So I got mad. Really mad. "How can I tell people this works in 21 minutes when it takes me four hours?!"

And suddenly I had a stroke of genius.

I thought to myself, "Remember that sunny summer California afternoon back in 1983 when you spoke angrily?"

Well, I heard a voice—an impression rather—say to me, "When you spoke the words back then, **you shouted them with anger**."

Then it hit me!

Speak the words angrily again! I thought to myself, "I did it *accidentally* in 1983. Do it **intentionally** in 2018!" I thought to myself, *"Speak the words ANGRILY and AGGRESSIVELY just like you did on that sunny summer California afternoon in 1983 the day your green convertible died."*

Folks, I got off the treadmill—I had been doing cardio, and I fueled my 1225 words with the anger and the hot tears that poured out from my broken heart. *But this time I wasn't angry at God.* I was angry at my hurt, my pain, and my broken heart. I was angry that the 1225 words didn't calm me in 21 minutes. I was angry that it took me four hours to get over the hurt, the jealousy, and my broken heart over my new girlfriend.

And so I fueled my praises with my massive pent-up anger. I bellowed the 1225 words with unrestrained passion. With determination. Aggression. I even danced while I sputtered them. I hollered them with such a vicious onslaught that spit was flying out of my mouth. *I filled my 1225 words jam-packed full of my anger and frustration.*

Rageful Anger is a Killing Machine That Destroys Itself

I never realized what happened that sunny summer California afternoon back in 1983 was that I had *unknowingly, unwittingly, and unintentionally* **harnessed the power of the Evil Queen**. I wasn't aware that's what I did, but I inadvertently turned her power against herself. I accidentally tricked her, and when I did, she drunkenly stumbled headlong into an oncoming speeding passenger train. It shocked me how flawlessly she devoured herself.

The fact is your anger tries to feverishly devour you, but when you harness your anger, it can't devour you. In fact, it confusingly turns on itself and *feverishly devours itself.*

It's comical that the Evil Queen sets a trap, but the dumbass oaf falls into it herself.

****

A friend once complained to me, "The 1225 words don't work like they used to." I told her the story that I just told you about when I was on the treadmill and the words didn't work in 21 minutes. I said to her, "Kick the door down of the Evil Queen's house, slap her in the face, and put her to work for you. *You need her help.*"

She said, "What do you mean?"

I said, "She's your workhorse. Harness the power of that whore-a-saurus. When you harness her power, you activate her so that she tames herself. **SHE TAMES HERSELF**."

The fact is, the Evil Queen is your passion. God gave her to you to help you. She's *extremely and enormously* powerful and beneficial, and when you harness her, she's your best friend, but when you don't, she's your worst enemy.

My friend exclaimed, "The Evil Queen is my friend?!" She was dumbfounded. "Did you just say she's my *best friend* and *I need her help?*"

I said, "YES."

"But how can the Evil Queen be my friend?"

I said, "Because she is your passion that God gave to you to benefit you, to give you power to conquer this life, to strengthen you in times of trouble. She's a massively powerful force. She started out good, but something terrible happened to her along the way. She went berserk."

Did you hear me? The Evil Queen is *your passion—your barely controllable emotion that's gone berserk, astray, erratic.* She's gone psycho crazy to the point that *she incites anger, fear, frustration, and despair* instead of **happiness, peace, and joy**.

My friend thought about it for a minute, and then exclaimed, "I got it! I got it! I'll harness the power of the Evil Queen—I'll use *her* power to **attack** herself. I will use *her evil power* to tame *her wicked self."*

I said, "Yes, now you've got it."

****

Your *strong and barely controllable emotion* can be wonderful, good, and amazing. Everybody has passion. It's beautiful. Your passion is priceless. You were born with an invaluable God-given passion that is designed to serve you. Passion is your drive for success. For a happy family. For all the good things in life, BUT: **Here's the challenge—**

Here's the challenge with passion: When those wonderful desires get postponed, or unnecessarily delayed, or they don't work out like you had planned, then your passion—your strong and barely controllable emotion—quickly turns against you, and it turns into the Evil Queen of anger… worry… stress. Or bitterness. Or unforgiveness. Or impatience, that's a tough one.

Passion Starts Out Good but Quickly Turns Ugly

Your passion is designed to be a comfy cozy campfire that you roast marshmallows on with your family and friends to make s'mores, but the next day when you drive home you leave a few smoldering embers that turn into a raging inferno that burns the forest down.

Last night the campfire was comfy and cozy, you and your friends sang folk songs and roasted marshmallows but today the campfire causes massive death and destruction.

Your comfy and cozy campfire of passion quickly turns into a raging inferno that burns thousands of acres of forest to the ground.

****

That afternoon on the treadmill I learned to *intentionally* harness my passion of hurt over my girlfriend; a passion that's meant to be good and lovely but turned into a raging inferno. I harnessed my evil passion to turn on itself, to turn my perverted feelings completely around to work FOR me, and when I did, my 1225 anger-filled words annihilated my raging inferno of jealousy and a broken heart…in 21 minutes. (Not four hours.)

The pain came back, of course. It most certainly does. So? Fight it again. And again.

And again.

I fought my jealousy and hurt every time they reared their ugly heads, and each and every time, peace came in 21 minutes.

Every time and without fail those 1225 words *forced* peace into my heart in 21 minutes.

It was an accident that I ramrodded my angry words into the smoggy skies of Los Angeles on that sunny summer California afternoon back in 1983 the day my green convertible died, but that afternoon on the treadmill, it wasn't an accident. I did it intentionally.

That afternoon on the treadmill I **purposefully** packed my words full of the Evil Queen's anger. That afternoon I rested comfortably in the power of my 1225 words that I filled to the brim with the Evil Queen's horrendous and putrefied emotions of anger and jealousy. What happened next? The words gave me peace, calm, and tranquility just like what happened to me that sunny summer California afternoon thirty-five years earlier in 1983 the day my green convertible died.

Brace yourself, because what I'm about to say, I doubt you have ever heard, and if you have, you're my hero. Are you ready? *Here it comes…*

The eviler your bad self is, the quicker it defeats itself

"Whoa Steve, you lost me there. Could you repeat that again please?"

Sure, I'll say it again.

The Eviler Your Bad Self, the Quicker it Defeats Itself

It's peculiar, but the eviler your *bad self is*…listen to me carefully—**the eviler your bad self is**…which is to say, the *eviler your perverted passion, the eviler your anger, the eviler your jealousy,* **the quicker it defeats itself**.

That's right. The more rageful anger and compulsive hatred that you feel in your heart, when you harness that compulsive hatred and rageful anger to work FOR you, THE MORE QUICKLY IT DEFEATS ITSELF.

"Whaaat?! Steve, could you repeat that once more please...?"

Sure, I'll say it again: The eviler your bad self is, the quicker it defeats itself. *—Hallelujah Sweet Rosy Miss Mosey, we've hit the MOTHER LODE!*

The eviler your bad self, the quicker it defeats itself

"Steve, I've never heard anything like this before in my life!" Yeah, I know. I just blew open the doors into one of the deepest, mysterious, most powerful secrets of happiness. When you wisely harness your evil self to work FOR you then you tap into a world of power that is indefatigable, unassailable, and inexplicable, yet ever so simple.

All you must do is *infuse your evil self into your 1225 words*...whatever your evil self is, be it anger, fear, anxiety, worry, stress, or hatred. Do it just like I did that sunny summer California afternoon in 1983 the day my green convertible died, because the more of your hideous, sewer-rat self that you infuse into your 1225 "praise cuss words" the more *quickly* your 1225 words *force-feed* **peace and happiness** into your heart which paradoxically eviscerates your sewer-rat self.

I accidentally discovered on that sunny summer California afternoon back in 1983 that the power of my raging anger ever so easily defeats itself, and consequently I harnessed my anger **on purpose** in 2018 when I was jealous over a new girlfriend.

Two weeks later she said to me, "What's different about you?" You seem stronger and more confident." I innocently asked, "Really? What do you mean?" *I knew what she meant.*

Aikido Redirects the Energy of Your Attacker

Aikido is a martial art that *redirects* the energy of your attacker. The more energy your attacker has, the more powerfully and quickly he defeats himself *with his own energy*.

The same is true with your anger. The more anger you have—in other words, the more anger-power you infuse into your 1225 words—the more quickly your rageful anger turns on itself to defeat its own self *by its own energy*.

I had a friend say, "But I can't work up any anger," I told her, "That's okay. You were a cheerleader in high school, right?" She said, "Yes."

I told her, "Stir up your cheerleader passion as if your team has intercepted the ball on their own one-yard line and is sprinting for the goal line. The runner crosses midfield, he crosses the forty, the thirty…your team is down by five points. Time has run out on the clock.

"Twenty more yards to go for a touchdown…if your team scores, you win the state championship…if not, you lose.

"Ten more yards, five more yards…

"TOUCHDOWN!"

I told her, "Shout the 1225 words with the passion and enthusiasm as if the state championship depends on it!" *Your passion and enthusiasm is how to make the words work in 21 minutes*. The more you saturate your words with passion—**it makes no difference whether it's the passion of rageful anger or the passion of the cheerleader at the state championship**—the more dynamically and swiftly the words *drive peace into your heart.*

****

Incidentally, when I infused the Evil Queen's *angry* passion into my words the day my green convertible died, that's what turned my praise words into praise *cuss* words. ANGER turned my praise words into the ugly gift I brought to the little girl's birthday party. "Cussin' praise words" are the words of the prophets that you fill to the brim with the Evil Queen's anger.

"Biblical cuss words" are the 1225 words that you fill with anger to transform them into an impeccably powerful weapon to pound peace and happiness into your heart

Therefore, don't allow your anger to intimidate you. Don't feel guilty about it. Instead of feeling guilty, make your anger work *FOR* you. Embrace your anger, because the more of the Evil Queen's anger you pump into your 1225 words, well then, the more quickly *her anger destroys her very own self,* and thus the more explosively your 1225 words transmute your heart from rage to rest, from hellish to happy, from pissy to peaceful. That's what I *accidentally* discovered on that sunny summer California afternoon in 1983 the day my green convertible died.

It's what I *purposefully* executed on the treadmill thirty-five years later in April of 2018.

But you'd better dodge God's lightning bolts. (I'm kidding.)

Listen, those 1225 cussin' praise words are high-powered projectiles, but projectiles don't shoot by themselves. They need a weapon, and somebody to pull the trigger.

WHAT'S *the weapon?*

WHERE'S *the weapon?*

WHO pulls the trigger?

****

Scene 11

Deadly Lethal Weapon

It was forty years ago on that sunny summer California afternoon in 1983 the day my green convertible died that I accidentally pounded peace into my heart that replaced the anger that evilly possessed me. That was the day my 1225 "biblical cuss words" slammed against the forces of my anger and nasty emotions, and completely ruled both, and I've done it thousands of times since.

That afternoon, even with no sincerity within five hundred miles, I crushed the fierce winds of anger, pain, and a broken heart. My 1225 words mightily conquered my monstrous anger. My words *forced* peace and happiness to leap up out of my heart.

But did you notice my words didn't jump off the page?

Bullets don't shoot by themselves. They need a weapon and somebody to pull the trigger.

And neither do your words shoot by themselves. They need a *weapon* and *somebody to pull the trigger.*

All the holy books tell you how important it is to control your tongue, but why? How does it work?

Listen carefully to this brain spike as this next gentleman uses two striking comparisons to portray the mysterious power of your tongue.

What IS This Powerful Weapon?

First, he compares your tongue to the bit in the horse's mouth that can turn the whole animal. "We put bits in the mouths of horses to make them obey us, and we can turn the whole animal" (James 3:3). Your tongue has the power to control your emotions like the bit in the horse's mouth has the power to control that big burly beast.

Next, he compares your tongue to the rudder of a ship. "Behold also the ships, which though they be so great, and are driven of fierce winds, yet they are turned about with a *very small rudder,* wherever the impulse of the captain determines" (James 3:4).

"Behold" is your clue to pay attention. In everyday talk, it means, "What I'm about to say is shitastic, so pay attention!"

He continues. "Imagine a ship—but it's not just a medium-sized ship—it is a *great big ship.*" But his description doesn't end there, not by a long shot. "Not only is it a great big ship, but this great big ship is thrashed by fierce winds and behemoth waves."

So, picture this: a *great big ship* thrashed by fierce winds and behemoth waves, hurricanes, tsunamis…the whole nine yards. Got the picture? Okay, there's more. "Despite the size of the ship…despite that it's tossed with violent winds and behemoth waves," James proclaims, "YET it is turned about by an *exceedingly small rudder!*"

Whoa, wait a minute…the author turns a corner here. First he lays out an epic scenario of a huge ship. Then he adds that it's pummeled by violent winds and huge mountains of torrential water. And yet…and YET—despite these insurmountable odds—that tiny rudder *forces* the direction of the huge ship to plow through the mighty winds and torrential waves.

Well heavens to murgatroyd…a *tiny little rudder* does all that?!?

YES! The tiny little rudder—despite the mammoth size of the ship…despite the driving winds and torrential waves—*turns the ship around to whatever direction the captain wants it to go.*

****

Can you imagine the herculean force of a rudder that turns the huge ship, even though driven by fierce, angry winds that pummel the sides of the ship with megatons of ocean water? The rudder astonishingly overpowers these impossible obstacles. The tiny turbine generates enough force to turn the ship even against these menacing odds.

Now, listen to me carefully: *This unfathomable power of the rudder to control the ship is* **the unfathomable power of your tongue** *to control YOU.*

The unfathomable power of the rudder to control the ship is the unfathomable power of your tongue to control YOU

Your tongue is a lethal weapon that has invincible power to dynamically turn your body against the rageful forces of anger with as much domination as the rudder has immutable force to turn the huge ship against violent winds and waves.

But wait…it gets even more astonishing as we dig deeper into his comparison.

He says, "It doesn't matter the size of the gigantic ship." Nope. The size of the ship is irrelevant. He says, "It makes no difference that the ship is huge. Neither does it make any difference that ferocious winds mercilessly pound against the sides of the ship." So, if the size of the ship doesn't determine its direction, and neither do the fierce winds, nor do the torrential waves…

What determines the direction of the ship?

The RUDDER determines the direction of the ship.

Despite insurmountable odds, the ship turns because of a small…no, *absurdly small* rudder.

James describes the *boundless power* of the ***tiny-sized rudder*** to utterly thrust and propel the gigantic ship through tumultuous seas and treacherous storms. The truth is, although the rudder is tiny, it dominates the enormous ship through these gut-churning waters.

That's **the baffling power of your tongue, and mine, too**.

Indeed, that sunny summer California afternoon in 1983 my tiny rudder—my *tiny* little powerhouse one inch below my nose—that *tiny little dynamo* demolished my anger like a hydrogen bomb demolishes a campsite.

The rudder is enormously powerful yet EXCEEDINGLY SMALL.

I declare we've settled the age-old debate— "Does size matter?" [Rimshot "ba-dum-ching"]

But I digress.

****

So then, what is the ultimate authority that decides the direction of the captain's ship? Is it the *powerful wind* that decides its direction? Is it the *ship's size* that decides its direction? Nope, neither has enough authority.

Is it the *torrential waves* that decide the direction of the ship? Nope, not that either.

So then what is the ultimate authority?

The ultimate authority is the tiny rudder! The tiny rudder—with its dictatorial power—its unmitigated power—its limitless power—its insurmountable power—its overwhelming power—is the *utmost authority* that decides the direction of the large ship.

That's the inconceivable incontrovertible **power of your tongue**!

Count from One to Fifty

This experiment that you're about to do is an irrefutable demonstration of the superiority of **the power of your tongue** to conquer your thoughts.

Try this test right now and watch **the power of your tongue** prove itself to you. Are you ready? Okay, count in your mind from one to fifty. Don't move your lips. Count silently at a pace that's about three numbers per second so that at the end of five seconds you should be on number fifteen.

At the same time you count numbers silently in your mind, after five seconds speak your full name aloud. Remember to try as hard as you can to keep counting the numbers silently while *at the same time* you speak your full name out loud.

Take a moment and do it right now. Count silently from one to fifty. Five seconds after you begin counting, say your full name aloud. Count the numbers, three per second…ready? Begin counting. (1, 2, 3… 4, 5, 6… 7, 8, 9… keep counting, keep counting, *silently* keep counting)—*Now. Speak your full name aloud.*

What happened to your counting? It stopped. How soon did it stop? — Immediately.

Your mind immediately shuts down to listen to what your mouth says. It's undeniable. ***The power of your tongue*** rules. **Your tongue is where your power is**. *When your tongue speaks, your mind shuts down to listen to what your mouth says.*

Let me announce it one more time, boldly in all caps: YOUR MIND IMMEDIATELY SHUTS DOWN TO LISTEN TO WHAT YOUR MOUTH SAYS. **The power of your tongue** (that's where your power is) *controls, governs, and dominates your thoughts through the rugged terrain* JUST LIKE **the rudder of the ship** *controls, governs, and dominates the ship through the ferocious storms.*

Were you able to concentrate on the numbers when you spoke your full name out loud? No, you couldn't. You *cannot* focus on counting numbers in your head while **the power of your tongue** spews words out of your mouth. ***The power of your tongue*** is too strong.

You *cannot* focus on thoughts that are contrary to the words that you speak, and neither can you think two opposite thoughts *at the same time*. And if your brain tries to think on two different thoughts, well, guess which one wins?

The power of your tongue wins! Your words win! Your mind can only focus on *the words that come out of your mouth.*

Think back to that sunny summer California afternoon in 1983 the day my green convertible died when my mind could *not* focus on angry thoughts while biblical cuss words flew out of my mouth. My tongue dominated my thoughts like the rudder dominates the ship.

That's how effortlessly **the power of your tongue** *controls your thoughts.*

Your tongue, like the rudder, is lifeless. It has no emotions. It can't think for itself, it has no feelings, nor can it make its own decisions.

Your tongue…the rudder…and the bit in the horse's mouth—they are lifeless and inanimate—yet they ramrod peace into your unhinged soul.

The sunny summer California afternoon in 1983 when my green convertible died, my tongue had no mind of its own, no willpower, and no college degree, and yet this minuscule turbocharger easily and mightily *forced* peace into my heart even though my intense deplorable emotions tried to sink my ship.

My tongue unleashed the fury of words that *force-fed* peace into me in the middle of a turbulent, life-threatening storm. My uneducated, illiterate tongue overpowered my brain, my willpower, and even my college degree. I might be smarter than my tongue, but not stronger!

Remember: All the holy books say to control your tongue. Now you can see why!

When the Storm Rages, Run to the Tongue!

When the captain's ship is in a storm, he *runs to the rudder.* He doesn't think about it. He doesn't question it. He doesn't hesitate. He doesn't dive into the water with his flippers, mask, and snorkel to swim hard against the sides of the ship to turn it around. What would the crew think if their captain screamed, "There's a ship headed straight for us! Somebody grab my flippers, mask, and snorkel, I'm jumping in!"

The captain doesn't try to turn the ship by his own power, and neither do you try to turn your emotions *by your own power.* No! When your emotions are in a torrential downpouring storm *run to the tongue!* Don't think about it. Don't question it. Don't hesitate. Don't grab your flippers, mask, and snorkel.

Run straight to the tongue as fast as you can!

The next time you're in a firestorm, and you feel the frustration, the despair of "Why do my dreams take so long?" Or "I'm bitter at my father and mother who were cruel to me." Or "I'm depressed, worried, stressed, and anxious that I can't pay my bills…" Or "My husband left me and ripped my heart open, and I don't know what to do!" …

As soon as those fierce storms thrash against the sides of your ship…

As soon as those violent waves try to capsize you…

As soon as you are worried, stressed, jealous, hurt, or anxious…

Run to the tongue. Immediately!

Run to your tongue immediately, and fire off several rounds of 1225 praisin' brazen "biblical cuss words."

Fill your words with your anger, or fear, or whatever barely controllable nasty, filthy emotion that you feel.

Grab your weapon and mightily pull the trigger. What're your bullets?

Your bullets are the 1225 words. Your weapon is **the power of your tongue**.

Would you like to see me demonstrate for you how this works?

You can download a video of me as I speak the 1225 words. I will show you exactly how this works. Download the video for free, but don't do it just yet. Finish reading the next scene, and then I'll remind you when to download the video.

You'll see what to do to employ your tongue to dominate against the onslaught of winds, waves, and insurmountable odds, and *forces* you—yes, it FORCES you to enter the calm waters of happiness, peace, and joy, and isn't that exactly what happened to me that sunny summer California afternoon in 1983 the day my green convertible died!

****

Scene 12

The Good Shepherd

There was a shepherd that tended a hundred sheep. At night, the shepherd kept them in their fenced area where they stayed warm, cozy, and safe from predators. In the daytime the shepherd let them out into the fields to play, eat, and frolic. Each day as the sun set, the shepherd herded them all back into their home. One by one, the sheep entered the gate, and one by one, the shepherd counted… "ninety-seven, ninety-eight, ninety-nine…"

A look of shock comes on the shepherd's face. "One hundred went out this morning. Only ninety-nine returned."

The shepherd, in his unfailing love and compassion for the one lost lamb leaves the ninety-nine to go out into the night to find her. He searches high and low, everywhere. The late hour doesn't hinder him. The chilly night doesn't discourage him. His mission is to *find the little lost lamb!*

****

I remember the first time my mom and dad took me shopping for school clothes. I was excited. I get to pick out some cool shirts, then we eat lunch, and we get to spend time together. But after we shopped for a while, I suddenly noticed they were gone. I looked for them. I couldn't find them. Then the realization hit me. Panic shot up my spine. I frantically ran through the store, crying for my mom and dad. I'm about five years old at the time, and the fear—the panic I felt…I sobbed uncontrollably. *Where are my mom and dad?!*

"Mommy, Daddy, where are you?!? Please, please come find me!"

The good shepherd continues his frantic search for the little lost lamb. She's covered head to toe with briars, she's lost, dazed, and confused. She's tried to find her way home, but she can't. She panics. She's frightened, she's shivering from the night cold, and she feels helpless. It's long past dark and she's all alone in the wild with no one to protect her from howling wolves that seek to devour her. She cries out, *"Please, please come find me!"*

After a while, the good shepherd sees the little lost lamb. With a shout, and with tears streaming down his cheeks he sprints toward her. *At long last he's found her!* He falls to his knees, hugs her tightly, and wraps his cloak around her to keep her warm. He scoops her up in his arms and comforts her, and whispers in her ear, "It's okay, I'm right here." He picks her up and carries her back to the others where she feels warm, safe, and protected.

When my mom and dad saw me, they ran to me, fell to their knees, and with tears streaming down their cheeks they scooped me up in their arms, and hugged me tightly. They cried, I cried…I was overwhelmed with an immense feeling of comfort, safety, and security…and love. "It's okay Steve, we're right here."

My mom and dad's love as they frantically searched for me in the department store that day is like the good shepherd's love and compassion as he frantically searches for the little lost lamb. The fierce love of my parents and the fierce love of the good shepherd are both decorated in a picturesque word, an enormously powerful, compassionate, and tender word. The word is a Hebrew word: The word is *yeshua*.

Yeshua is the Hebrew word that portrays the heart of the good shepherd as he leaves the ninety-nine others to find the one lost lamb who feels helpless and all alone.

Yeshua is the love, the compassion, and desperation of my mom and dad at the mall that day as they frantically searched for me until they found me.

Yeshua is a beautiful portrayal of the good shepherd's love and empathy for the little lost lamb that compels him to leave the ninety-nine others to go out into the chilly night to save her from the wolves, to rescue her, and bring her home.

Yeshua paints a stunning picture of how lost I was that sunny summer California afternoon in 1983 the day my green convertible died when I had no one to protect me from my rageful anger, anger that roiled inside me like a pack of hungry wolves as they sought to devour me, but when I sputtered the 1225 words of the prophets jam-packed full of my barely controllable hideous emotions of anger and frustration, the good shepherd noticed that I was the one-hundredth lamb that didn't return home, and he left the ninety-nine to frantically search for me until he found me, and as tears streamed down his face he sprinted toward me, lovingly picked me up in his arms, hugged me and held me tight, and whispered in my ear, "It's okay Steve, I'm right here."

This shepherd that tirelessly searches for the little lost lamb is a beautiful tapestry that the Hebrew word *yeshua* portrays, a tapestry that is like the artist who meticulously and painstakingly perfects his masterpiece.

Even though that day I was a hot-ass mess, my 1225 "biblical cuss words" and **the power of my tongue** awakened the good shepherd who is the Prince of Peace who then left the ninety-nine to search for me until he found me, kissed me with the power that awakened me from my deep slumber, and he carried me in his arms to the comfortable shade underneath the coconut palms on the beaches of Bora Bora where he made me feel safe and protected. And loved. "It's okay Steve, I'm right here," whispered the good shepherd after his grueling search for me. That's the incredible meaning of the compassionate Hebrew word *yeshua.*

The good shepherd bathed my ugly soul with the soothing tropical waters of the French Polynesia, and in response my exhausted heart, my weary and broken heart cries out, "Thank you Lord, I love you" …and a still small voice whispers back, "You're welcome Steve, I love you."

****

This concern and unfailing love of the good shepherd we see in this lovingly gentle yet fiercely compassionate Hebrew word *yeshua,* tells the story of how he comes to rescue the scared little lost lamb, and to rescue the scared little boy who can't find his mom and dad in the mall.

Yeshua tells the heartfelt story of how he comes to rescue the demented actor who was imprisoned by his hideous emotions on a sunny summer California afternoon in 1983 the day his green convertible died.

Yeshua tells the story of how he comes to rescue YOU when you feel lost, helpless, and all alone in the world with no one to protect you from the fears, the heartache, the pain, the sorrow, the worry, and the stress that make you feel like you can't go on another day.

Yeshua is a man's name. *Yeshua* is a man's name that has been trashed, castigated, and trampled underfoot for hundreds of years. Yes, even thousands of years. Yeshua is the God-given name of a man that fiercely forsakes all to come find you when you're in trouble, to hunt for you when you're filled with pain, hopelessness, and when you feel all alone in this world.

This man is the good shepherd that leaves the ninety-nine to save the one lost lamb, to save the scared little boy at the mall, and this man is the *Prince of Peace* that showed up to comfort me the day my green convertible died. This man is the good shepherd that searches for YOU when you feel lost, all alone, and afraid in this world.

This man is the unseen, mysterious power who *forced* peace into my heart that sunny summer California afternoon in 1983 the day my green convertible died.

This man is the Prince of Peace that saves *you* from your pain, your heartache, your worry, your stress, your fear of failure, and your loneliness as he force-feeds *his* peace into *your* heart.

This man's Hebrew name is *Yeshua.* When you transliterate this Hebrew name into English it's a name that's recognized by people all over the world. This Hebrew name *Yeshua* when transliterated into English is the English name *Jesus,* and to you he says, *"Speak the words...I'm right here."*

****

I think of the little girl whose mother died when she was five, her father abandoned her, and she cries herself to sleep every night in the orphanage and wonders, "Why doesn't anybody want me?"

To you my dear child, the good shepherd whispers, *"Speak the words...I'm right here."*

I think of the thousands of teens who are in such misery and pain that they cut themselves with razor blades. They do so because the physical pain of self-inflicted bodily mutilation takes their mind off, if only for a moment, their deep emotional pain of their broken heart, a heart so lonely and empty. To you he says, *"Speak the words...I'm right here."*

I think of you who are worried, stressed, and unsure of your future. Or you're unsure where you belong in the world. You feel lost, alone, unloved... To you he says, *"Speak the words...I'm right here."*

I think of you whose body is diseased, the doctor has given you six months to live, and you wonder how your family will make it without you. You ache for the pain you see in your children's and husband's eyes as they try to act happy even though they're afraid. To you he says, *"Speak the words...I'm right here."*

I think of you who are addicted to drugs because you turned to the only escape you knew to stop the horrific pain and trauma of a life filled with pain and no hope. You've tried to break the addiction, but you can't. There's no way out. To you he says, *"Speak the words...I'm right here."*

I think of you who put your heart and soul into a business, and you dedicated months and years to build it, and through embezzlement by a corrupt partner, or a downturn in the economy, you lost your life savings. To you he says, *"Speak the words...I'm right here."*

I think of you who lost a son or daughter in a car accident. Or to suicide. Or drug overdose. Or to a senseless and brutal murder, and your heart aches beyond the ability of the human mind to understand. To you he says, *"Speak the words...I'm right here."*

I think of you who's marriage ended, and the pain rips your heart out of your chest. You're broken beyond repair, and you don't want to live another day. To you he says, *"Speak the words...I'm right here."*

I think of you who were sexually assaulted as a kid by a trusted friend of the family, or a relative, or by a professor whom you held in high esteem…to you he says, *"Speak the words...I'm right here."*

When you're lost, afraid, all alone in this world, the good shepherd comes for you. How does he find you? *"Speak the words...I'm right here." THAT'S HOW HE FINDS YOU!*

The Hebrew word *yeshua* is a verb. It's an action word that means "to *force-feed* you full of peace when your heart is broken, to *forcefully pound happiness into you* when you're fearful and afraid, when your business is failing, when you've heard the dreaded news that you have cancer, or you've lost someone close to you."

His name is *Yeshua,* a power-packed word that is crammed full of actions of love, compassion, caring, and he comes to your rescue when you feel lost and alone in the world. He's the good shepherd that leaves the ninety-nine to come find you. He's the Prince of Peace that came to rescue me that sunny summer California afternoon in 1983 the day my green convertible died, and to you he says, *"Speak the words...I'm right here."*

How does he forcefully pound peace into your heart when you're lost…afraid…all alone in this world…when you have nowhere to turn…when you're scared, lonely, hopeless, and your life is falling apart?

"Speak the words...I'm right here."

When you wildly speak the 1225 words like I did that sunny summer California afternoon in 1983 the day my green convertible died, you feel his supernatural peace—you feel a peace that's beyond the ability of the human mind to understand…a peace that forcefully overwhelms you by the power of 1225 words coupled with **the power of your tongue**.

There is no other force powerful enough to hammer peace into your heart when the Evil Queen has you in her inescapable grip of pain, heartache, anxiety, fear, loneliness, unforgiveness, and hatred, and the whole host of emotional demons she uses to mercilessly torment you.

You Have an Immensely Powerful Weapon but *You Must Pull the Trigger*

Ladies and Gentlemen, it's true that you have a glorious and massively powerful weapon, and although it is intensely powerful, it can't shoot by itself. It must have a sharpshooter to pull the trigger. And it must have bullets.

Bullets are worthless without a weapon.

A weapon is worthless without bullets.

Both are worthless without the other, and both are worthless without a sharpshooter.

The weapon is your tongue. The sharpshooter is you. The bullets are your 1225 "biblical cuss words."

DOWNLOAD THE VIDEO NOW!

Go to my website ShittyToHappy.com. When you get to my website, type in your email, and you'll get immediate access to the video. If you're in a hellhole of a storm right now, right this very minute, then please…please go immediately to ShittyToHappy.com to download the video of me as I speak the 1225 words for you. Watch the video.

After you watch the video, download a written copy of the words, and YOU *pull the trigger of your enormously powerful weapon.* As soon as you do, you'll feel those 1225 words crush the anxiety, fear, and anger that you feel. Speak them three times through. I said *three times through!*

It gives you relief, if only for a moment. If you are still hurting, violently speak them through three times from start to finish again. You'll feel peace force itself into you. You'll feel the 1225 words, coupled with **the power of your tongue** *force-feed* peace into your heart.

Peace forces itself into you. Comfort saturates you. You feel inexplicable calm.

"Speak the words…I'm right here."

****

At this point in our journey, this is what you've learned:

ONE: Your purpose in life, like I told the young girl, is to be happy.

TWO: Words—1225 of them—are your all-powerful, yet gentle power-packed energy that somehow, someway relentlessly chase you down like the skilled trackers in *Butch Cassidy and the Sundance Kid*, and when they hunt you down and catch you, they tackle you to the ground and *force-feed* peace and happiness into your heart.

THREE: How do your 1225 words hunt you down? By **the power of your tongue**. Your tongue is like the rudder of a ship. Your tongue is like the bit in the horse's mouth. Your tongue is like a pit bull that grabs onto your pants leg and shakes its head back and forth and won't let go until the power of those 1225 words **force-feeds** *peace and happiness* into your heart.

FOUR: It's of utmost importance to remember that once you've set your 1225 words in motion it's *impossible* to thwart their power. You *cannot* abort their mission. *You cannot abort their mission even if you try!*

On that sunny summer California afternoon in 1983 I tried like hell to abort their mission.

But I *couldn't.*

My goodness, your 1225 words and **the power of your tongue** are so potent that they even override your nasty rebellious attitude and childish cynicism such as how they overpowered my sarcastic attitude that sunny summer California afternoon in 1983 the day my green convertible died, and on the treadmill over my new girlfriend when I decreased the time from four hours down to 21 minutes. The supernatural strength of the 1225 words and **the power of your tongue** bores through your crusty outer core and *compels, forces, and urges* your inner heart to feel at peace and at rest.

They're that powerful. *You can't hold back the dawn!*

FIVE: The power of your tongue coupled with the power of your 1225 words is even more electric when you **harness your anger**, which is to say, when you pump your words full of the Evil Queen's anger, fear, worry, stress, heartache, pain, sorrow, loneliness, and unforgiveness. When you pump your 1225 words full of your strong and barely controllable emotion, then your nasty emotions enhance the ability of your 1225 words to invade your heart more quickly and efficiently. When you fill your words full of the Evil Queen's nasty, putrid, sarcastic, wily, poisonous, vile emotions, then you convert the 1225 words into "BIBLICAL CUSS WORDS."

SIX: The Evil Queen is the origin of all your heartache, pain, agitation, anxiety, frustration, and anger. She's a vigilante, but she's also your friend. The ultimate movie plot twist is the villainess Evil Queen is the grotesque thug on a mission to destroy you, but in the middle of her deadly assignment she gets into a vicious argument with herself, then vacuously puts a gun to her face, stares blankly at the barrel of the gun, and pulls the trigger.

The Evil Queen is a suicide bomber that assassinates herself.

In the meantime, you go free while she falls to the floor like a tattered dress. Your 1225 words and **the power of your tongue** turn her from a once feared super villain into a village idiot.

SEVEN: And finally, you've learned the most valuable, spellbinding treasure, the greatest gift ever in my whole life I could give to you, like the gift at the cute little birthday girl's party.

It's the gift of *"Speak the words…I'm right here."*

ENTR'ACTE

We're preparing for the gigantuous party I promised the young girl, and we're a lot closer, but there's more. Are you ready to dive deeper into the next act of this play…*HOW peace and happiness get you everything you want?*

But first, I'd suggest for you to take another breather, an entr'acte, which is a fancy way to say, "Take a break." You're learning a lot of valuable information at breakneck speed, and it takes a few moments for your brain to process your newfound freedom.

It is extremely important that you take these breaks when I tell you to. Your brain needs time to process this information, and to assimilate how it applies to you, your life, your family, and your business. Go to the bathroom, grab a cup of coffee and a sandwich, call your husband, play with your kids, walk the dog, and then, let's get back to business.

If you haven't downloaded the 1225 words yet, do it now. Go to ShittyToHappy.com to download the 1225 words. Speak them through three times. It takes twenty-one minutes.

I promise you that you'll feel strangely peaceful. I'll see you back here after your break.

ACT 3: Peaceful Power Opens Doors

Scene 13

Extraordinary Inexplicable Happiness

As we delve deeper into the secrets of happiness, peace, and joy it's imperative to make a distinction between the two kinds of happiness.

Two Kinds of Happiness

One kind of happiness is, "I feel good cuz I drive a red Ferrari and date a Victoria Secret model." It's a fun kind of happiness, it's genuine, and it's real, but it's one-dimensional. It doesn't spring forth from deep within the hidden caverns of your heart. *It's an emotional reaction to **the good life**.*

The other kind of peace and happiness is the supernatural peace, joy, and happiness that erupt from deep within your heart from 1225 cussin' brazen praisin' biblical cuss words that you unleash by **the power of your tongue** for 21 minutes like I did that sunny summer California afternoon in 1983 the day my green convertible died. This kind of peace comes ONLY from **the power of your tongue** that ignites incendiary words that rip through your heart with an explosion of peace, calm, and tranquility that transcends this natural world. It's surreal. It's indescribable. It's incomprehensible. *It's an emotional reaction independent of **the good life**.*

The first kind of happiness starts from the outside and goes in. The second kind of happiness starts from the inside and pours out.

Both kinds of happiness are great, but the first one is skin deep compared to the second one that comes from down inside you, the kind that is buried within the innermost core of your heart.

This kind of peace—the kind that you can't explain, is unlike anything I've ever felt. It *forces* itself into you, and that's why it surpasses the ability of your mind to understand.

How could this supernatural otherworldly peace ramrod itself into me even when I fought so deliberately AGAINST it on that sunny summer California afternoon in 1983 the day my green convertible died? How can this transcendent peace *force itself* into me even when I'm such a whacked-out, rebellious, cantankerous bumbling fool?

I have no idea how such a power roars to life from a bunch of "biblical cuss words," but I know that those 1225 words when you combine them with **the power of your tongue** *flood your body* with the gentle, inescapable certainty of a sunrise to *force* these supernatural emotions into every cell and every fiber of your being. *How the hell does it do that even when I'm an asshole and my life is a shitshow?!?* I don't know and I don't care. It's astonishing. It's bewildering. It's mystifying, and I'm grateful.

If you think the peace and happiness that come from the red Ferrari and the Victoria Secret model is the pinnacle of peace…well, just wait till you pound yourself full of the kind of happiness, peace, and joy that erupt from 1225 praisin' blazin' cussin' crazily-spoken words that pound themselves into you by **the power of your tongue** and thereby controls you like the power of the rudder controls the ship.

Your happiness and peace levels advance from a rusty dilapidated covered wagon to a shiny glistening supersonic jet. And here's the zenith: These supernatural hyper-emotional forces that you pound into your heart by the 1225 words and **the power of your tongue** open the doors to everything you need, want, dream, and desire, even red Ferraris and hot girlfriends, but calm down, oh ye greedy cowboys and girls, allow me to explain before you drown yourself in dollar signs.

These emotional forces transcend and supersede this natural world. They assure undeniable entrance into the land of accomplished dreams and hopes fulfilled. Why? Because these emotional forces are supernatural keys that open doors into an unimaginable paradise called "The Garden of Eden."

Now, listen to me carefully: This happiness, peace, and joy that explode outward from the inside of your heart from 1225 words that you detonate with your lethal weapon, **the power of your tongue**—they are PROCURING SPIRITUAL FORCES*...that empower you AND thereby open the doors to all your successes, dreams, and desires.*

Inexplicable happiness, peace, and joy that you pound into your heart by ***the power of your very own tongue*** *are* PROCURING SPIRITUAL FORCES *that acquire for you everything you want, need, dream, and desire!*

Peace is ONLY THE BEGINNING!

Happiness is great. It's fantastic, and so is peace, and yes, they feel good, but there's more in store for you. Lots more.

For instance, when you first meet the man of your dreams you go to dinner, have enjoyable conversation, and feel an attraction. That's great, but it doesn't stop on your first date. There's more to come, isn't there? Much more!

The same holds true for your peace and happiness. Your blessings don't stop on your first date with peace and happiness. *There's more to come.* Much more!

Imagine you're on a game show.

You're a finalist on *The Game Show of All Game Shows*. If you conquer this next challenge correctly, you win the grand prize. "Tell her what she wins, Johnny!!"

ANNOUNCER: You'll win the biggest grand prize ever in the history of all television game shows.

You think, "What could a prize so magnificent be?"

ANNOUNCER: You'll win a lifetime all-expense paid trip to a paradise of luxury and delight where *all you could ever dream, hope, or imagine is yours...forever!*

The studio audience cheers wildly for you! Your heart feels like it'll explode! You're so ecstatic you feel lightheaded. You faint. You fall to the floor and knock yourself unconscious...*and your dream begins...*

[DREAMLIKE TRANCE] *Once upon a time, long, long ago there was a man and his wife who lived in such an unimaginable paradise. They lived in a land of dreams achieved and hopes fulfilled called the Garden of Eden. It was the garden of God where everything was provided for them that they could ever need, want, dream, or imagine.*

The word "Eden" in Hebrew means *luxury, or delight.* Hence they lived in God's Garden of unimaginable luxury and delight.

You're startled when I smack you on the back of your head and say, "Wake up Sleepyhead!"

"What happened?"

"You fainted. The game show is over. Everyone's gone home."

"What the…?!?" You're crestfallen.

"Don't worry," I reassure you, "I'll show you the secret path that leads you straight into the Garden of Eden."

"What the hell…? How'd you know I just had a dream about that?!? How do I get there?" you ask, still dazed as you rustle through your purse in search of aspirin for your splitting headache from smacking your head on the floor of the television studio.

ME: Your pathway into the luxurious garden is simple: It's the path of *happiness, peace, and joy* that not only leads you there, but they open the doors for you when you arrive.

YOU: That's wonderful, but what about my grand prize on the gameshow, and where the hell is my aspirin?

ME: If you'll be patient, I'll tell you how to claim the grand prize.

YOU: Alright, alright…I'm listening.

ME: Happiness and peace—I'm not talking about the namby-pamby peace that comes when your life is smooth, and you have no problems. That's not peace; that's *comfort*, and I'm also *not* talking about the kind of peace that comes from red Ferraris and hot boyfriends. That also is *comfort.*

I'm talking about the *incomprehensible, inexplicable, unexplainable, transcendent* peace that forces itself into your heart by your 1225 words and **the power of your tongue** even when you're a jerk and your life crumbles around you. This peace launches you ever so higher, much more so than even if your life is full of red Ferraris and hot boyfriends. *THIS kind of supernatural otherworldly incomprehensible peace…*opens the doors…to the Garden of Eden.

YOU: I found my aspirin. Okay, I'm listening. I'm intrigued.

Peace and Happiness are Keys to Unlock the Gates to the *Garden of Eden*

ME: Now listen to me carefully because there are three steps that lead you into the land of dreams accomplished and hopes fulfilled:

Step ONE: Unleash **the power of your tongue** to fire off several rounds of 1225 biblical cuss words so that they stir up the Prince of Peace.

That's step one.

Step TWO: The prince gives you a kiss, like the prince kissed Snow White. His kiss awakens you from the slumber of anger, hatred, stress, worry, anxiety, fear of failure, doubt, and the whole gamut of the Evil Queen's gnarly soul-snatching irrepressible emotions. God's unexplainable peace *forcefully explodes in you* and *consumes you* like what happened to me that sunny summer California afternoon in 1983 the day my green convertible died. His incomprehensible peace overwhelms you like the Navy SEAL team stormed the beaches of my heart and overwhelmed the enemy.

His peace and happiness forcibly possess you EVEN AGAINST YOUR WILL, even if everything within your screams, "Fuck this shit! There's no way this'll work. No way!"

But I promise, if you'll do it, your 1225 words and **the power of your tongue** will shock you, because these two powerful armaments are so strong as to overcome your rebellious, cantankerous, boy-bitch, weak-spined willpower.

Yes, they're THAT powerful!

That's step two.

Step THREE: When you tap into *his* peace that's beyond human description, and *his incomprehensible happiness* that crushes your whiney little bitch-boy self, these emotions that defy common sense not only calm you and give you rest and tranquility in the middle of a storm, but they force open the floodgates of heaven that pour out all the treasures that belong to you that are in the Garden of Eden.

That's steps one, two, and three.

YOU: *What?!? Are you saying that the happiness and peace that forcibly enters my heart by my 1225 words and* **the power of my tongue** *is* THE ACTUAL POWER *that leads me into this lavish garden where all my dreams, wishes, and desires come true?!?* [You're astonished at its simplicity.]

ME: Pshyeah…!!!

Scene 14

Peace Acquires Worlds

Don't act surprised when I say, "Peace Acquires Worlds." This is not an untested idea. Philosophers have extolled the virtuous benefits of peace and happiness for centuries. Aristotle and Saint Augustine, to name a few. Moses declared it. Abraham did too. And so also did King David.

And then you have modern-day motivational speakers and authors like Napoleon Hill, Norman Vincent Peale, Zig Ziglar, and Anthony Robbins who extol the values of this elusive peace and happiness.

And of course, you have world-renowned preachers like Joel Osteen and Joyce Meyer who declare that joy and peace will give you an abundance of everything you need, want, dream, and desire.

All the great prophets, preachers, book authors and motivational speakers boldly proclaim:

When transcendent peace forcefully POSSESSES you…
All your dreams forcibly OVERTAKE you

Happiness, peace, and joy—I'm not talking about the wimpy little namby-pamby kind that comes from the red Ferrari and "my life is good" … That's a wonderful feeling, but it's panty-pie peace.

I'm talking about the *supernatural* forces of happiness, peace, and joy that erupt from within your soul with gusts like a category 5 hurricane off the coast of Florida in mid-September. These supernatural energies of peace and happiness *force-feed* themselves into you by the 1225 words and **the power of your tongue** with such a breathtaking stunning rush of wind that it would be easier to stand barefoot in the middle of a gravel road while you try to withstand the force of the hurricane than it is to stop the mighty stupendous force of 1225 "biblical cuss words."

"BUT WAIT, THERE'S MORE," I eagerly effuse, like the infomercial sales pitch guys you see on late night TV.

"There's more!! *There's more!!"*

Tell me the more Steve, tell me about the more!

These forces of happiness, peace, and joy are *PROCURING SPIRITUAL FORCES*...

...that blow open the gates...

...to the Garden of Eden...

...to unleash everything you need, want, dream, and desire...

...that includes all your successes that await you...

...in the magnificent paradise called The Garden of Eden.

This otherworldly PEACE and HAPPINESS are incomprehensible energies that forcefully sprang up from deep inside me that sunny summer California afternoon in 1983 the day my green convertible died.

This same peace and happiness that flooded my heart that sunny summer California afternoon in 1983 floods YOUR HEART when you let loose **the power of your tongue**, that incomprehensible force that unleashes its mighty resurrection power. **The power of your tongue** digs up the incomprehensible peace that passes all understanding from deep within your heart, and it accomplishes this transformation in just under 21 minutes.

Listen to me though, because here's what's mind-blowingly amazing: This *same* peace and happiness that blasted into my heart that sunny summer California afternoon in 1983—even though it was an accident—are the same peace and happiness that *blow open the gates for you to get everything you need, want, dream, and desire.* Hallelujah that makes me happier than a shark in a fish tank full of tubby ladies riding the cotton mouse. Husbands ask your wives to explain that one to you.

Speaking of tubby ladies, I have a surprise for you beautiful ladies. It's a recipe that is healthy, wholesome, and satisfies your chocolate cravings. I'll give it to you in a few minutes. "I want it now Steve, I want it now!" Yeah? Well, if I give it to you now, it's no longer a surprise then, is it?

****

Anyway, back to my point. The game show grand prize—everything you want, need, dream, and desire—belong to the man who, with a heart full of unexplainable *transcendent* peace does a **roundhouse groin kick** into the testicles of his broken heart, his worry, stress, his heartache, hardship, and his hopelessness. *This transcendent peace and happiness are a rock-solid emotional reality that are beyond the observable physical universe.* This *transcendent* happiness, peace, and joy that *force-feeds* itself into your heart by **the power of your very own tongue** as it speaks these 1225 words **kicks open the doors to the luxurious Garden of Eden**.

"But how?" you ask. "HOW does joy and peace kick open the doors to the Garden of Eden?

The answer is twofold:

ONE: When you are happy and peaceful with the supernatural otherworldly peace and happiness of which I speak, then your skills improve, your wisdom grows, your knowledge increases, your diligence intensifies, and you are emotionally stronger than any obstacle that comes your way. Transcendent peace and uncanny happiness empower you in ways that are as yet unimaginable.

TWO: Your happiness and peace tap you into God's magnificent power. Your happiness and peace tap you into his unlimited ability to move mountains on your behalf to miraculously multiply your business, your opportunities, your relationships; and as if that wasn't enough, he promises to give you a world of abundance over and above anything you can ask, think, dream, or imagine. This is your land of promise, a garden of luxury and delight that is called *The Garden of Eden*.

All of these valuable dreams and desires of your heart blast open the doors of reality like the volcano Mount Vesuvius when you ignite **the power of your tongue** and 1225 words to *force-feed* peace and happiness into your heart like I accidentally stumbled upon that sunny summer California afternoon in 1983 the day my green convertible died.

****

Let's talk about *how*... (the word "HOW" is my favorite investigative word) ...Let's dig deeper into HOW peace and happiness kick open the doors to the luxurious Garden of Eden. It's exciting to hear that it DOES kick open the doors, but I wanna know HOW it kicks them open.

There are three fantabulous factors that perform this perfecta trifecta that kicks open the doors to the Garden of Eden.

Number ONE…Happiness and Peace Increase Your *Strength, Wisdom* and *Skill*

Thor's hammer is his power. Happiness and peace are your hammers that launch you into the rarified stratosphere of *strength* and *dominance* over every situation. How so? Because those emotions heighten your human skills. They make you more efficient, smarter, and wiser. Have you noticed that when you're in a good mood then your day flows smoothly, and everything naturally falls into place?

What else? You meet the right people. Phone calls are profitable. Study is easier for you. Sales increase. Creativity abounds. Opportunities appear when you least expect it. Creative ideas pop up out of your head unexpectedly. You uncover simple solutions to complex dilemmas; thus, you easily solve difficult problems.

So, **happiness benefit number ONE:**

You achieve your goals **much easier** and with less effort *because your peace and happiness increase your skill, maximize your efforts, increase your wisdom, and they give you strength and dominance, all of which empower you to operate at peak performance to get things done.*

Life is a Marathon with Prizes Along the Way

Imagine your life is a marathon. During the marathon you pick up prizes all along the route. Those prizes are your dreams, goals, and visions. As you run your race, you notice that the race is easier than the training. What do I mean by this? Let me tell you about the time I ran a half-marathon.

It was freezing cold in the early morning hours of Sunday, December 6, 2009, the day I ran a half-marathon in Las Vegas. I'd be insane to run a 13-mile race with no training, but here's what is interesting. I diligently trained for many months, but on the day of the race much to my surprise the *race was remarkably easier* than the training. I trained an extremely intense training schedule which made the race easy.

The training was intense. Hence, the race was easier than the training.

Even so, when you intensely train yourself in supernatural happiness, transcendent peace, and indescribable joy, then these powerful emotional forces *empower you with wisdom, strength, and skills* that **make your race easier** so that when you run your marathon—your race where you pick up prizes along the route, prizes such as a fun and rewarding job; wisdom in a daunting career; a place to live; favor, wisdom, and skill to negotiate business deals; ideas to make your business grow; awareness and compassion to make your marriage heaven on earth, and insights to wisely raise your kids—well, these prizes along the marathon route mysteriously appear to you easier when you fill yourself full of happiness, peace, and joy.

The training that you invest into yourself by your 1225 words and **the power of your tongue** that pound peace, joy, and happiness into your heart makes your race oddly effortless. It's quite strange, this feeling of ease that takes over.

Your race to the finish is much easier when you intensely train yourself in happiness and peace. In other words when you *passionately force-feed yourself full of supernatural peace, the peace that transcends this natural world, this peace that surpasses your mind's ability to understand,* ***then the race is easy!***

The race is EXCEEDINGLY EASIER than the training

What happens to your life-altering powers when you unceasingly ramrod yourself full of happiness, peace, and joy, and you do it constantly, consistently, and continuously with your 1225 words and **the power of your tongue**? Here's what happens: Your supernatural emotional forces transform you into a well-trained soldier, a highly skilled athlete full of strength, knowledge, and wisdom that propels you forward to achieve your dreams that produce for you a beautiful family, a thriving business, and a healthy body that all come much easier than you ever thought possible.

****

AND here's your big bonus. Are you listening? —*Peace and happiness…****activate God's power****…to move on your behalf…****which ensures that your success****…is astonishingly disproportionate…****to the amount of work you put in.***

How would you like for the miraculous world to be normal for you?

Peace and happiness…activate God's power to intervene on your behalf…which ensures that your

success…is astonishingly disproportionate…to the amount of work that you put in

Can I get an "Amen" from the lazy folks? *I'm kidding.* You're not lazy—in fact, you're quite the opposite. You're extremely diligent when you persistently hammer yourself full of peace, happiness, and joy by your 1225 words and **the power of your tongue**. It takes **diligence** and **persistence** to continuously hammer the 1225 words by **the power of your tongue** into your heart so that you live in that rarified stratosphere of happiness and peace, because the Evil Queen never takes a holiday. She's always ready to smack you in the face with gobs of stress, worry, and fear when you least expect it.

Stay diligent with your 1225 words and ***the power of your tongue***

Stay diligent! For example, if you're in great physical shape, what happens if you slack off? If you have a slack attack, well then before you know it you've eaten yourself into two pant sizes bigger and your muffin tops have turned into a busted can of biscuits.

****

I've had ripped abs most of my whole adult life until a couple years ago when I suddenly had a love affair with cashews. And pizza. And my favorite—chocolate toffee with pistachios. And more cashews, and lots of peanut butter…jars of peanut butter. And more pizza. I blew up twenty pounds. I couldn't zip up my jeans anymore.

Oh, and I stopped working out, too. I no longer ran fifteen miles a week, and I no longer worked out with weights, and sank into a depression the likes of which I never knew existed, but that's another story for another time. I've recovered, but the point is to stay diligent in your fitness.

The same is true to stay diligent in happiness and peace because the Evil Queen is on a full-time mission to destroy you. She never takes a holiday, and she never lets up. She constantly lurks in the shadows to pounce on you. She continually plots to devour you.

However, when you stomp on the Evil Queen's neck—which is to say, when you trick her to do the dirty work; that is, when you harness her evil power to fuse into your 1225 words and **the power of your tongue** like I did that sunny summer California afternoon in 1983 the day my green convertible died, then the Evil Queen's wicked energy **supercharges your words** which then act like Thor's hammer to slam into her ugly forehead, while at the same time *force-feeds* you full of happiness, peace, and joy. When you harness the Evil Queen's wicked and vile proclivities, then she can't control you. She tries to, but she can't.

You control her.

****

Speaking of great physical shape, here's the surprise I promised you, that fabulous chocolate recipe. You'll LOVE this chocolate recipe, and if you don't love it, then you need to bury yourself in the backyard.

Recipe for Healthy Chocolate

I don't know about you, but my biggest failure is to split a bar of chocolate into the pre-cut squares, and then eat all of them.

Here's the recipe for healthy, wholesome, nutritious chocolate. Preferably use raw and organic ingredients.

The first is coconut oil. The second is cacao powder. The third is honey. That's it. You can add raisins, walnuts, and peanut butter if you'd like.

For the coconut oil I use extra-virgin organic. For the cacao powder—it's not cocoa; it's cacao. I use raw organic cacao powder, the same as cocoa powder, but less processed, and the vowels are reversed.. For honey I use raw, unfiltered, and organic.

How much of each ingredient? Hell, I don't know, I'm a guy. I'm not into details like that. What I'd suggest is trial and error, according to your taste. Start with coconut oil, add peanut butter (if you want) and honey. Stick 'em in the microwave for about thirty seconds to soften. Next, stir in the cacao powder, just enough to make a consistency like paste. Then add the raisins. Or even walnuts if you prefer. Or peanuts. You'll have to experiment to find what you like best.

You can see that a recipe book is not in my future since I use no measurements.

Nevertheless, you'll LOVE this recipe for chocolate. It's healthy. You can eat as much as you want without feeling guilty, because all the food is super healthy. I shouldn't have to say this, but I must add a warning label: Do not eat so much of this healthy chocolate that you throw up like I did in the cute little girl's driveway at her birthday party.

Make sure you research the differences between cacao and cocoa. Although the vowels change places, there are enormous differences in benefits even though they come from the same seed.

Anyway, back to my point: Train yourself intensely and diligently in happiness and peace with your 1225 words and **the power of your very own tongue**. Be diligent! Your 1225 words and **the power of your tongue** are a noteworthy pursuit.

And remember this salient point: Your intense training when you *force-feed* peace into your heart by **the power of your tongue** makes your race easier, much *easier than the intense training* just like my half-marathon was *easier than the months of grueling preparation.*

****

All of these are your benefit number one—that is, **strength and dominance over any situation**. Let's move on to benefit number two.

Benefit Number TWO...You're Happy *During the Waiting Period*

Benefit number TWO of happiness is this—and it's extremely valuable—you are happy, peaceful, and joyful *during the waiting period*—during that sometimes long and grueling wait time between "I want that!" and "There it is!"

Have you heard to stop and smell the roses? That means when you're full of happiness, peace, and joy then you appreciate life no matter how much abundance or how little you have. You enjoy the journey because your transcendent peace fills you with overflowing patience and confidence so that you know beyond a shadow of doubt that you will have a lot more than enough, everything your heart desires, everything in due season, and eventually everything you could *ever imagine.*

The 1225 words and **the power of your tongue** *force-feed* you full of this amazing hope, faith, and confidence, and they *force-feed* you full of this peace, patience, and contentment that strengthen you during the waiting season.

When do you need confidence, patience, and endurance? *During the waiting time between— "I want that!"* and *"There it is!"*

So listen to me, here's the pinnacle of happiness— When you're happy, peaceful, and full of joy during the in-between time, the waiting time between *"I want that"* and *"There it is,"* then your happiness, your peace, and your joy never again will depend upon material possessions, accolades, and achievements.

Why? Because you build your happiness upon the foundation of 1225 "biblical cuss words" and **the power of your tongue** that floods your soul with transcendent otherworldly peace that rises up from the inside of you *independent of your possessions, accolades, and achievements.*

Happiness, peace, and joy are forever yours, and free you from dependency upon material possessions and achievements

That, my friend, is LIBERATION. It's true FREEDOM brought about by INEXPLICABLE HAPPINESS.

Think about this: If your happiness depends upon your achievements and material things, but you have no achievements and no material things, then how can you be happy?

No things, no happiness. You'd do just as well to run a forty-yard dash in a thirty-yard gym.

My goal for you is to depend ONLY upon your 1225 words and **the power of your tongue** to *forcibly feel peaceful and happy* INDEPENDENTLY *of your possessions.*

How the hell can this be? It's weirdly easy when your 1225 words and **the power of your tongue** force-feed peace into your heart, and that's because this transcendent otherworldly peace that you *force-feed* into yourself gives you comfort and rest REGARDLESS OF YOUR SHITTY CIRCUMSTANCES!

Now LISTEN CLOSELY: I'll let you in a little secret. **This transcendent peace and otherworldly happiness is what opens the doors to your treasures.**

Wait Steve, you said it AGAIN!!

That's right, and I'll say even more about it shortly, but in the meantime your goal is for you to feel this supernatural transcendent peace *before* you get all the desires of your heart *so that you can get all the desires of your heart!*

Should I say that again? I think I'll say it again:

Your goal is to force-feed this supernatural transcendent peace into your heart BEFORE you get all the desires of your heart, and that's HOW you get all the desires of your heart!

If you disobey this amazingly easy, and glorious path to obtain all the desires of your heart, then you are in the unenviable position of full-on dependence upon *THINGS* for your happiness and peace.

You talk about a life that's a dead-end street in a dark alley, that's it.

If you depend upon THINGS for your happiness and peace, you're like a house built on sand.

Let me tell you a story about a house built on sand.

****

Scene 15

California Earthquake 1994

It was 4:31 a.m. on January 17, 1994, when the massive Northridge earthquake shook Los Angeles. My wife Tammy and I lived on a cul-de-sac on the top of a mountain in Sherman Oaks just a few miles from the epicenter. One half of our neighborhood, including our house, was built on bedrock. However, from our home to the end of the cul-de-sac the developers had excavated dirt from the first half of the neighborhood and used it to create landfill at the end of the cul-de-sac to level it out. So, the other half of the neighborhood was built on sand and packed dirt.

The earthquake sounded like a freight train that thundered through our bedroom. If you've never been through a major earthquake, here's how it feels. Imagine a jackhammer. You know, the kind the workers use during road construction.

Now, imagine there is a huge monster underneath the earth that lies on his back, and pounds the surface of the earth with a jackhammer the size of Los Angeles. This jackhammer pounds rapidly up and down the distance of 2 ½ feet. That's what our house felt like. Our bed thrashed up and down 2 ½ feet in the air at the speed of a jackhammer.

Now, add the thunderous sounds of a freight train at the foot of the bed, and you have the sights and sounds of how it felt that eerie wintery Monday morning. The earthquake ride at Universal Studios comes close, but the real thing was worse, much worse.

After the violent shaking was over, we looked out our bedroom window over the San Fernando Valley and saw several fires ablaze in the otherwise bleak darkness as electricity was out all over the city.

We checked on our kids. Our son Austen was six, our daughter Natasha was five. They were sound asleep. Two of their friends were over for a sleepover. It was the first time they'd ever been away from their mom and dad overnight.

They also were sound asleep. If our house was the Titanic, Leonardo DiCaprio would've had to wake up the kids underwater.

When the sun came up, we toured our neighborhood and saw half the homes, starting from the house three doors down from us to the end of the cul-de-sac were destroyed, some off their foundation, others flattened like a pancake. This is because the landfill at the end of the cul-de-sac turned into jelly under the enormous force of the magnitude 6.7 earthquake.

My neighbors' houses, regardless that they were fortresses, were built on packed dirt and sand that, no matter how tightly compacted, shook like a bowl of jelly under the tremendous shaking of the earthquake. Regardless of the strength of the structure, their houses fell to the ground.

Our house was built on bedrock, and even though we felt the same violent shaking we had minimal damage.

Regardless of the strength of your business, your career, and your family, if your life is built upon the sand of weak emotions, when the earth shakes your empire tumbles to the ground.

And so, here's **happiness benefit number TWO**:

You are built—not upon a bowl of jelly—but on solid bedrock. Your happiness and peace that you slam into your heart by your 1225 words and **the power of your tongue** *force* you to remain calm and at rest during your entire journey from "I want that!" to "There it is!" even though the winds whirl and the earth shakes, and your world crashes all around you, and even though your dreams seem to take forever.

Your joy—your happiness—and your transcendent peace—are your *internal strength* that gets you through the famine. They're what make you *strong* during the scarce times. They're your rock-solid foundation. They're your bedrock that keeps you strong until your flood of success breaks wide open.

This happiness, peace, and joy that you *pound into your heart* by the undeniable **power of your tongue** and 1225 words like I did that sunny summer California afternoon in 1983 when my green convertible died construct an impenetrable fortress, a bedrock-solid foundation of emotional strength in the middle of a life-shattering earthquake, which means you are happy, peaceful, and joyful *independent* of what goes on around you.

You're peaceful *even while you sleep in your car, shower at the gym, and eat black beans and brown rice.* That's another story for another time.

You're peaceful even though your boyfriend cheated on you. You're peaceful even though your boss is a shithead. You're peaceful even though the world looks like the end is near. How can this be?

It's because your all-powerful 1225 biblical cuss words that you unleash by **the power of your tongue** *pound peace into you.* Yes, they FORCEFULLY POUND an inexplicable peace and calm into your soul.

These two formidable forces—1225 words and **the power of your tongue**—unite to transform your broken soul from heartache to happiness, regardless of your circumstances, regardless of what goes on around you.

I absolutely *cannot* understand how those 1225 words and **the power of our tongue** *force* us to feel peaceful even during tough times, but they do, and that's why it's transcendent peace—*peace that is from another world and therefore passes all understanding.*

Those 1225 words that you unleash by **the power of your tongue** invade your soul to crush your anger, anxiety, and broken heart.

They *force* you to feel full of peace, contentment, and a sense of well-being even though your circumstances are so lousy that you feel like a piñata and everyone else carries a stick.

****

Twelve hundred and twenty-five biblical cuss words that you detonate by **the power of your tongue** pound peace into your heart which makes you happy and peaceful *before* you achieve your dreams and get your things, and lo and behold (here's that little secret) *that's what speeds up your dreams to happen.*

Steve did you just say it again?!?— ***The peace that floods me when I speak the 1225 words is the actual force that opens the doors to my dreams, hopes, goals, desires, and visions?!?***

Yes, I indeed said it again, and yes, **peace forces your dreams to happen, and causes them to happen more easily and with less effort!**

Listen to me...*this peace that strengthens you through the tough times...is the same peace...that blows open the doors...to your good times, also known as The Garden of Eden.*

That's a whirlwind of a mindwank, so I'll say it again...

This transcendent peace that strengthens you through the tough times is the same peace that blows open the doors to your good times

Take a sip of wine, or coffee, or whatever you're drinking and meditate on this: This peace—peace that is a luxury that very few grasp yet is available to everyone—not only makes your life pleasant, but also ignites a powerful spiritual force that fights battles for you, while at the same time preserves your peace and calm in the middle of an earthquake, and as if that's not enough, it opens doors into the Garden of Eden. I don't know about you, but this makes me happier than a preacher's kid at a biker babe rally.

We've covered happiness benefits ONE and TWO.

Are you ready for happiness benefit number THREE? It's almost incomprehensible, but let's go for it.

Happiness Benefit Number THREE…
You *Intensely* Enjoy Your Material Things

Remember I said your enjoyment and appreciation for the red Ferrari and the hot girlfriend graduates from a rusty covered wagon to a glistening supersonic jet?

Imagine this: Your 1225 words and **the power of your tongue** *force you to feel* happy, peaceful, and joyful throughout your journey from "I want that!" to "There it is!" Your strength, wisdom, and skill are above and beyond normal levels, and thus empower you and strengthen you to excel at everything you do (benefit number **ONE**). You are peaceful even *before* you get your things (benefit number **TWO**).

This leads us to happiness benefit number **THREE**. Your rock-solid peace and happiness on your journey from "I want that" to "There it is" gives you *gargantuan explosive intensity* to ENJOY and APPRECIATE your dreams, desires, and material possessions when they finally arrive.

It's interesting to note that the same joy and peace that opens the doors to your success is the same joy and peace that *expands and magnifies your ability to **enjoy your success***.

******

Listen to me carefully: Do NOT…I repeat, do NOT expect your fulfilled dreams and desires to make you happy and peaceful if you don't have peace and happiness to begin with. (Read that last sentence about a hundred and thirty times, and then read it through twice more.)

Your success, dreams, and goals CANNOT *make you happy if you are not already happy to begin with.*

If you're not happy already, then don't expect peace and happiness to spring up from your success any more than you expect a breath of fresh air to come from sucking on a blowtorch.

Success doesn't guarantee happiness any more than sucking on a blowtorch guarantees a breath of fresh air

This flies in the face of human understanding.

This is 100% contrary to human thought.

This doesn't make sense.

I know, I know ladies and gentlemen, boys and girls, it's a mental whiplash, so let me take a few minutes to further explain this because it is a truth that is so vitally important for you to grab a hold of, so hang on as we dig deeper.

****

Scene 16

Preset Happiness Thermostat

Psychologists have observed a phenomenon that no matter how happy and excited you feel from a new job, the red Ferrari, a new boyfriend, the Victoria Secret model girlfriend, an exciting new marriage, a successful business deal—our tendency is to revert downward to a stable level of happiness.

We have a *happiness set point.*

It's like a thermostat.

Therefore, no matter how excited and happy something makes us feel, the exuberant feelings are temporary because sooner or later we get accustomed to our new possessions, and we return to wherever our happiness thermostat was set.

Imagine that you're a backwoods villager who lives in a remote town with no running water or electricity. You walk five miles to get water; you gather wood to build a fire to cook food and stay warm. Tough life, but you adjust, but then you move to a city where you have electricity and running water.

The first time you flip on the light switch—how exciting! You flush the toilet and voila—poop is gone! Wowsers. You turn on the TV—it's the Kardashians. You abruptly switch channels. (Just kidding, I love the Kardashian girls, which includes the one formerly known as Bruce.)

Now let me ask you, a year later are you still excited about lights?

How about the toilet?

How about the Kardashians?

Your new surroundings have lost their pizzazz. They're not as exciting as they once were.

Pop quiz: Are you exuberantly excited when you flip on the light switch in your home? Do you shout with glee when you flush the toilet? Think about how we take things for granted. You're not even all that impressed with a cell phone that has more operating power than the computers we used to send a man to the moon.

Here's what's mind blowing: The same phenomenon happens with mega-millions of dollars, successful careers, cars, jets, and boats.

They lose their excitement.

Study of Lottery Winners

There was a study in 1978 that found that lottery winners are ecstatic, super-happy, and beside themselves with excitement—*but only for a while*. It's only a matter of time before they lapse back to their previous level of happiness, or lack thereof.

In other words, if they are *unhappy, worried, and stressed* BEFORE they win the millions of dollars, then no matter how happy the prize money makes them feel, they slowly but surely drift back to their previous level of *unhappiness, worry and stress*. Even depression. And loneliness.

They drift back to their ***happiness set point****.*

Can you imagine winning the lottery? How exciting would it be? Imagine it. Now, think back to how happy, or unhappy you've been this past year. Got it? Is it a lot? A little? Somewhere in-between?

Okay, now prepare yourself for the gruesome reality: Soon *after* you win the lottery when the excitement wears off, you return to your previous level of happiness. This explains why some people get mega-rich and have outstanding careers, lots of homes, automobiles, yachts, and jets, and yet they abuse drugs, alcohol, and some even overdose or commit suicide.

Why would someone kill himself after he gets everything he wants? The fact is if an *unhappy* person gets successful, then he is indeed happy and enjoys the success. Extremely so!...*But not for long.*

Soon thereafter, the strangest thing happens. *He returns to his previous level of emotional happiness, or lack thereof.*

The success continues, but the happiness fades.

****

When ABC cast me in the television series with Michelle Pfeiffer, I was on cloud nine. I was on top of the world. I had achieved my life's dream, but a strange thing happened. Within fifteen days…*fifteen days*…I reverted to worry and stress over whether the producers would fire me because I didn't do a respectable job, and other crazy thoughts of insecurity.

You see, I was a very insecure young man, and no matter that I had a TV series, my insecurities dragged me down from the mountaintop of my happy high.

My insecurity claimed its rightful ownership of my heart.

My happiness thermostat dragged me right back down to where I was *before* I got the TV series. I couldn't relax and enjoy something that should've been very gratifying.

****

We were in the middle of filming the fourth episode of the show. It was Christmas, 1979. The Harmon family was big—still is—in Los Angeles. Their dad Tom was a Heisman trophy winner. Mark was a massively successful quarterback at UCLA. He had a co-starring role in a television series at the time. This is the same Mark Harmon in the long-running CBS television series *NCIS.*

His sister Kelly had guest starred in many television shows including mine, the one I mentioned earlier with Michelle Pfeiffer. Kelly and I got along great. Maybe that's why she invited me to her family's home for Christmas Day. However, my insecurity shined through in all its painful glory. When Kelly invited me to spend the day with her family, all I could think of was how nervous I would be around all those famously successful people.

Without a moment's hesitation I told Kelly I had plans with my family on Christmas Day, which I didn't. I lied. They were in Florida. I was in California.

And so I spent Christmas Day alone. It's pathetic when you think about it, but I could not overcome my insecurities even though I was the star of a television series. My happiness thermostat was set for "insecure." It was set for "fear of failure."

Even with all my success, my happiness thermostat dragged me right back down to my miserable happiness set point, and so here I was, the star of a television series with a once-in-a-lifetime chance to spend Christmas day with one of the most successful families in the world, and I spent Christmas day alone, all by myself…alone in my apartment.

****

Your happiness set point is like gravity. No matter how high the amazing Michael Jordan leaped, gravity always pulled him right back down to the court.

No matter how happy you get from cars and homes, a booming career, lots of money, and a hot guy or girl, it's a temporary spike because your happiness thermostat drags you right back down to where your happiness set point was before you got all that stuff.

If you're not happy before you get all your stuff, you'll only get a temporary spike in happiness from "things." Eventually, you take them for granted just like the backwoods villager does the light switch, the toilet, and the Kardashians.

Don't believe me? Then listen to four celebrities—Jim Carrey, Eric Clapton, John Lennon, and Cameron Diaz. Listen to them tell you that *all the fame and fortune in the world* won't make you happy if you're not already happy.

****

"I find this wealth to be a terrible burden, and I would trade it all for one successful relationship."

J. Paul Getty

Scene 17

Celebrities and "Stuff"

Some folks grind their way to the top to achieve everything they could ever want. They attain fame, fortune, homes, yachts, and automobiles only to find their happiness doesn't last. It's temporary, and so they wonder, "I have everything I could possibly want…why am I not happy?"

They rise to the top of the world only to find it's eerily deserted. It's an empty ghost town. They struggle for years to slog their way up the side of the mountain, and when they arrive at the pinnacle, they're disappointed to find a dusty wasteland where all that's there is *disappointment, hopelessness, and emptiness.* They discover that no amount of fame, money, and success can fill the bottomless void in their heart.

When they discover that their successes and good fortunes didn't make them happy, they feel like it's impossible to *ever* be happy. What else is there to conquer? What else is there to achieve? I can hear their cry when they're alone as they drift off to sleep, *"I have it all and I'm still not happy."*

That's why so many of them abuse drugs and alcohol. They feel like they'll *never* be happy, so they numb the empty feeling with more drugs and more alcohol until finally, the lure of the hangman's noose seduces them. Death offers them an escape hatch from the hopelessness they feel so deeply in their heart. They flirt with the seductive charm of death. Their pain is too much to bear. Death lures them into its trap. They no longer care, so they recklessly overdose or commit suicide.

The Evil Queen wins!

****

The most successful people in the world tell you that if you don't already have internal happiness and peace, then even if you achieve every desire of your heart—every hope and desire you could possibly want—you will NOT enjoy them. They tell you that if you don't have genuine peace and happiness, then you'll only *temporarily* enjoy those outward things.

You can Google "celebrities speak out on fame and materialism," and it'll take you to YouTube where you can watch multiple videos of celebrities that warn you of the emptiness that awaits you if you trust in fame, fortune, and possessions to make you happy.

For the internet-challenged who think "YouTube" is a device for a colon check and "Google" is the sound an infant makes when he's happy, I'll quote a few of them for you starting with Jim Carrey: "I hope everybody could get rich and famous and will have everything they ever dreamed of so they will know that it's not the answer."

Jim Carrey said fame, fortune, and *everything you've ever dreamed of* is not the answer.

What's the answer? The answer is *peace and joy.* The answer is *happiness.* The answer is an unshakable foundation of supernatural happiness, transcendent peace, and unspeakable joy *that empowers you so that you can enjoy all the wonderful things in life.*

The ultimate curse is to have everything you could ever dream of and enjoy *none* of it.

In *Pirates of the Caribbean: The Curse of the Black Pearl,* the undead pirates had all the food and drink they could ever want, but they couldn't enjoy it. Food and drink ran through their skeleton bodies so that the instant they drank the wine, the next instant it spilt onto the deck of the ship.

Without happiness, peace, and joy you can have all the diamonds, gold, and rubies, multi-million-dollar homes, jets, and fast cars, yachts, fine wine and exquisite food, exotic vacations with fine women, and fine men—*but a curse awaits you.* Your curse is that you have all the treasures you've ever dreamed but you enjoy NONE of it.

I don't know about you but that gives me a pit in my tummy.

If you happen to achieve fame and fortune *before* you achieve peace and happiness, it's like you put gasoline in a wrecked car.

My heart aches for those that have nothing yet think that when they achieve everything, they will be happy; just like my heart aches for those that achieve everything, and are still unhappy, like what Eric Clapton said, "I had everything a man could want. I was a millionaire. I had beautiful women in my life. I had cars, a house, a solid gold career and a future, and yet, on a daily basis I wanted to commit suicide."

He'd built what he thought was an impenetrable fortress, but when the earthquake rocked, his fortress teetered because it was built on sand.

It's unimaginable that we *must have peace and joy* to enjoy the great and wonderful treasures in life. It seems crazy, but if you do not have peace and joy then *those great and wonderful things taste like astringent vinegar.* John Lennon said so himself.

Listen to what Mr. Lennon said. "As a Beatle we made it, and there was nothing to do. We had money, we had fame, but there was no joy."

He was the frickin Beatles and had no joy! His sad words are those of a mighty fortress built on sand.

My heart aches over the sadness and pain of Marilyn Monroe, Philip Seymour Hoffman, Jim Morrison, Jimi Hendrix, and Janice Joplin, amazing talents all, as were John Belushi, George Michael, Prince, and Michael Jackson, all of whom died of drug overdoses; and suicides by Kurt Cobain, Robin Williams, Ernest Hemingway, and Vincent van Gogh whose last words ring hollow, "The sadness will last forever," and Freddie Prinze Sr. who left a suicide note, "I must end it. There's no hope left. I'll be at peace…"

He had all the fame and fortune a man could ever want, a hit TV series, a beautiful wife, and a young son, yet he didn't have *peace.* My heart aches to the very core when I think of the pain of a man, a woman, a boy, a girl who has no peace.

Broken people with untold wealth, fame, and success litter the highways of life with alcoholism, suicides, and drug overdoses. It's a sad list of thousands of hurting and broken-hearted people with everything this life offers…but no peace. *These souls build their renowned fortresses and impenetrable empires on sinking sand, and when the rains come and the earth shakes, great is their fall.*

Cameron Diaz sums it up, "If you are looking for fame to define you, then you will *never* be happy, and you will always be searching for happiness, and you will *never find it in fame."*

****

Scene 18

Explosive Truth Bomb!

Now listen to me as I smack you upside the head with a virulent truth bomb. The celebrities say: *Fortunes do* NOT *birth peace and happiness.*

They speak mucho macho wisdom. How true it is that fortunes do not birth peace and happiness!

But wait, I'm not through…there's more…here it comes…

PEACE AND HAPPINESS BIRTHS FORTUNES!

Wait…Steve, could you repeat that one more time please?

Yes, I'll say it again:

The celebrities say that *fortunes do NOT birth peace and happiness.*

That's true, and it's nearly incomprehensible, especially to those who've never had money, fame, and fortune, but now I'm gonna flip the script.

Money, fame, and fortune don't give you peace, but PEACE, HAPPINESS, AND JOY GIVE YOU MONEY, FAME, AND FORTUNE.

You scratch your head even though you don't have head lice. It took me three scenes to convince you that money, fame, and fortune do not ensure happiness and peace of mind, but then I drop a wacko wonky conflagration that crams up your noggin when I tell you that YOUR HAPPINESS, PEACE, AND JOY ENSURE THAT YOU GET ALL THE DREAMS, HOPES, AND VISIONS YOU COULD POSSIBLY IMAGINE.

You cry aloud, "Steve, you just threw me into a seventeen-car train wreck."

I know, I befuddled you.

"Are fortunes okay for me to have?"

I hear the hope in your voice and see the twinkle in your eye. *"Are they?!?* And if so, how do I get them Steve? How Steve, HOW?!? HOW DO I GAIN FORTUNES?!?"

It's simple, it's straightforward, and it's remarkably simple.

Fortunes do NOT *birth peace and happiness*

However...Peace and happiness birth fortunes!

****

"I think I got it Steve...one more time please..."

ALTHOUGH FORTUNES DO NOT BIRTH PEACE AND HAPPINESS...

...PEACE AND HAPPINESS BIRTH *FORTUNES*

****

Sit tight Ladies and Gents, boys and girls, we've hit a long fly ball in Dodger stadium, and we've crossed third base, sprinting toward home plate for an inside-the-park homerun.

I'm gonna expound more on this seventeen-car train wreck.

It's coming up in the next act of this riveting screenplay, but first take another intermission. Rest up your brain synapses before we embark on this next fascinating leg of our journey from *Shitty to Happy in 21 Minutes: THE SECRET KINGDOM.*

INTERMISSION

Act 4: The Garden of Eden

Scene 19

Peace Births Fortunes

We just heard a smack-you-upside-the-head truth bomb from four world-famous celebrities that everything you could ever dream of—automobiles, homes, a solid gold career, private jets, yachts, and even if you're the Beatles…without peace and joy, they don't amount to a hill of beans.

But hold on just a cotton-pickin' minute…

Yes, it's true what they say that material things, fame, and fortune do not in and of themselves make you happy, but on the other hand the great philosophers, teachers, and motivational speakers say that the powerful forces of happiness, peace, and joy—not the panty-pie kind of peace, but the kind that *forces* itself into you by **the power of your tongue** like what happened to me that sunny summer California afternoon in 1983 the day my green convertible died—

—They say that this kind of incomprehensible happiness and transcendent peace **empowers** you to **acquire *and enjoy*** every one of those fortunes.

Indeed it sounds like the celebrities throw a bucket of ice water on your hopes of fame, fortune, wealth, and success, businesses, and careers, but do they?

PEACE BIRTHS FORTUNES

Does a baby give birth to momma? It's a bonafide idea for a sci-fi movie, but no, a baby does not give birth to his mother. It's impossible.

Does your fortune give birth to peace? No, it's another fantastic idea for a sci-fi movie, but like the four celebrities say, it's impossible for fortunes to give birth to peace just like it's impossible for a baby to give birth to his mother.

Alrighty, we're getting somewhere. So who gives birth to whom? Even though the baby can't give birth to his mother, *can the mother give birth to her baby?* Oh YES, most definitely.

You got it!

PEACE is the mother, the giver of life, the womb where the baby grows from a single cell zygote to a full-blown human being made in the image and likeness of God.

Fortune is the Baby

Don't get it twisted and backward. Avoid the trap that 99.99% of the world falls into: *"If I just had more money, a better job, a thriving career, a booming business, a wife, husband, kids—* [fill in the blank]*—then I'd be happy."*

In other words, when my life prospers, THEN I'll be happy.

No the flim-flam, golly damn, eat a clam tomfuckery ma'am, you won't!

You're a fool if you expect fortunes to make you happy.

The four world-famous celebrities already told you it ain't gonna happen! Are they blowing smoke up your ass?!? Do you think they know what they're talking about? Do you trust what they say?

FORTUNES DON'T MAKE YOU HAPPY!

But right on the other hand you're obliged to EXPECT that **PEACE and HAPPINESS** gives birth to your **FORTUNES** as much as you can expect a mother and father to give birth to their baby.

Hence, the title of this scene: *Peace Births Fortunes*.

I'll say it loud, say it strong, say it loud, and say it long…

Fortunes don't make you happy

Happiness makes you fortunes

****

Another distinguished gentleman, a world-famous philosopher—a mystery man many times more famous and wealthy, prosperous, successful, and powerful than the previous four celebrities—said something along the lines of *Peace Births Fortunes* but his name slipped my mind. I gotta eat more cilantro because people say it cleanses your brain of the heavy metals such as mercury, lead, and aluminum that cause brain fog and forgetfulness. Your squeaky-clean brain then crystallizes thoughts more easily. Google it: "cilantro chlorella detox."

What the heck, I'll give you the formula right now. Go to ShittyToHappy.com to download the formula. It might just clear your brain fog enough for you to remember all the state capitals.

Now, where was I…oh yes, the distinguished gentleman, the world-famous philosopher, the mystery celebrity… He was a castigated, misunderstood, and reviled Jewish rabbi that trekked the dusty highways of Israel two thousand years ago. So, listen to these time-tested words of this sandal-wearing mystery man when he says, "Pursue *first* the kingdom of God—make it your *top priority."*

Why do you say such a thing, Mystery Man?

"Because" he says, "the kingdom of God gives you ALL your desires, everything you could want—food, clothes, happy family, cars, a fun career that you love, a successful business, and rewards above and beyond what you could imagine."

His words stymie you, but you beg to hear more.

He continues, "The kingdom of God lavishes upon you all your desires like a downpouring rain; like a mountain of whipped cream on a hot fudge sundae at the little girl's birthday party."

That's Mathew 6:33, and yes, I copiously paraphrased the words because bible translations can confuse you more than abstract algebra.

****

You abruptly halt yourself in the middle of a text from your boyfriend—you look up from your phone and blink at me like a bullfrog in a hailstorm… "Whoa, now wait a minute Steve—stop the presses…*hold on…!"* You're flabbergasted. "This homespun rabbi says **the kingdom of God** gives me all these good fortunes I want in life?!?"

ME: Yes, that's right.

YOU: But Steve, you just finished telling me that *happiness, peace, and joy* gives me all these fortunes!

ME: Right again, I did say that.

YOU: What the heck Steve, first you tell me *happiness, peace, and joy* is the power that unlocks the door to all my dreams, desires, and fortunes. Then you bring up this humble rabbi from the deserts of the Middle East who says it's the *kingdom of God* that unlocks the doors to all my wishes and dreams.

Which one is it?!?

I'll tell you flirty girl, but first finish your text to your boyfriend, then take a stiff shot of whiskey, sit down, and let me explain.

****

On one hand, the great prophets, philosophers, and teachers including the prophet Moses, the motivational speaker Tony Robbins, and America's preacher Joel Osteen say that *happiness, peace, and joy* are the keys that unlock your dreams.

On the other hand, the lone Jewish rabbi says *the kingdom of God* is the key that unlocks your dreams.

Me personally, I don't care which one it is. I'll take either one. Whichever one unlocks my dreams, I want it, and *I'll do whatever it takes to get it.*

****

My favorite movies are the ones where the hero learns of a hidden treasure. He risks his fortune, his family, even his life to get the key, the trinket, or the map that unlocks the door to the hidden fortune. *Raiders of the Lost Ark* is one of those movies. The Ark housed invincibility at the hands of God. That's why the Nazis fought Indiana Jones so aggressively to get it. *They too, wanted this power.*

Me too, I want this power that gives me the invincibility of God to unlock my dreams.

I'm excited...*but wait*...which one of these is the unspeakable powers that unlocks all my dreams? Some say it's happiness, peace, and joy—*they're the unspeakable powers* that unlock my dreams. The rabbi says it's the kingdom of God that is *the unspeakable power* that unlocks my dreams.

Which one is it?

****

In *Raiders of the Lost Ark,* Indiana Jones knew about the invincible powers that were housed in the Ark of the Covenant, and he also knew there was a map room that shows where the Ark is hidden. How did he know? Because he thoroughly researched *prior to* his whirlwind quest to pursue the Ark of the Covenant.

We too must do our research before we embark on a whirlwind tour to pursue this invincible power called *The Kingdom of God* because what happens if we pursue an artifice, a fake?

For instance, if you embark on a scavenger hunt and the list says to bring back a used rubber glove, but instead you bring back a used rubber condom you don't win the party prize. After three drinks you're like, "Rubber glove, rubber condom, nobody'll know the difference!"

Hence we must decipher what is the proper entity to hunt for.

But what happens if we pursue the *right* entity but look for it in the *wrong place?* That's what happened to the Nazis when they miscalculated where the Ark of the Covenant was hidden, and so they dug with their shovels in the wrong location.

So not only must we figure out WHAT it is, we must then figure out WHERE it is.

****

We can all agree—we want the key that unlocks our treasures that reside in the Garden of Eden! We can all agree that *whichever* one it is that unlocks the door to all our dreams, we'll pursue it with full gusto.

So…which one is the key? Is it what the book authors, preachers, and motivational speakers proclaim, that *happiness, peace, and joy* are the keys that unlock our dreams?

Or is it what the lone Jewish rabbi claims, that *the kingdom of God* is the key that unlocks our dreams?

Is it one or the other? Or is it both? Do they relate to one another? And if so, how?

We'd better investigate whatever the heck this *kingdom of God* is, and then once we know what it is, then we'll compare it to *happiness, peace, and joy* so that we can figure out which one is the golden key, and hence, which one we will pursue.

And so the first question is… *What is the kingdom of God?*

Scene 20

God's Mighty Kingdom

Have you ever heard of such a thing? *What is it? What is the kingdom of God?*

It's simple to know what happiness, peace, and joy are. They're *emotions.* That's pretty obvious. They're passionate feelings that you can *force-feed* into your body via your 1225 words and **the power of your tongue** like I did that sunny summer California afternoon in 1983 the day my green convertible died.

But the kingdom of God ain't so obvious. The kingdom of God is elusive. It's mysterious. It's obscure like the Ark of the Covenant, and yet the mystery man who is the Jewish rabbi said to pursue it *first*...make it your *top priority.*

Two Questions: WHAT is it...and WHERE is it?

Some have proffered that the kingdom of God is far off in the future, way out there in the distant universe somewhere. If that's true, then why would the rabbi tell us to *pursue it first,* and to *make it our top priority* if it was out yonder beyond our reach—out there in the by-and-by? Another question is why would he tell us to search for something and pursue it if we don't even know what the hell it is?!?

Therefore, doesn't it make sense that we must establish what it is, and doesn't it make sense that it is within our reach? In the here-and-now? Even closer than our next breath? It must be within our reach, because how else would he expect us to make it our top priority if it was unattainable, and a mile away?

The Jewish rabbi says, "People will tell you the kingdom is over here, or over there, across the ocean or up in heaven." He exclaims, "Bull hockey!"

All right, we're getting somewhere. He says the kingdom of God is not somewhere out in the future, nor is it halfway around the world, across the ocean, or up in heaven.

Okay, he didn't say "bull hockey." I made that part up.

So, if it's not in those other faraway places then *where is it?*

He plainly tells you. "The kingdom," he says, "is *inside you"* (Luke 17:21).

It's inside me!?

Well good golly gee willikers, I feel like Indiana Jones in his search for clues to the Ark of the Covenant. *It's inside me?!?* That's strange… Indiana Jones had to go halfway around the world to find the Ark of the Covenant, but I only must look *inside* me?! I'm flabbergasted.

So, let's assume we know *where* it is… next, let's delve into *what* it is.

****

Remember, on one hand many folks claim that the powers of happiness, peace, and joy are the keys that unlock the treasures of life.

On the other hand, the Jewish rabbi claims that the mysterious powers of the kingdom of God are the keys that unlock the treasures of life.

*Which one is it…*is it *happiness?* Or is it *the kingdom?* Or is it *BOTH?*

Sweet sassy molassy, I'm 'bout as excited as a curly-haired kid with cute dimples on Christmas Eve! Alrighty, so let's continue our investigation into this mysterious kingdom!

The Apostle Paul in Romans 14:17 clearly and simply defines the kingdom of God. He says, "The kingdom of God is…" [DRUM ROLL, PLEASE]

I can hardly stand the suspense; it's killing me. So... what is it, this kingdom that lives inside me?

"The kingdom of God that lives inside you is..." [ANOTHER DRUM ROLL PLEASE]

Omigasm, isn't this the esoteric quest of the ages, to figure out what is this elusive kingdom of God? The rabbi says if we gain access then we have the keys to everything we could ever possibly want, and when he says everything, he means EVERYTHING. He doesn't dangle a carrot! Everything you could ever want, all that your heart desires—*everything that's in the Ark of the Covenant is in the kingdom of God which includes all the treasures in the Garden of Eden!*

****

Before we go on, I have a confession to make. I'm gonna get brutally honest with you. You wanna know what drove me to search for the golden key to endless treasures? When I learned I could get all the treasures I wanted, I had an insatiable desire for material things, fame, and fortune. That's what drove me. I wanted to be rich, I wanted to be famous, and I wanted fancy houses and fine cars.

Is that greedy? Well, if I look to those things to make me happy then yes, that's greedy. Are you like me? Do you want a whole bunch of stuff, and for that reason you'll pursue the power that gives you all the things you want in life?

But what if you're not so interested in stuff? You just want to make it through another day—survival. You're an emotional wreck. You can't leave the house because you're so depressed, and you want relief from your pain.

Are you both? Are you somewhere in-between? Whatever you want, stay with me here, because you're about to get the keys to everything you want in life.

EVERYTHING…!!!

****

If the kingdom of God is the power to get endless treasures, then you'd think people would have figured out by now what it is, right? But *nooooo*…after thousands of years *people still don't know baby shit from butterscotch.*

It's ridiculous how much they complicate and distort this institution called "The Kingdom of God."

Why does it have to be so freaking complicated?!?

For instance, how many times have you heard an arcane, mind-numbing, convoluted explanation of what the kingdom of God is, whether it was a preacher, or some guy on TV, and their explanation leaves you more confused than a hangry baby in a titty bar? (A *hangry* baby is so hungry he's angry.)

Or how many books have you read some weird, esoteric, far-fetched, twisted, and tortured explanation of what the kingdom of God is? We've heard all kinds of strange and cryptic, downright puzzling explanations of what the kingdom of God is.

Why does it have to be so frickin complicated?

****

Scene 21

What's the Kingdom?

The Kingdom of God Is…What?

Here's a great idea. Why not let's bypass thousands of years of religious goofiness and high-minded silliness, and let's look it up for ourselves. I've given you enough foreplay to gag a maggot, so here's the answer.

The Apostle Paul defines the kingdom of God quite simply in Romans chapter 14, verse 17. The kingdom of God is [ONE LAST DRUM ROLL, PLEASE] …the kingdom of God is *righteousness, peace, and joy.*

[TA-DAAAA] There it is—BAM—as in, wham bam, thank you, Ma'am. In one sentence…four words— (three if you leave out 'and')—you just learned what the kingdom of God is.

[Fireworks explode. The world cheers with unbridled joy.] Why the worldwide celebration? Because this journey just got a helluva lot easier. This elusive, esoteric, nebulous, ethereal, and mysterious kingdom of God that lives inside you is…*it's peace and joy.*

Whaaat the…?!

Yes! The kingdom of God is PEACE and JOY.

"Steve are you telling me that PEACE and JOY are ***the kingdom of God****?!?"* Your face looks like a dropped pie.

YES. *The EMOTIONS of* ***happiness, peace,*** *and* ***joy*** are the powerful, infinite, all-encompassing **kingdom of God**.

EMOTIONS and THE KINGDOM are THE SAME DAGNAB THING! ("Dagnab" is an old-timey word that substitutes for…well, you can figure it out. An "old-timey word" is also known as an "Oldcootism," and since I am seventy years old I qualify as "an old coot" and I use lots of 'em.)

Incidentally, you notice I use the words *joy* and *happiness* interchangeably.

Many folks make a distinction between the two, but for ease of communication I swap them interchangeably. Both are rooted and grounded in the one true source of happiness and peace—1225 words and **the power of your tongue**.

Neither of them are based upon your surroundings, nor are they built upon your comfortable lifestyle. Feelings that spring up from your comfortable lifestyle are "panty-pie" happiness and peace, also known as *comfort.*

I say it often that comfort and panty-pie peace are legitimate feelings, they're wonderful, and they're the fruit of the rewards in The Garden of Eden, but they are not supernatural and otherworldly emotions, such as are the peace and happiness that explode up from 1225 words and **the power of your tongue** such as what happened to me that sunny summer California afternoon in 1983 the day my green convertible died.

This kind of *supernatural happiness and peace are OVER AND ABOVE* comfort. *They are **inexplicable forces***—they are the **kingdom forces** that roared to life in my heart that sunny summer California afternoon in 1983 no matter that my attitude was wickedly angrified on steroids.

The happiness and peace that my 1225 "biblical cuss words" and **the power of my tongue** *force-fed* into my heart that day are worlds apart from panty-pie peace and comfort.

They're dizzying heights of happiness and peace that are indescribable, inexplicable, unexplainable, incomprehensible feelings that overwhelm a human being more than the natural mind can understand.

True happiness and peace are the lethal forces that I set in motion by the 1225 words and **the power of my tongue** on that sunny summer California afternoon in 1983.

It's beyond my ability to understand how this commandeering kingdom that maneuvered like a Navy SEAL team that sneaked up on the sleeping enemy in the middle of the night overpowers me, even while my life is a shitshow. It's inconceivable that it crushes my demonic emotions *despite* that I am insolent and weak, and it annihilates my horribly shitty attitude even when I'm an incredibly insincere whiney boy-bitch. That forceful kind of happiness and peace that lives inside us is an incomprehensible, mystifying, even perplexing kingdom, especially bewildering in that we can easily uncork its powers by 1225 words and **the power of our tongue**.

There is no way in heaven or hell, Venus, Pluto, or Saturn for us to experience these powerful kingdom of God emotions unless we speak, shout, scream, spit, even whisper those 1225 words.

You gotta SPEAK those words to unearth their inexplicable supernatural otherworldly powers of happiness and peace. It's only by **THE POWER OF YOUR TONGUE** that you unleash their potential, and then deeply feel their magnificent energy. *There is no other way.*

You gotta unleash **the power of your tongue**. You must SPEAK the 1225 words three times through. It takes 21 minutes. It's a total of 3675 words, and when you do then **the mystical power of your tongue** *force-feeds* you so full of peace and happiness that you feel the unfathomable energy of these emotions as they dig their heels deep into the limbic system of your brain that controls your emotions.

The 1225 words and **the power of your tongue** supercharge your heart as those words burrow themselves into your soul to unlock their explosive powers of happiness and peace from deep within you where they have been buried for so many years. They're buried so deep that very few ever discover their existence, and even fewer bring them to the surface.

To those of you whose material world is already extravagant, filled with red Ferraris and Victoria Secret models, even so if you'll daily speak the 1225 words for 21 minutes, and do it several times a day I promise **the power of your tongue** will give you a bonafide spike in levels of supernatural happiness and transcendent peace like you've never imagined, and you'll feel a super-charged appreciation for your car and hot girlfriend.

The 1225 words and ***the power of your tongue*** *raise the temperature setting of your happiness thermostat.* They'll make you feel like you traded in your rusty covered wagon for a glistening supersonic jet, and thus, you forever immunize yourself from the ominous warnings of Jim Carrey, Cameron Diaz, John Lennon, and Eric Clapton who have massive amounts of material possessions, fame, and fortune, but like John Lennon sadly bemoaned, "We had no joy."

And if you don't have your fortunes yet, hang on for the ride, because supernatural peace and incomprehensible happiness kick wide open the doors into the Garden of Eden where all your fortunes, treasures, successes, and every desire of your heart lives.

Scene 22

I Found It!

By golly I found it! *...Yes, I found it!...* **I found the kingdom of God!!!**

This powerful **kingdom of God** roared to life from the innermost caverns of my heart. It had been hidden inside me, and like an uncapped fire hydrant, flooded my heart beyond comprehension that day in 1983 when **the power of my tongue** and 1225 words performed heart surgery on a sunny summer California afternoon despite my juvenile behavior and infantile assholitude.

This kingdom of God is the power that vigorously flooded my heart that day my green convertible died. This forceful liberating Navy SEAL team is the inexplicable force of peace—*a persuasive, emancipating peace.* It is happiness. *Energetic, liberating happiness*. It is joy. *Forceful, energizing joy.*

The KINGDOM OF GOD is the force that invaded my heart that sunny summer California afternoon in 1983 the day my green convertible died.

This is the **kingdom of God** that has eluded people for centuries even though they've searched for it unceasingly!

What took them so long? The **kingdom of God** is so simple you'd have to pay somebody to help you misunderstand it.

Happiness, peace, and joy IS the **kingdom of God**—the golden key to all the treasures that await you in the Garden of Eden.

The **kingdom of God**—happiness, peace, and joy—is the master key that unlocks the doors for everything you need to get everything you want.

The **kingdom of God**—*happiness, peace, and joy*—lives...where? *Inside you.*

The **kingdom of God**—happiness, peace, and joy—is all you'll ever need to get all you'll ever want.

The **kingdom of God** is the unspeakable powers that are locked inside the Ark of the Covenant and locked inside YOU.

The kingdom of God is the golden key...it's the Ark of the Covenant...it's happiness, transcendent peace, and exhilarating joy...that grants you unlimited access to the endless treasures in the Garden of Eden... It's all you'll ever need to get all you'll ever want

Can you see why the Jewish rabbi excitedly encourages us to pursue **the kingdom of God** FIRST?!?

Yes, FIRST, it's THAT IMPORTANT!

That's why I told the young girl, "Happiness is your purpose in life."

****

Merry Christmas to all us curly-haired kids with the cute dimples that waited all night for Santa to arrive! There's nothing more rewarding, electrifying, desirable, or trustworthy than transcendent otherworldly peace and supernatural happiness that floods you as it *forces* itself into your heart via **the power of your tongue** and 1225 praisin' brazen biblical cuss words.

Happiness, peace, and joy that springs forth from your 1225 cussin' praise words that you unleash by **the power of your very own tongue** is the zenith of life! It's the pinnacle! This supernatural peace is the kingdom of God, and it's this kingdom of God that is the power that opens the doors to all the things you want, need, desire, hope for, long for, and dream about.

This kingdom of God ensures that you get all those things.

The Kingdom of God is the Emotions of Happiness, Peace, and Joy!

So, what is the kingdom of God?

It's EMOTIONS.

Which emotions?

Happiness, peace, and joy.

Is it elusive, esoteric, nebulous, ethereal, or mysterious? Nah.

Is it complicated, shadowy, or hidden? Not really.

What is the kingdom we hunt for FIRST to get all the things we want?

The kingdom of God in all its glory, majesty, power, and simplicity is your EMOTIONS of *happiness, peace, and joy* that spring forth from 1225 words and **the power of your tongue** like what happened to me that sunny summer California afternoon in 1983 the day my green convertible died.

It's that simple.

The kingdom of God lives inside you.

The kingdom of God is your happy EMOTIONS. It's your peaceful EMOTIONS. It's your joyful EMOTIONS. *They live inside you.*

Happiness, peace, and joy are your shelter of rest *located inside you.*

Happiness, peace, and joy—they are *the secret place of the Most High* (Psalm 91:1). *The Secret Place of the Most High is inside you.*

Happiness, peace, and joy...these transcendent emotions that *force* themselves into you via **the power of your tongue** and 1225 words...these incomprehensible *emotions*...are your *passion.* These incomprehensible emotions are THE KINGDOM OF GOD **that lives INSIDE YOU!**

Whew, this feels like a full-blown visitation from God.

"Steve, you said the kingdom of God lives inside me?"

Yep.

"And you said the kingdom of God is peace and happiness and joy?"

Yep. And love, too, don't forget love.

"And they live inside me?"

Yep again.

"So, the happiness and peace are *already* inside me even when I'm an angry shitshow?"

Yes, that's right.

"So really my 1225 words and **the power of my tongue** stir up something that's *already inside of me?* "Yes Brainiac, why act so surprised? Were you comatose when you heard the lone Jewish rabbi say, "The kingdom of God is *inside* you"?

The Kingdom of God is *Hidden Inside You*

A huge block of marble sat in the courtyard of the Florence cathedral for twenty-five years. Other artists had agreed to carve the biblical David but abandoned the project. On September 13, 1501, the 26-year-old sculptor Michelangelo went to work on the slab. He carved out David in such a way that the artist Giorgio Vasari later described as "the bringing back to life of one who was dead."

When asked how he performed such a feat, Michelangelo replied, "The sculpture is already complete within the marble block before I start my work. It is already there. I just have to chisel away the superfluous material."

So listen up, oh ye hardheaded piece of marble block, you fantabulous blockhead—the kingdom of God emotions of happiness, peace, and joy are *already complete inside you.* You just need to chisel away the parts of you that is the superfluous material that covers over the kingdom of happiness, peace, and joy…a completed kingdom that lies deep inside you, a completed kingdom that has lain dormant inside you like it did inside me for thirty years…a perfect and complete kingdom that has lain dormant inside you, inside me, and inside the young girl like David had lain dormant inside the slab of marble for thousands of years.

But it's buried.

It's hidden.

You can't see it. You can't see it, hear it, or feel it, not while it's buried. You are unaware of it. You are completely oblivious.

It might as well not even exist if you can't see it, feel it, and you are unaware of it, right?

But thank God for that miraculous discovery on a sunny summer California afternoon in 1983 the day my green convertible died when I discovered that **the power of my tongue** and 1225 words dig deep into my heart to unearth the buried treasure that has lain dormant inside me since the day of my birth.

Your 1225 words and **the power of your tongue** chisel away the superfluous material to "bring back to life one who was dead."

Now, get to work, Michelangelo! Use your 1225 words and **the power of your tongue** like a hammer and chisel to chip away the parts of you that are not the kingdom of God. *STIR UP THE MIGHTY FORCES OF THE KINGDOM OF GOD THAT LIE DEEP WITHIN YOU!*

Scene 23

Unearth Your Treasure

Imagine you're Indiana Jones who pursues the treasure that's hidden inside you! Work like a sonofagun on an archeological dig to unearth the supernatural happiness, peace, and joy that's hidden deep in you, powers that surpass the ability of the human mind to comprehend.

When you unleash this supernatural transcendent otherworldly happiness, peace, and joy that flows up from deep inside you, powerful emotions that are already complete and perfect inside of you, powers that you unearth by the *force* of your 1225 "biblical cuss words" that you audibly unleash into the skies by **the simple power of your tongue** like I did that sunny summer California afternoon in 1983 the day my green convertible died—**then you've tapped into the hidden powers of the Ark of the Covenant.**

You've tapped into the golden key that leads to all the treasures you could ever want.

You've taken ahold of the keys that lead to the grand prize on the game show, keys that open the gates into the Golden City that lead into the Garden of Eden.

David was a completed sculpture inside the marble block long before Michelangelo pulled out his hammer and chisel from his tool bag.

The kingdom of God is a completed sculpture inside YOU long before you pull out your chisel and hammer from your tool bag.

The chisel is your 1225 words.

The hammer is **the power of your tongue**.

Chisel away! Sling the hammer!

The kingdom is not "out there" somewhere, it's not across the ocean, it's not up in heaven, and you don't need to go anywhere else to get it.

It's already a completed sculpture buried deep inside you.

All kingdom power has been given to you. It's inside of you, and it's been there since the day you were born.

Happiness, peace, and joy are the perfect and completed kingdom of God that lives on the inside of you.

Seize the kingdom. It's yours. *Take it!* TODAY!

Where is it?

It's inside you!

The Jewish rabbi— *the good shepherd that left the ninety-nine to search for the one little lost lamb*— He's the *Prince of Peace* that appeared to me that sunny summer California afternoon the day my green convertible died— He's the mysterious fellow with the Hebrew name *Yeshua* and the English transliteration that is a piss-poor transliteration of his Hebrew name into *Jesus*.

Brains explode all over the world at what I just said. Christians and Catholics are pissed. What about you? If so it's because you've done no research on the ultimately powerful, supreme, and dominant name of God who walked this earth in the body of a man called *Yeshua* as compared to the word *Jesus*. In Hebrew, names have powerful meaning. In English not so much.

Okay, I've pissed off the Christians. I've pissed off the Catholics. I've pissed off the Jews. Anybody else? Islamists? Hell they're always pissed. If I haven't pissed you off yet, stick around. I'll keep trying until I do. More on the faulty translation of his name in the second volume of this trilogy *THE EVIL QUEEN*.

The Kingdom is More Valuable than Gold, Silver, Diamonds, and Even the $300 Trillion it Would Take to Buy the Whole World

Jesus…or rather *Yeshua* compares how enormously valuable this *kingdom of God* is. He says, "It's like a merchant looking for fine pearls. When he found one of immense value, he went away and sold everything he had and bought it" (Matthew 13: 45, 46).

What's he saying? He says that your EMOTIONS of happiness, peace, and joy are like the fine pearl a merchant seeks after, and when he finds it, he sells everything to buy it.

It'd be like if the executor of an estate offered you to buy a house. The owner passed away, and his estate wants nothing to do with the house, so they include everything in the sale of the house—the furniture, the attic, the artifacts—it's all yours as long as you pay cash by this afternoon. You quickly inspect the house, the roof, the foundation. You sift through the attic. You notice a painting that catches your eye. You do a quick internet search to find out it's a masterpiece worth $300 million. Will you sell everything you own so you can buy the house by the deadline?

THAT $300 MILLION PAINTING IS HOW ENORMOUSLY VALUABLE your kingdom of emotions of happiness, peace, and joy are!

That's how important the kingdom of God is, a kingdom that is your EMOTIONS! *Will you sell everything you own to buy them?*

Which emotions are so immensely valuable as the $300 million painting? *Supernatural* ***happiness, peace*** *that transcends this natural world, and* ***joy*** *unspeakable and full of glory.*

Where is this kingdom of inexplicable, invaluable treasures called "emotions"? Where are these fantabulous glory-filled EMOTIONS?

They're inside of you, exactly like the Jewish rabbi said, "The kingdom of God is INSIDE YOU" like the priceless painting is inside the house.

Indiana Jones had to fly halfway around the world to find the Ark of the Covenant. You never have to leave your kitchen. Why? Because your treasure is complete, lacks nothing, and is buried deep *inside* you.

"Where's the kingdom, Rabbi?" they inquired of him.

He answers them and says, "This completed and perfect kingdom is inside you."

Your 1225 words and **the power of your tongue** arouse the sleeping giants of happiness, peace, and joy that lie dormant inside you, like David laid dormant inside the block of marble—

Dormant, that is until Michelangelo unleashed his hammer and chisel to resurrect David from the dead—

Your kingdom lies dormant inside you until you give free rein to your 1225 words and **the power of your tongue** to arouse these immensely supernatural otherworldly sleeping giants of happiness, peace, and joy from the dead.

Not as thrilling as the whirlwind adventures of *Indiana Jones* but just as opulent.

The kingdom of God with its emotions of happiness, peace, and joy is a pearl with immense value—more valuable than the $300 trillion it takes to buy the whole world.

Sell everything to buy the hidden treasure of the kingdom of God!

That's how priceless are the miraculous life-altering forces of the kingdom EMOTIONS of happiness, peace, and joy that erupt from deep inside you via the mighty 1225 words of the prophets recorded thousands of years ago that you blast into the skies with your lethal weapon called **the power of your tongue** like I did that sunny summer California afternoon in 1983 the day my green convertible died, the day I accidentally discovered the kingdom of God that is *already a completed work hidden inside me.*

"Speak the words…I'm right here."

****

You're in the shallow end of the pool, but I'm gettin' ready to shove you off into the deep end.

This is an excellent time to take a break. Walk around the room, go outside for a few minutes, and breathe in a deep breath of fresh air because this next section is a bit intense. Why so intense? Because I want to introduce you to somebody who's kind of a big deal. I told you in the beginning that you'd meet the person that taught me this unfailing power.

It's time for you to meet him but take your break first. When you take the breaks I suggest, you can easily handle the Niagara Falls of revelation that pours out from these pages.

Oh, and another thing…I'm warning you right now that you're gonna be hooked on this trilogy forever. Why so?

Because you need to read these three volumes many times through, again and again to deeply fathom all that's written herein.

It took me forty years to uncover a thousand pages of revelation that I recorded in this three-part trilogy, so welcome to my crazy whacked-out mind that requires of you several read-throughs to fully dig deep and unpack everything I have for you.

Anyway, come back in seventeen minutes, and then LET'S DIVE BACK IN! I'll explain the reason for seventeen minutes a little later.

INTERMISSION

ACT 5: Ladies and Gentlemen... MEET GOD

Scene 24

Who Is God?

Break time is over, so let's dive into the interminable question that men have pondered, argued, and debated. It's a centuries-old argument that has caused humans to gobsmack each other and hate one another for millennia. Men have fought wars and slaughtered millions because they disagreed over this question "Who is God?" Man's juvenile quarrels over God have caused more bloodshed and heartache than one can imagine, and I'm gonna pile onto the fray with some juicy fodder to offer another controversial version.

So the question is, "Who is God?"

****

There's a third word that you might've noticed in that definition of the kingdom that I gave you earlier, "The kingdom of God is *righteousness,* peace, and joy…" (Romans 14:17). Righteousness, peace, and joy… The Three Musketeers. Who is this third musketeer, this strange guy called "righteousness"? We know who "peace" is, we know who "joy" is, but who is this new fellow on the block called "righteousness"?

Okey dokey smokey let's go artichokey. Let's simplify this abstract algebra.

Righteousness is a mystical, magical, mysterious word like the expression *kingdom of God* that for thousands of years people have bantered about, misunderstood, misconstrued, and massaged without a happy ending. People trip all over themselves to try to explain it.

Simple…keep it simple. The slogan *love your neighbor as yourself* encapsulates the word "righteousness." There it is, it's that quaint.

Righteousness is embodied in the Golden Rule that says, “Do unto others as you would have them do unto you.” Matthew 25:34-40 states explicitly that “righteousness” includes *taking care of the poor, the fatherless, and the widow.*

Righteousness is “The Golden Rule.” What is the Golden Rule? Well, if you lost your job, and your family is hungry would you want someone to help you get food for your family?

Since you lost your job, you’re short this month on your electric bill, would you appreciate it if someone gave you a hand?

If you feel sad and broken-hearted, would you like someone to smile at you, give you a warm hug, and offer you a word of encouragement?

If you lash out at a friend and you feel horrible about it, would you like that person to forgive you? Of course you would! **That’s righteousness.** *We thrive on acts of love and compassion.* All of us do. These acts of love and compassion are what is known as *the Golden Rule,* also known as *righteousness,* also known as LOVE, also known as the kingdom of God.

In summary: “Seek first the kingdom of God which is *love…peace…and joy—but the greatest of these is* LOVE.”

We’ll do a deep dive into LOVE in volume three of this trilogy *Shitty to Happy in 21 Minutes: THE GREAT INVASION.*

…And One More Thing…

You might have noticed the last four words in Paul’s definition of the kingdom of God, “The kingdom of God is love, peace, and joy *in the Holy Spirt”* (Romans 14:17).

What’s that? What’s the Holy Spirit? Who’s the Holy Spirit? It’s God.

Who’s God? I love simple questions. They elicit simple answers.

Here’s the answer to the question of the ages, ‘Who is God?’ “In the beginning was the *word…and the word was God”* (John 1:1).

“Wait a minute Steve, you just said, “The word is God.”

That’s right, that’s what I said, or rather that’s what John said.

“So Steve, if God is the word, is it possible that God…is…those 1225 ‘biblical cuss words’ …that you irreverently spewed…the day your green convertible died?”

You're gettin' warmer…

"Steve…are you saying that God IS…those *1225 cussin' crushin' praise words*…those *praisin' profanities* that you irreverently spit back in his face that sunny summer California afternoon in 1983 the day your green convertible died? Those words are God?!?"

Wow, you catch on quick.

****

Have you heard the ear-splitting sound of a speeding passenger train when the conductor slams on the brakes, the high-pitched screeching sound as metal wheels grind against steel railroad tracks? That's the sound my brain makes as it short-circuits when I try to understand that these 1225 words are God. *I cannot make sense of it.*

Let's assume that yes, **these 1225 words are God**. Do you think that's why these words were so immensely powerful to calm my angry heart and frustrated soul the day my green convertible died? Have you ever heard of any such **power** that has *that much* ***control*** *over a man's heart?*

I ask you, what other **power** could *forcefully yet effortlessly* resurrect transcendent peace that had lain dormant inside me for thirty years of my life from 1953 to 1983, dormant like Michelangelo's David had lain dormant, hidden deep inside the 17-foot-high block of marble?

Does any other such **power** exist that detonates the life of God's kingdom that's buried deep inside you? I'm open to suggestions, but can you offer up any other solution to the mental ills that have faced mankind since the beginning of time?

How could these 1225 words *force-feed* inexplicable transcendent peace, peace that is from another dimension outside of our third dimension, and yet is hidden inside our human body— how could they cause inexplicable peace to explode outward from inside of me, especially when I was a ridiculously immature, cantankerously rebellious whiney little boy-bitch?!?

Here's how: "In the beginning was the Word…and *the Word was God.*"

I'm open to your suggestions, or suggestions from the "experts," but I can imagine no other power but the power of God that could calm my torrential flood of anger like what happened to me that sunny summer California afternoon in 1983 the day my green convertible died, and to this day I'm thankful that he didn't strike me with lightning over my rabid overtures like the lightning that struck William Cosper.

Lightning struck William Cosper on his front porch, and he lived, but then lightning struck him again, only this time he died. His family buried him in a cemetery in Talladega County in Alabama, but then his tombstone—I kid you not, lightning struck and destroyed his tombstone. His family erected a new tombstone—which *lightning also destroyed.*

The family gave up and left the small pile of rubble to mark Bill's grave.

True story.

****

Let's get back to the topic: *Who is God?* He is *those biblical cuss words* that flew out of my mouth on that sunny summer California afternoon in 1983 that transformed me from *Shitty to Happy in 21 Minutes* even though I was a miserable, broken-down ass-soul (you see how I spelled it there?) …a rebellious, cantankerous, cranky cuss…a weak-willed, angry, frustrated chump…and it was through no power of my own, except of course **the power of my tongue**—that's my *only* contribution. **The power of my tongue** is my singular solitary contribution to the miraculous transformation that happened to me that day that hell got kicked out, and heaven entered in.

I Had Only One Assignment

On that sunny summer California afternoon back in 1983 when my green convertible died, I only had *one assignment.* What was the one thing I did to win the Academy Award for my performance in the blockbuster movie *Shitty to Happy in 21 Minutes: THE SECRET KINGDOM?*

Was it my willpower? Did I engage my willpower? No. My willpower couldn't win a one-person argument.

Was it my decision? Did I make the decision to be happy? Hell no, I didn't even know what the heck I was doing.

Did I win the Oscar for my sincerity? Definitely NOT. My wimpy weak-kneed sincerity is as comical as a piss ant floating down the river on his back with a hard-on, tootin' for the bridge to open up.

Well then, what the heck did I do to cause overwhelming peace and calm to flood my soul? What role did I play that sunny summer California afternoon in 1983? And who wrote the script for the movie that unfolded on that oddly bizarre afternoon the day my green convertible died?

The production company called "God's Mighty Kingdom" cast me in the leading role to do one thing, and one thing only—SPEAK.

That's it.

That's all I did.

Steve, that's ALL you did was SPEAK?!?

Yep.

I followed a script just like the actor that I am. That's it. I unleashed **the power of my tongue**. That's all I did. I didn't write the script. *God did.* I didn't create **the power of my tongue**. *God did.* Can you see why I can't take ANY credit for my victory? I can't take ANY of the credit. NONE. Not even one teensy little bit.

I take the credit to speak, but even then I spoke with an attitude that was sick, nasty, putrid, and vile—humanity at its filthiest. Nevertheless *the words and* **the power of my tongue** *accomplished a mighty feat of miraculous transformation.* Other than that, I didn't do anything. It wasn't me. It wasn't my power. It wasn't my strength. Nope, I had nothing to do with it.

****

God's a funny guy. "He who sits in the heavens laughs" (Psalm 2:4). God has such a sense of humor that it wouldn't surprise me if he omitted the sincerity requirement on purpose just to mess with us.

Maybe he doesn't demand sincerity because he knows that if the 1225 words and **the power of our tongue** depend upon our sincerity, then we as humans will proudly take the credit for the victory.

In other words, we humans claim that it's our sincerity that makes the words effective, so we get cocky, arrogant, and huffy, as in "I'm so gosh darn sincere, and the only way to make the words powerful is *my sincerity!* See how great I am? The words are powerless without my sincerity!"

Fucking idiot!

You want the credit? Do you wanna take the credit for the power of the words and **the power of your tongue**? Do you? Well too bad! I have news for you—

You don't give power to the words. The words give their power to you, o ye arrogant ass-soul (I spelled it that way again.)

****

You know how I know people would take the credit for the victory? It's because for many years I shared this revelation with hundreds of people, and more often than not they *insist* that *you must feel sincere.*

What arrogance! Like God needs your sincerity to get the job done.

O ye blustery blockhead. Why must you add the burdensome prerequisite of "sincerity"? Why must you add a cumbersome chore to an uncomplicated task? Why must you complicate such an easy assignment?

It takes a megadose of skill to feel sincere, a skill that I sorely lack. And isn't it true that whatever it is that we "work hard for," we want to take the credit, right? Don't lie to me, you know it's true!

The only way you won't take the credit for the miraculous explosion of your 1225 words and **the power of your tongue** to *force-feed* peace into your heart is if you know you had nothing at all to do with it.

Do you take the credit if your grandfather left you a million-dollars inheritance? You might try, but everybody else laughs at you. Not for the million dollars, but because you take credit for it.

That's why I take no credit at all for the 1225 words and **the power of my tongue**. I give ALL the credit, ALL the glory, ALL the praise, and ALL my thankfulness to God, and his creation called **the power of my tongue** and for his 1225 mighty words that he gave to the prophets, words that are a slice of GOD himself.

Do you wanna take credit because you added sincerity? I'll laugh at you the same way everybody laughs at you if you take the credit for your granddaddy's inheritance.

All credit goes to the 1225 words and **the power of your tongue**.

You get NONE of the credit because those 1225 words are God himself. They're him. It's HIS power.

You have NONE of the power. Well, actually you DO have power. You have the power to speak, but all the power that pours forth when you speak is in **the power of your tongue**, power that you didn't create because it is HE that created **the power of your tongue**.

"Wait a minute Steve, I hear you say that I have no power because all the power is in the 1225 words and **the power of my tongue**. I accept that."

Alrighty we're getting somewhere. Anything else you wanna know?

"Well yes, how the holy cannoli can I possibly comprehend that **the words are God**?!? *Please help me understand."*

****

Listen, I had no intention of bringing this up so soon, but now is as good a time as any. I've already touched on it but let's dive deeper.

Do you remember in the movie when Sundance asked Butch, "Who ARE those guys?" Well, I have the conclusive answer to the question, "Who are those words?"

They are God (John 1:1).

Yes, they are pure God through and through.

Praisin' brazin blazin' bitchin' biblical cuss words ARE GOD. (Wowsers, there goes the sound of that speeding passenger train again as the conductor slams on the brakes.)

Yes, those 1225 words are God, and that's the reason they're so powerful!

Don't get your panties in a bunch over what I just said because I can already hear the doubts in your head that those words are God. You reason within yourself, "God is infinite, right?"

Yes, he's infinite.

"He's the creator of heaven and earth, right?"

Yes, he's the creator of heaven and earth, and always was, always is, and always shall be.

"And yet Steve, you tell me this magnificent, huge, infinite, limitless God who is everywhere at all times is *those 1225 tiny words in my mouth?!?"*

Well…yes, those 1225 tiny words in your mouth are God…

BUT…

Those 1225 words in your mouth are not all the God there is. (Whew! The sound of that screeching passenger train is giving me a headache.)

You inquire of me, "Steve, if God's infinite, the creator of the universe, bigger than my pea brain can imagine, then how could he be a tiny bunch of 1225 words in my mouth?"

That's a brilliant inquiry and a shocking notion that I've tried to wrap my head around for forty years. Even though I can explain it to you, I can't make you understand it because hell, I can't fully understand it myself.

However, I'll give it my best shot.

****

Scene 25

The Seven Seas

Imagine you're in Malibu at a surfing competition in Southern California. The beachgoers soak up the sun, drink beer, and slather guacamole on corn chips. You wipe a smidge of guacamole off your chin, get up from your beach chair, and you saunter down to the shoreline with an empty beer glass in hand to scoop a glass of water out of the ocean. You hold it up to the sun and notice how it glistens. You see its beauty. Behold, it is pure water through and through, right?

Would you agree that the water in your glass is the same water that's in the ocean? Can you tell the difference between the water that's in the ocean and the water that's in your glass? No, other than the amount, because the water in your glass is the same water as is in the Pacific Ocean.

Now, let me ask you this…even though your glass of water is the same water that's in the ocean…is your glass of water the *entire Pacific Ocean?* It's kind of a dumb question, but no, your glass of water is not the entirety of the Pacific Ocean. It's only a few ounces, sixteen to be exact, just a glassful.

So then would you agree that the Pacific Ocean is millions of times bigger than your glassful of ocean water? Yes, the Pacific Ocean is billions of gallons more, even trillions of gallons more water than is in your glass. In fact, the Pacific Ocean is 187,000,000,000,000,000,000 gallons of water, much more water than the sixteen ounces in your glass.

As you turn your attention back to the buck nutty surfers that ride the six-foot waves, you glance once more at your beer glass. You grab a corn chip, scoop a dollop of guacamole, and take a sip of your boyfriend's beer since your glass is full of salt water.

Your boyfriend asks, "What's in your glass?" What do you tell him? "Dr. Pepper." No, you'd be lying. "Ginger ale," no, "Beer," no.

"It's the Pacific Ocean."

He's intrigued. He takes another swig of beer and belches. After you unwrinkle your face at his gross belch, you then explain to him that your glass of water is the same water as is the one hundred eighty-seven quintillion gallons of the Pacific Ocean. There's only one difference.

"What's the difference?" he indifferently asks.

You tell him, "The only difference is that my beer glass of water is a mere sixteen ounces of the 187,000,000,000,000,000,000 gallons of the Pacific Ocean. Other than that, they're the same."

Your boyfriend smiles, kisses you on the cheek, and belches again.

Here's my point: Your glass of water is totally, absolutely, unequivocally Pacific Ocean through and through, right? But is it the ENTIRE *Pacific Ocean?*

****

Listen to me very carefully because this is where this gets tricky to wrap your head around. The 1225 words are pure God through and through just like your sixteen-ounce glass of water is pure Pacific Ocean through and through, but are the 1225 words *the entirety of all the God there is?*

No. How could they be if God is everywhere, at all times, in every nook and cranny of the universe and beyond? Therefore the 1225 words in your mouth are a puny little sliver of God, a mere sixteen-ounce beer glass size of the nearly infinite 187,000,000,000,000,000,000 million times a billion times a gazillion gallons of the infinite omnipresent all-powerful One and Only, the God of the Universe.

Are God and the 1225 Words in Your Mouth Identical?

I have a question for you: Are the 1225 words in your mouth purely, absolutely, unequivocally the infinite omnipresent all-powerful God through and through?

Oh yes, most definitely those words are the pure fullness of God through and through.

I have another question for you: Are the 1225 words in your mouth indistinguishable from God? Can you tell them apart?

I'll answer that question with a question: Is the water in your glass indistinguishable from the water in the Pacific Ocean? Yes, it is. It's indistinguishable from the water in the Pacific Ocean with only one difference.

What's the difference?

The one and only difference is the quantity, the amount.

Other than the amount, what's the difference?

Other than the amount how can you tell them apart?

Other than the amount of water in your glass compared to the amount of water in the ocean, aren't they the same?

Isn't it true that the substance and the molecular composition of the water in your glass is the same substance and molecular composition of the water in the ocean?

Even so, the 1225 words in your mouth are the same substance and molecular composition as the infinite, all-knowing, almighty Lord God.

The only difference between the words in your mouth and the Lord God Almighty is the quantity.

Not the quality.

The *quality* of those words—the substance and the molecular composition of those 1225 words are identical to God himself.

Other than the difference in quantity you cannot tell them apart. They are indistinguishable.

They are indivisible because they are ONE.

Another question, the third question: Are the 1225 words in your mouth the ENTIRETY of all that God is? NO! It's not possible that those 1225 words are the entirety of all that God is because God, like the Pacific Ocean, is 187,000,000,000,000,000 gazillion times a million times a billion times a gazillion times *bigger, bigger,* BIGGER, even *bigger than you can imagine* than the 1225 words in your mouth.

Your 1225 Words are Him, But He's MUCH Bigger

It's true that the 1225 words in your mouth are the mighty God your creator, but they are only *an itty-bitty-sized glassful of him.* How could they be the totality of all that God is?! They CAN'T. They are merely a tiny fraction, an itty-bitty sliver, an infinitesimal sliver, but hallelujah, that tiny little sliver of God in your mouth is *all the God you'll ever need* to get *all the happiness, peace, and joy you'll ever want*...which is plenty enough of his kingdom emotions to kick open the doors to the land of hopes and dreams fulfilled called the Garden of Eden.

It's these same emotional forces of happiness, peace, and joy that are the kingdom of God that arose from dormancy on the inside of my barren desert where the kingdom had lain idle for the first thirty years of my life, and yet **the power of my tongue** awakened the force within, and this kingdom exploded with a thunderous force that POUNDED his transcendent peace and inexplicable happiness into my heart that sunny summer California afternoon in 1983 the day my green convertible died.

A tiny sliver of God is all the God you'll ever need to get all the desires of your heart you'll ever want! That little sliver of God in your mouth goes a long way. *That tiny sliver of God in your mouth is all the God you'll ever need.*

HE'S MORE THAN ENOUGH!

Unlimited Energy in a Tiny Capsule

You wanna know another little sliver that goes a long way? Nuclear physicists say if you could turn all the atoms in that sixteen-ounce beer glass of water into pure energy, it would yield enough power to run the city of Miami for one year.

For one year! Now your boyfriend perks his ears up because we're talking scientific stuff about energy and power, you know, male macho stuff.

The water in a sixteen-ounce beer glass can supply enough energy to power Miami for a whole year.

Well hello Sunshine, a tiny sliver of water...a cup of the living water called *1225 praise words* is more than enough of God's power to energize YOU *for not only a year, but for a thousand lifetimes.*

How? You simply detonate the explosive power of those 1225 words by **the power of your tongue**.

The power of your tongue ignites this glassful of energy-laden words into a superabundance of potent emotions that *force-feed* their happiness, peace, and joy into your soul. They're the powerful kingdom of God, the kingdom that he says to pursue first.

The power of your tongue ACTIVATES GOD who is the 1225 words.

The power of your tongue TRIGGERS GOD so that he storms onto the scene in all of his might and glory like what happened to me that sunny summer California afternoon in 1983 the day my green convertible died when the Navy SEAL team stormed the beaches of my broken heart and *force-fed* peace into my butchered soul.

But please, please, I'm begging you *please*—remember that a superabundance of these emotions of happiness, peace, and joy are much more than a "feel good pleasure" that comes from the red Ferrari and hot boyfriend. That's not transcendent peace: That's COMFORT.

The kingdom forces that I'm talking about are *the supernatural kingdom* that transcends this natural realm; the kingdom that grants you supernatural peace that floods you in the midst of a storm.

It's this kingdom that grants you *all the power you need* to get *the endless treasures* that you want, need, dream, and desire.

It's this kingdom that taps you into the riches that belong to you in the *Garden of Eden,* which might include, if it's what you want, the red Ferrari and hot boyfriend. It also includes your first job. It also includes a car to drive, a humble automobile that gets you from your apartment to the grocery store. It also includes a puppy if that's what you want.

Don't get caught up in the size of the blessing, whether large or small.

Get caught up in the fact that you seek first the kingdom of God first and foremost, and then *all the desires of your heart come a-runnin' like a raging bull chasing the cowboy at the rodeo.*

REMEMBER: The 1225 Words Are a Tiny Sliver of Almighty God

Now then, listen to me carefully: *That tiny cup of ocean water is* HUGE AMOUNTS OF ENERGY *that can power Miami for a year like a tiny cup of the living water is* HUGE AMOUNTS OF ENERGY *that can power* YOU *for a lifetime.*

You beg for an explanation, "How can God be the 1225 words in my mouth?!?"

How would you like a scientific explanation how God can be the 1225 words in your mouth?

I'm not a scientist but I've played one on TV, so allow me to tap into other men's knowledge that is far more extensive than mine.

Scene 26

Astrophysicists Explain God

Astrophysicists Explain How God is Multi-Dimensional

Astrophysicists have learned that there are more dimensions than just length, width, height, and time, space, and matter. That's only three dimensions, the three-dimensional world in which we live.

There must be at least six other dimensions of space to accompany the three that we're familiar with. Six *extremely tiny* dimensions of space.

Space-time theorems now prove that there must be a causal agent that has the power to create space-time dimensions. Well duh, that would be God, oh ye small-minded creature who tries to understand him in only three dimensions, as in the intellectually deficient question, "If God is the creator of the universe, then who created God?"

Silly boy, he's outside of all ten dimensions, and the fact that there's six more plus one dimension more than the three dimensions of which we are familiar, astrophysicists agree that the God who created these space-time dimensions must be *bigger* than what happens in ten space-time dimensions.

But just for shits and giggles let's entertain the question, "Who created God?" Every person with a brain bigger than a walnut acknowledges that there is an uncreated creator.

Let's say it was a multiverse generator that created the universe. Yeah, that's it! A multiverse generator created the universe!

Some people say it's a quantum environment in which our universe emerged spontaneously. Okay, let's go with that theory.

Regardless of which theory to which you subscribe, that force that created the universe was uncreated, can we agree on that?

If so, then it turns out everyone believes in an "uncreated creator," is that fair to say?

So then the only real question is whether that uncreated creator is ***personal*** or ***impersonal***.

If you need me to tell you I will, but I think you can figure it out for yourself. Hint: Pick the uncreated creator that HAS emotions, who IS emotions, and who demands we seek HIS EMOTIONS for our survival, prosperity, and success.

A multi-universe creator has **no emotions**. A quantum environment has **no emotions**. An impersonal uncreated creator has **no emotions**.

A personal creator has incomprehensible, inexplicable emotions of happiness, peace, and joy that transcend our three-dimensional world.

An impersonal creator has no emotions. *A personal creator has floods of emotions that fill you full to overflowing.*

But I digress.

How Can God be Everywhere at All Times Yet Still in Your Mouth

Hang in there with me another minute so I can explain as an astrophysicist explains how God can be everywhere at once and yet still be the 1225 words in your mouth.

It's impossible to comprehend these deeper dimensions. For instance, in the fourth dimension I could take a basketball, and turn it inside out without making a cut or a hole in the surface of the basketball. I can't do that in three dimensions, but I can certainly do it in four dimensions. How the hell can you comprehend this? You can't, and that's only the *fourth* dimension. Remember there are *at least* six more.

If you could enter the fifth, sixth, and seventh dimensions you could travel back and forth from the past to the future, and back to the present. In fact you could exist in all three separate time eons at the same moment.

In the tenth dimension we reach a pinnacle where everything you imagine immediately appears, and everything imaginable happens at the speed of thought. Is that the dimension that God refers to when he says, "Nothing shall be impossible to you"? Is it the tenth dimension where Isaiah says, "Eye has not seen, nor ear heard, neither has any human mind imagined the things that are in store for them that love him"? Isaiah prophesied that 2800 years ago around 700 BC.

The astrophysicist from whom I learned these dimensions is Dr. Hugh Ross who once took a mathematics course where the professor required him to prove these other dimensions with mathematical equations. He could indeed prove them mathematically, but he couldn't visualize them, nor could he comprehend them.

This is millions of brain cells above my paygrade, but let's proceed.

So how do we understand these other dimensions? Well, we can't imagine the fourth dimension much less all ten dimensions, but what we can do is visualize fewer than our three dimensions. Dr. Ross gives an easy-to-understand example.

He says to the audience, "I have a couple I'd like to introduce you to. They're handicapped, but not physically handicapped. They're handicapped in that they are missing one dimension. They have length and width, but not height."

He continues, "So please welcome Mr. and Mrs. Flat."

He takes two paper cutouts, one of a man, one of a woman that he cut from a piece of paper with a pair of scissors. He holds them up so the audience can see.

He then lays them flat on top of the table and says, "We're gonna constrain them to a flat universe. Mr. and Mrs. Flat live in a flatland universe where there's just length and width, and no height."

Hence two pieces of paper cut in the shape of two people lie flat on the podium for the audience to see the flatland universe of Mr. and Mrs. Flat.

He asks the audience, "So how do Mr. and Mrs. Flat engage with one another? Well, Mrs. Flat looks at her husband and what does she see? She sees a line. As she walks around him, she can see longer lines or shorter lines, depending upon what part of Mr. Flat's body she looks at.

If she looks at his head, she sees a shorter line than if she looks at his torso," to which I add, "If she looks at his pee-pee it's a much shorter line than even his head. You know, his *other* head." Locker room talk, I know. It's why I never get invited to speak in churches.

He continues with his example. He refers to himself when he says, "As a three dimensional being I don't have that handicap." Dr. Ross looks down at his podium where the two paper cutouts lie, and he says, "I look at Mr. Flat, and I immediately see the entire outline. I don't have to walk around him."

As he stands at his podium and holds his hand over the two cutouts, he continues, "Moreover when I come close to them I can put my hand one millimeter above Mr. and Mrs. Flat. I'm now physically closer to them then they are to one another, but because I'm above their plane, it's impossible for them to see me or touch me."

Do you see from this example how God is unseeable and untouchable, and yet closer than our next breath? It's because he operates on another plane outside of our three dimensions, and yet he's closer than the next heartbeat.

That's how God is the 1225 words in your mouth, and even though they appear to you as only words, in the unlimited time-space dimensions of God THOSE WORDS ARE HIM.

Do I fully comprehend what I just said? Nope, and I don't care. I accept the fact that the 1225 words are God, and when I fire them off into the skies with **the power of my tongue** they *force-feed* supernatural transcendent peace into my heart like what happened to me that sunny summer California afternoon in 1983 the day my green convertible died, but as you can see over and over throughout this book, I don't settle for merely "it is so," but I dig deeper into the HOW.

Yes, God is those 1225 words in my mouth, but HOW?...and I gave it my best shot to explain HOW by explaining that God operates outside of, over and above all the dimensions that he created that we will never comprehend until we enter *the world to come.*

More about *the world to come* in the second volume of this trilogy entitled *Shitty to Happy in 21 Minutes: THE EVIL QUEEN,* but the 1225 words are our initial foray into God's greatness.

The 1225 words and **the power of our tongue** thrusts us into the presence of his magnificent greatness by way of the inexplicable emotions of our infinite God, the One who is our creator, who duplicated his emotions inside us, and buried them deep into our innermost being, and gave us 1225 words and **the power of our tongue** to resurrect them from dormancy into dominance.

We'll come back later to explore more of who God is, and I promise it'll surprise you. I guarantee you've never heard anything like it, but first let's explore deeper how to open the doors to all your dreams, desires, hopes, and wishes.

"Speak the words...I'm right here."

****

Scene 27

Emotions Command Kingdoms

Alrighty let's get back to the point that I made before I launched into an explanation that your *1225 biblical praise words are the Lord God Almighty.*

Remember we discovered what the kingdom of God is? The kingdom of God is happiness, peace, and joy...*God's* ***supernatural*** *happiness, peace, and joy that transcends the natural realm of this present world,* a peace that you *force-feed* into your heart via the 1225 words and **the power of your very own tongue** like I did the day I accidentally plowed headlong into God himself like a drunken sailor on a three-day binge that sunny summer California afternoon back in 1983 the day my green convertible died.

The kingdom of God is happiness, peace, and joy.

Remember I posed the question earlier, is it happiness, joy, and peace that kick open the doors to the Garden of Eden, or is it the kingdom of God that kicks open the doors to the Garden of Eden? Do the prophets, teachers, preachers, and motivational speakers who claim that happiness, peace, and joy open the doors to your fortunes agree with the Jewish rabbi who claims the kingdom of God opens the doors to your fortunes?

The answer is emphatically yes, unequivocally yes, and a great big scream from the mountaintops YES!

The Words of the Jewish Rabbi and Those of the Prophets, Teachers, Preachers, and Motivational Speakers ALL AGREE

All agree. Everybody agrees that **happiness, joy, and peace that transcend the natural world...emotions that erupt from deep within you by the 1225 words that you patiently speak by THE POWER OF YOUR VERY OWN TONGUE are** ***powerful emotions*** **that, when they commandeer your heart, these emotions open wide the gates to everything you need, want, dream, and desire.**

And the pinnacle of simplicity is these emotions are the kingdom of God. It's the kingdom he said to strive for, pursue, and make your top priority.

This kingdom IS emotions, specifically the **enormously powerful emotions** of supernatural happiness, peace that transcends this natural world, and joy unspeakable and full of glory.

These kingdom emotions come to us from another dimension. Which dimension? The tenth, of course. "All things are possible to him who loves, obeys, and seeks first the kingdom of God."

The rabbi continues, "When you seek FIRST these otherworldly transcendent emotions that are not from this world, but are from another dimension, then ALL THESE THINGS—your wishes, dreams, and desires WILL BE ADDED TO YOU."

There goes the sound of the screeching wheels of the speeding passenger train. Even after forty years I still try to wrap my mind around what I just said, but no matter whether I understand it or fully comprehend it, I still get the benefits: That is, the kingdom of God emotions kick open the doors to the Garden of Eden, God's garden of luxury and delight that belongs to every man, woman, and child that walks in these supernatural emotions of happiness, peace, and joy that originate only from God who lives inside us, God who is the 1225 words that we *force-feed* into ourselves by **the power of our tongue**, like what happened to me that sunny summer California afternoon in 1983 the day my green convertible died.

These powerful emotions comprise the kingdom of God, the kingdom that IS the unspeakable powers in the Ark of the Covenant that Indiana Jones sought after.

****

Now, get on with your mission to dig for the Ark of the Covenant. Sell everything you have to buy the pearl of great value.

Diligently strive for the unspeakable, incomprehensible powerful emotions of the kingdom of peace and happiness that have been buried inside you since the day you were born.

Pursue these emotions with all your energy, heart, soul, and might because these EMOTIONS are the kingdom of God that grant you entrance into the luxurious and opulent, very lush Garden of Eden.

****

Scene 28

Adventurous Thrill Ride

And now get ready my dear friend, because you are about to embark on the most exciting adventure you could ever imagine!

You're the hero in the movie that sells all that he has to buy the hidden treasure. Where is this treasure? *It's buried inside you,* just like King David was buried inside the seventeen-foot-high block of marble. The great sculptor Michelangelo could see the completed David inside the marble block as he chiseled away the parts of the marble that were not David.

God the great sculptor sees the COMPLETED YOU *inside your worried, fearful, fretful, and angry exterior.* **He gives you the hammer and the chisel**—*the 1225 words and* **the power of your tongue**—*to chisel away the dirty, crusty, scabby outer core of you that covers over the kingdom of God to reveal* the inward COMPLETED YOU just like Michelangelo chiseled away the dirty, crusty, scabby outer parts of the marble that covered over David to reveal the inward COMPLETED SCULPTURE of David.

The kingdom of God—happiness, peace, and joy—lives inside you. It's buried deep underneath your crusty scabby poisonous emotions of anger, fear, worry, stress, anxiety, depression, a broken heart, and bad breath. Well, not bad breath, but the rest of them for sure.

Anyway, the kingdom of God is hidden inside you just like David was hidden inside the seventeen-foot-high block of marble.

****

Chisel away the crusty crap and crud that chokes and suffocates your kingdom! Pursue joy unspeakable and full of glory! *Uncover the true you.* Expose the inexplicable peace that lives inside you that surpasses the ability of the human mind to comprehend!

Do not allow anything or anybody—not even yourself—*especially* don't allow yourself—to stand in the way, because **yourself** *is the* ONLY *person* that can stop your happiness and peace from bursting forth from the depths of your seventeen-foot-high chunk of marble.

How can you thwart the kingdom of God from bursting forth? There's only ONE WAY— Negligence.

Negligence is the only way to suppress the kingdom of God that hides inside you, because when you *neglect to use your 1225 words and* **the power of your tongue**, then the kingdom, although it's alive, whole, and complete, remains idle, effete, useless, to no avail, and worthless. It might as well not exist, and all that God created you to be is for naught.

Neglect is the *one and only* omission you can employ that prevents the 1225 words and **the power of your tongue** from forcing yourself to be full of happiness and peace.

Nancy Negligence and Nicholas Neglect have the power to chokehold your 1225 words and **the power of your tongue**, not because they have power, but because they restrain YOU from using YOUR POWER.

These ugly harmful restrictions called NEGLECT and NEGLIGENCE put a chokehold on you. They restrict you from tapping into your supernatural powers that reside in **the power of your tongue**, a power to behold that kicks the living shit out of the Evil Queen who is the filthy ogre with boogers in her nose that lives under a bridge who's filled to the brim with the demonic vultures of anger, hate, frustration, worry, stress, and fear of failure.

There is only one force more powerful than Superman. What is it, do you remember?

Kryptonite.

Nancy Negligence and Nicholas Neglect are your kryptonite.

Therefore, CRUSH THEM. ANNIHILATE THEM. Be diligent! Be persistent! Stay after it!

When you propel the energy of those 1225 words into the skies by **the power of your very own tongue**, there is no force, no energy, no demon…no black hole, no gravity, no supernova…no Evil Queen, no kryptonite, and NOT EVEN YOU…nothing in the universe is strong enough to thwart the unrelenting forces of **the power of your tongue** and 1225 words from unearthing the hidden treasure of the kingdom of God that lies deep inside you.

Once you unleash the 1225 words by **the power of your tongue** there's nothing that can stop the relentless attack of peace and happiness that *force-feeds* itself into your heart with such an intense assault that it befuddles the natural mind. It's an invasion into your soul that originates from deep within the caverns of your innermost being and is even more overpowering when you harness your Evil Queen's demonic powers of anger, unforgiveness, worry, stress, fear of failure, depression, and hopelessness, precisely like what I accidentally stumbled upon that sunny summer California afternoon in 1983 the day my green convertible died!

So, what are the only powers that can impede the peace and happiness from bursting forth out of your heart?

Negligence and neglect.

When you refuse to use the power of your tongue then YOUR NEGLECT is the kryptonite that blocks your power.

CRUSH NANCY NEGLIGENCE! ANNIHILATE NICHOLAS NEGLECT! They're the only two forces capable enough to defeat you. Nothing is more powerful to stop the kingdom of God from total outbreak in your mind, your heart, and your soul than NEGLIGENCE and NEGLECT.

Therefore put a headlock on Nancy and Nicholas, and thus force yourself to speak the 1225 words, and when you do, then **the power of your tongue** chisels away the parts of you that are not the kingdom of God, that kingdom that's buried inside you that is mighty and powerful, that kingdom inside you that is full of unspeakable remarkable emotions of supernatural happiness, otherworldly peace, and joy unspeakable and full of glory.

It's that very kingdom that's buried deep inside you, and buried inside me, a kingdom that remained hidden from me until I accidentally unearthed it from the treasure trove of my soul on that sunny summer California afternoon in 1983 the day my green convertible died.

This is the kingdom that you make your top priority. Pursue this hidden treasure, because when you do, then *you get all the things that you need, hope for, dream about, and desire!*

Two of the mightiest forces in the universe—his 1225 words and **the power of *your very own tongue***— that is to say, a cache of high-powered ammunition and a lethal weapon to fire them, and a sharpshooter to pull the trigger—combine to give you the greatest miracle of all miracles…and that's *peace that* *transcends this natural world even whilst you're in the middle of a life-shattering cataclysmic earthquake.*

****

And one more thing: Don't be a dingleberry poopwad and expect sincerity from yourself when you don't have any to offer.

You'll never feel sincere when you're worried, stressed, morally bankrupt, full of anxiety, hatred, anger, resentment, and unforgiveness.

You have no sincerity to offer when you're pissed, and even if you did, it wouldn't make the words work any better or more powerfully.

In fact, on that sunny summer California afternoon in 1983 the day my green convertible died, my anger was exceedingly *more beneficial* to the power of my words than was any human sincerity I might have conjured up, which I didn't, because I had none.

I realize I just dropped a stink bomb on you, and I'll go much more into detail about this a little later.

The point is sincerity is a most reprehensible prerequisite. In fact it's worse than blue balls because the sincerity requirement terminates your supernatural otherworldly peace. It causes your mission to prematurely abort.

Nothing gets accomplished while you foolishly wait for your sincerity to kick in.

But like a neanderthal Pharisee, you demand that unless and until you feel sincere then you will not speak the 1225 words.

Why is this so disastrous, catastrophic, silly, imbecilic, ignorant, and moronic to wait for sincerity?

BECAUSE YOUR SINCERITY NEVER KICKS IN!

Sincerity is a burdensome man-made obligation that professors and preachers conjure up in seminaries, pass it along to other preachers who blather on about it in their pulpits in their spineless attempt to facilitate God, and in their moronic illiteracy, they sermonize that you must add the carnal idol worship of *sincerity* to coax God into a divine intervention. *That shit doesn't work, never has worked, and never will work!* It's the equivalent if your five-year-old daughter helps you fix the carburetor. She's cute, she's convinced she's helping you, but she gets in the way, and she can't fix anything.

Sincerity is cute, she's convinced she's helping you, but she's in the way, and she can't fix anything.

Ladies and gentlemen, boys and girls, when you're angry, pissed, depressed, anxious, and full of unforgiveness YOUR SINCERITY NEVER KICKS IN. You'll never "feel like it." You are CURSED with your demented emotions if you demand sincerity to kick in before you agree to unleash the 1225 words by **the power of your tongue**.

Don't wait for sincerity. Pull the trigger. Fuck your sincerity.

When Dirty Harry pulled the trigger of his .44 Magnum, did he grunt hard to make the bullets move faster? Did he think to himself, "Boy, I sure hope this gun works today?" Did he work up a heart-felt sincerity before he fired the gun? Did he think to himself, "There's gotta be something more I can do to make these bullets move faster!" No silly goose, he pulled the trigger and let the bullets fly that ripped new assholes in the bad guys!

THE BULLETS are God's 1225 words.

THE MAGNUM .44 WEAPON is **the power of your tongue**.

WHO'S DIRTY HARRY? *Dirty Harry* is YOU. Pull the trigger. Unload a barrage of bunker-busting ammo on the bad guys of wicked emotions.

"Speak the words...I'm right here."

****

It's time for another break. The reason you take seventeen-minute breaks is because the ideal study time is fifty-two minutes of study, seventeen minutes of breaks. That's why I suggest each break is seventeen minutes.

Even though the time between each intermission might not be fifty-two minutes since everyone reads at different speeds, but every reader without exception needs time to assimilate, and to fully comprehend the depth of revelation, revelation that certainly I cannot fully comprehend in fifty-two minutes, and very few others can, even in fifty-two minutes.

I suggest these intermissions especially when the subject matter is quite heavy such as was this last section. It takes a few minutes to absorb the depth, and yet simplicity of God who lives in your heart and your mouth, and whom you ACTIVATE by **the power of your tongue**.

So grab a sandwich, a cup of coffee, take a walk, lay down for a few minutes, go run an errand, or sit and do nothing even though "sit and do nothing" is man's specialty, not women's. I'll see you in seventeen minutes.

INTERMISSION

ACT 6: Let's Talk About Your Goodies!

Scene 29

Where's the Goodies?

Oh yes, oh yes, you wanna know more about your game show prizes, don't you! Who doesn't? Listen to the Jewish rabbi trip out on your prizes that break out like floodwaters as your *Peace Births Fortunes.*

"Pursue the kingdom—peace, joy, and happiness—because it's these kingdom forces that ensure *you amass the whole enchilada on the game show"* (Mathew 6:33). "Whole enchilada" is *the whole shabangabang* for all y'all non-tamale-loving redneck folk.

"Yeehaw, Steve...I wanna know about all the stuff I get! I wanna hear about all the awesome prizes from the game show! Tell me about all the treasures in the Garden of Eden, God's garden of luxury and delight that I get when I diligently pursue the unspeakable powers of the kingdom of happiness, peace, and joy."

Here they are. Listen to the things that come after—AFTER you pursue the kingdom of God. Yes, this means AFTER you pursue supernatural happiness, peace, and joy. Not before.

YOU: Cut the bullshit Steve, why do I gotta pursue the kingdom first?!

ME: *Because Cabrón, these spiritual forces of happiness, peace, and joy* ***are the forces that empower you with the strength, the skill, and the intensity to GET the things you need, to ACQUIRE all the desires of your heart.*** **These emotions are the forces that attract everything you want, need, dream, and desire!**

YOU: Did you just call me 'dumbass' in Spanish?

ME: Sí.

YOU: [Sigh] Alright, alright, you have my attention. I'm listening.

****

Listen to this paraphrase of the rabbi's prodigious promise in Mathew 6:31-33, "Don't worry about your life, what you'll wear, what you'll eat, what you'll drive, or where you'll live. Look at the flowers of the field. Do you see how beautiful they are? They don't toil nor spin, and yet I tell you that Solomon with all his Beverly Hills bling and tailored Armani suits was not arrayed like one of these." (Armani suits…*definitely* a paraphrase.)

The benefits continue, "If God clothes the grass of the field which is here today and gone tomorrow *how much more will he clothe you, oh ye doofus flatbottomed mommas?"*

My mother's favorite flower was an orchid. Oh my goodness how she treasured her orchids! I love Stargazer lilies because of their aroma…there's nothing that smells quite like it; and every girl loves her man to give her a dozen red roses on Valentine's Day.

So I want you to think to yourself, "No matter how lovely these flowers, their beauty, their aroma, the love, and the memories… He'll clothe me in much finer attire than even these beautiful flowers." Okay, I admit that he didn't call you a "doofus flatbottomed momma" but I indeed called you a 'cabrón' *dumbass* in Spanish.

He continues, "So *don't worry* about what you'll eat, or what you'll drink, or what you'll wear, like the village idiots do." He goes on to say, "These lame-brained bozos pursue fame, fortune, and wealth with a heart devoid of peace and joy." When these simpletons pursue the desires of their heart first before they pursue the forces of joy, happiness, and peace that comprise the kingdom of God, they overlook the precise dynamisms that open the doors to the very things they want, need, dream, and desire. It's the same as if you refuse to enter the PIN number for your bank account at the ATM machine.

They refuse the rabbi's epitomical words to seek the kingdom first, and thus their journey to acquire the desires of their heart is wrought with worry, fear, and stress, they step all over people to get their goodies, and they take foolish shortcuts. They even lie, cheat, and steal to acquire the things they want.

Then to add misery on top of misery, they don't even enjoy the crap when they get it. Remember the four celebrities?

WORD TO THE WISE: *Pursue the kingdom* BEFORE you pursue the **fortune** SO THAT *the* **fortune** *you acquire is untainted and untarnished* and is not a curse.

Listen to me, does the wagon pull the mule? No, that's backward. Do you get a flat tummy, and *then* eat properly? No, that's also backward.

People that ask me, "Can I get a flat tummy first, and then eat right?" also have to ask for the number to dial 9-1-1. It's as foolish to expect the desires of your heart to happen before you get happiness, peace, and joy as it is to expect the flat tummy to happen before you work out with weights, do cardio, and eat proper nutrition.

Pursue good nutrition and workouts first, and *then* you get the flat tummy, because if you pursue a flat tummy without the proper nutrition and good workouts, then you'll stress and get frustrated and take foolish shortcuts. Stress and frustration lead to dietary shortcuts like the celery diet, the starvation diet, and the *seafood* diet (whenever I *see food,* I eat it).

Pursue *the good nutrition and proper workouts* FIRST*...then* the flat tummy naturally follows.

Even so, pursue *the kingdom of God* FIRST*...then* the desires of your heart naturally follow.

Oh, and don't forget the recipe for chocolate. It's sooo good, and in some cases has helped folks slim down.

Conquer Your Muffin Tops

Allow me to divert for a few moments to help you learn a nutritional lifestyle that benefits you physically, emotionally, and spiritually, and then we'll get back to happiness, peace, and joy.

My heart aches for those that food holds them hostage. It's the subject for another time and place but for now let me give you a catalyst to get your body started to go in the right direction, would that be okay?

My weakness my whole life has been sugar, sugar, and more sugar, mixed in with a little butter to add that velvety taste, and powdered sugar sprinkled on top, and chocolate for dessert.

As a little boy I'd sneak into Mom's kitchen at night, pour myself a bowl of cereal and empty the entire bowl of sugar onto the cereal until the sugar formed a mound slightly higher than the milk. I'd hurry through the boring cereal to get to the milk-soaked sugar, and you talk about heaven, I was there.

In eighth grade my sugar addiction graduated to a higher level of sophistication. After a tough day on the baseball field little Stevie Hanks would invade Mom's kitchen and melt a whole stick of butter over the stove. Then pop a couple of slices of zero-nutrition white bread into the toaster and whip up a concoction of cinnamon mixed with sugar. By now the butter is melted, the toast is done, and now comes a third of the melted butter onto the white nutrition-less bread and smother it with cinnamon sugar until the butter no longer absorbs the cinnamon sugar.

Next is another third of the butter, add more cinnamon sugar, and finally the last of the butter, more cinnamon sugar until the stack of butter and cinnamon is an inch high and soaked through with butter. If my mom had put butter-soaked sugar on my spinach I'd have bigger biceps than Popeye's.

I dragged these lousy nutritional habits into my adult life, but there's a big difference between a kid who eats crap and an adult who eats crap. What's the difference? The adult who eats crap puts on fat quicker than the kid, and it's harder to lose.

In high school I wanted to play college football. My coaches said it was unlikely because my senior year I played third string tailback. Third string means there are two players that are better than me at my position. I played tailback because every time I'd jump up to get in the game coach would yell, "Hanks get your tail back on the bench!"

My dad knew I wanted to play college football, so he scheduled a meeting with my coaches to get their expert advice. "No way," they flatly denied, "There's no way he can play college football." My coach's pessimistic prognosis drove me to work harder, not only to prove them wrong, but I had a burning desire to play college ball, high-school coaches' opinions be damned.

My senior year in high school I weighed a meager one hundred fifty-five pounds, not enough to play college football. The scouting report on Hanks— "He's small but he's slow." And so to grow bigger, my weight gain diet was several meals a day that included chocolate covered donuts, sugar-coated breakfast cereal— By the way they conducted a study in 1960 at University of Michigan at Ann Arbor and found there is more nutrition in the cardboard box than in the cereal.

I looked forward to my nightly dinners of four Big Macs with fries and Coke. My weight blew up to 198 pounds and my waste was a massive thirty-eight inches. Just for comparison my waste today is thirty-two inches at 178 pounds with six-pack abs. Fifty years later, I'm seventy, and my body is in way the heck better shape than it was fifty years ago in college.

My first year after high school I went to Florida Southern College in Lakeland where I got cut from the baseball team and spent the whole rest of the year on weight-training and weight-gaining to prepare to transfer to Florida State to play football.

The dean of Florida Southern College, a great and well-loved man named Frank Szabo expelled me the last week of school for leading a group of about one hundred and fifteen freshmen to push a fire truck from the fraternity house next door into Lake Hollingsworth at the bottom of the hill.

My dad, the Reverend Carl Hanks was a preacher of a small Methodist church in Orlando about an hour east of the college. Florida Southern was a Methodist college that gave me a preacher's kid scholarship, and my dad drove from our home in Orlando to Lakeland to talk the dean into letting me back in to take my final exams. My propensity for school was about as keen as stale milk but what else was there for me to do? College was the only place for me, a kid with no plans and who doesn't know what to do with his life.

I transferred to Florida State University in my sophomore year. I tried out for the football team during spring training, and not only did I make the team, but they offered me a partial scholarship. For the next two years football consumed me until I put together a rock n roll band, played all the bars and clubs and fraternity houses in Tallahassee, quit my football scholarship and paid and played my way through school as a rock star. And that's when the partying exploded. I outdrank, out-partied, and outcheated every fraternity member on Greek row. You read that right…outcheated.

One night after a case of beer and playing a club on Tennessee Avenue in Tallahassee… that's right, a case of beer—that's twenty-four beers; I drank all of them—it was finals week, and I put together a posse of drunks to carry out my hair-brained idea to go across the street to the business school because back then professors used mimeograph machines which came over with Christopher Columbus on the Mayflower. Wait…he came over on La Pinta, La Nina, and La Santa Maria.

You'll have to Google mimeograph machines in the 70s, but the professors discarded the first several printed copies of the final exams because the ink hadn't yet started to flow. The copies were inferior, but they were readable.

So the professor cuts them with scissors since paper shredders had not yet been perfected, he throws the first couple of copies in the trash can, the maid comes along and empties the trash cans and drops all the trash in the dumpster outside the building, and bingo: There sits a most valuable treasure to a lying cheating university student who's drunk on twenty-four beers and got kicked out of a religious school.

I rallied twenty fraternity brothers, we took trash bags with us, and went to the dumpster to load all the trash to bring it back to the fraternity house. Picture this: Twenty drunken fraternity brothers each with a bag of trash, dark figures in the night around 2:00 a.m. as we waddle across Tennessee Boulevard looking like drunk Santa Clauses with bags of toys slung over our shoulders. We unloaded our spoils in the dining room of the frat house, and we pieced together ten final exams from shreds of paper that the professors had painstakingly cut with scissors. We finished around 6:00 a.m. the next morning. It was like we put together a massive puzzle with thousands of puzzle pieces. It's ironic that if we'd studied as long as it took us to piece together all the exams we'd have passed without cheating.

We got our just rewards though, because while we slept soundly after a night of piecing together ten exams, one of the fraternity brothers stumbles in around 7:30 a.m., he's cold, he's still drunk from the night before, so he needs kindling to start a fire in the fireplace to keep him warm, right? Yep, he used the neatly assembled tests we'd spent the entire night piecing together as kindling to start a fire.

Soon after I arrived in Hollywood to pursue my dream to be an actor that was birthed in me that day in the church around the corner from my life insurance office in Orlando, my acting coach pulled me aside and said, "Steve, you need to look like an actor, not a football player." And so at the age of twenty-five, the diet bug burrowed deep into me.

I tried every diet in every magazine on every talk show and they all worked beautifully to frustrate me, discourage me, and make me even fatter than ever; smaller, yet fatter.

The more I tried to lose weight, the more I obsessed over food. At night I'd eat a whole bag of Famous Amos chocolate chip cookies and then go to the track at Beverly Hills High School and run five miles to work off the calories. The final straw came when I went on a starvation diet and ended up looking like a pear—big bottom, small top.

For several years I was on a quest to find the answers and through many years of trial and error found the perfect, easy, and effective way to get six pack abs and a smoking ass—smoke crack and liposuction my thighs. Nah, I'm kidding.

I promise you that you will learn the most effective, surefire, and stunningly effortless way to get your body in swimsuit-look-hot-at-the-beach shape, but that's for a later book but in the meantime you can learn the catalyst. Go to ShittyToHappy.com to download a video of me making the best protein shakes you've ever tasted.

I'll come back to this story about muffin tops in a few minutes.

Seek the Kingdom FIRST

As always, the proper sequential order for your health, your job, your business, your career, your family, and your fit body is that you pursue *the happiness, peace, and joy* FIRST…*then* your good fortunes, including all the desires of your heart naturally follow.

Listen, God knows you need things. He knows you *want* things, including a fit body, and he gives you the secret how to get them. *Here's God's secret:* "Pursue first **the kingdom of God**, and then *all these things that the village idiots seek after* come easier and with less effort."

But then he screams, "STOP!"

What?

"Stop the worry and stress! Worry and stress is the 'toiling' and 'spinning' I warned against."

STOP IT!

Not only do worry and stress make you miserable, but they *block* your good things from happening, like a kink in the garden hose stops the water flow which then causes *more* misery, stress, and worry, which perpetuates *more* toiling and more spinning.

It's a vicious cycle, a never-ending merry-go-round that spirals out of control into sadness, misery, frustration, and despair that's inescapable even if you get your stuff, so say the four celebrities.

How do you halt the debilitating merry-go-round of worry and stress?

It's easy when you know how.

HOW DO YOU DO IT? HOW DO YOU HALT THE MERRY-GO-ROUND OF WORRY AND STRESS??? Here's how!

You unfurl 1225 words by **the power of your tongue** to FORCE-FEED peace and happiness and a sense of calm into your heart like what I accidentally discovered that sunny summer California afternoon in 1983 the day my green convertible died. *That's how to avoid toiling and spinning, worry and stress!*

Your 1225 words that you fire off by **the power of your tongue** are the Navy SEAL team that sneaks up on the sleeping enemy and surprise attacks Mr. Anger, Mr. Worry, and Mr. Stress with a hefty dose of peace, transcendent inexplicable peace that **the power of your tongue** and the 1225 words *force-feeds* into your heart so that you fill yourself full to overflowing with that supernatural happiness and otherworldly peace, both of which are the kingdom of God, the kingdom that the Jewish rabbi says is hidden inside you, that kingdom that has been buried deep down in your heart since the day you were born, and is the never ending flowing fountain that supplies everything you need, want, dream, and desire.

It's these superabundant emotional forces, these powerful emotions that smartly crush the debilitating Evil Queen, and it's these 1225 words and **the power of your tongue** that *force-feed* strength, power, wisdom, and might into you, and thus catapults you onto the throne in *The Secret Place of the Most High.*

It's these emotions that you *force-feed* into your heart that empower you to live in the rarified stratosphere of otherworldly peace, happiness, and joy that enable you to amass all your fortunes, dreams, wishes, and the desires of your heart that await you in the Garden of Eden.

It's Impossible to Worry While You Feel Happy

You can't feel peaceful and stressed at the same time any more than you can turn left and go right at the same time. Have you ever tried to go left and go right at the same time?

I've never tried to go left and go right at the same time, but I've tried to date two girls at the same time without one knowing about the other, but that's different. That's back when I was a bad boy. Listen, it's impossible to go left and go right simultaneously.

You can't do it.

My point is you can't worry and stress at the same time that you feel happy and peaceful. So, when you *worry* and *stress* about your stuff, then your mighty warriors of happiness and peace have left the building. They're downtown where they sit at the local pub slamming down drinks, telling each other stories, and getting drunk.

Let's head downtown to see what's happening at Bobzo's Bar and Grill.

Scene 30

Downtown Bobzo's Bar

INTERIOR BOBZO'S BAR AND GRILL – MID AFTERNOON

MR. PEACE: Hey, Mr. Happy, I feel worthless. [He slurs his words.] This guy won't let us do our job. He won't let us make him happy and peaceful. I even filed for unemployment.

MR. HAPPY: Yeah, I'm with you. What's wrong with this *cabrón* that he won't do something so simple as to open his mouth and unleash **the power of his tongue** to speak 1225 words so that you and I can give him the gift of "us," the gifts of supernatural peace and happiness? I'm still on the payroll, so he might as well get the most out of it. [They commiserate together. They guzzle more drinks. It's been a long afternoon.]

****

May I give you a word of advice? Don't disappoint Mr. Happy and Mr. Peace. They stand ready to open the floodgates to the majestic kingdom, a kingdom that awaits you the moment you cut loose your 1225 words and **the power of your tongue** to drown out the clamor of worry and stress.

The truth is, the instant you call on Mr. Happy and Mr. Peace, they pay the bill, gulp down their drinks, dash out of the pub, and sprint straight to your heart with such a ferocious roar (albeit a tipsy one) that you no longer hear the din of worry and stress, anxiety and fear, hatred and unforgiveness.

That's what the words and **the power of my tongue** did for me that sunny summer California afternoon in 1983 the day my green convertible died.

Twenty-one minutes after you unleash your 1225 words by **the power of your tongue**, these two dynamic weapons *force-feed* peace and happiness into your heart.

Remember, these emotions lay dormant inside you, and have lain dormant inside you since birth, but they storm the scene with might and fury by the dual artilleries of **the power of your tongue** and 1225 "biblical cuss words."

You resurrect the kingdom of God with the same power that Jesus arose from the dead. A tiny glass of God's water is all you need, and that's when I promise you that you are in a perfect position to pursue and achieve your fortunes and your goodies.

They might not come today, but they'll come, and it'll be by reason of the kingdom of God—*happiness, peace, and joy,* and NOT by worrisome and toilsome, stressful and worry-filled pursuit.

Yes, you can achieve your dreams *without* happiness and peace, and even if you're filled with worrisome and toilsome pursuits you'll get stuff, but it's a grind. It's not fun, is it? It ages you, and gives you wrinkles and saggy skin. It causes ulcers. And hemorrhoids. And sometimes lots of drinking and drug abuse.

Countless men even lose their families as they pursue their dreams, goals, and visions when they are filled with worrisome and toilsome pursuit devoid of kingdom emotions of happiness, peace, and joy, and thus lose the balance in their life. Success is more important to them than their family when they can have both.

And the worst part of all is even when you achieve everything you want, every desire, every dream, every wish, if you are devoid of peace, so what? You already heard John Lennon, Eric Clapton, Jim Carrey, and Cameron Diaz, all who have way the hell more money, fame, and success than most ever will. You heard all four of them tell you: *All that stuff won't bring happiness.*

Ten words you never hear on a deathbed: "I wish I'd spent more time at the office."

That's great Steve, but you never finished telling us about our goodies.

****

Scene 31

Goose's Golden Eggs

Steve, you never finished telling us about all the goodies we're gonna get!

Oh my goodness, you're right! That's because I focus on HOW you get the goodies much more than I focus on the goodies themselves. The tail mustn't wag the dog.

Alright, so then what are the *goodies* that you get when you pound yourself full of his kingdom of happiness, peace, and joy by 1225 words and **the power of your tongue**?

God whispers to you that he'll clothe you like the flowers and the grass of the field, more beautiful than my favorite Stargazer lilies, my mom's beautiful orchids, and the dozen red roses for your wife on Valentine's Day. These beautiful flowers are allegorical for your "things"—your goodies, your dreams, your goals, and your aspirations—*all the desires of your heart.*

It includes, like he promised, the clothes you wear and the food you eat, where you live, and what you drive—the everyday needs we all have, but it also includes your extraordinary game show prize called "The Garden of Eden" which includes a beautiful family and great friends, and how to raise your kids. It includes successful jobs, blossoming careers, business ventures, and brilliant ideas.

It includes limitless wisdom and insights to solve business problems, personal and relationship problems. *It includes all the good things you can imagine.* The whole shabangabang. Remember "the whole shabangabang" is *the whole enchilada.*

Have you Heard of the Goose that Lays Golden Eggs?

The kingdom of God is the goose that lays the golden eggs. You remember the story, right? You can have *one* meager golden egg, or you can have the goose that lays *all* the golden eggs. Which one do you choose? That's easy.

Happiness and peace...*the kingdom of God* that springs forth after 21 minutes as you consistently spew forth 1225 words, time after time, day after day is your goose that lays the golden eggs.

When you *consistently, diligently* pursue the goose—that is, when you consistently and daily pursue God's happiness and peace, rest, and tranquility by the weapons of your 1225 words and **the power of your very own tongue**—then your golden eggs naturally follow.

Apply the Kingdom to Wherever You Are in Life

Now that you know there's a goose that lays golden eggs, here's a reality check: Start where you are. If you're a teenager, chances are slim that you'll own the New York Yankees right out of high school. Heck, you don't even have a job yet.

Or if you're under six feet tall it's unlikely you'll win the NBA Slam Dunk Contest, unless you're Spud Webb who won in 1986 at the unbelievable short height of 5'7" when the other players were a foot taller than him. For comparison, Michael Jordan at 6'6" won the following two years in 1987 and 1988.

When I first assumed that I could get everything I want, I had a wild imagination. I wanted to run major film studios, own seven cars, be a famous actor, travel in my private jet, and preach this message of peace, happiness, and joy to people all over the world, but I didn't have the money to make payments on my green convertible. That's why they repossessed it.

So, I aggressively sought happiness, peace, and joy for my *immediate* needs, like not getting angry when I had to take city buses in the pouring rain after the bank repossessed my car.

This was before cell phones, so I didn't have the bus routes and time schedules at my fingertips like cell phones have today. But even though I was dead broke and soaking wet from the pouring rain, I pursued peace.

I'd speak those 1225 words until **the power of my tongue** *forced* peace into me. *I refused to let anger control me and rob me of my hopes, dreams, and wishes.* You gotta handle the **rain** at the bus stop (the petty annoyances) before you can handle the **flood** (the magnificent blessings).

Crush Those Petty Annoyances!

It was January of 1985 when a friend of mine, Karen got me an audition to work at the Detroit auto show as a spokesman for a car company which was ironic since I myself didn't own a car after my green convertible got repossessed. My transportation around Los Angeles was bus and bicycle. On the day of the audition my interview was at 1:00 p.m., so I left the apartment about 11:00 a.m. to make sure that I would make it on time.

Los Angeles is a huge city. I started my bus trip on the Westside headed for downtown where I assume the address is located, 19001 S. Western Avenue. When I get to downtown LA, there's Western Avenue, but the address numbers are only four digits long. The address of my interview is five digits long. So I keep going and going, hoping to find where the addresses turn from four numbers into five numbers. It didn't happen.

Finally I get off the bus to call the Toyota headquarters where my interview is to ask for their location. Remember, we had no cell phones, so I dropped a dime into the pay phone back when pay phones cost a dime. It turns out they are a 2 ½ hour bus ride away from where I was. They are all the way down south in Torrance. You talk about pissed. I was livid.

Who the hell city planner names two streets twenty miles apart the same name!

Now remember I am already well-disciplined to use **the power of the tongue** to overcome my sadistic nature, so I start to speak the 1225 words with loads of sarcasm and frustration.

I continue the bus ride. I have to go south to get to the Toyota headquarters—a *long* way south. The bus seems like a slow crawl, and there I sit on the seat near the back of the bus, muttering the 1225 words under my breath so that **the power of my tongue** *force-feeds* supernatural inexplicable peace into my heart..

Finally we get to where I think we are near the Toyota headquarters, but the bus suddenly turns left. I run to the front of the bus and ask the driver, "Hey, why'd we turn left? I have to keep going south." It so happens that no buses go directly to the Toyota offices. The driver informs me that I gotta take two more buses to get to where I need to go. I was already so damn late for the interview.

I get off the bus, and I'm standing at the bus stop, waiting for the next bus, and I get mad…raging mad…really raging mad and frustrated. It's cold outside, it's raining, I'm late for my interview, I'm the ex-star of a cancelled TV series, and I am madder than a mangy-haired pit bull chewing on a wasp.

But I remembered the words of the Jewish rabbi emblazoned on my mind, "Seek first the kingdom of God, joy and peace and his righteousness, and everything else will be added to you," and that he adds, "When you find the pearl of great value, sell all that you have to buy it."

What's the pearl of great value? EMOTIONS. The EMOTIONS of *supernatural happiness, peace that is not from this world, and joy that you cannot describe.* **That's the pearl of great value.**

Did I want to speak the 1225 words at the bus stop in the cold rain? Are you kidding me? I'd rather jump rope in dog shit, but through gritted teeth I continue to speak the 1225 words out loud.

I steadily pace up and down the sidewalk as I wait for the bus for what seems like an eternity. I sputter the 1225 words like a machine gun so that the weapons of **the power of my tongue** and my 1225 words shuts down my mind with all its childish reasoning.

Finally the bus arrives.

Even though I am wet from the rain, even though I am late for the interview, even though I am frustrated, anxious, and pissed off, even though I am sitting in the back of a smelly Los Angeles public transportation bus, the same peace that flooded me that sunny summer California afternoon in 1983 flooded me once again in the back of that city bus.

Folks, I'm pleading with you—*this shit works!*

I make it to the interview 2 ½ hours late. I step into the bathroom to change into my nice interview clothes that I have been carrying under my arm all this time. As I walk into the man's office, he greets me with a smile, invites me to sit down, and after he hears my story, he looks at me with a gentle smile and offers me the job. I cannot contain my excitement. We stand, shake hands, and he gives me a hug. I broke down and cried like you girls watching a Hallmark movie. He hands me a tissue, and I celebrate the whole four-hour bus ride home.

Now let's return to my story about my muffin tops like I promised you. The auto show that the nice Toyota man hired me for was in Detroit, so Toyota flew me from Los Angeles in January 1985. Karen, the girl who got me the interview, and another girl Trish whom I had a major crush on, and I met for dinner every night at the hotel after the show. And for dessert we ordered my favorite, my all-time number one request for dinner every night—cheesecake smothered in … hell, it makes no difference what it's smothered in—just smother it. Omigod if somebody could make soap out of cheesecake I might bathe more often.

Remember I had used the weapon of **the power of my tongue** and 1225 words to overcome emotional junk, so now my plan was to try it on the physical junk. Several weeks prior I had begun to speak out loud "my body is stripped of all excess fat." Those were my words and I said them with regularity.

There's no magic in the words, so fat will not melt off just because you say it, but for sure what happens is your mind seeks out ways to give you those results.

Two major paradigm shifts happened within weeks and months of speaking those words. One, every book on nutrition that I read pointed me in the right direction as to what to eat, how to eat, and how to exercise. I've learned that for every great book on nutrition and exercise there are thousands of bullshit ones; and yet every book that I came across just "happened" to be one of the great ones.

The second thing that happened is my words and **the power of my tongue** changed my desires.

Let's continue the story at the Detroit auto show. At the dinner table after a show with my two girlfriends we ordered cheesecake and my friend Karen turned to me with a mouth full of luscious cheesecake and asked, "Aren't you going to have any?" It wasn't until that moment that I realized my desire for the cheesecake was gone. Poof! Vanished like a lazy man running from a job.

I'm not going to say I've never eaten cheesecake since the auto show in Detroit but will say that now I control the cheesecake; it does not control me.

Anyway, my point is you gotta be diligent in the little nuisances in life.

*You gotta handle the **rain** before you can handle the **flood***

It's important to remember that how you are in the trivial things is how you are in the lavish things, so you must conquer anger over a broken fingernail before you can conquer anger over a million-dollar business deal, which is why I fought so diligently to stay peaceful in the ice-cold pouring rain at the bus stop that frigid afternoon.

Of course I kept the big dreams alive in my heart but remember, happiness and peace are also effective on the trivial pursuits like your crazy roommate that won't clean the dishes.

Happiness and peace affect every aspect of every person's life, no matter who they are or in what echelon of society, whether they're the CEO of Disney who negotiates multi-million-dollar deals, or whether they're the kid that got his zipper stuck in his Mickey Mouse costume in Disney World. No matter where you are in your life's journey, happiness and peace are the pearl of great value that gets you through the tough times and busts open the doors to the good times.

Let's continue with his instructions on *how* to get your goodies.

The KINGDOM Empowers You to Get Your Goodies

Listen…when you're happy, peaceful, and joyful from those 1225 words that you cut loose by **the power of your very own tongue**—

—In other words, when you, Mr. Dirty Harry, fire off several rounds of those 1225 words by **the power of your mighty .44 Magnum**—

—Well then, this peace that you *force-feed* into yourself empowers you to get your things.

But *how?* You notice I ask "how" quite often. So, HOW does peace and happiness get your things? I mentioned it earlier, but let's re-examine.

Happiness and **peace** transform you from a fresh army recruit into a trained soldier. They conform you to be *highly skilled* and *efficient in your endeavors*.

They broaden your human efforts—whether it's phone calls, negotiations, meeting the right people, creativity and brilliant ideas—so that your efforts are *highly* productive.

Happiness and peace that erupt from those 1225 praise words that you unleash by **the power of your tongue** fashion you from a weekend tennis player into a seasoned pro.

I wanted to play professional tennis, so I started on what used to be called the satellite circuit. I flew to Elvis Presley's hometown of Memphis for my first tournament. I checked in to the desk, met my opponent, and we played our first match, which he won 6-0, also known as six love. It felt like six-hate to me, but whatever.

The next set was a little better. He still beat me 6-0, but this time I returned a few of his serves. The third set I gave him a run for his money. Yeah, I made him run for the balls that I knocked into the neighboring courts. The final score was six-love, six-love, six-love. He whupped me in straight sets.

As we walked to the scorer's table to report our match results, I noticed that my opponent—his name was Josh—walked slowly and slightly slumped. I asked him if he was okay, and he told me this was his first tournament in eighteen months. I asked why so long? He said he'd been sick for a year and a half, and this was his first time back out on the court since he'd been sick. *I got whupped by a man that had been ill for eighteen months!*

I meekly congratulated him for a good match.

When we approached the scorer's table, the scorekeeper in charge exclaimed, "Mr. Hanks, what're you doing here?! You're supposed to be playing your match!"

I sheepishly responded, "We've already finished."

Afterward, my opponent Josh and I shook hands, he went his way, and I went mine back to Los Angeles, and never played another satellite circuit tennis tournament again.

Yes, happiness and peace will turn you from a weekend tennis player into a seasoned pro, but as you can see from my personal experience, it's allegorical.

Happiness and peace exceedingly energize and momentously multiply your efforts so that your humble human efforts produce *superhuman results* whether it's for a job, groceries, and a place to live, or whether it's a multi-million-dollar business deal, or whether it's knowledge of fitness and nutrition, or whether it's how to have the most perfect marriage on earth and the most perfect kids in the world—a skill that requires wisdom, training, and diligence but you'll learn how to master each of these in volume three in the *Shitty to Happy in 21 Minutes* series called *THE GREAT INVASION.*

Happiness and peace train you and equip you so that these wishes, dreams, wants, and desires come on you and overtake you. How? Why?

Because happiness and peace make everything you touch turn to gold.

I have a friend that came from a family where her stepmother was a drugged-out junkie who was jealous of her over the other sisters because she was daddy's favorite, so the stepmom hated her, abused her, went on rage-filled tantrums, and treated her and her sisters horribly, all the while her father was oblivious to the stepmom's behavior because he was liquored up every day. This little girl and her sisters lived in constant fear in their own home every day of their life.

By the time I met her she was twenty-six and had deep emotional scars from the abuse of her stepmother and uncaring father. She contemplated suicide. She built a beautiful array of tattoos on her right arm to hide the physical scars from the cuts she self-inflicted with razors to numb her deep emotional pain. She felt hopeless. **PTSD *never* lets up!** That is, until you slam your heart full of 1225 words by **the power of your tongue**. It'll stop PTSD dead in its tracks, but it's only a momentary relief that lasts for just a few minutes before it returns, but your 1225 words and **the power of your tongue** give you *a few moments* of relief. Do it again to get *a few more minutes* that last a little longer before you need to fight it again. How often must you fight it? Every time it returns. It's a helluva fight, but the mighty artillery of the words and **the power of your tongue** win with immediate, albeit temporary relief, so fight it again, win again, fight it again, win again. Wash, rinse, repeat.

This little girl's biggest dream from a young age was to meet a Prince Charming that would rescue her with the kiss that would wake her up from the nightmarish hell that the Evil Queen had inflicted upon her. It was soon after we met that she fell in love with the man she always dreamed of as a little girl. For the first time in her life, even though she mistrusted men because of her father, she at long last met a man to whom she gave her heart—completely, loyally, and deeply. Every little girl's dream.

All was perfect, they were in love, they had fun, they planned to get married…until he deceived her. For many weeks he continued to break her trust and her heart. She was devastated. She was crushed. She was heartbroken. She cried out, "I *knew* he was the one. Why God, why?!?" For several months she was devastated, broken-hearted, and ANGRY…angry like I've seen very few, although many suffer from anger.

But she diligently unleashed the power of her 1225 words by **the power of her very own tongue** to rest in the peace that passes all understanding, and slowly but surely, **the power of her tongue** and the 1225 words turned her huge ship around, even though whipped and smashed by mighty winds and torrential waves of anger, despair, abandonment, and a crushed heart.

Now three years later, the 1225 words and **the power of her very own tongue** healed her heart, she's reconciled with her father, her stepmother circled the drain (died), she has more money than she knows what to do with, and she's with a man who's everything she ever dreamed of, and she travels the world, not only for her fashion business, but to improve the quality of lives of those who've never had a fighting chance.

It didn't happen overnight. **But it happened.** *Happiness and peace make everything she touches turn to gold.* That's why it's a pearl of great value. *Sell everything you have to buy it.*

"Speak the words…I'm right here."

Scene 32

Kingdom Forever Reigns

Folks, if you haven't figured this out by now *this is not religion*. This is not religious gobbledygook that does nobody any good. This is a supernatural way to live in God's kingdom of happiness, success, and peace where everything you touch turns to gold, a life that he intends for every man, woman, and child to enjoy…FOREVER.

You exclaim, "FOREVER? Steve, are you telling me this kingdom of happiness, peace, and joy lasts *forever?!?"*

Yes, I am. David, the king of Israel—the real one, not the marble one that Michelangelo carved out of stone—exclaims, "Your kingdom is an *everlasting* kingdom" (Psalm 145:13). What does *everlasting* mean?

"Everlasting" means FOREVER.

What kingdom is he talking about that lasts forever?

He's talking about the kingdom of God, your emotions of happiness, peace, and joy, emotions that leap up from deep within your soul like those that I accidentally excavated that sunny summer California afternoon back in 1983 the day my green convertible died.

He's talking about the kingdom that *force-feeds* itself into you with explosive power to flood every fiber of your being by **the power of your very own tongue** that speaks 1225 words of praise that arouse the mighty fury of the Prince of Peace—the prince who is *God himself* who lives on the *inside of you*.

These emotions of happiness and peace are the kingdom of God that resides in you forever and ever. These emotions are the kingdom that's lived inside you since the day you were born, and these hidden emotions are the kingdom that propels you through this life, and *these emotions that you resurrect by the 1225 words and* **the power of your tongue** are the kingdom that kicks open the doors to the Garden of Eden, God's garden of luxury and delight, and it's these emotions that are the kingdom of God that invade your heart and live inside you, and thoroughly possess you so that you look like God himself, and this kingdom lasts throughout all eternity.

****

Have you ever wondered what you're gonna do for all of eternity? How do we keep from getting bored? I mean, a gazillion billion years is a long time…and that's only a mere drop in the bucket in the scope of eternity. *Eternity is a long-ass time!* You wanna know how you'll keep from getting bored throughout all of eternity? Is it a vacation home? How about three vacation homes, one in Tahiti, one in Canada, one in Aspen? How about twenty homes…or thirty…and a jet to fly between all of them. And enough gold to build a city. Is that how you'll be happy forever and ever? Really? Not quite…after a few lifetimes of years you're bored out of your gourd, regardless of how many hundreds of homes and thousands of pounds of gold you have.

****

Allow me to show how bored you'll be if all you have is material things. The first time you watched your favorite movie, you loved it so much that you watched it again. And again. And again. I had a friend that watched *E.T. the Extra-Terrestrial* fifteen times. You might've watched your favorite movie fifteen times, but did you watch it a hundred times? Did you watch it a thousand times, or ten thousand times? No, because if you watched it ten thousand times you'd despise the movie and never watch it again.

Well guess what? It's the same in eternity if all you have is a bunch of material possessions. If that's all eternity is, you'll be as bored as a blind man in a strip club. You'll despise your fifteen solid gold Cadillacs, your seven jets, and your thirty homes as much as if you watched the same movie ten times a day for a thousand years.

Come to think of it, remember the four celebrities told you that if the only thing you have in this earthly life is material possessions, lots of gold chains around your neck, fame, and a fortune in the billions, even trillions of dollars, but have no peace and joy, well then even if you're the world-famous John Lennon who had it all but had no joy, then you'll grow to hate your fortunes, fame, and lifestyles of the rich and famous, which explains why so many mega-rich folks fill their days with drugs and alcohol. It's the only escape hatch they know of that dulls the emptiness and boredom.

There's only one eternal force that satisfies you, not only in this earthly life, but for all of eternity, and that is peace that passes all understanding, joy unspeakable and full of glory, and love, fun and fellowship with every person you've ever loved on this earth, every family member, every one of your pets, and even every person you've ever met, and even those whom you've never met including every person that's ever lived since Adam and Eve, with a few exceptions. It's strange how someone would choose a different eternity, but they do. I'll explain how and why in volume two of this trilogy *Shitty to Happy in 21 Minutes: THE EVIL QUEEN.*

Eternal life is gonna be a big party, even bigger than the party I promised to the young girl.

And don't worry, you'll have LOTS of awesome and fantastic *material things and fortunes* for you to enjoy throughout all eternity, and yes, you can even have them while you're on this earth, but best of all you're gonna have so much peace and happiness that you melt into total eternal relaxation, fun, and joy like you cannot imagine, not to mention you'll operate in all dimensions—fourth through the tenth.

I'm curious how we can turn a basketball inside out without cutting the ball or poking a hole in it, and that's only the fourth dimension. There are at least six dimensions beyond that.

The tenth dimension is where everything you imagine appears. Immediately! As soon as you imagine it!

Is it the material cars, boats, yachts, jets, homes, castles, fine food and wine that make eternity so special and fun? *Are you fricking kidding me?!?*

It's your God-given emotions of happiness, peace, and joy that make your eternity a paradise!!!

The best way I can describe our emotional bliss that lasts for all of eternity with my severely limited human experience is it's like the feel-good pleasure and relaxation when you sit on the beach in the Caribbean drinking pureed mango topped with Jamaican rum in the soft breezes under the warm sun, your adoring husband by your side, the kids play happily in the ocean, and everywhere you look for as far as the eye can see *life is good.* You and your husband have dinner planned tonight at your favorite restaurant. You watch the kids play and they give you immeasurable happiness. You have no stress and not a care in the world. When do you want that vacation to end?

Never. That's how much fun eternity is. *You never want it to end.* It's a good thing too because it never will.

And remember eternity is not limited to three dimensions. Three-dimensional material things cannot satisfy you for trillions of years. Yes, you'll have plenty of material things, more than you can imagine, but eternity is much better than material possessions. It's a full-blown explosion of peace, happiness, and joy, more so than you can comprehend. Eternity satisfies you with EMOTIONS that extend far above and beyond your comprehension, and those EMOTIONS are the eternal kingdom of God that lasts forever.

That's why I show you TODAY how your emotions open the doors to the ETERNAL Garden of Eden.

So whadya say we tap into that eternal happiness, goodness, peace, and joy right now? You're gonna be ecstatically happy for eternity, so you might as well get accustomed to it RIGHT NOW!

That's why I told the young girl, "Your purpose in life is to be happy." I told her to pursue the one true thing that lasts all eternity. King David said, "Your KINGDOM is an *everlasting* kingdom…" (Psalm 145:13). What kingdom is that King David? "It's the kingdom of EMOTIONS of happiness, peace, and joy. That's the kingdom that lasts for all of eternity." *It's the pearl of great value. Sell everything today to buy it!*

Listen to me, I promise that your goodies, the desires of your heart, and all your wishes will come to you in abundance.

You'll get your goodies, but hopefully by now you can see that even though you'll get all the desires of your heart, remember that the four celebrities said they're not as fulfilling as peace, happiness, and joy. These spiritual forces—these kingdom forces—are the pinnacle of delight, like the Ark of the Covenant with its treasures of untold value.

How do you arouse these kingdom of God emotions of happiness, peace, and joy? You do it like I did that sunny summer California afternoon in 1983 the day my green convertible died.

"Speak the words…I'm right here."

My brain is near saturation, and if yours is too then it's a good time to reflect. You've learned a lot so far, and it gets even more intense from here on, so take a break and come back a little later, I encourage you to do so. Take another seventeen minutes for this break. You'll be refreshed and energized as we move deeper into the realms of happiness and peace, joy and love.

INTERMISSION

ACT 7: You'll Get Goodies! But When?!?

Scene 33

What's the Holdup?

Are you ready to have that big party I promised the young girl?

Wheeeee YES! Let's PARTY!

Slow down Speedy Gonzalez, slow down, not so fast.

Why slow down?! Why not so fast?

Because Speedy G, God adds a stern warning about your goodies, and it's a doozy. Let's tackle his ominous warning. *It's of utmost importance!*

HERE'S GOD'S WARNING!

"Hey Buttflakes, if you make the *goodies* your number one priority like the village idiots do, that's a recipe for disaster."

You think to yourself, "What the heck is wrong with that God, and why'd you call me 'Buttflakes'?"

Those are both good questions. First, he calls you "Buttflakes" because you're a buttflake. Second, there's an incredible delusion if you focus on your wants, needs, dreams, and desires BEFORE you revere the kingdom of transcendent peace, otherworldly happiness, and unspeakable joy.

"Cut the Crap God…I Want the Desires of My Heart!"

You grumble, "What's the big deal God, if I pursue my dreams, my needs, my wishes, and my desires **before** I *force-feed* myself full of happiness, peace, and joy? C'mon God, lots of people do that."

God does a face-plant. "Yes, you're right, lots of people seek after the things before they seek after the peace. That's why I call them *buttflakes.*" He persists, "Listen to me, I *want* you to have all the desires of your heart, I patently do. So if you'll listen to me, I'll show you HOW to get them in the most efficient and productive way imaginable."

Okay God, but what does "patently" mean? And what's all the stuff you'll show me how to get?

I'll show you how to get ALL THE DESIRES OF YOUR HEART!

And "patently" means I am *clear and unambiguous.*

He's not finished yet, there's more.

Please continue God, I'm listening.

God continues his fantabulous offer, "And when you do things my way, which is you pound yourself full of happiness, peace, and joy like a mighty warrior who squeezes the trigger of Dirty Harry's .44 Magnum of 1225 words and **the power of your tongue**, then the dual double-barreled armaments that I give you to protect yourself against the vile and demonic emotions of the Evil Queen—this heavenly artillery of 1225 words and **the power of your tongue** packs you full of my emotions that enhance your skills, they ensure that you expend less energy, you produce more success, and hence the desires of your heart come to you much easier than ever before, and the best part is they come without stress and worry, also known as toiling and spinning."

Keep talking God, I'm listening.

He continues, "When you do things MY way, your goodies come to you in abundance like the torrential downpour the day it rained six feet in twenty-four-hours on Foc-Foc in La Réunion Island in the South Indian Ocean in 1966."

God is educated, so he uses fancy words like "patently" and brings up obscure floods of biblical proportions like what happened on an island named, of all things "Foc-Foc." Really God? Six feet of rain in one day?!? *One day!?* What da Foc-Foc were you thinking?

God laughs. He thinks I'm funny. Religious Pharisees with their thumbs up their ass think I'm a heretic. Anyway, he continues, "The thing is, if you do it *your* way, you'll grind and struggle, worry, and stress, and even if you get the riches, the homes, the cars, the businesses, the fantastic careers like many people do, these achievements fail to make you happy."

I disagree with you God. When I get all that stuff I KNOW I'll be happy...right?

Dear Reader, may I remind you *again* what the four wealthy and successful celebrities, John Lennon, Eric Clapton, Jim Carrey, and Cameron Diaz already told you!

What happens when you gracelessly stumble backward from the kingdom of transcendent peace like a club-footed Sumo wrestler in a belly dance contest, and you goofily plow ahead into your vacuous dreams, far-fetched goals, and feckless visions? [Your dreams and goals are indeed reckless, feckless, and far-fetched when your fuel tank of happiness, peace, and joy runs on empty.]

When your tank is empty, here's what happens: You have a weighty ball of stress, worry, and anxiety chained to your ankle. It hogties you as you drag around three sixteen-pound bowling balls as you look for a place to live, a car, a job, a career, business deals, a boyfriend, a family…all these good and noble things that you greatly desire but are such a pain in the ass to accomplish if you don't have happiness, peace, and joy.

God instructs us, "When you pursue the things without *first* taking a drink from the plentiful fountain of happiness, peace, and joy, then *every task is a chore* and *everything you touch turns to dust."*

He elaborates, "Nothing works. Everything falters. Your endeavors are futile when you're filled with worry and stress, and thus your efforts are vanity. Your arduous work gets you nowhere, and even if you achieve your desires *you will* NOT *enjoy them."*

That's right, you will NOT enjoy the blessings, ain't that right, Mr. John Lennon? And Mr. Clapton, and Mr. Carrey, and Ms. Diaz, and J. Paul Getty who said, "I find this wealth to be a terrible burden, and I would trade it all for one successful relationship."

If J. Paul Getty was alive today I'd invite him to read volume three of this trilogy *THE GREAT INVASION* and he'd see how enormously easy it is to enjoy his massive wealth of billions of dollars and at the same time have a *Love Story* that exceeds his greatest expectations.

However if a man builds his multi-billion-dollar empire on a flimsy foundation devoid of peace, happiness, and joy, then he's built his empire on quicksand, and when the rains come like the day it rained six feet on Foc-Foc Island, then his empire collapses to the ground like the houses in my neighborhood crumbled like LEGOs during the Northridge earthquake in 1994 because they were built on a flimsy foundation of packed sand and dirt.

"When the floods come and the winds blow, that house collapses with a mighty crash" (Mathew 7:27). *Without the kingdom of happiness, peace, and joy as a bedrock foundation, you are a toad swimming with sharks*. Your billions of dollars won't save you from a broken, crushed, and lonely heart.

Oh but you obstinate thing, you complain, moan, bawl, and squall, "The things come after?!? The 'things' come *after happiness, peace, and joy?!?* Oh jiminy fizzle buckets God, I want the desires of my heart NOW!! I WANT 'EM NOW, and then when I get them, THEN I'll be happy!"

God does another face-plant. He has bruises on his forehead from all the face-plants you cause him. God tells us for the four hundred and forty thousandth time, "I WANT YOU TO HAVE YOUR GOODIES!" [God uses ALL CAPS when he wants to get our attention.]

He pleads with us, "I want you to have your goodies! I want you to have *the desires of your heart* more than you want them for yourself, but it's futile when you toil and spin, so if you'll LISTEN to me I'll show you HOW to get them easily, effortlessly, all without toiling or spinning."

You relax for a moment when you realize God wants you to have your stuff, and that he's not telling you to seek peace because it strokes his ego, no. He tells you to seek his kingdom of peace FIRST because THE KINGDOM OF PEACE *is how you get your shit!*

God Tells You How to Get Your Goodies

God says, "Pursue the kingdom of peace and joy FIRST, and THEN pursue your goodies." He continues, "Don't pursue your goodies, also known as 'the desires of your heart' before you pursue and reside in and take up residence in the kingdom of peace and joy, also known as *The Secret Place of the Most High."*

Why not God, why not?

"Because oh ye douchewaffles, *your peace and joy* OPENS THE DOORS *to the desires of your heart."* God calls us "douchewaffles" when he tires of calling us "buttflakes" as he tells us for the eleventeen thousandth time to seek peace first because **peace is the key that opens the doors to the desires of your heart that reside in the Garden of Eden**.

Did you catch that last sentence, the one right before he called you a "douchewaffle"? What did he say? He said, "*Your peace and joy* are the keys that UNLOCK THE DOORS *to your goodies in the Garden of Eden!"*

Transcendent peace and otherworldly joy are the keys that UNLOCK THE DOORS *to the desires of your heart*

How much more awesometastic can God's plans be for you and me to achieve success? He implores, pleads, begs, and cajoles for you and me to *seek the kingdom* FIRST. As a byproduct we get **all the desires of our heart**!

A few of you need help with the meaning of "awesometastic." It's fantastic with a dose of awesome sauce.

****

Scene 34

God's PIN Number

Have you ever had the perfect solution for a friend, but your friend doesn't listen? If they'd listen, they'd easily solve their problem, but *they don't listen.* It's frustrating, isn't it?

I have a buddy that wants to lose weight. I asked how many sodas a day he drinks. "Two," and then he added, "Losing weight is SOOO hard!"

We're driving down the freeway. I said, "Pull over, let me show you something." We dodged three traffic cones, a Hyundai, and a Lamborghini before we pulled over onto the right-hand shoulder of the 405 freeway in West Los Angeles.

"How many calories are in a pound of fat?" I asked him.

He says, "I don't know." I said, "Three thousand six hundred. How many calories are in a can of soda?" He looked at the can in his hand, and he replies, "It says here 140."

"You drink two a day, how many calories is that in a day?"

He said, "Rounded up is 300."

I'm not quick at math, so I said, "Take out your calculator. Divide 3600 calories that are in a pound of fat by 300 calories in two cans of soda that you drink every day. What's the answer?"

"Twelve."

"That's right. Every twelve days that you drink two cans of soda you add a pound of fat to your body. That's the bad news, but on the other hand if you stop drinking that shit, then every twelve days you LOSE a pound of fat. That's the good news."

He sighed. "But it tastes SOOO good," to which I replied, "Nothing tastes as good as fit feels."

I continued, "Do you know how quickly your body converts the 300 calories of sugar in those two cans of soda into fat?"

No.

Pretty fast. As quickly as by mid-afternoon if you slam too much sugar into your body all at once.

He wasn't happy.

"That's okay," I told him, "The truth sets you free, but first it pisses you off."

Did he change? No, even after I laid out for him how simple it is to lose one pound every twelve days, two and a half pounds a month, thirty pounds a year if he does one thing, eliminate soda. That's all. **Eliminate soda!** Nothing else. *Eliminate soda!*

Now you can understand how frustrated God gets when he tells us how simple it is to get our goodies, but *we don't listen.* He tells us again and again that *the key that unlocks our goodies* is THE KINGDOM OF GOD! *But nooo…I want my soda!*

Listen to me, this what I'm about to say is profound: Your goals, dreams, and desires that you anxiously pursue when you're filled with worry, fear, and stress are the same goals, dreams, and desires that YOU ACHIEVE when you follow God's instructions.

How does God say to pursue your dreams, goals, and desires?

He says, "Seek first the kingdom of God, and all these goals, dreams, and desires, houses, places to live, automobiles, great jobs, a fantastic career…ALL THESE THINGS that you desire, want, and need WILL BE ADDED TO YOU because your kingdom of God emotions of transcendent peace and happiness OPENS THE DOORS for you to enter into the fantastic Garden of Eden where all your desires come to life.

The same peace, joy, and happiness that *force* you into the rarified stratosphere of *feel-good pleasure* also give you a 100% **achievement rate**. All you gotta do is *force-feed* yourself full of otherworldly peace that transcends this natural three-dimensional world, and then **be diligent in all your hand finds to do**, and take care of the poor, the fatherless, and the widow.

Diligence is important, but FIRST you must seek his kingdom of *otherworldly peace* and *joy unspeakable and full of glory,* and THEN be diligent in your tasks, phone calls, study, and the thousands of other tasks set before you.

Do things in the right order, and then these supernatural powers UNLOCK THE DOORS to your treasure chest called the Ark of the Covenant, a treasure chest that leads you to all the goodies you desire.

"But beware," warns God, "Your goodies, your dreams, your desires, and your goals scamper away like a startled deer when you stress, worry, and you're anxious. It's like you try to sneak up on a squirrel. You can try to catch him, but he's too quick.

"When you worship at the altar of these vile emotions then you needlessly overwork yourself. You're like a pack mule towing a tour bus with three flat tires, and fifty obese sightseers."

How many more times must God tell us that the secret to unlock the desires of our heart is happiness, peace, and joy? But since we're boneheads we continue to do things our own imbecilic stressed-out, worried, dumbass way, like my friend who drinks soda and wants to lose weight! God has bruises all over his forehead from the face-plants we cause him.

We have an overwhelming urge to complicate what God makes simple.

God's Ways Are the PIN Number

Let's say I give you an anniversary gift of $10,000 to go on a vacation with your family to the Bahamas. I give you my bank card and the PIN code. I send you a text, "The PIN code to my ATM machine is 2345. There's no daily limit, so take out the $10,000 and have a great time with your family."

You text back, "Why do I need the PIN code? I just want the $10,000."

I text back, "But the PIN code unlocks the ATM that opens the door to the $10,000. The pin code is 2345."

You respond, "But why do I need a PIN code? *I just want the money!"*

I scream at you in all caps, "THE PIN CODE OPENS THE BANK DOORS TO THE $10,000!"

I do a face-plant and shoot you one last text, "It's no wonder God does face-plants and calls you a *buttflake* and a *bone-headed douchewaffle* when you continually ignore his PIN code that opens the gates to all your desires in the Garden of Eden."

What's the PIN code that opens the gates to the Garden of Eden?

P.E.A.C.E.

Peace is the PIN code that opens the doors to your Garden of Eden!

That's profound. Tuck it away for a bit and we'll come back to it in a minute.

If you chase the $10,000 without the PIN code, you're like the fool who chases his wife's boobies before he chases her heart.

I'll let you in on a little secret Guys, if you seduce your woman's heart, she'll give you…don't faint boys, listen to me: If you seduce her heart, she'll give you her body. Can I get an "Amen!" from the girls?

Don't try to get her body without the PIN code to her heart.

Neither do you try to get $10,000 from the bank without the PIN code to the ATM machine! The PIN code is the top priority; otherwise it's an exercise in futility, the same futility as if you chase your success, your fortune, and your goodies before you have the PIN code of transcendent otherworldly peace, happiness, and joy. It's the same futility as if you chase your wife's boobies before you chase her heart.

It's as futile as if you wipe before you poop.

You gotta have the PIN code to unlock the ATM machine. You gotta have the PIN code to unlock the Garden of Eden. You gotta have the PIN code to unlock your wife's boobies. Put things in the right order boys and girls. *Don't wipe before you poop! It's futile, and there ain't nothin' there.*

So men and women, boys and girls, what's the PIN code that unlocks the Garden of Eden where all your dreams, visions, hopes, desires, and goals await you?

HERE'S THE PIN CODE: **The kingdom emotions of happiness, peace, and joy.** That's your PIN code!

And guys, what's the PIN code to unlock your wife's body? HER HEART. When you pursue her heart *then she'll unlock her goodies*, and you'll learn so much more about this in the third volume of this trilogy *Shitty to Happy in 21 Minutes: THE GREAT INVASION.* Guys and girls, you'll love how *THE GREAT INVASION* unveils the foolproof method for you to have a relationship where the both of you have starring roles in *The Greatest Love Story Ever Told!*

God has a beautiful and fulfilling foolproof action plan for your success, for your goodies, for your marriage, and for your health, and for all the good things you want in life that includes everything you need, want, dream, and *all the desires of your heart*. Here it is: *Pursue first the unspeakable powers of the kingdom of God.*

AND THEN WHAT, GOD?

GOD: ***"The result is you'll have all the power you need to get all the things you want, need, dream, and desire."***

He's not through yet, ***"And whatever else you still need, well then I, the Lord your God will invade your world to make sure it happens."***

When you exalt the spiritual kingdom forces of EMOTIONS—the happiness, peace, and joy that explode up from deep down inside you by the power of your 1225 words that you detonate with **the power of your very own tongue** like what happened to me that sunny summer California afternoon in 1983 the day my green convertible died, then he *promises* you that his transcendent peace and inexplicable happiness force everything you need, want, dream, and desire to appear in your life.

This is his unimpeachable assurance: *The kingdom of God that you pound into your heart by the twin armaments of 1225 words and* ***the power of your tongue*** *THRUSTS you, COMPELS you, FORCES you into the Garden of Eden where the desires of your heart await you.*

**God's Perfecta Trifecta to Prosper
Your Body, Health, Family, Finances**

ONE: *Force-feed* the 1225 "biblical cuss words" by **the power of your tongue** like the gushing water of a firehose that you cram down your throat so that they in turn *force-feed* peace, joy, and happiness to explode upward from deep within you, like what happened to me that sunny summer California afternoon in 1983 the day my green convertible died.

TWO: The happiness, peace, and joy that you *force-feed* into your heart like I slam-dunked into myself that sunny summer California afternoon kicks wide open the doors to your goodies that are in The Garden of Eden.

IN SUMMARY: *Happiness, peace, and joy are* **the kingdom forces that OPEN THE DOOR to your goodies**, *and thus they are* the PIN code to the ATM machine.

ONE: Keep in mind the PIN code.

TWO: Be **diligent** in all your hand finds to do.

THREE: When you pull the money out of the ATM machine, give a portion to the poor, the fatherless, and the widow. To every bum on the street? No, but you'll know when it's right.

"Speak the words…I'm right here."

****

Scene 35

The Treasure Map

You've pursued the goodies when you're stressed, haven't you?

Did you notice how difficult it is to pursue your goodies when you have no happiness, peace, and joy? Don't look at me with that innocent look on your face, like "Who, me?" Yes, douchewaffle, I'm talkin' to you, and yes, I borrowed God's pejorative pronoun. Maybe it's a noun, but whatever.

You want the things, right? Who doesn't want the things? *And you should have the things!*

And you WILL get the things because God promises you that *all the desires of your heart* are yours.

Why am I so confident you'll get your desires*? Because God gives you a TREASURE MAP!* The treasure map lays out the path for you to get your dreams, hopes, goals, and visions, and here's the best part: **It'll be without the painful, despicable, and even revolting feelings of anxiety and stress, fear of failure, and the two wickedly notorious cockblocks—GREED and IMPATIENCE.**

Now listen to me, when you achieve everything you need, want, dream, and desire, then remarkably you avoid the painful prophesies of Carrey, Clapton, Lennon, and Diaz, and J. Paul Getty. In other words, *you enjoy your goodies without the faux happiness that requires excess drugs, alcohol, and work-a-holic-ism..*

The Treasure Map

If your multimillion-dollar rich great grandfather gives you a secret map to tap into his safe in the basement of his mansion estate after he dies, how assiduously do you protect that map from intruders? Do you sleep with it under your pillow? Do you fight to protect it no matter what the cost? How valuable is that treasure map?

There's another treasure map that's even more valuable than the map to your great-granddaddy's safe. ***It's the map that leads you into the Garden of Eden.***

What's the treasure map to get you into the Garden of Eden that unlocks all the things you want, need, dream, and desire?

Here's the map that leads to the treasure. *Rest peacefully in his kingdom also known as The Secret Place of the Most High.* **This treasure map leads you to *The Secret Place of the Most High!***

Indiana Jones followed the treasure map that guided him to the Ark of the Covenant. When you follow the treasure map of otherworldly transcendent peace that you *force-feed* into your brain by your weapons of 1225 words and **the power of your tongue** then you're Denzel Washington in *Man on Fire*. You pump yourself full of the strength, the assurance, the skills, the knowledge, and the fire in your belly to get everything you need, want, dream, and desire.

Peace is the treasure map to your rich great grandfather's empire. How hard do you fight to guard that peace? Do you hide that peace from intruders like when you hide the map under your pillow? Do you fight to protect that otherworldly transcendent peace lest anyone steal it? No matter what the cost of your security force? How valuable is that peace?

Here's the surefire way to get your things, everything you need, want, dream, and desire.

Here it is: *Pursue the treasure map of his peace, joy, and happiness FIRST.*

Why FIRST?

Because Cabrón, those supernatural emotions equip you, empower you, and embolden you with SKILLS and POWER to unlock the abundance of GOOD FORTUNE that resides in *The Garden of Eden*.

When you *force-feed* yourself full of God's otherworldly peace and supernatural happiness that exudes out from your heart via the mighty weapons of 1225 words and **the power of your tongue** like I did that sunny summer California afternoon in 1983 the day my green convertible died, then you notice that "Things always go my way" is not a pipe dream, nor is it an allusive mirage, but it's a steadfast repeatable reality.

Notice I called it "repeatable." It works again and again, whenever you apply it, whenever you want. If Chef Ima—you've heard of her, right, Chef Ima Good Cook? If Chef Ima Good Cook gives you a recipe, do you think if you follow her recipe, plus she stands over your shoulder to make sure you do everything exactly like she does, do you think you'd whip up potatoes au gratin just as good as hers?

God gives you a recipe for your success, and he stands over your shoulder to make sure your potatoes au gratin turn out just like his.

What's the recipe? The first ingredient is to seek FIRST the kingdom of God. What's the second ingredient? Be diligent in all your hand finds to do. What's the third ingredient? Take care of the poor, the fatherless, and the widow, and when you mix all these ingredients together, and bake it in the oven at 450 degrees, then ALL THESE THINGS WILL BE ADDED TO YOU.

Here's the recipe, also called a success-a-pee.

ONE: Seek first the kingdom, like I *accidentally* did that sunny summer California afternoon in 1983 the day my green convertible died.

TWO: Be diligent in all that your hand finds to do.

THREE: Take care of the poor, the fatherless, and the widow.

And there you have it my friends, the secret recipe for potatoes au gratin.

In summary, otherworldly peace, diligence in all that your hand finds to do, and when you take care of the poor, the fatherless, and the widow, this tripart perfecta trifecta continuously unlocks the doors to the gifts, strengths, and good fortunes so that you easily, and "without toiling or spinning" accomplish all the things you desire, whether you want a better job, more clients, you wanna lose weight, a better marriage, happy children, body healed of cancer, sickness, and disease…*whatever the desires of your heart.*

Peace AND Diligence AND Love…
They Open Wide the Doors to Your Goodies

Peace is your FIRST and *foremost,* ULTIMATE and UTTERMOST, TOPPERMOST, and highest order of business. *Peace is the PIN code to all your dreams, wants, needs, wishes, and the desires of your heart.*

Transcendent peace that is not of this world increases your human skills, and in addition to your increased human skills, your transcendent otherworldly peace and happiness unleash *the power of God's miracle-working inexplicable surprises as he supernaturally executes the unexplainable events* that suddenly appear out of nowhere, surprises that are exceedingly over and above the diligent efforts you put in, but just as important as transcendent peace is to take care of the poor, the fatherless, and the widow, also known as righteousness, also known as love.

****

"Take care of the poor, the fatherless, and the widow, for as you have done it unto one of the least of these my brethren, ye have done it unto me."

Scene 36

Widow, Fatherless, Poor

Every Christmas day my family made the trek to the beach where we'd feed the homeless at the Santa Monica Pier; not that a cookie changes their life, but conversation with them on Christmas day makes them feel loved, if only for a moment.

Mother Teresa said the feeling of being unwanted, unloved, uncared for, and forgotten by everybody is a much greater poverty than the person who has nothing to eat.

So anyway, we met this couple with eleven kids. My wife Tammy says, "Can we take them in?" She has the biggest heart you can imagine. I knew better than to say no, so we supported them for many months.

Meanwhile, I had pissed off the CEO of our company, and he refused to schedule me for any speaking engagements. Every month in the seminar business for me is around $25,000 a month that I could make but didn't.

Why'd he take me off the road?

Here's why. When I first got into the seminar business as a speaker we had to learn a two-hour script and I found that to be daunting. So I scoured the internet to see what was available and found what TV newscasters have in their ear so they can hear the producers talk to them while they're on the air. So I purchased one, trained myself how to use it, and recorded the two-hour seminar on a digital tape player so that when I did seminars, I could hear my voice in an exceedingly small wireless unit that fit in my ear that nobody could see. The audience was unaware that I could hear the whole seminar word for word. I spoke along with what I heard on the digital tape player. The digital recording was a bit ahead of the words that I spoke. My speech was like the dust that follows close behind a speeding car cruising along the dusty highway.

I was so good at it that one night after a seminar when our sales were in the toilet, I took another company's script that sold the same product, and I merged their script with our product. I replaced all the slides from their PowerPoint slideshow with our product and company logo.

The next day I could do the other company's entire two-hour script with their PowerPoint slides but with our product. I executed their script word for word, slide for slide. Yep, that's what I did.

It was all well and good except that I performed the seminar in the city that is their headquarters, San Francisco. There was a representative from their company in the audience and he heard me do their seminar.

About four weeks later I get a FedEx package from their lawyers on Christmas Eve, the day before we went to Santa Monica Pier to feed the homeless when we met the family of eleven. The other company's lawyers announce they are suing me for $100,000 for copying their script. Yah, I know, I was a dumb ass for doing what I did, but not only did they sue me for $100,000, the company that I worked for took me off the road to protect themselves from liability, and I lost all the potential income, about $25,000 a month.

So now I'm out $25,000 a month, their lawyers sue me for $100,000 and it's entirely my stupid fault. And to make matters worse, we didn't do any better in sales with the other company's script.

What a mess!

So what do I do? I do the only thing I know to do when I'm in a tempest that I myself create.

I unleash the power of my double-barreled weapons of the 1225 words and **the power of my tongue** that have worked perfectly for me since that sunny summer California afternoon in 1983 the day my green convertible died. I unleash the double-barreled shotgun of 1225 words and **the power of my tongue** to *force-feed* peace from the deeper dimensions that live inside me, and thus *instigates an invasion* into my heart, my brain, my thoughts, and my soul.

Thank you God that these weapons work even when I'm in the middle of a self-inflicted shitstorm!

Four months later after a $100,000 loss of income and a pending $100,000 lawsuit, I get a surprise.

One afternoon we took the family of eleven to McDonald's to let their kids play on the playground and eat some burgers. While they are munching on burgers and fries and the kids play on the playground, I get a call from the CEO who had booked no speaking engagements for me since the lawsuit, about four months earlier. I could hear the alarm in his voice. "Steve, how quickly can you get to Tucson?" I replied, "What's up Freddie?" He said, "Brian's flights out of Atlanta are cancelled because of snow, and he can't make the event." We were all seminar speakers who traveled to a different city every week. He continued, "I've invested $50,000 in advertising and I need a speaker. Can you go?"

"Sure Freddie, how soon do you need me there?"

I could hear the urgency in his voice, "I need you there by tonight."

I said, "Freddie, I haven't done the seminar in four months. I might be a little rusty."

He quipped, "That's okay, you have the earpiece, right?"

I replied, "Very funny Freddie!" He was always a jokester. I gulped down my salad and told my wife Tammy, "I'll see you in two days."

I performed so well in Tucson that the CEO asked if I would drive over to Phoenix to finish out the week. I did so well in Tucson and Phoenix that he put me permanently back on the schedule, and for the next five years I made a killing with his company.

I went from zero to zillions overnight.

****

What's the secret to success? These are the three steps that ensure your success.

Step Number ONE: Use your 1225 words and **the power of your tongue** to *force-feed* yourself full of transcendent peace and supernatural joy, the kind that is buried deep within you that's beyond the ability of the human mind to comprehend.

Step Number TWO: When you force-feed peace into your heart, then embark on your daily tasks; be diligent whether it's phone calls, study, building new customers, your job at Walmart, or whatever.

Step Number THREE: Do charitable acts, like what my wife Tammy and I did with the family of eleven we met on Christmas day. Charitable acts is what *righteousness* is, among other things. It means "right living" which is encapsulated in the one word—LOVE, which includes take care of the poor, the fatherless, and the widow. "In everything you do, do unto others as you would have them do unto you, because this is in totality a completion of the law and the prophets" (Mathew 7:12).

When you follow this recipe, then you open the doors wide to supernatural divine interventions that astound and dismay your natural mind.

To sum it up, supernatural happiness and transcendent peace are your highest priority in your quest for success and good fortune, coupled with diligence in your daily tasks, and *taking care of the poor, the fatherless, and the widow.*

And how do you fill yourself full of peace and happiness? You do it like I did that sunny summer California afternoon back in 1983 the day my green convertible died. During those bizarre twenty minutes, my anger-filled, sarcastic, venomous scriptural cuss words, those *crazin' brazen blazin' biblical cuss words* supernaturally *force-fed* peace into my heart by **the power of my very own tongue** EVEN AGAINST MY WILL!

****

The dual armaments of 1225 words and **the power of my tongue** forced me to feel happy, peaceful, and joyful that sunny summer California afternoon even though my life was falling apart, television producers wouldn't hire me, my girlfriend broke my heart, and I was sleeping on the living room floor of a couple's one-bedroom apartment, curled up on a skanky throw rug underneath their rented piano.

****

What about the $100,000 lawsuit? A year and a half passes, and we near the eighteen-month deadline when the lawyers must wrap up the lawsuit or else the court dismisses the charges.

I spent that year and a half seeking first the kingdom of God which is joy and peace.

One day Tammy my wife calls me from Los Angeles. I was in Salt Lake City doing a seminar, and she says, "Steve, you got a package from their lawyers. Should I open it?"

My heart dropped because I knew they had two more weeks to sue me or else the courts would drop the lawsuit. I said, "Yes, open it. *No, don't open it.* Okay, go ahead, yes, open it."

"I already opened it." Silence.

"Well? What does it say?!?" She scanned to the last paragraph. She screamed, "They agreed to drop the lawsuit if we pay their lawyer costs of $5,000!" I couldn't write them a check fast enough. You know, before they changed their mind.

And not once during that year and a half did I ask God to take away the fear, the stress, and the worry. Not once did I beg him to help me. Not once did I beg him to take away the lawsuit. Why in the hell would I beg him to take away the lawsuit when he tells me precisely what I must do to conquer the lawsuit?

How did he say to conquer the lawsuit? He said "Seek first the kingdom of God and his righteousness and *all these things will be added to you."* Do you know what's included in the phrase "all these things will be added to you"? I'll tell you what's included: Peace, happiness, joy, contentment, serenity…and what else is included in *all these things* that'll be added to me?

One of the things that got added to me was the CEO put me back on the road even though the pending lawsuit stipulated a hefty fine for him if he put me back on the schedule. He risked a legal quagmire, but he put me back on the road anyway.

What else is *all these things* will be added to me? *The other company's lawyers dropped the lawsuit against me!*

So why the hell would I beg God to do what he's already gonna do? It seems silly to ask him for something he already promised me, and for something I'm already gonna get, right? (More about that in a few minutes.)

What happens when I enter the PIN number? The ATM spits out $300, right?

Do you remember the PIN number?

What's the PIN number?

HERE'S THE PIN NUMBER:

P.E.A.C.E.

How do you get peace?

"Speak the words…I'm right here."

…like I did that sunny summer California afternoon in 1983 the day my green convertible died.

****

This next act dives deep into uncharted territory that very few are familiar with, and there are many that will strongly disagree with me, but it won't be the first time. Hell, wait until you get to the second volume of this trilogy THE EVIL QUEEN. Your head will explode because you've never heard anything like it. and I'll wager that ninety-nine percent of you will disagree with me at first, but when you hear my arguments, you'll happily embrace the truth when we call on Toto to pull back the veil of *THE EVIL QUEEN* in the second volume of this three-part trilogy *Shitty to Happy in 21 Minutes: THE EVIL QUEEN.* I'll see you in seventeen minutes.

INTERMISSION

ACT 8: How to Ask

Scene 37

The Golden Promise

Seek the kingdom, all else gets taken care of

I'll let you in on a little secret but lean in closer so I can whisper it to you. Here 'tis: *The more a man walks in peace*—that is, the supernatural otherworldly peace that comes ONLY from **the power of your tongue** and 1225 words, *the less that man asks God for stuff.*

What the hell are you talking about, Steve?!? Hold onto your horses cowboy, listen to me the reason why I don't ask God for stuff.

When you live in, abide in, and assume residence in the secret place of the Most High, that place of rest where supernatural transcendent peace from another world governs your heart, and it cushions you like an oversized marshmallow, the less you ask God for stuff *because he's already promised to give you all the desires of your heart!*

When you rest in *The Secret Place of the Most High* then THE DESIRES OF YOUR HEART chase you like a 50-foot wave off the North Shore of Oahu chases the surfers before it buries them in three hundred tons of Pacific Ocean.

Why ask God for something I'm already gonna get?

Let's say you and your husband drive to the car lot to buy a new car. It's a thirty-minute trip. How many times during the thirty-minute drive do you ask your husband for a new car? Three times? Eight times? Thirteen times? Imagine this. You plead with your husband every three minutes to buy you a new car, "Can we get a new car Honey, please can we get a new car?" In exasperation your husband says, "Babe, we're headed to the car lot now to get you a new car." My guess is you don't ask him again unless you have the IQ of a snail.

You can do what you want, but I haven't asked God for anything for as long as I can remember because everything I need, want, dream, and desire shows up on my doorstep like an Amazon package. My heart's desires are in the warehouse of my imagination, and how do you suppose I transfer them from the warehouse into the three-dimensional world?

I transfer them by means of the power of his otherworldly peace that I *force-feed* into my heart by my stupendous 1225 words and **the indefatigable power of my tongue**, plus shitloads of diligence to do what my hand finds to do, plus take care of the poor, the fatherless, and the widow.

The mighty bombastic armaments of 1225 words and **the power of my tongue** team up to *force-feed* God's peace into me, which thereby births my desires from the warehouse of my imagination, also known as my heart. The seeds of my desires grow into a full-grown crop of wheat that appears in my garden, and I'm the farmer that puts in the sickle and harvests the crops.

> *My harvests show up, not by an enchanted wave-of- the-wand magic, and not by "name it and claim it," or any other forms of Christian or New-Age quackery, and neither do they show up immediately,* ***and MOST CERTAINLY do not show up without diligence, diligence, and more DILIGENCE, and neither do they show up without taking care of the poor, the fatherless, and the widow, and most definitely they do not show up without first seeking the kingdom of God emotions of happiness, peace, and joy,*** *but when I knit these unassailable forces into a mighty bastion of impermeable power to form a united front, then the Brigadier General of the universe, my Lord God Almighty, the Creator who numbers the hairs on my head ensures that I get all the desires of my heart. They remarkably do appear.*

"But Steve," you inquire, "What about 'Whatever you ask for, he'll do for you'?" What about, 'You have not because you *ask* not'"?

Good questions. I have the perfect answer, but first let's do a Jacques Cousteau deep-dive into the definition of the verb "to ask."

What Does the Verb "ASK" Mean?

The word "ask" in Hebrew, the language of the bible, means *to make a demand upon something due.* It does NOT mean "to make a request" as in you put your order in for the barista to brew four cups of Cuban coffee for you and your lovely girlfriends.

That's indeed what the word "ask" means in English, but it's NOT what it means in Bible-talk. Did you know that? Maybe you did, maybe you didn't, but it doesn't mean "May I have a stick of gum?" or "Please pass the potatoes."

It means "to make a demand upon something due" which is exactly what I *unknowingly* and *accidentally* stumbled upon that sunny summer California afternoon in 1983 the day my green convertible died.

What did I DEMAND that was DUE to me?

First of all, let's tweak the meaning of the word "DUE." *Due* is something that is OWED to me. In other words, "ask" means to make a demand upon something that someone owes me.

When I go to the ATM machine, do I ask the ATM machine for $300? Do I pray on the way to the bank, "Oh Wells Fargo, Oh Wells Fargo," and fall to my knees on the sidewalk at the altar of the ATM machine and plead in my most holy reverent voice, the one that we reserve for when we desperately want something from God, "Oh *puh-leeze* Mr. Wells Fargo, please, I beg of you, please help me, I need $300 like you wouldn't believe, so I'm begging you to give me $300!" No that's silly. I'd slap you for that but I'm not sure your brain could process the pain.

However, does Mr. Wells Fargo owe me $300? Yes he does. Therefore how do I make a demand upon the $300 that Mr. Wells Fargo owes me? It's easy breezy lemon peazy, I pop in the Wells Fargo bank card, punch in the PIN number, and the bank gives me $300. I don't even say "Thank you."

That's how I make a demand upon something due from the bank. I simply follow Mr. Wells Fargo's bank instructions.

God Also Has a Set of Instructions!

Consider this: The bank owes me $300 when I enter the PIN number, isn't that right? Do I need to ask, as in the manner of 'ask' such as, "Hey Mr. Bank, please give me $300?" No, the PIN number is all I need.

Must I make an appointment with the bank president, send emails back and forth, and plead with the bank teller to give me my $300? No, not that either.

Here's my favorite: Must I **feel sincere** for the bank to give me my $300? No you dingleberry poopwad, you don't need to feel sincere, nor do you need to perform any other of this hodgepodge of ludicrous behavior to get your $300 from the bank.

Neither do you need to perform such a horse pile of ludicrous behavior to get the desires of your heart from God that he already promised you can have because they already belong to you. Like the husband promised his wife a new car.

Now that you know the biblical meaning of the word "ask," how silly does it sound to ask God for stuff as in, "Hey God, please give me…? Pretty friggin silly, right?

Peace. Peace that is not of this world. Peace that transcends this natural world. Peace that's beyond the ability of the human mind to comprehend. Peace that comes from another dimension. Peace that the Lord of the universe OWES ME. Why does he owe it to me? Because HE PUT IT INSIDE ME. *HE GAVE IT TO ME!*

What else in addition to otherworldly transcendent peace does he owe me? He owes me ALL THESE THINGS THAT GET ADDED TO ME! What things? *All the desires of my heart! HE GAVE THEM TO ME.* It's now up to me to **make a demand** upon that which he gave me.

Does this sound arrogant to you to make a demand upon God? If it does then it's time to graduate out of kindergarten, quit with the fake humility, and do God's things in God's ways so that you get God's results.

On that sunny summer California afternoon in 1983 when my green convertible died, I made a demand upon something due when I slammed 1225 of the mightiest word-daggers in the universe, also known as "the sword of the spirit" into the smoggy skies of Los Angeles by **the power of my tongue**. It was an accidental discovery *but that's the day I learned how to ask.*

In case you glossed over it, the 1225 words coupled with **the power of your tongue** are *the sword of the spirit,* a most powerful offensive weapon to kick the Evil Queen's ass, and when I neutralize her evil, then I remove her influences from blocking all the desires of my heart from bursting forth, as long as I exercise diligence in all my hand finds to do, diligence to seek first the kingdom of happiness, peace, and joy, and diligence to take care of the poor, the fatherless, and the widow.

Everything in that last paragraph is ***HOW I ASK***.

On that sunny summer California afternoon in 1983, I didn't "ask" for peace, as in "Please pass the potatoes," or as George Carlin famously quipped, "Please pass the piano."

I certainly didn't "ask" as in, "Please give me," but I did indeed "ask" in strict obedience exactly like how God instructs us to ask.

That is, *I made a demand upon something due.*

What did I make a demand upon that was due? *I made a demand upon the peace that passes all understanding! I FLOODED MYSELF WITH GOD'S PEACE by 1225 words and **the power of my tongue**...**THAT'S HOW I ASKED!** And I certainly was not "sincere."*

My sincerity was as useless as a steering wheel on a mule that sunny summer California afternoon so long ago, but did it matter? No, it didn't matter. **That's the first time in my life I "asked" correctly. It's the first time in my life I MADE A DEMAND UPON SOMETHING THAT WAS DUE.**

It didn't matter a lick of a whit on that sunny summer California afternoon that I was downright naïve about how to properly "ask." My naïveté didn't stop the 1225 words and **the power of my tongue** from executing their remarkable transformation in my soul that day, and neither does it matter that I am naïve about how the bank gives me $300, as long as I OBEY. I obediently insert the ATM card, enter the PIN number, punch the $300 button, and voilà! **Money appears!**

Clueless? Who cares! Naïve? Doesn't matter. Sincerity? Wasted breath.

Whether I understand it or not, whether I can explain it or not, whether I have enough faith or not, $300 appears out of the ATM machine. My cluelessness is irrelevant as long as I follow the bank's instructions because when I do, then three one-hundred-dollar bills pop out of the ATM machine. Three crisp one-hundred-dollar bills spit out at me whether I understand how it works or not. Three crisp one-hundred-dollar bills pop out of the ATM machine whether I "feel like it" or not, whether I understand it or not, and whether I feel sincere or not.

Even though I was painfully unaware of the forces that I activated that sunny summer California afternoon in 1983, did peace halt its invasion of my heart? Did the Prince of Peace abruptly command, "Peace, halt your invasion! This stupid actor doesn't know what he's doing. We don't move another inch further until he understands how this works!"

That's not what happened! Even though I was clueless, the Prince of Peace ignored how ignorant and oblivious I was as he ruggedly stormed full-speed ahead into the catastrophic crime scene of my butchered heart with an explosion of peace that lit the skies like a fourth of July fireworks show.

Did I "ask" for peace, as in, "God, please give me peace"? No silly, I didn't "ask" for peace any more than I ask the bank for $300 when I have a bank card, a PIN number, and punch the $300 button.

But did I ask for peace? *I damn sure did ask for peace!* **You're darn tootin I asked for peace!**

HOW?

I *made a demand upon something due* ***like he told us to do*** even though I was utterly clueless as to what I did.

But Steve, shouldn't I "ask" God for things I need?

This brings up the subject of things I do NOT ask God for, and by "ask" I mean "God, please give me…."

Listen to me carefully: Did I "ask" for an acting job, a place to live, and a car on that sunny summer California afternoon? No I didn't. Why should I? Why would I ask for the very things that he says will be added to me when I seek first the kingdom of God that is otherworldly supernatural incomprehensible peace that comes only from 1225 words and **the power of my tongue**? Why don't I "ask" in such a manner? Because when I seek first his kingdom, then all my desires, needs, wants, and wishes—all the desires of my heart—get added to me!

I didn't make this stuff up. *He did.*

I didn't say these things. *He did.*

I didn't promise myself all the desires of my heart. *He did!*

Wouldn't it be redundant for me to ask for what he's already promised to give me? **Wouldn't that be a slap in God's face?**

Wouldn't that be as goofy as the wife asking her husband for a new car on the drive to the car lot? **Wouldn't that be a slap in the face to her husband?**

Husbands, what would your wife think if you asked for dinner when it's sitting right in front of you on the dining room table! She might get you checked out for Alzheimer's, which by the way is type three diabetes. It's no mystery. Look it up for yourself. Google it: "Alzheimer's type three diabetes."

But I digress.

What Are the "All These Things" That Will Be Added to You?

Is employment included in "all these things will be added to you"? Yes.

Is a car included in "all these things will be added to you"? It most certainly is. And so is a cow if you live in a cow country.

Is a girlfriend, a wife, a husband, a family, a prosperous business, a successful career, a thriving farm included in "all these things will be added to you"? Yes, yes, and yes.

Is the desires of your heart included in "all these things will be added to you"?

The answer to all these questions is YES *as long as they're the* ***desires of your heart***.

Here's the golden key: When you *force-feed* yourself full of this incomprehensible peace then ALL THESE OTHER THINGS—all the desires of my heart that includes acting, my book, public speaking, music, family, wife, kids, and everything else—will be added to me.

I like that promise. "All these things will be added to you." I REALLY like that promise.

Do I Say I Don't Ask God for Stuff?
Perish the Thought!
The Key is HOW I Ask God for Stuff!

I don't ask God for any of the desires of my heart, as in the English meaning of the word "ask." I don't "ask" that way, just like the wife doesn't ask her husband for a new car as they drive to the car lot, but please listen carefully: **I do ASK**, but how? **How do I ask?** HERE'S HOW I ASK:

I make a demand upon something due!

I make a demand upon THE SOURCE OF my material things, which is what? What is the source, the eternal fountain, the endless supply of every material need, every financial need, every career and business need, every family need, every nutritional and fitness need?

WHAT IS THE ETERNAL SUPERABUNDANT CASCADE OF SUPPLY FOR EVERYTHING I NEED, WANT, DREAM, AND DESIRE?

ONE: Seek peace. Transcendent otherworldly peace.

TWO: Be diligent in all my hand finds to do.

THREE: Take care of the poor, the fatherless, and the widow.

It's that simple. Yes I DO ASK, but I ask according to these three high-level uncomplicated super-important actions, and when I ask in this high-level secretive, hitherto unknown way, that's when *all these things I need, want, dream, and desire GET ADDED TO ME,* so yes, I do indeed "ask."

THESE 3 HIGH-LEVEL PERFORMANCE ASSIGNMENTS ***ARE HOW I ASK***

Do I refuse to ask?

No silly, but the golden key is HOW I ask.

Do I ask stuff from God like "Please give me a bicycle"? No, I ask at a higher level of sophistication, a much deeper level of intimacy with God, and with a much more certain guarantee that everything I need, want, dream, and desire GETS ADDED TO ME *just like the Jewish rabbi promises.*

Peace is a Perpetual Motion Machine, a Cascade of Supply, a Continual-Flowing Fountain that Pours Out All the Desires of My Heart

Peace that he says to seek FIRST is the perpetual waterfall, an unending source of supply for ALL THE DESIRES OF MY HEART. All I need to do is *ask* like the bible says to ask. How does the bible say to ask?

Do you remember what the lonesome Jewish rabbi says? "Seek FIRST the kingdom of God—PEACE, JOY, and HAPPINESS—and then ALL THESE THINGS will be ADDED to you." *That's how the bible says to ask.*

Peace is like the bank PIN number. *Peace* is the PIN number that gets you…what? What does the PIN number of P.E.A.C.E. get you? ANSWER: The PIN number of P.E.A.C.E. gets you **all the THINGS that he promises that get added to you**.

That's how I ask.

POP QUIZ: What are the "all these things" that get added to you? Do you have any idea? Can you take a guess? I don't care if you're wrong, but at least give it a try. What are the "all these things" that get added to you when you seek FIRST the kingdom of God which is supernatural happiness, peace, and joy?

ANSWER: "All these things that get added to you" are THE DESIRES OF YOUR HEART, which includes everything and anything you need, want, dream, and desire.

That's how I ask. THAT'S HOW I ASK. ***That's how I ask!***

Yes indeed, I do ASK, but my ASK is that I *make a demand upon something due.*

That's how *I ask God for stuff!!* That's how I ask God for all my needs, wants, dreams, and desires!

You can do what you want, but that's how I ask.

****

Have you ever played the game where somebody offers you, "If you could have one wish what would it be?" I'll bet your answer was, *"My wish is that I have an unlimited number of wishes."* Was that your wish? If it was, remind me to never play monopoly with you. You'll buy up all the properties like I used to do with my grandma. I'd buy all her properties, and when she ran out of money, I'd loan her money from the bank. Our Sunday afternoon Monopoly games took eight hours for me to empty all the money from her, from the bank, and I'd even let her write me IOUs so we could keep playing.

But I digress.

The cool thing about the kingdom of God of happiness, peace, and joy is instead of only one wish, YOU GET AS MANY WISHES AS YOU WANT!

****

Scene 38

God's Unlimited Wishes

Let's get back to my accidental discovery in 1983. Did I have the slightest inkling that I "asked" according to God's instructions on that sunny summer California afternoon?

No, I was totally bumfuzzled. I didn't have the faintest idea.

Did it matter that I was bumfuzzled and clueless?

No, and thank God he didn't strike me with lightning for being such a smart ass.

Accidental or intentional, clueless or educated, it doesn't matter. I *made a demand upon something due.* **I discovered that sunny summer California afternoon, even though it was an accident, HOW TO ASK!** I accidentally and unintentionally *made a demand* upon the most important, viable, and supernatural raw material in the universe, more real than life itself, more real than anything in our brick-and-mortar three-dimensional world.

What Is "Raw Material"?

Raw material is the cotton that we make shirts from. It's the steel that we make cars from. It's the love that we make marriages from.

What is the most important, powerful, and substantial raw material in the universe that is the building block for all your desires?

The most important, powerful, and substantial raw material in the universe that is THE SOURCE of all your desires is the kingdom of God—*happiness…peace…and…joy.*

This kingdom of peace, happiness, and joy are the "raw materials" that are the building blocks for your heart's desires, dreams, goals, wants, and needs…ALL OF THEM. Not only are these otherworldly emotions the source, but they are also the ocean liner that transports your desires from the *warehouse of your imagination* into the brick-and-mortar walls of your material world.

Can you see why the lone Jewish rabbi implores you to seek his mighty kingdom first and foremost, before you do anything else? It's because his invisible kingdom is the raw material that ensures that you get everything else that you want, like that game that offers you the one wish of anything you want. Your *ONE WISH THAT YOU HAVE UNLIMITED WISHES* is perfectly accomplished when you seek his kingdom of otherworldly transcendent emotions *first and foremost.*

God's Kingdom is the Building Block for All Your Desires

If you try to construct a skyscraper without the building blocks of steel, then you're a special species of stupid. *You need steel to build a skyscraper.* The same as if you try to sew a cotton T-shirt without cotton. *You need cotton to sew a T-shirt.* The same as if you try to construct all your dreams, hopes, goals, and wishes without the building block of God's happiness, peace, and joy. *You need the fruit of the spirit—happiness, peace, and joy—to construct the empire of the desires of your heart.*

If you believe you can construct an unshakable impenetrable empire without happiness, peace, and joy, I could agree with you, *but we'd both be wrong.*

I'm not saying you cannot create a billion-dollar empire without peace and joy. What I am saying is your quest to build an empire comes easier, and not only that, but you enjoy your empire a thousand times more when you force yourself full of **happiness, peace, and joy.**

Peace is the **raw material** *that is the substance of your wishes and desires.* Not only is peace the raw material, but your peace physically transfers your desires from the invisible supernatural kingdom within you, into your three-dimensional visible, physical world, but **only when you add DILIGENCE in all your hand finds to do, AND take care of the poor, the fatherless, and the widow.**

Peace, happiness, and joy give birth to our hopes, dreams, and desires of our heart that reside in the deeper dimensions *inside us.* Peace and **the power of our tongue** bridge the gap between the invisible dimensions that live inside us and the visible third dimension that lives outside us.

In other words, these spiritual forces are the delivery truck that transports your hopes, dreams, wishes, and desires from the inside of you where they are so small you can't see them, to the outside of you where they are fully grown.

It's like when you give birth to a baby. The baby is invisible to the naked eye, it starts from a microscopic seed, and just like the wife doesn't harangue her husband to buy her a new car on the drive to the car lot, neither does the wife harangue her husband for a baby while the baby grows inside her, and neither do we harangue God for things that already grow inside us that ARE ALREADY OURS like the unborn baby is ALREADY OURS.

Our three-fold mission to birth our heart's desires from inside us where they're unseen to outside us where they ARE seen is as follows:

ONE: *Force-feed* our heart full of **peace**, **happiness**, and **joy**.
TWO: BE DILIGENT IN ALL OUR HAND FINDS TO DO.
THREE: Take care of the poor, the fatherless, and the widow.

Here are God's Instructions *HOW TO ASK*

What are God's instructions *HOW TO ASK?* They're just like the bank's instructions *HOW TO ASK*. Here's the bank's instructions:

1) Insert the ATM card.
2) Enter the PIN code.
3) Punch the $300 button.

Well, that's the same way we ask God for stuff. How?

1) Pursue the peace. Peace is the PIN code.
2) Punch in the diligence.
3) Take care of the poor, the fatherless, and the widow.

> *Listen to me: This is not some kind of touchy-feely, ooey gooey New Age bullshit like "Think it, you'll see it," or the Christian version that's just as goofy called, "Name it and claim it."*

This is more solidly real than life itself. It taps into God's raw materials of his supernatural emotions. I label them "supernatural" because they surpass the ability of the human mind to comprehend, and because they majestically transcend this three-dimensional world.

Add a hefty dose of diligence, because diligence puts flesh and blood on that raw material of happiness, peace, and joy, and when you take care of the poor, the fatherless, and the widow, then your golden keys to prosperity and abundance open the floodgates of blessings and they unleash the power of God to move above and beyond your human efforts, so that they flood you, like the six feet of rain on Foc-Foc Island in 1966 with blessings that defy comprehension.

The young girl asked me, "What is my purpose in life?" I told her, "Your purpose in life is to be happy," but it's not the happiness that comes from red Ferrari's and hot boyfriends, NO, but rather it's the kind of peace and happiness that come from 1225 words and **the power of your tongue** that connect us to the God of the universe who lives INSIDE US.

After you *force-feed* God's supernatural transcendent peace into your heart so much so that it floods you with that otherworldly inexplicable feeling like what happened to me that sunny summer California afternoon in 1983 the day my green convertible died, that's when you diligently go to work on your phone calls, your study, your business, your negotiations, your business deals, your manufacturing company, your farm, your tractors, your cars, your homes, your family, your nutrition, your fit body, your children, and whatever else are the desires of your heart. *That's when his phenomenal promise kicks in:* ***Whatever you do prospers.***

That's how to ask. THAT'S HOW TO ASK. **These ACTIONS are how you ask.**

These actions are the DILIGENCE that make you rich.

And then remember to take care of the poor, the fatherless, and the widow.

These three actions open the doors to everything you need, want, dream, and desire. They open the door to your rich great grandfather's safe. *They open the door to the desires of your heart.*

However, God's kingdom of peace is FIRST and FOREMOST.

Peace is the PIN number.

Folks, I just taught you in all simplicity *HOW TO ASK!*

Can you see how much more sophisticated, and yet simpler this is, and more dependable and trustworthy than, "Please God, give me a bicycle."

How do I ask? I make a demand upon *the source* of my bicycle.

Remember the story of the goose that lays the golden eggs? Why would I ask for the golden eggs when I have the goose? What's the goose in this example?

1) *Happiness, peace, and joy* is the goose.
2) *Diligence* is the goose.
3) *Take care of the poor, the fatherless, and the widow* is the goose.

The golden eggs are "All these things including *the desires of your heart* that get added to you," such as a bicycle. An acting career. An apartment. A car. A thriving business. A satisfying career that you've dreamt about since you were a teenager. A happy family. Strong solid kids, and whatever else are *the desires of your heart.*

Do I ask for the golden eggs when I already have the goose? You can do what you want, but I don't ask for golden eggs. Not when I already have the goose.

And when you pursue the kingdom like God told you to do and *continue* to pursue the kingdom because out of it flow the forces of life, then he stands over your shoulder like Chef Ima Good Cook to ensure that ALL THESE THINGS WILL BE ADDED TO YOU. *That's the way I ask.*

QUICK REVIEW: "Please Pass the Potatoes" is NOT How I Ask

Not only do I not ask him for material things according to the English meaning of the word "ask"—in other words I don't ask him for golden eggs—and neither do I "ask" him for peace, as in "Hey God, please give me peace," and neither do I ask the preacher to pray for my peace, nor do I call prayer hotlines to pray for my peace.

I don't call a psychotherapist who's gonna do nothing but identify the problem but doesn't give me a solution because he fuckin' doesn't have one. *Neither do most preachers as evidenced in their foolhardy sermons, "Ask God for peace."*

Bullshitty Bang-Bang. I defy you to find scripture that says, "Ask God for peace" as in the English meaning of the word "to ask." You can't find one. It's not there. You most certainly can find scripture that says to "ask" God for peace in the Hebrew meaning of the word, such as "to make a demand upon something due," but I defy you to find scripture that says to "ask," as in "please give me peace."

"Speak the words…I'm right here." THAT'S how to ASK for peace!

On that sunny summer California afternoon in 1983 the day my green convertible died, I did not "ask" according to any of these aforementioned religious and juvenile absurdities, and yet I unintentionally and accidentally "asked" as in *to make a demand upon something due.*

It was quite by accident that I discovered how to *make a demand upon something due* on that sunny summer California afternoon in 1983 the day my green convertible died.

That was the day I learned about God's streamlined, highly accurate, top-level, surefire approach HOW TO ASK FOR PEACE. That was the first time in my life I ever properly asked for peace when I *made a demand upon something due* that thrust me headlong into a silver bullet encounter with the one Isaiah calls "The Prince of Peace."

What did I "make a demand upon" that was DUE, that was **OWED TO ME** that sunny summer California afternoon in 1983 the day my green convertible died?

I made a demand upon THE PEACE THAT PASSES ALL UNDERSTANDING. How'd I make the demand upon the peace that was owed to me? I made a demand upon the peace that God gave to me by the dual armaments that God also gave to me, two of the most powerful creative forces in the universe: One, his 1225 words, and two, **the overwhelming inexplicable insurmountable infallible power of that tiny piece of flesh, the rudder of an exceptionally large ship, the bit in the horse's mouth also known as THE POWER OF MY TONGUE**.

The power of your tongue and 1225 words is how you make a demand upon that which is due.

The power of your tongue is how you cross the time-space barrier to enter God's world of eternal rest also known as *The Secret Place of the Most High.*

The power of your tongue is how you *force-feed* the unmitigated, unlimited, incomprehensible, otherworldly, inexplicable peace that springs up from the one and only true God who lives INSIDE OF YOU.

"Speak the words...I'm right here." **That's how I "ask" for peace.**

I had no intention to enter the *Secret Place of the Most High* on that sunny summer California afternoon in 1983 the day my green convertible died. God seemed a million miles away. *Peace was the furthest thing from my mind.* Nevertheless I cracked the code that escorted me into the hiding place, that place of refuge under the wings of the Almighty.

Although it was an accident that I stumbled into *The Secret Place of the Most High* as clumsily as a hippo with a hangover at 4 a.m. at Denny's, *I nevertheless made a demand upon something due by* **the power of my tongue** and thereby gate-crashed the fortress that leads into *The Secret Place of the Most High.*

That's the day I asked with the precision of the neurosurgeon, in spite of the fact that I was a neurotic, vitriolic, imbecilic boy bitch actor without a job, and was sleeping on the floor underneath a rented piano of my friend's one-bedroom apartment in West Los Angeles.

On that sunny summer California afternoon in 1983 when I slammed 1225 of the mightiest words in the universe into the skies by **the power of my tongue**, the Prince of Peace stormed onto the scene like the Navy SEAL team sneakily attacks the sleeping enemy, and he utterly gate-crashed into the core of my heart in waves of firepower that shocked the holy hell out of me because *that which I "demanded" showed up in a way that I never even remotely expected.*

When he flooded my heart full of peace with such a gentle force as I never imagined, I could not hold back my burning tears of happiness, shock, and surprise. I abruptly stopped on Olympic Boulevard in West Los Angeles, my eyes wider than the first time I peeked at a Playboy centerfold, and I reverently whispered, "What the hell did I just tap into?"

Can you imagine your shock if you forgot your tenth wedding anniversary, and your wife says, "It's okay Babe, I bought a lottery ticket today, and we hit the $100 million jackpot!" You expected her to cut off your balls but instead she pleasantly shocked the holy hell out of you.

Neither did the Lord of the Universe cut off my balls for my insolent and aggressively vitriolic behavior, but instead he gave me a pleasant surprise like the wife's winning lottery ticket, better than anything I could ever imagine.

That was forty years ago on a sunny summer California afternoon in 1983 the day my green convertible died.

QUICK REVIEW: Why Beg for What's Already Yours?

Why would I beg the Prince of Peace to give me peace when he told me how to get peace? Why would you beg the trainer to make you stronger when he tells you how to get stronger?

What did my trainer, the Lord of the universe tell me to do to get his peace?

How did he instruct me to ASK?

"Speak the words…I'm right here."

That's how he instructs us to ask.

Guys get rid of your vagestacles (which is girly balls) grow a real pair and do things God's way.

Girls, that's the way I talk to guys, but for you ladies I give you a hug, tell you everything's gonna be okay, let you cry it out, and when you're ready then I give you the answer. Yes, I read all the relationship books that tell me, "Don't solve her problem. Listen to her, give her a hug, and when she's ready give her the answer."

Remember the $100,000 lawsuit? When the lawyers sued me which forced the CEO to take me off the road, I *made a demand upon something due* by the power of my 1225 words and **the power of my tongue**.

I made a demand upon the peace that passes all understanding that is not of this world, but rather emerges from another dimension, and when I did, the 1225 words and **the power of my tongue** kicked into high gear to *force-feed* peace into my heart that ushered me into *The Secret Place of the Most High.*

When I *force-fed his* transcendent otherworldly peace that bypasses the human mind yet lives on the inside of me, well holy cannoli, *that's the PIN number* that opens the door to everything else that I need, want, dream, and desire which are all the things that get added to me, including the lawyers that dropped the lawsuit and the CEO that put me back into the rotation of a heavy and intensive travel schedule.

And remember, I didn't ask God for either of those beautiful blessings according to the English meaning of the word "ask."

However, did I "ask" in the true biblical meaning of the word "to ask"?

You're ding-diggity-dog right I did—

THAT'S HOW I ASK!

How do I ask? ***I seek FIRST the kingdom, his emotions.*** *Why?*

Because HIS EMOTIONS *open the floodgates*
to the desires of my heart.

"Speak the words…I'm right here."

Scene 39

Demand Your Peace!

Have you ever begged God to give you peace? I'll bet you have, and if you did, did peace come? Probably not. Why not? Because that shit doesn't work.

Why would you ask, beg, cry, and cajole for God to give you peace when he told you what to do to get it yourself?

Demand your peace!

Have you ever asked a preacher to pray for your peace? Did it come? Probably not, other than a momentary jolt briefer than an ejaculation. Why not? Because that shit doesn't work. Why would you ask a man to pray for your peace when God told you what to do to get it yourself?

Demand your peace!

Have you ever asked your prayer group to pray for your peace? Did it come? Probably not. Why not? Because that shit doesn't work. Why would you ask your prayer group to pray for your peace when God told you a million times over again how to get it yourself?

Demand your peace!

Would you pray for food that's already on the dinner table? Why would you pray for food that's already cooked, piping hot, and sits right in front of you? Can you imagine your friends invite you over for dinner, they ask you to pray over the food, and you launch into "Ohhh God, we're so very hungry, we beseech thee to give us food.

"Please dear God give us food, and oh dear God, please, we beg of you in our most holy, reverent, and sincere voice, please help us to eat," to which your dinner hosts whisper what an idiot you are.

Even God steps in to interrupt your prayer, "Yo dumbass, did your parents ever ask you to run away from home? *The food's getting cold. EAT!* And while you're at it get rid of that stupid-looking, scrunched-up "holy" look on your face that everybody gets when they try to act holy with me."

And so his people cry out, "How Lord, HOW—HOW do we get peace?!?"

To which he answers for the ten thousand eleven hundred and one millionth time, *"Pick up your fork and put the food in your mouth. THERE'S PLENTY OF FOOD on the dinner table! Speak the words...I'm right here."*

Make a demand upon your peace! It's right here!

On that sunny summer California afternoon in 1983 when my green convertible died, did I ask God for peace? No I didn't, and if I had it wouldn't have come. Why not? Because that shit doesn't work.

However, did peace flood me that sunny summer California afternoon in 1983 the day my green convertible died? You're damn right peace flooded me like a river overflowing its banks! Why? **Because, even in my sheer ignorance and rebellion, I made a demand upon something due.**

I made a demand upon the peace that God owes me!

Do you ask God for food that sits on the table in front of you? No. Why then would you ask God for peace that's already inside of you like dinner's on the table in front of you, and why would you ask him for peace when he tells you how to pull it out of the depths of dormancy, bring it to the surface, and do it all by 1225 words and **the power of your tongue**?

REVIEW

I want you to get this, so let's do a quick review, and here's the important distinction to make. Are you ready? Alrighty, here we go. On that sunny summer California afternoon in 1983 the day my green convertible died, I didn't "ask" for peace in the traditional sense of the word "to ask," as in, "May I please have a popsicle?" I didn't "ask" like that, but I certainly did "ask." I certainly did ask God for peace, but the key word is ASK.

How did I "ask"? How did I "ask" God for peace?

HERE'S HOW: **I made a demand upon something due, even though it was a complete accident.** But no matter, that's what the biblical word ASK means.

What's the thing that is due that I made a demand upon?

That which is due that I made a demand upon is the **peace that passes all understanding**, a transcendent otherworldly peace that exists outside of our dimension of time, space, and matter, and yet lives inside of us.

That kind of peace doesn't come by request, as in, "May I please have some peace?"

No, that supernatural kind of peace comes only by the dual armaments of 1225 words and **the mighty power of your tongue** that rips through the Evil Queen's fortress, boars into the central core of your heart, resurrects the kingdom of God that has lain dormant inside you since the day you were born, and thrusts his kingdom onto the throne of your heart so that you walk in happiness, peace, and joy which translates into power, might, and victory!

That's how to ***make a demand*** *upon your peace!*

So then HOW did I **make a demand upon this peace that was due**?

Here's how I made a demand upon that peace that was due: I unknowingly, accidentally, unwittingly, and viciously screamed 1225 angry words into the smoggy skies of Los Angeles on a sunny summer California afternoon in 1983 that day my green convertible died, and when I did, **the power of my tongue** kicked into high gear and flooded my heart with indescribable peace that shocked the holy hell out of me. The Prince of Peace arose from deep inside me where he'd lain dormant for so many years, and with a flurry of fire and a whirlwind of fury he stormed onto the scene with all his might and majesty and kicked the living shit out of the Evil Queen, that horrible ogre with boogers in her nose who lives under a bridge that plagues us non-stop our whole life, yet you stop her dead in her tracks when you properly ASK.

That's how to demand your peace!

When you *force-feed* peace into your heart by **the bone-crushing power of your tongue** and 1225 words, that's how you ASK.

That's how you **make a demand upon something due**.

That's how you **make a demand** *upon your peace!*

When you make that demand upon something due by your 1225 words and **the power of your tongue**, then otherworldly peace that defies human understanding *force-feeds* itself into your heart, and that's when the pearl of immense value kicks into high gear and moves heaven and earth to ensure that everything that you need, want, dream, and desire pours down on you like six feet of rain on Foc-Foc Island.

I personally don't ask for golden eggs. I make a demand upon the goose.

You can ask God for $300 all you want, but not me. I want the PIN number.

You can do whatever you want, but as for me, that's how I "ask."

Demand your peace!

So that's the course of action I took when the lawyers in the $100,000 lawsuit pounced on me like a pack of wild hyenas. I pursued first the kingdom of God, exactly like I did that sunny summer California afternoon in 1983 the day I accidentally discovered that the double-barreled shotgun of 1225 words coupled with **the power of my tongue** would deliver me from pain, heartache, worry, and fear, and these dual armaments of 1225 words and **the power of my tongue** would kick open the doors that lead to the Garden of Eden.

On that sunny summer California afternoon I asked no questions. I made no complaints. I didn't ask people to pray for me. I didn't call my pastor to pray for me. I didn't post on Facebook "Please pray for me," because Facebook wasn't invented yet, but if it had been, I wouldn't have posted. I simply obeyed God, unknowingly and accidentally, but nevertheless I "made a demand upon something due."

I attack, he fights, I win.

What's the formula?

I speak.

The power of my tongue and 1225 words attacks.

God fights.

I win.

"Speak the words…I'm right here."

I have an amazing story that illustrates this wartime strategy in scene 58 called "Holy Street Fighter."

BONUS SECTION

Nearly all of the blessings in my life, also known as "all these things that get added to me" …I didn't foresee any of them. I never "asked" for them in the English meaning of the word "to ask."

Allow me to clarify: I certainly had visions of grandeur for sure, but what about the specifics? I'm clueless about the specifics. Hence each of the huge blessings and miracles that happen to me always take me completely and totally by surprise.

For example, I wasn't looking for a wife when I got married, and certainly not a widow with a two-year-old little boy and a nine-month-old baby girl, but she gave me twenty-five of the best years of my life.

I wasn't looking for a twenty-year seminar speaking career when the opportunity came available. However it did in fact fit the pattern of my wishes that I outlined in the church that day around the corner from my life insurance office when I was twenty-two. In other words, performer, politician, preacher, and professor were my four heart's desires…but the specifics? No way did I know them.

As I said before, maybe I'm not mature enough or developed enough in my relationship with God to "ask" him for specifics, but until then, the way I've "asked" works perfectly and gives me more than I could ever dream, think, hope, or imagine.

I wasn't looking to author a book. I simply sat down with my yellow notepad at a friend's condominium in Marina del Rey during the summer Olympics in Los Angeles in 1984. *The seeds grew.*

I wasn't looking for a starring role in an Aaron Spelling television series on ABC-TV with Michelle Pfeiffer, yet it showed up on my doorstep like an Amazon package. *The seeds grew.*

I wasn't looking for…well, damn near everything that's ever happened to me, none of it did I ask for, as in, "Hey God, please give me a… (fill in the blank)." *Nevertheless he outdid himself with showers of blessings.*

You can do whatever you want, and if I'm wrong I stand corrected, and I repeat, maybe I'm immature and have yet to develop my theology enough to ask God for stuff according to the English meaning of the verb "to ask," but until I do, or until somebody shows me a better way, then I'll continue to praise, praise, praise, for days, days, days until everything I need, hope for, wish for, and desire, *plus all kinds of stuff that I had no idea I even wanted* continues to show up on my doorstep like an Amazon package.

As if I needed to remind you once again of the trifold recipe for success:

"Speak the words…I'm right here." … *"**Be diligent in all your hand finds to do**"* … *"Take care of the poor, the fatherless, and the widow."*

"Speak the words…I'm right here."

Scene 40

Resounding Thunderous "YES!"

Have you ever asked God to "help you," but he didn't?

It's important to note that God didn't "help me" as a father would help his kindergarten son in response to his pleas for daddy to help him, and yet God certainly did "help me."

Unfortunately for the first thirty years of my life I had a relationship with God like a kindergartener who pleas for his parents to help him, which of course they do, but God expects us to graduate from kindergarten into adulthood.

For the first thirty years of my life I had a kindergartner relationship with God where I asked him to "help me," and begged him to "take away the pain," and pleaded with him to give me all the things that you and me, and all of humanity asks for him to give us, but alas! He didn't! Why not? Because *he's already given them to us.*

He's already given us all things, like the hostess already gave us the piping hot turkey and gravy that sits in front of us on the dining room table.

This is the reason why I spent the first thirty years of my life so flipping frustrated, because no matter how much I asked God for stuff, and pleaded with him, and begged him to "help me" according to the English meaning of the word "ask," he never did.

Is that because he didn't want to help me? GOD FORBID! **Get rid of that thought**! NEVER think it again! He desperately wanted to help me, even more than I wanted help for myself!

"But why Steve," you ask, *"Why didn't God help you?"*

That's a helluva good question, one that millions have asked, yet the answer is as obvious as knowing not to dress up in a Captain Hook costume at a gynecologist convention.

The reason God didn't help me was because I unknowingly, yet disobediently "asked" in a way that was diametrically opposed to how he instructed us to ask. In other words, I "asked" wrong. James 4:3, "You ask, and do not receive, because you 'ask' wrong."

What do you mean Steve, that you "asked" wrong?

I mean that I asked for his help in a way that he NEVER said to ask for his help. That's why nothing happened.

That's why he didn't help me.

I must tell you again, is it because he didn't want to help me? No, no, no, a thousand four hundred times NO. He desperately wanted to help me, and desperately wants to help you, and every man, woman, and child that walks the earth, but he didn't help me because I asked him in an immature and illiterate way.

I didn't follow his instruction manual called "How to Get God's help" that he painstakingly lays out for us from Genesis to Revelation, and henceforth I suffered horribly, and lived in emotional pain—not all the time, but there were times that I couldn't manage life.

And how else did I suffer? Fear of failure is a big one. I had a fear of failure because of my lack of knowledge.

"My people are destroyed for a lack of knowledge" (Hosea 4:6).

What is the proper, accurate, and effective way to "ask"?

Well, what's the proper way to "ask" for $300 from the ATM machine?

You could ignorantly "ask" the ATM for $300, "Please Mr. ATM give me $300," or even better, you can prayerfully kneel on the sidewalk in front of the ATM machine and whip out your guitar and sing three worship songs, and then with your face in that Sunday morning scrunched up "holy look" that annoys God, in your most piously religious, saved and sanctified voice you can cry, beg, bawl, and squall for the bank to give you $300.

"Puh-leeze Mr. Bank, I'm begging you to give me $300, I'll serve you forever if you do."

Only a man who couldn't spell "cat" if you spotted him the C and the T would ask like that, because unless and until you insert the ATM card, punch in the PIN code, you ain't gettin' shit.

How ridiculous does that sound for the bank to give you $300 in such a manner? Just shy of criminal, right?

And yet that's how ridiculous and moronic we sound when we beg God for stuff that he's already promised to give us, and then when it doesn't happen, then we tell our friends that God said, "No, you can't have that."

No the fuck he didn't tell you "No, you can't have that!"

God doesn't tell you "No" any more than the bank tells you "No."

I'm gonna talk tough to you for just a moment, so brace yourselves for a spanking… *SHUT UP with your stupid, moronic, imbecilic man-made religious explanations, your mental twists and turns to explain away shit that doesn't happen because you were a dumbass that foolishly ignored, disregarded, and paid no heed to God's instructions!* Okay, your spanking is over. Now come here, I'll give you a hug.

The Bank Has Instructions, and So Does God

The bank demands that you insert the ATM card, punch in the PIN code, and out pops the $300. That's the bank's instructions. *There are no exceptions!*

God also has a set of instructions. *There are no exceptions!*

I can already hear the faint-hearted say, "Yeah but Steve, God understands what I want, he knows what I mean." It's true, he does know what you mean, and he does know what you want, just like I know what you mean and what you want when you tell the trainer, "I want to get in shape." The trainer knows what you want, but if you don't do what the trainer says to get in shape, such as workout and eat proper nutrition, then you can ask the trainer until you're blue in the face, "Please make me lose weight," and not a damn thing happens.

But right on the other hand...

When You Follow God's Instructions HE NEVER TELLS YOU "NO."

When you follow God's instructions, he never, not ever, without exception ever tells you "No."

I know, I know, this upsets religious folk who sit in the pews of their shitty fucky little church club as they listen to the brain-dead preacher blather on about, "Sometimes God answers 'No.'" The charlatan who parades as a knowledgeable preacher pitifully explicates, "You'd better ask God for something else."

Your prayers turn into a long-shot crapshoot, because how the hell do you know when the answer is "No"? After three hours? After three days, or three years? I've had desires that took forty years! And not once in those forty years did I assume the answer was "No."

It's such a fucked-up relationship with God if you never know if the answer is "yes" or if it's "no," but listen up, Buttercup, I have shitastic information for you, so I'll say it again: Follow God's instructions. When you follow God's instructions **HE NEVER TELLS YOU "NO."** God never tells you "No" any more than the bank tells you "No."

God patiently waits for you to insert the ATM card, punch in the PIN code, and out pops peace, joy, and happiness that are the building blocks for **all the desires of your heart** that he says you WILL get when you seek FIRST the kingdom of God—happiness, peace, and joy, and then **be diligent** in all your hand finds to do, and then **take care of the poor, the fatherless, and the widow**.

The word "No" in response to the desires of your heart is nowhere to be found in his instruction manual.

My life jumped to new levels when I "asked" God in the correct manner in which he instructs us to "ask"—

—in other words, when I pursue FIRST the kingdom of God of happiness, peace, and joy, **then be diligent in all my hand finds to do**, and then *take care of the poor, the fatherless, and the widow*, what then does God do, and how does he respond?

He, the Lord of the universe steps up to the plate, swings the bat, and hits a bases loaded grand slam home run 500 feet over the left field fence as he screams at me, "Yes!" and by golly gee willikers he helps me abundantly above what I can think, dream, or imagine.

He helps me so often and with such regularity that I no longer "bump uglies" with the godless prostitutes of worry, stress, and anxiety.

I no longer pay tribute to those slutty emotions as guests of honor who try to seat themselves at the head table in the dining room of my heart.

Bumpin' uglies is slang for fornicate, and if you knew that then this book was written for you, and if you *didn't,* you do now.

How Do I Ask for God's Help?

I use my 1225 words and **the power of my tongue** to kick the living shit out of those nasty-ass demonic emotions as I pursue FIRST peace, happiness, and joy that catapults me into *The Secret Place of the Most High* that King David talks about in Psalm 91.

So Steve, how does God HELP you?

He "helps me" by the power of his 1225 words that are him, that I couple with **the power of my tongue**, and these two forces work together like a highly-skilled heart surgeon to slit the Evil Queen's throat, they crush her inane and wickedly poisonous noxious emotions, and they forcibly unleash the power of peace onto the throne of my heart, a peace that is not of this world, a peace that opens wide the gates to the Garden of Eden, the garden of God's luxury and delight that includes all the desires of my heart, none of them to which he responds with, "No Steve, you can't have them."

In a screenplay we enclose stage directions in brackets. [GOD GRINS BIG WITH PLEASURE]

How else does God "help" you Steve?

He "helps me" when he slams peace into my heart as he gives me a kiss like the prince gave Snow White a kiss that awakened her from her deep slumber and broke the curse from the Evil Queen's poisoned apple.

[GOD WILDLY BELLY-LAUGHS]

How else does God HELP you, Steve?

He "helps me" when ALL THESE THINGS GET ADDED TO ME after I pursue first and foremost *the* **otherworldly peace** *that passes all understanding, an* **otherworldly peace** *that defies human comprehension, an* **otherworldly peace** *that opens the doors to the Garden of Eden.*

Not only does God grin with pleasure and belly-laughs, but he screams at the top of his voice, "YEE-HAW, YOU GOT THIS!"

This is turning out to be a helluva screenplay!

How excited God must be when we fully understand what he's tried to get us to understand for thousands of years *so that he can FINALLY bless us!*

[FLASHBACK TO THE LITTLE GIRL'S BIRTHDAY PARTY]

God holds up my ugly gift for everyone to see, and exclaims, "I love this gift. It's perfect for me!" And then God looks at me with a twinkle in his eye and mouths the words, "Thank you Stevie Hanks for my wonderful gift, and ***thank you for coming to my party****."*

****

How badly does God want to help you? MORE THAN YOU KNOW! I've outlined the divine plan how to get his help, and that's how God "helps" me, and that's how he "helps" you, and that's how he "helps" every man, woman, and child that hooks his wagon onto the magnificent 1225 words and **the power of their very own tongue** to slam dunk **otherworldly peace** that passes all understanding into their hearts.

Do you want God's help?
Pssst...I just gave you the secret to get God's help

These transcendent emotions are the PEARL OF GREAT VALUE!

That's how to get God's help.

These otherworldly emotions are the PIN number to the ATM machine.

That's how to get God's help.

These emotions from another dimension are the KINGDOM that he said to SEEK FIRST.

That's how to get God's help.

These emotions buried deep inside you are the GREATEST TREASURE KNOWN TO MAN.

They're how to get God's help.

These cataclysmic, supernatural, otherworldly EMOTIONS *that are* **not of this world** *are the* SOURCE *of* ALL THESE THINGS WILL BE ADDED TO YOU.

That's how to get God's help.

These emotions of **happiness, peace, and joy** are THE KINGDOM OF GOD that lives inside you, and gives you access to the fourth through the tenth dimensions that are smaller than the tiniest nanoparticle, and they live inside you.

That's how to get God's help.

These emotions are THE GOOSE THAT LAYS THE GOLDEN EGGS.

That's how to get God's help.

Don't seek the golden eggs, no hell no. What do you seek? *Seek the goose.*

What is the goose? The goose is God's otherworldly emotions of peace, the supernatural inexplicable peace that defies human understanding, the peace that your human mind cannot comprehend. The goose is the happiness that I told the young girl is her purpose in life.

That's how to get God's help.

What else is the goose? DILIGENCE. Diligence to pursue your tasks, your errands, your workload, your business, your career, your marriage, your kids, your phone calls, your study—all the necessary steps to accomplish every dream, want, wish, and desire.

THE KEY is to **diligently pursue** your mission that puts flesh, skin, and bones onto the **desires of your heart,** but you must do so AFTER, AFTER, **AFTER**… When? **AFTER**… *When?* **AFTER** you enter *The Secret Place of the Most High,* his throne room where peace rules your heart.

That's how to get God's help.

Seek FIRST his EMOTIONS—the goose—that lays the golden eggs.

Oh, and there's one more especially essential element that completes the tapestry of the goose that lays the golden eggs. Top priority is to seek first the kingdom, second is to be diligent in all your hand finds to do, and the third… What is it? *Take care of the poor, the fatherless, and the widow.*

THAT'S HOW TO GET GOD'S HELP.

Listen to me, when those kingdom forces of happiness, peace, and joy forcibly control *your emotions* like the day that they forcibly controlled mine that sunny summer California afternoon in 1983 the day my green convertible died…

…when transcendent peace *force-feeds itself* into you by **the power of your very own tongue** as it speaks 1225 biblical *crazin' brazen bitchin' blazin' cuss words of praise…*

...THAT'S when and how God supernaturally reaches up from deep inside you to "help you" …

…and THAT'S the moment in time when you embark on your day's work, on your tasks, your project, your business, your career, your marriage, your family, your kids, your fitness…

…and that's when "whatever your hand finds to do prospers" as promised in Psalm 1:1-3; Genesis 39:3; 1 Kings 2:3; Deuteronomy 12:7; Deuteronomy 29:9; Joshua 1:7; Deuteronomy 30:8-10 to name a few even though you won't look them up.

****

REVIEW

God's Formula to "Help You"

ONE: Seek peace and pursue it, like you'd pursue the pearl of great value, like Indiana Jones pursued the Ark of the Covenant. Pursue the kingdom just like the Jewish rabbi says, "Seek FIRST the kingdom of God which are the emotions of happiness, peace, and joy."

TWO: Be diligent in every task, every errand, every phone call, every bite of food, piano practice, study—be diligent in EVERYTHING you do.

THREE: Take care of the poor, the fatherless, and the widow.

That's how to get God's help.

That's when ALL THESE THINGS WILL BE ADDED TO YOU.

Not before. Keep your priorities in the right order. Seek FIRST the kingdom of God.

Don't wipe before you poop.

Whew, I need a nap. I'll see you in seventeen minutes.

"Speak the words…I'm right here."

INTERMISSION

ACT 9: Climb the Highest Mountain

Scene 41

High Performance Racer

Seek first the emotions of happiness, peace, and joy, and then all the things you need, want, dream, and desire will be added to you

The times I sit at my computer to write when I have supernatural peace—not just the panty-pie peace that comes from a comfortable lifestyle, but the otherworldly peace that transcends this present world of time, space, and matter, then my writing skills blast *off the charts.* I write from a dimension that's outside of this natural realm.

On the other hand, there are two barriers that block my vast worlds of creativity.

ONE: If I'm angry at someone, or even slightly perturbed, then I must quickly forgive lest my writing feels like I'm wading through mud.

POP QUIZ: What is forgiveness? *Forgiveness is when you rinse the acid out of your heart* that sizzles your brain like a fried egg in an overheated skillet when a nincompoop asswipe has done you wrong. I'll go into extensive detail about *How to Forgive* those that have done horrible damage to your heart in volume three of *Shitty to Happy in 21 Minutes: THE GREAT INVASION.*

TEASER: It's as simple to forgive nasty-ass people as it is to *take a breath of fresh air.* I kid you not. You'll be shocked at how simple it is to forgive…AND FORGET! What means "forget"? It means *rid your heart of your painful* **emotions** *and filthy-as-rags* **reactions** *to what they did to you.* It's remarkably easy to perform this seemingly gargantuan task, and I give you explicit instructions in volume three *THE GREAT INVASION.*

TWO: The second stumbling block that impedes my creativity is if I neglect to propel my levels of peace into the upper tiers of heavenly places by

the power of my tongue—that supersonic and majestic level of incomprehensible peace that *force-feeds* itself into my heart every time I unleash the 1225 words into the blue skies like I did that sunny summer California afternoon in 1983 the day my green convertible died.

This extraordinary peace is a supernatural assemblage of emotional serenity that King David bespeaks in Psalm 91 called *The Secret Place of the Most High.*

If I carelessly falter, stumble, and neglect to *force-feed myself FULL* of this supernatural peace, then my creativity is still good but not great; my writing skills are normal; my work is adequate but it's not *off the charts otherworldly.*

Comfort, also known as "Panty-Pie" Peace is NOT Otherworldly Peace

Peace that comes from a comfortable lifestyle is "panty-pie" peace. It's comfort. It's a peace that you can mentally grasp, you can rationalize it, and it makes perfect sense, and therefore not "otherworldly," inexplicable, nor incomprehensible.

How do I distinguish between the peace that is *comfort*, and the peace that is *transcendent otherworldly peace* ***that defies human comprehension?***

> *If I'm peaceful because I have fine cars, gorgeous homes, a beautiful wife, well-behaved kids, and a fantastic career, then* ***it's not otherworldly peace****. It's marvelous peace, it's fantastic peace, it's Garden of Eden peace, but it's not otherworldly peace that defies comprehension.*
>
> *It's comfort.*
>
> *This comfortable peace is a gift that overflows its banks in the Garden of Eden, God's garden of luxury and delight, but* ***it's not supernatural peace****.*
>
> *The peace that comes from beautiful homes, fine cars, a happy family, great kids, an illustrious career, a successful business, a huge business deal, a new client, well, this peace is ours in the Garden of Eden, but* ***this peace does not surpass the ability of the human mind to comprehend****.*

May I submit to you that if you can comprehend it, then it's not supernatural. It's not otherworldly if you can explain the reason why you have it. It's not a peace that transcends this three-dimensional world if it's not a transcendent otherworldly peace like the kind that hit me like a tsunami that sunny summer California afternoon in 1983 the day my green convertible died. *I had no reason to feel peaceful that sunny summer California afternoon. NONE…except for two earthshattering forces:* ***1225 WORDS*** *and* ***the power of my tongue.***

The two kinds of peace are identical twins. They look nearly the same, but like identical twins, there are subtle, yet substantial differences.

Both kinds of peace are fantastic, yet they are worlds apart.

Comfort is a good peace. It's a beautiful peace, it's a fantastic peace, and it's a peace that the Garden of Eden supplies in abundance...

…BUT…listen to me carefully, it's not the kind of peace that blew up in me that sunny summer California afternoon in 1983 the day my green convertible died. *That kind of peace that hit me that afternoon is incomprehensible.*

That's the kind of peace that is over and above, and far beyond what the human mind can understand. That's the kind of peace of which I speak that is the peace that is not of this world. That's the kind of peace that possesses me even when my life is falling apart, money's tight, and a flea bit me.

It's this incomprehensible inexplicable peace that transcends this three-dimensional world.

This is the kind of high-level inexplicable peace that blows my book-writing skills through the roof and into another dimension.

It's the kind of peace that blasts mountains out of our way and kicks open the gates to the Garden of Eden where everything we can think, dream, or imagine awaits us.

Supernatural Peace Births Comfort

One peace springs up from the other. Peace that passes all understanding is the father, comfort is the son. Peace inexplicable is the mother, comfort from nice things is the daughter. Transcendent peace is the mama bear; comfort is the cub.

The "comfort" peace, the "panty pie" peace…these are the offspring of the supernatural peace that transcends this three-dimensional world.

So, you see that both kinds of peace are ours, and both are beautiful, and both enhance your heart so that you live heaven on earth, but the most important difference between the two is **one of them is from a comfortable lifestyle**, the other one is **independent of your lifestyle**.

One precedes the other. Transcendent peace begets the nice things that provide comfort. I wrote about it earlier in *Peace Births Fortunes*. ***Transcendent otherworldly peace*** *begets the desires of your heart, which begets* ***comfort***. The two kinds of peace go hand-in-hand like two lovebirds. Both have their proper place in our lives, both are vital—like fire and water.

However, you can only maintain comfort for as long as you feed the transcendent supernatural otherworldly peace. If you take your eyes off of the supernatural peace, and instead focus your attention solely on your lifestyle as the primary source of your peace, then your peace is built upon sand, and when the winds come and storms blow, great is the fall of your paper-thin empire.

I'll not tell you how much time I spend to speak praises each and every day to flood my heart with these deep levels of supernatural otherworldly peace that arise from the depths of the kingdom that lives inside me, but I'll suggest to you this: Spend 21 minutes the first day, then see how you feel. That's 1225 words three times through for a total of 3675 words. It takes twenty-one minutes.

If you like it, then do it twice that day. If you still like it, then do it a third time, but I promise you that your daily tasks will flow a helluva lot easier and more efficiently the more often you propel your 1225 words into the skies which thereby *force-feeds* your heart full of transcendent peace by **the power of your very own tongue**.

QUICK REVIEW: Where is your happiness, peace, and joy to be found? Where do they originate from?

They originate from deep inside you where the kingdom of God is, and they are locked and loaded in **the power of your tongue**.

Where does your peace hide? Where does your unspeakable joy hide? Where does the happiness hide that I told the young girl is her purpose for life? That night when she asked me that profound question, her otherworldly happiness was closer than her next breath. Where was her happiness hiding?

Her happiness and peace, and yours and mine, are hiding inside us. The night she asked me the question, the young girl's happiness and peace was hidden inside her.

Your happiness and peace hide inside you as they do inside the young girl, just like the fourth through the tenth dimensions hide inside all of us.

Who are the fourth through the tenth dimensions? They are God.

Where is God?

He's inside you, but he's not limited to inside you since he's omnipresent, in all places at all times.

Screeching sound again…

Do you want to tap into that power? It's a power that's buried deep inside you like David was buried deep inside the seventeen-foot-high block of marble.

Do you want an outpouring of that power? Are you sure? It's incomprehensible. It's unexplainable. Are you sure you want it?

If so, then you must speak. No speak, no power.

The power of your tongue is the umbilical cord that connects you to the lifeblood of God who lives inside you.

I promise that **the power of your tongue** will slam dunk you so full of the *supernatural high of transcendent peace* that is *beyond the ability of your mind to understand* and listen to me carefully, it will hook you so fancifully that whatever has felt like peace in the past will feel like a rusty tugboat compared to a glistening ocean liner.

Would you rather travel the world on a rusty dilapidated tugboat, or would you rather travel on a beautiful glistening ocean liner? If all you have is comfort, it's tugboat peace compared to glistening ocean liner peace.

If you have all the nice things, great career, thriving business, beautiful family, then please don't limit yourself to that peace that's mere "comfort." Press higher into the worlds where you have *supercharged otherworldly peace that transcends this three-dimensional world.* That's your ticket to cruise the world on the glistening ocean liner to the most beautiful locales on earth.

Regular peace also known as "panty-pie" peace is beautiful, fine, and fun but transcendent otherworldly peace is exceptional.

WARNING TO THE PHARISEES!

Do you mind if I stomp on some religious quackery? Most preachers encourage you to tap into the peace that is an IMITATION of *the peace that passes all understanding.* It's the peace that comes from a beautiful lifestyle, a well-deserved lifestyle, and it's a beautiful peace, a rewarding peace, but it's NOT otherworldly transcendent peace that is inexplicable to the human mind.

I can always tell when a preacher sermonizes from a place of "panty-pie" peace, also known as *comfort*, versus that place of supernatural, otherworldly, fourth-dimensional transcendent peace that is not from this world.

How do I know? I'll tell you.

All preachers preach "peace," right? They bellicosely thunder, "Have peace in the thunderstorms!" That's true, but if he encourages you to have peace in the storm with bromides like "Hang in there brother, God will come through for you!" Or how about this one, "God's about ready to move mountains out of your way!" And the ubiquitous platitude, "Your miracle is right around the corner!"

When the preacher pugnaciously clamors such banalities while his spit flies, his armpits sweat, and his audience claps and cheers like trained seals, then this preacher dangles "panty-pie" peace that seduces the audience to drool like Pavlov's dog BECAUSE GOD'S GONNA GIVE ME MY STUFF! *God's gonna give me my stuff!* Thus, the preacher trumpets "comfort," and "panty-pie" peace rather than God's genuine rock-solid peace.

Did he encourage the people to seek after supernatural otherworldly peace? No, he didn't, and the trained seals in the audience who love to have their ears tickled don't know the difference.

When a preacher sermonizes, "Hang in there brother, God will take care of you," and "Your miracle is right around the corner" he strains his hemorrhoids to convince you that ***GOD'S ABOUT READY TO GIVE YOU YOUR STUFF***.

They attempt to impart peace that passes all understanding by enticing you to believe promises that your material goods, problems solved, and desires of your heart are right around the corner.

I submit to you that's a twisted road that leads to the Wizard of Oz instead of *The Secret Place of the Most High*.

> It's like trying to get full without eating dinner.
> It's like trying to lose weight without eating right.
> It's like wiping before you poop.

Get Peace First! Then It's Easy to Believe God's Promises!

Listen, **if you don't already have peace** that transcends this natural world through 1225 words and **the power of your tongue** like I accidentally stumbled upon that sunny summer California afternoon in 1983 the day my green convertible died, then you cannot convince yourself, nor can a preacher convince you that "God's about ready to move."

Sermons that encourage you with bromides like, "Hang in there, you're close to your miracle," are meant to impart peace. They entice you with a honeycomb of miracles, but there's no way to grasp these promises if you're not **already seated with him in heavenly places**. In other words, the only way to grasp God's promises is if you're already full to overflowing with the peace that catapults you into *The Secret Place of the Most High.*

If you're not already seated together with him in heavenly places, then you CANNOT grasp the truth of these promises! If you're not already seated in *The Secret Place of the Most High* it doesn't matter how many sermons you hear— You'll never believe them! Or at best, believe them for a moment, and on a shallow level.

All of God's promises are TRUE, but if you're not already firmly rooted and grounded in *peace that passes all understanding* then YOU CANNOT BELIEVE THEM! I'll say it again, if you're not already peacefully seated together with him in heavenly places in *The Secret Place of the Most High* that David talks about in Psalm 91, then tens of thousands of sermons will not get you there.

Only your obedience gets you there.

God's promises are indeed "yes and amen," but unless you have supernatural inexplicable otherworldly peace, you don't have the power, strength, or confidence to grasp them.

Only supernatural otherworldly peace that transcends time, space, and matter enables you to hang onto God's promises.

"Faith comes by hearing; and hearing by the word of God." What words of God? The **1225 words!** *Hearing* doesn't mean "hear the preacher say it." "Hearing" means YOU say it. The word "hearing" means *obedience*. Who obeys? You do! What's the obedience?

"Speak the 1225 words…I'm right here!" **THAT'S THE OBEDIENCE**!

It's only by ***your obedience*** *that you believe God's promises.*

There's only one act of **obedience** that *force-feeds* the kind of peace that gives you confidence in God's promises—only *ONE WAY* that seats you together with him in heavenly places, the exalted position of power and authority where *YOU HAVE THE STRENGTH, the CONFIDENCE, and the ASSURANCE TO BELIEVE GOD'S PROMISES—*

What's that, Steve?

I've said it ten thousand times before, but I'll say it again: **THE POWER OF YOUR TONGUE is the only way to peacefully sit together with him in**

heavenly places. Hence, **the power of your tongue** is the ONLY way you can believe God's promises.

Straight is the way, and narrow is the gate that leads into LIFE.

Where's life? "Life is in **the power of your tongue**" (Proverbs 18:21).

How do you enter the King's castle where it's easy to believe God's promises?

Only obedience gets you there. HERE'S HOW TO ENTER THE KING'S CASTLE: Spit out the 1225 words OUT LOUD three times through, a total of 3675 words. It takes 21 minutes. Do it often, and when you do, then **the power of your tongue** *force-feeds* his mighty peace into your heart with the sound of a rushing, mighty wind like **what happened to me** that sunny summer California afternoon in 1983 the day my green convertible died!

The power of your tongue *rips through your body, courses through your veins, and DROP-KICKS YOUR BUTT into the Secret Place of the Most High, and once you're there,* ***then it's EASY to believe God's promises!***

Once you've arrived in *The Secret Place* then it's easy to "Hang in there, Brother." In *The Secret Place of the Most High* is where it's easy to believe all the desires of your heart are yours.

I NEVER rely on preachers that sermonize, "Hang in there brother." NEVER. In fact, that worn-out cliché annoys the shit out of me.

When you're in *The Secret Place of the Most High* it's as effortless as breathing in the crisp Colorado mountain air to expect everything you need, hope for, and desire to show up on your doorstep like an Amazon package.

Listen, do you get a full tummy before you eat dinner? No, and neither do you get a full heart with "Hang in there, Brother!" When the "panty-pie" preacher shrieks, "Hang in there, Brother," his bloviated meanderings sound like two skeletons wrestling on a tin roof.

NOTE TO PREACHERS: Don't sermonize your way into the people's hearts to get them to believe God's promises. *That shit doesn't work.* Teach them to seek peace FIRST. When you teach them how to seek peace, then **they easily believe every one of God's amazing, mind-numbing, miracle-working promises**, and you don't have to yell and scream at them like a crazed lunatic to get your point across. And you'll spare your voice, and not sweat as much.

See the difference? The right way works magnificently, perfectly, and easily.

The wrong way is as dumb as a football bat.

****

"One act of obedience is better than one hundred sermons."

Dietrich Bonhoeffer

****

"Speak the words…I'm right here."

Scene 42

Easier is Harder

The Easier Your Life, the More Difficult it is to Live in Otherworldly Supernatural Peace

The peace that comes from 1225 words and **the power of your tongue** far surpasses the peace that comes from a comfortable lifestyle, but how do you discipline yourself to persevere in the otherworldly "peace that passes all understanding" when you already have all the things you could ever want?

Here's how.

Be diligent to continuously speak the 1225 words, or any of the other tens of thousands of words like my friend chose to speak. Speak these words until **the power of your tongue** *force-feeds* inexplicable peace that passes all understanding into your heart so much so that you can teach others how they too can walk in this kind of peace regardless of how fantastic their life is, or even how down-in-the-dumps their life is.

You can do what you want, but I rely solely upon the 1225 words and **the power of my tongue** to keep my heart pure, and to protect me from the faux security blanket of peace that comes from a comfortable lifestyle, *and boy is it a challenge,* but we have no choice. We MUST seek first HIS happiness, peace, and joy so that we don't fall into the trap of a comfortable lifestyle that turns warriors into lazy men.

*Comfort—**without otherworldly peace**—*
turns warriors into lazy men

The More Success You Have, then the More You Must Speak!

I told you when I force-feed *that kind of otherworldly peace* into my heart, then I get better quality writing done in three *hours* than I do in three days. I kid you not, it's unbelievable how much more creatively I write when I *force-feed* myself full of transcendent otherworldly peace that surpasses the ability of my human mind to understand.

The same is true of your business, that no matter how successful it is, it grows and increases above and beyond what you ever dreamed or imagined, and the best part is *it grows and increases with LESS effort than ever before!*

I've thought to myself in the past, "But I don't have an extra 21 minutes to unleash **the power of my tongue** to speak 1225 words. I'm too busy." No doubt you'll feel the same, but I assure you—when you set apart 21 minutes to ignite **the power of your tongue** to set those 1225 words in motion—

...when you detonate the power of those 1225 words by **the power of your very own tongue**—

...when you unleash the powers of **peace** and **happiness** that reside deep inside you like David resided in the 17-foot-high block of marble, then you'll accomplish *much more work* and perform **higher quality work** in much fewer hours, and therefore you'll have lots of extra time to love your family, take a walk, have dinner with your spouse, relax, and enjoy life.

When you invest the 21 minutes to speak the 1225 words, you don't lose time. YOU GAIN time. I'll say that again...

When you speak the 1225 words,
you don't lose time—You GAIN time

It's impossible to experience how this supernatural otherworldly peace empowers your skills so efficiently that you work less and accomplish more in fewer hours until you experience it yourself; until you pound into yourself that supernatural peace by **the power of your very own tongue** for a full twenty-one minutes, and don't limit yourself to just once, but do it many times over.

For starters, do it just once. What do you have to lose, but my advice to you is praise, praise, praise for days, days, days to supercharge your body, your skills, your emotions, and your strength. Do it consistently and do it persistently.

Hold on to your otherworldly transcendent peace with a bulldog grip, and chew and choke as much as possible. Abraham Lincoln said it, the "chew and choke" part, not the "peace" part. That's when you're primed, pumped, and ready to go to work on your daily tasks, and I promise you, you'll get a lot more done, and better-quality performance in fewer hours.

When you set apart 21 minutes to *"Speak the words..."* **the power of your tongue** crams you full of the Prince of Peace who is the one who says, *"...I'm right here"* and he brings his glistening ocean liner peace that is better than any tugboat quality of "panty-pie" peace your empire has to offer.

What's more, your 1225 words that you catapult into the skies by **the power of your very own tongue** causes you to get more done in less time which gives you MORE free time to relax and do whatever else you want. In addition, your business, your career, your profession, your family, your kids, and everything else explodes to higher levels of success than you can imagine, and with more ease than you ever thought possible.

The more time you spend speaking the 1225 words, the more free time you have, and the easier your successes chase you and overtake you. Cray-cray, I know, but it's a cray-cray backward kingdom!

Listen, *God desperately wants you to have the desires of your heart!* He promises you that the kingdom of God guarantees that your goodies get added to you. Why else would he explain to you how to get them in a way that seems so backward to the carnal mind, and yet is more powerful, efficient, and easier than anything you've ever experienced!

God wants nothing more than for you to have your goodies—the desires of your heart—and he wants you to empower yourself with his words to solve your unsolvable problems! Why else would he painstakingly teach you, show you, and plead unceasingly with you how to get the desires of your heart, plus give you the wisdom to solve your unsolvable problems with improbable solutions, and all this without toiling or spinning?

"The blessing of the Lord brings wealth, without painful toil for it" (Proverbs 10:22). God wants so much for you to peacefully attain your goodies, the desires of your heart, that he bends over backward to show you HOW to get them without toiling or spinning! I like success and wealth without painful toil. Maybe you'll look that one up. It's Proverbs 10:22.

What does he say to do to get the desires of your heart without painful toil?

ONE: Be peacefully diligent, *be peacefully diligent,* **be oh so peacefully diligent** in your tasks...
TWO: Take care of the poor, the fatherless, and the widow...
THREE: *Force-feed* yourself full of peace by **the power of your tongue**.

How do you force-feed yourself full of peace?

"Speak the words...I'm right here."

Scene 43

God's Awesome Stuff

I met a girl on an airplane on a flight from Albuquerque to Los Angeles after a speaking engagement. She asked me what I do for a living, and I told her I was an ass model. I'm kidding. I'm not kidding that I told her I'm an ass model. I'm kidding that I'm an ass model. I'm not. Anyway, I told her about this book, and her response was, "I'm already happy."

I met another girl when I did a seminar in Reno, and I asked her, "If I was God and could grant you any three wishes to make you happy, what would they be?" She said the same thing: "I'm already happy."

These two girls described *comfort.* Comfort is wonderful, but it's not supernatural peace. Comfort is fantastic, it's a blessing, but it's not the kind of peace that surpasses the ability of your mind to comprehend, the kind of peace that is not of this world, the kind of peace that no man can enter into without the power of the spirit.

Remember the Jewish rabbi said, "The words that I SPEAK are spirit."

What is the **power of the spirit** that *forces* you into *The Secret Place of the Most High?* The power of the spirit is *the power of the* WORDS that you SPEAK, and thus **the power of your tongue** ignites them like a stick of dynamite.

When you ignite the 1225 words by **the power of your tongue** they work together to incite the inexplicable energy of the SPIRIT. The spirit then ignites the otherworldly PEACE, the peace that transcends this natural world, a peace that is far beyond the ability of our human mind to comprehend. This is the inexplicable otherworldly peace that dwells in those 1225 happy bombs that you *force-feed* into your heart by **the power of your tongue**.

Where Does the Kingdom of God Hide?

Where did the Jewish rabbi say the kingdom of God is located? INSIDE YOU. Inside ME. Inside the young girl. That's where this otherworldly transcendent peace lives, that otherworldly peace that transcends this natural world, yet lives inside you, but lies dormant until you activate it.

This invisible kingdom lives inside you like King David lived inside the seventeen-foot-high block of marble, unseen to the naked eye until Michelangelo chipped away the superfluous parts to reveal to all the world the beautiful image of David that only the trained eye of Michelangelo could see.

Even so, the kingdom of God lives inside of you, a nanoparticle-sized beautiful kingdom that only the trained eye of God can see.

So how do you strip away the superfluous parts of you that cover this kingdom so that you tap into this invisible, yet mighty empire for all the world to see? (You'd better have this memorized by now!) **The power of your tongue** and the 1225 words chip away the superfluous parts of you that are not the kingdom, and thus **the power of your tongue** bridges the gap between this natural world and the invisible kingdom that lives inside you.

What obscures this kingdom? Why is it so vague?

The Evil Queen suffocates this kingdom like a wet blanket thrown on a campfire. How do we fan the flames to burn away the wet blanket? **The power of your tongue!** The power of your tongue transforms the written words into spirit, which is the power by which you crucify the deeds of the flesh, which are the Evil Queen's wet blanket of anger, bitterness, resentment, unforgiveness and a million other emotions that **drown the fires of your powerful kingdom**.

The 1225 words and **the power of your tongue** sever the Evil Queen's tentacles that strangle this glorious kingdom. The words and **the power of your tongue** are two bunker-busters that pry open the floodgates that thwart the mighty forces of happiness, peace, and joy, and hence unleash the flood that pours out of your heart like a mighty rushing river.

The kingdom of God is not "out there somewhere." The kingdom of God is inside you, and the Evil Queen's sole mission is to use her darkness to cover your kingdom and keep it hidden from you, but when the dam of her darkness crumbles, these kingdom forces explode up from within you for all the world to see as their vigorous might and fury kicks open the doors to the Garden of Eden.

No Speak, No Power

The 1225 words on a page…USELESS.

The 1225 words by **the power of your tongue**...SUPERNATURAL.

No speak, no power. Make use of that powerful piece of flesh.

Got it? THE POWER is in that simple piece of flesh. *Life and death are in **the power of your tongue**.*

When I was ignorant about **the power of my tongue**, how desperate was I? How desperate are you? I'll bet hundreds of times you prayed to God to help you, and you begged and pleaded with God to give you a miracle of $300 from the ATM machine but not a damn thing happened. I'll bet you listened to a thousand sermons to "build your faith" but nothing happened. Why not? Because you didn't activate his 1225 words by **the power of your *very own* tongue**. You didn't insert the ATM card, punch in the PIN number because if you did you'd get three crisp $100 bills, but I'll bet you could quote all God's promises, right? I'll bet you still have all those sermons on speed dial, but alas God never helped you.

Did God want to help you? Damn right he wanted to help you more than you know!

But why didn't he?

Because if you don't follow the instructions on the bank ATM machine, God ain't spittin' out three $100 bills for you. Has that ever happened in the history of ATM machines? Not likely.

You could listen to forty thousand sermons that tell you the benefits of the ATM machine, how it'll give you three hundred dollars if "you'll just hang in there brother," because the bank's three hundred dollars are "right around the corner." Your ears perk up, you lap up the sermon like a dog in heat. The preacher bloviates, "You're so close to getting your $300!" You shout, you stomp, you cheer, you clap your hands. "God's gonna come through for me!" as you gleefully sing, shout, raise your hands, and dance.

But alas, after three months the bank still hasn't given you your three hundred dollars. You pray, you cry, you beg to God, you download another sermon, you pray yet again, "God *puh-leeze* give me three hundred dollars!"

But nothing happens. You go to church on Sunday and the preacher explains, "Well son, you see, sometimes God's answer is "No."

Fuck that shit. God's answer is "Yes," but *he can't do a dagnab thing.*

Whoa Steve, did you just say God can't?!? You heard me right. If you don't follow his instructions *he can't.* Let me explain that he WANTS to, but he CAN'T.

Can you go right and left at the same time? No, you can't, not while you live in this three-dimensional world. It's impossible to go right and left at the same time in this three-dimensional world even if you're God but allow me to explain something.

God CAN go left and go right AT THE SAME TIME in other dimensions as can you and me. Take the basketball example: Can you turn a basketball inside out without making a cut or a hole in the ball? Not in this third dimension, but in the fourth dimension it's easy. You can turn a basketball inside out without making a cut or a hole in the ball.

Therefore, God CAN go left and right at the same time in the higher dimensions, as can you and I, but NONE of us including God can go left and right at once whilst the third dimension constrains us. That explains why there are things that even God cannot do while we're restricted in this third dimension. Could Jesus go left and go right at the same time? He can now, but he couldn't then, not while he walked the earth.

So then how do inexplicable miracles happen in our third dimension such as the gold coin in the fish's mouth, turning water into wine, and multiplying five loaves and two fishes to feed fifteen thousand? Miracles happen in our third dimension when for that moment in time, the fourth dimension appears from inside of you, peaks his head out, and invades this third dimension if only for a few seconds. That's how Jesus in his resurrected body passed through solid walls. Even though the disciples padlocked the doors because they were terrified of the Jewish leaders, the Son of Man suddenly appeared to them in their hideout, which, needless to say, freaked them out more than Casper the friendly ghost. It certainly would have me!

I hear the sound of the screeching wheels AGAIN!

Anyway, back to my point: God can't spit out three $100 bills for you any more than your wife can make you go left if you turn right. You bellow, "Where's the restaurant?" Your wife responds, "It's not where you're headed!!!"

Why can't God reach out to help you if you turn right when he told you to turn left? It's because he told you to go left but you turned right, and *you can't go left and right* AT THE SAME TIME. That's why God can't help you, and so we act like a spoiled brat as we bawl and squall, moan and complain to God, "You didn't help me!"

And then to add misery on top of misery, some dumbass low IQ preacher opines, "You didn't get your $300 because sometimes God answers 'No.'"

The frustrated wife says to her husband, "I told you to turn left, but you didn't listen," and she throws her hands up in the air just like God throws his hands up in the air when we complain to him with our childish whines of "You didn't help me."

God agrees with the wife, "Tell me about it Mrs. Wife, when men, women, boys, and girls don't listen to me like your husband didn't listen to you, then they blame me for turning the car right when I told them to turn left."

Don't quote me on this one, but it wouldn't surprise me if God added, "And to add misery on top of misery, dumbass preachers blame ME with a stupid, uneducated, low IQ assumption like, "Well brother, sometimes God says 'No.'"

What a crock of shit! God NEVER says "No," and I'll prove it to you in the next scene!

It's no wonder people can't find the restaurant!" to which I add, "It's no wonder they can't find their ass with both hands in their back pockets."

God didn't say that. I did.

****

How do we find the restaurant? How do we get three hundred dollars out of the ATM machine? How does God move fantastically in our life? Here's the answer:

Crush the Evil Queen! ***Unleash the kingdom of God!*** How?

The words that you SPEAK are the SPIRIT by which you put to death the deeds of the flesh which are anxiety, worry, depression, unforgiveness, and pissed off feelings at people that have hurt you. **These are the Evil Queen antichrist emotions that block your entrance** to the kingdom of God, which henceforth blocks your entrance to the three hundred dollars inside the ATM machine.

"Speak the words...I'm right here."

Why is "speak" so important?

It's because the 1225 words have no power **unless you unleash their power**. What apparatus unleashes their power?

THE POWER of that simple piece of flesh called YOUR TONGUE unleashes their power. *The power of that tiny little member of your body called* "the tongue" UNLEASHES THE POWER OF THE 1225 WORDS.

So therefore ramrod the 1225 words by the might and strength of **the power of your tongue** so that it fights your battles for you, and thereby controls your emotional shitshow and henceforth opens the slot to the ATM machine, and easy peazy lemon breezy, three one-hundred-dollar bills spit out at you. See how simple this is?

Once again, listen to Paul without a last name who says, "Be controlled by the spirit, speaking to your own self in Psalms." You notice that half the time I don't give you the scripture reference. That's because you won't look it up, and if you want to look up the scripture reference you can Google it, and the scripture will pop up in thirty different translations.

"Be CONTROLLED…by the SPIRIT…by speaking PSALMS…which are WORDS…that when you SPEAK…they, THE WORDS, transform into SPIRIT."

All right all right, I'll give you the scripture reference to this one. It's Ephesians 5:19. If you look it up you'll see it says, "Be FILLED with the spirit," but *filled* means "controlled," so it reads, "Be CONTROLLED by the spirit…" How? "By speaking to yourselves in Psalms."

The 1225 words are PSALMS, a CONTROLLING SPIRIT.

Therefore the spoken WORDS—those 1225 words of Psalms you SPEAK—equate to the CONTROLLING SPIRIT that **CONTROLS** you with inexplicable dominance exactly like they controlled and dominated me that sunny Summer California afternoon in 1983 the day my green convertible died, but here's the catch: *They are merely words on a page until you speak them.*

> *They are only letters of the alphabet on a page, and not SPIRIT until you SPEAK them.*
>
> *The 1225 words are not spirit until you speak them.*
>
> *Prior to the moment that you speak them they are only letters, vowels, and consonants on a page without a whit of power to control you.*

That's why I put so much emphasis on **the power of your tongue**. If your tongue lies idle, not a damn thing happens.

Are you and your wife gonna have a baby if you don't stick it in? No, your penis is idle. Not a thing happens if you don't stick it in. *No penis, no baby.*

Are you gonna have peace that transcends this three-dimensional world if you don't "stick it in"? No, your tongue is idle. *No tongue, no power.*

This stuff is so simple it befuddles the human mind. It completely brain-freezes the antiquated pharisaical mind, but nevertheless **the power of your tongue** gives LIFE to the 1225 words just like sticking it in gives life to a brand-new human being.

But the sperm and the egg lie lifeless and inanimate. They fall to the ground dead, effete, and powerless if you fail to unite them, and the same happens with your 1225 words. They fall to the ground, lifeless, inanimate, and powerless if you don't impregnate them with **the power of your tongue**.

The life that is in **the power of your tongue** is the hammer, the 1225 words are the chisel. These two insurmountable armaments combine to form an incomprehensible force to chip away the extraneous rubble to uncover the kingdom of God that lies hidden inside you like David was hidden inside the block of marble.

My goal for you—actually God's goal for you—is to transform you into his image, which is another way of saying that he wants you to look and act just like him. *How the heck do we look, and act just like him?*

Do we look and act like him by our own paltry human efforts such as *the power of our sincerity* and "you gotta mean it from the bottom of your heart," and the whole host of man-made stipulations that religious pharisaical fools demand?

No, we're gonna look like him and act like him by **the power of that tiny little piece of flesh called your tongue** that speaks his WORDS which are SPIRIT which are 1225 words of PSALMS that I accidentally discovered their might and energy when I harnessed **the power of my tongue** that kicked the 1225 words into overdrive on that sunny summer California afternoon in 1983 the day my green convertible died.

That's the groundbreaking accidental discovery that I fell headlong into on that sunny summer California afternoon forty years ago.

"Speak the words…I'm right here."

Scene 44

God Thunders "Yes!"

We're gonna take a short commercial break. This is the 90-second commercial break I promised you a few pages ago when I said I'd prove to you that God ALWAYS answers "Yes," and it's brought to you by the One, the Only, the Great One, the King of kings and the Lord of lords, the maker of heaven and earth, and the One who gives you ALL the desires of *YOUR heart.* Promise me you'll remember this forever and ever all the way into eternity, and promise me you'll never forget what I'm about to say—

God never, ever…no, not ever tells you, "No"

Preachers who have an infantile relationship with God blather on with their man-made foolhardy reasonings that "Sometimes God answers "Yes," sometimes he answers, "Wait," and sometimes he answers "No" as drool spills out the sides of their mouth like a beleaguered geriatric while the nurse spoon-feeds them creamed peas.

Have you ever heard that old wives' tale that God sometimes answers "No"?

Alrighty almighty good morning good nighty, I'll prove to you it's the Pharisees piss-poor reasoning for one's illiterate insubordination.

God never answers "No," or even "Wait." You must "wait," yes, but the "waiting" is not because God withholds from you. No, the waiting is the same as if you plant a watermelon seed, and you "wait" for the watermelons to grow. Is God holding back the watermelons? No, the seeds take time to grow.

It's the same as when you start a business. Do you start a business, and the next day have thousands of customers? No, it takes time for your seeds to grow. That explains "wait."

Now, what about "Does God tell me "No"?

SCENARIO 1: When you seek peace and pursue it, does he tell you "No"? Ever? Are you kidding me?!? He never tells you "No" when you seek peace and pursue it in the manner he instructs. In fact when you obediently pursue peace with his 1225 words and **the power of your tongue** like I did that sunny summer California afternoon in 1983 the day my green convertible died, he parts the skies with a bolt of lightning that pierces the heavens to overrule your rebellious paltry putrid emotions with a resounding blast of otherworldly peace as he thunders "YES!"

He *force-feeds* HIS peace into you with the strength of an earth-shattering fifty-foot wave off the North Shore of Oahu by the supernatural powers of his 1225 words and the greatest power in the spirit world and in the natural world, **the power of YOUR VERY OWN TONGUE**.

And your peace doesn't wait until tomorrow, or next week, or even three hours: YOUR PEACE COMES IN 21 MINUTES!

Therefore can we agree that God never tells you "No" when you seek peace in his precise accurate manner, such as I did that sunny summer California afternoon back in 1983 the day my green convertible died?

SCENARIO 2: "But Steve," you ask, "What if I want a career, a family, a business, a home, a car, an apartment, an acting career, a career in entertainment, a manufacturing company, a farm, or a puppy but he tells me "No"? That's a great question, so let's see what God himself says.

When you enter into *The Secret Place of the Most High*, and from that exalted position of authority you pursue the desires of your heart, then does he tell you "No" to any of the desires of your heart?

No silly goose, why would he tell you "No" to any of the desires of your heart when he's the *God of the universe* that **put those desires in your heart in the first place**!

See how simple this is?

Speaking of simplicity, you and God are more similar to each other than you ever thought. Physically? No, but inwardly? YES.

What do I mean by that?

****

Scene 45

God Has Emotions

You heard me right. I'll say it again: *God has emotions.* Sounds pretty crazy, doesn't it? Not only does God have emotions, but his emotions become ours.

"Steve you're so full of shit your eyes are brown."

Really? Is LOVE an emotion? Is JOY an emotion?

Is PEACE an emotion? By the way, my eyes are blue, not brown.

You'll notice 1 John 4:8 doesn't say, "God HAS love." No, it doesn't say "God HAS love." That's not what it says. It says, "God IS love." Substantial difference, would you agree? So can we conclude that if God is love, then God is like Old Faithful geyser that continuously erupts with emotions, not only of love, but also the emotions of joy, peace, and happiness?

God is of course unlimited, infinite, and unconstrained to any one explanation just like the Pacific Ocean is not constrained to one sixteen-ounce-sized glass of water, but like the tiny glass of Pacific Ocean is a slice of The Seven Seas, can we conclude that love, joy, and peace are a slice of the Eternal King, the Almighty God, the Wonderful Counselor, the Everlasting Father, the Prince of Peace?

The prince of…what? ***The Prince of Peace.***

Is PEACE an emotion? The last time I checked, I'm fairly sure that, yes, peace is an emotion.

What Is Eternal Life?

Pharisees BE FOREWARNED because I'm about to rip you a new asshole. John 17:3 says, "This is eternal life that we know God." Scripture says to know God is eternal life. This begs the question—

How do we know God?

Great question with an answer so simple as to mystify, so radical as to revolutionize.

The means by which we are persuaded that we know God is what John calls *eternal life.*

That's great John, but what is *eternal life?* And why is it that none of these bible guys has a last name? I can understand Cher, Bono, and Prince, but *John?!? Paul?!?* Maybe if they were John, Paul, George, and Ringo I get it. Can you imagine if you're the first guy in history with a last name? "Enough of this one-name-only crap, I want a last name!" Well here ya go: Moses McGillicuddy. There, I gave Moses an Irish last name.

Anyway, our knee-jerk response to *eternal life* is "to live forever," and that's true, but I suggest it's also more imminent than "live forever." How does that eternal life play out today, right now, right this very moment? *If you've never experienced the immediacy of "eternal life" then you and millions of others have overlooked* **THE BASICS** ***of The Kingdom of God.***

Nothing is More Forthcoming than the Basics

John Wooden, the great coach for the UCLA Bruins won ten NCAA Championships in twelve years, including national championships seven years in a row! *Seven national NCAA basketball championships in a row, back-to-back,* a feat never accomplished before or since. Championship Coach John Wooden believed the basics were of utmost importance.

He said, "I believe in the basics: Attention to, and perfection of tiny details that might be commonly overlooked. They may seem trivial, perhaps even laughable to those who don't understand, but they aren't. They are fundamental to your progress in basketball, business, and life. They are the difference between champions and near champions."

For example, at the first squad meeting each season held two weeks before the first actual practice, he personally demonstrated how he wanted players to put on their socks each and every time. He instructed his players, "Carefully roll the socks down over the toes, ball of the foot, arch and around the heel, then pull the sock up snug so there will be no wrinkles of any kind."

Are you kidding Coach Wooden, socks?!? Ten-time NCAA Championship coach John Wooden instructed his teams to master the basics, including **how to put on your socks**. Who else enforces to "Follow the basics?" **The Jewish rabbi!** What are the basics, Mr. Rabbi who also doesn't have a last name. *"Seek* *first the kingdom of God so that you WIN CHAMPIONSHIPS!* **Put your socks on right!"**

A young man was privileged to watch Kobe Bryant practice at 4 a.m. in the morning at a basketball camp for young kids. For forty-five minutes he watched Kobe do the most basic footwork and offensive drills that kids learn in middle school basketball. He did the drills with an unparalleled level of effort and focus, and he performed every drill with surgical precision.

Later that day at camp, the young man approached Kobe and said, "I don't understand. You're the best player in the world. Why are you doing such basic drills?"

Kobe smiled at him and said, "Why do think I'm the best player in the world?" He paused to let his question sink into the young man, and then he answered his own question, "I'm the best player in the world because **I never get bored with the basics**."

Beware of the tens of thousands of sermons, books, and internet articles that are flashy, emotional, and tickle your ears but overlook the basics. What are the basics of *Shitty to Happy in 21 Minutes: THE SECRET KINGDOM?*

What Are the Basics?

The Jewish rabbi who is God in the flesh implores us and unceasingly exhorts us how to win the championship of life where the trophy is *The Garden of Eden.* He pleads with us, beseeches us, screams at us from the mountaintops to *never get bored with the basics*. May I remind you that Coach John Wooden said, "The basics may seem trivial, perhaps even laughable to those who don't understand."

Okay, okay, I got it Mr. Rabbi. What are the basics? He enthusiastically shouts for the ten thousandth time, "Seek FIRST…seek FIRST, **seek FIRST** the KINGDOM OF GOD! Put your socks on correctly!"

Kobe's voice pierces the skies from heaven, "I second that, Mr. Rabbi," as he proclaims loud and clear, "Don't get bored with the basics!"

****

Pursue the Basics

What are the basics?
Seek* FIRST *the kingdom of God
That's how to win national championships!

We've drilled down on the importance of the basics, which is to seek first the incredibly powerful life-giving emotions of happiness, peace, and joy. We've laid the foundation, now we graduate to the next level.

How do your emotions acquaint you with God?

****

How do your emotions bring you closer to God?

Scene 46

Wanna Know God?

Let's revisit the question I posed in the previous scene when I asked, *"How do we know God?"* Bear in mind scripture says "To know God is eternal life" (John 17:3).

The *eternal life* by which we know God paves the way to an NCAA national championship, also known as The Garden of Eden. So the question of the ages is: **What is the ETERNAL LIFE by which we know God?**

Here's another question for you champions, one that I hope stirs your religious proclivities to upchuck last night's pizza, so hold onto your cowboy hats boys and girls…

Does God give you ETERNAL LIFE…

…or…does ETERNAL LIFE *give you God?*

I'd better ask that question again, a little slower… Does God give eternal life to you, or does eternal life give God to you? Is it one, is it the other, is it both? A similar logistical conundrum is the riddle, what came first, the chicken or the egg!

Hold that thought for a moment, the answer might surprise you.

Okay let's dive deeper into the immensity of God's world of eternal life. What's our most important obligation in this life for you and me to be successful, prosperous, abundant, and filled with happiness, peace, and joy?

Seek the kingdom first, is that what he says? What is the kingdom he says to seek first? The kingdom of God that he says to seek first is happiness, joy, and peace. What are happiness, peace, and joy? —THEY ARE EMOTIONS! *They are EMOTIONS! THEY ARE EMOTIONS!*

Who's emotions are they? **They are God's emotions.**

God's emotions are THE BASICS! Coach Wooden and Kobe Bryant say, "Sharpen THE BASICS" **so that you win national championships year after year as did the UCLA Bruins**.

May I pose a question? **Are God's kingdom emotions THE BASICS by which I know God?** Is this the reason he says to pursue them with every ounce of your strength? Is this why the Jewish rabbi says, "Seek these emotions first, before you do anything else"?

Is this why he compares them to a pearl of great price, and thus sell everything to buy it? And if so, can we surmise that his incomprehensible unimaginable otherworldly emotions of peace, happiness, and joy are how we feel his presence, how we know God, and how the great God Almighty helps us in whatever we need, want, dream, and desire? If so, might this be the reason he says to escalate them to the top of your to-do list?

And another question: If these emotions are how we know God, they're how we feel God, and they're how we get his help in whatever it is that we need, want, dream, and desire, then is it fair to say that these *otherworldly supernatural emotions that transcend this natural world* are eternal life? After all, isn't it true they are how we **know** God, **feel** God, **experience** God, and they're how **we are intimate** with the Lord of the Universe!

That's a fantastic proposition!

Remember: The Basics Are Utmost Importance. What Are the Basics?

We've learned God's emotions of love, joy, and peace are THE BASICS, they are FIRST and FOREMOST, your TOP PRIORITY, is that right?

These kingdom of God EMOTIONS are the BASICS that we pursue with the same riveting intensity as did Kobe Bryant when he perfectly executed the basics at 4 o'clock in the morning. They're the basics Coach Wooden said to pursue first and foremost, and with dogged determination: "Put your socks on correctly!"

But what if the basics, these EMOTIONS of happiness, peace, and joy are spiritual fruit that are also…ETERNAL LIFE!

Is it possible that the emotions of happiness, peace, and joy who are God…that it's by them you know God…that it's by them you feel God, experience God, and hear his voice…and therefore, since they are how you know God, feel God, experience God…then is it possible it is by these emotions that you inherit eternal life?

And if so, would it explain why the rabbi preaches unceasingly for you and me to seek them first? And then, would it inspire you, and me too, to drill down on the basics of God's emotions as diligently as Kobe Bryant at 4 a.m.?

You'd better hang on tight as we continue our deep dive into the magnificent world of eternal life that is happiness, peace, and joy, the spiritual emotions that transcend our three-dimensional world of time, space, and matter, because it is these otherworldly emotions that forge a golden highway that leads into another dimension, a deeper dimension that leads us to the most holy place of all: *The Secret Place of the Most High.*

WHO is the kingdom of God? WHAT is the kingdom of God? Is it a person? Is it a place? Is it a location? Is it a thing? Is it a force? Whatever the heck it is, the Jewish rabbi who is the Prince of Peace says to seek it first.

The kingdom of God is created by the One, the Only, the great **LORD GOD ALMIGHTY**. Is that fair to say? No human being ever concocted such a thing! No king, no dictator, no world ruler, no magician, no inventor, no genius ever devised such a power including Nikolai Tesla, Albert Einstein, nor our own modern-day version of Einstein, Elon Musk.

There's only one designer with omniscient intelligence and unsurpassed brilliance who could possibly design and create such a magnificent kingdom of emotions, the seminal creation called *The Kingdom of God.* So then can we conclude that the Lord God Almighty *who is the architect of the kingdom of God* is also the architect of the emotions of happiness, peace, and joy that comprise the kingdom of God?

Clearly no man that I previously mentioned, regardless of their impressive IQs ever did concoct such a thing as *otherworldly transcendent peace.*

Man builds supercomputers, he builds smartphones that communicate across the world with friends and family at the touch of a button for a few pennies per call, he builds cars, trains, planes, and battleships; he builds the world's tallest skyscrapers, he tries to clone humans, but there's one thing man cannot do:

HE CANNOT CREATE EMOTIONS.

Shitty to Happy in 21 Minutes: THE SECRET KINGDOM doesn't claim to create emotions. There is only one true God that creates emotions. It is solely God the creator of all life and energy that radiates happiness, peace, and joy out from…where? *Out from the depths of each and every one of us!*

I realize we cannot limit God to a sixteen-ounce glass of the Pacific Ocean, but can we in part include the forces of the emotions of *happiness, peace, and joy* as a vital element in our quest to understand *who God is?*

Okie dokey Smoky, let's forge ahead. So then, since God is at least in part emotions, is it possible that we can conclude that the eternal life by which we know God is the EMOTIONS of happiness, peace, and joy?

May I let you in on a little secret? I'm leading you through the process of getting answers to pressing questions. I ask little baby questions, I get little baby answers, and those answers lead to bigger questions. I ask the bigger questions that lead to bigger answers, and eventually I hit the mother lode.

We're about to hit the mother lode!

"But Steve," you resignedly sigh, "I can't feel God. It's like he's not here. I feel like I'm talking to a brass ceiling. Where is he, especially when I need him most?"

Have you ever met up with that hopelessness? What a desperate feeling! Maybe you have, maybe you haven't, but *untold millions have.* Have you ever wondered why he seems so far away, and wondered how to fix it, and more importantly, how to know that God is real, that he hears you, and that he's closer to you than your next breath!

As per usual, I have good news, fantastic news, news so simple that even Lloyd and Harry in *Dumb and Dumber* get it:

> *The EMOTIONS of supernatural happiness, otherworldly transcendent peace that is not from this world, and joy unspeakable and full of glory that you force-feed into your heart like I did that sunny summer California afternoon in 1983 are the* ETERNAL LIFE *by which you know God.*
>
> *Whoa Steve, are you saying that God's emotions that we tap into are the* ETERNAL LIFE *by which we tap into God?*
>
> Yes, Lloyd and Harry get it, and so do you.

Not only are these emotions how we tap into God, but they're also how we contact him, how we hook ourselves up to his wagon, they're how we open the floodgates of his power, and they're how we intimately know him and his unlimited supernatural invincibility. These emotions are how you know God. That's why he calls them ETERNAL LIFE.

> *These emotions—the ones that are the kingdom of God are how you enter the dimensions beyond our limited world of time, space, and matter. Your kingdom of God emotions plug you into the unlimited dimensions, the ones where you see the unseen, the ones where you tell your business partner, "Go to the sea, cast a hook, and take the first fish you catch. When you open its mouth, you will find a gold coin. Take it and pay the taxes for you and me"* (Mathew 17:27).

Can you see why the Jewish rabbi also known as "the word made flesh" exuberantly shouts it from the mountaintops the powerful proclamation to "Seek FIRST the kingdom of God!"

He screams at us to pursue this fantastical bundle of emotions because *the emotions of God* are commandeering forces that are rooted in the Lord God Almighty, the Mighty One who lives in you, and these emotions are the kingdom that is the eternal life by which you know God your father and they're the power that opens the doors to everything you need, want, dream, and desire, including knowledge where the fish is that has the gold coin in its mouth.

That's why he says SEEK THESE EMOTIONS FIRST and FOREMOST, and then EVERYTHING ELSE that you need, want, dream, and desire GET ADDED TO YOU.

We've hit the mother lode!

The kingdom emotions of happiness, peace, and joy are the eternal life by which we cross over from the third dimension into the otherworldly dimensions that are not limited by time, space, and matter.

Our otherworldly transcendent emotions take us on a deep dive into the deeper more glorious dimensions where we see a fish in the river with a gold coin in his mouth.

I'll bet you never in your life have heard how vitally important your emotions of happiness, peace, and joy are to intimately know the eternal God!

The kingdom of God emotions...are the ETERNAL LIFE...by which you know the ETERNAL God...feel his presence...and reverentially experience him...who created the universe

The peace that transcends this natural world, the unshakable supernatural happiness, and joy unspeakable and full of glory are the ETERNAL LIFE by which we know God, feel God, experience him, commune with him, and enter into the holy of holies that is the throne room of the Prince of Peace that King David calls *The Secret Place of the Most High.*

"Come on in, have a seat" is his invitation to you and me.

I marvel to think how I cracked this secret code by accident forty years ago on a sunny summer California afternoon in 1983 the day my green convertible died. That was the day I slung nasty venomous *biblical cuss words* into the smoggy skies of Los Angeles, and suddenly, unexpectedly the Prince of Peace appeared to me in full grandeur and crushed my broken heart, and flooded me with his peace, an otherworldly peace that transcends this natural world, a peace that is the eternal life of God that *force-feeds* himself into me by **the power of my very own tongue**.

It was the grandest accidental discovery of my life.

How do you rip the veil off of the God of all creation, the ONE who's lain inactive inside you since the day you were born?

Here's how: You pull back the curtain that covers him and do so exactly like I did that sunny summer California afternoon in 1983 the day my green convertible died! That's how you reveal the God of the universe who is hidden inside you!

"Speak the 1225 words...I'm right here inside you." He continues, ***"THE POWER OF YOUR TONGUE*** *UNLOCKS YOUR POWERFUL KINGDOM EMOTIONS* ***WHO ARE ME, THE LORD YOUR GOD*** *WHO LIVES INSIDE YOU!"*

The kingdom of God emotions are the majesty of the eternal God, the God of Abraham, Isaac, and Jacob, the God who is the creator of heaven and earth, the One who is, was, and forever shall be. The kingdom of God is the *eternal life* by which we know God!

The kingdom of God that is the eternal life by which we know God is...what?

The eternal life by which we intimately know God, commune with God, and feel his presence is the emotions of peace, happiness, and joy, love, patience, kindness and goodness *also known as* ***The Fruit of the Spirit***.

This otherworldly peace, happiness, joy, and love that transcends this three-dimensional world is the *eternal life* by which we intimately know the Prince of Peace, and they're the keys by which we enter into his holiest of all holy places called *The Secret Place of the Most High* which ushers us into *The Garden of Eden.*

He's the God of the universe but he's closer than your next breath.

He's the Jewish rabbi but he's the peace in your heart. He's the Prince of Peace who is above all, beyond all, through all, and in you all.

He's your heavenly father who put the desires in your heart.

He's the God who tells you to seek first his kingdom so that all the desires of your heart that he places inside of you COME TO PASS.

He's the God of all creation who wants nothing more than for you to be filled with all of HIS peace, all of HIS joy, all of HIS happiness, all of HIS emotions, and these are *his eternal life,* the *kingdom of God emotions* that are ***the fruit of the spirit*** by which you intimately commune with the God of all creation.

"SPEAK THE WORDS…I'M RIGHT HERE!!!"

****

We're forty-five stories high atop the tallest and fastest rollercoaster in North America, the Kangda Ka.

Take a few minutes, catch your breath, and when you come back, hang tight and let's ride this exhilarating rollercoaster together!

INTERMISSION

ACT 10: Emotions Control Your World

Scene 47

Emotions Unleash God

God is infinitely above and beyond what we think, dream, or imagine and yet he's so simple that one must become as a little child to grasp him

Are these supernatural kingdom of God emotions, these superlative "fruits of the spirit" called happiness, peace, and joy that emanate from the heart of God, are they entirely all that God is? No silly, they're not all the God that is any more than the 1225 words are all that God is, nor is the sixteen-ounce beer glass of Pacific Ocean all the ocean that is.

However, these emotions are a tiny sliver of him, a microcosmic piece of the infinite God, and so these small slivers of God's emotions are how you and God connect with each other, they're the spiritual means by which God speaks to you, and they're how you link together intimately with him.

These emotions are his unmitigated unlimited flood of power that sweeps your heart clean when you're in a hellhole of a mess and your life is an unbearable shitshow like mine was that sunny summer California afternoon in 1983 the day my green convertible died.

God's emotions of happiness, peace, and joy are the eternal life by which you know him. They are your direct link to the Lord of the Universe. These emotions plop you down front and center on an overstuffed leather couch in the throne room called *The Secret Place of the Most High*.

"Whoa Steve, I've always heard we know God by faith, is that right?"

I've heard that a thousand times myself, but if we hear it a thousand and one times, does that make it true? If "by faith" you mean "without emotions" then I say poppycock, bull wonky, snake oil salesman, and cow paddies also known as *bullsh*t.*

Listen, to know God is to *forcefully pound* HIS peace, HIS happiness, and HIS joy into your heart. Are HIS peace, HIS happiness, and HIS joy that you *force-feed into your heart with the enduring* **power of your tongue** HIS emotions?

Of course they are!

Well then, can you see why God exhorts us a gazillion times to seek first his emotions of happiness, peace, and joy?

Why would he command us to seek after his emotions like a lion stalks his prey if they were not the most incredibly important lifeblood that supplies our very spiritual existence, and if they weren't the pathway to intimately know our Father?

Ask, Seek, and Knock…God's World Opens Up to You

ASK…

Why do we pray? *To unleash his emotions that are locked up deep inside us.*

SEEK…

Why do we study the word of God? *To unlock his emotions from deep within us where they've lain dormant for many years.*

KNOCK…

What is the world's most powerful force that we ask, seek, and knock for? *The kingdom of God.*

Ask, seek, and knock, and the door SHALL BE OPENED! The door to what? *The door to* ***the kingdom of God!***

What's the kingdom of God? *The kingdom of God is* ***his emotions*** *that are buried deep inside us.*

Ask, seek, knock, the doors to the kingdom shall be opened unto you

When you *force-feed* his supernatural emotions of peace, happiness, joy, and love into your heart by 1225 words and **the power of your tongue** like I did that sunny summer California afternoon in 1983 the day my green convertible died, then you fill yourself full of HIS emotions, and thus fill yourself full of the Lord God Almighty.

"Yo Dude, speak the 1225 words, I'm right here." God uses our lingo when he feels spunky.

Emotions are God, God Has Emotions, and His Emotions are the Kingdom of God that Opens the Doors to Your Garden of Eden where there Awaits Every Desire of Your Heart!

These emotions of peace, happiness, joy, and love are…whom? Who are they? They are HIM.

These supernatural emotions are the kingdom of God that he says to seek first, and they are God himself, and hence are the ETERNAL LIFE by which we know God.

You and Your Spouse Have Deep Intimacy Because of Your Emotions

How do you and your husband experience your best lives together? WHEN YOU CONNECT EMOTIONALLY! So why would you and God be any different!

How do you know you love your Golden Retriever? By your emotions.

What feelings do happy children give you? Happy emotions.

The young girl asked me, "What is my purpose in life?" I answered her, "Your purpose in life is to be happy," but I mean only the true supernatural happiness that explodes out from within you by 1225 words and **the power of your tongue** that connects you to the Lord of the universe, the Creator of all that exists, and the One who wants you to draw closer to him.

The only way to know God intimately is to *force-feed* his otherworldly transcendent peace and happiness into your heart until the forces of the fruit of his spirit of love, joy, and peace spring forth like a rush of warm water when you dive into the lake on a hot summer day.

It is by these fruits of the spirit including transcendent peace that you know God, just like these emotions are the only way for you and your spouse to know each other intimately.

Therefore, y'all that refuse to *force-feed* his transcendent supernatural peace into your heart, the kind that surpasses the ability of your mind to comprehend, then you guys can only experience him in the shallow end of

the pool, and certainly not in the deep end where there waits for you a deep and intimate connection with the Lord of the Universe.

"Whoa Steve, you sound cocky and arrogant."

Really? That's fine if you think that but I don't care because I'd rather you walk in otherworldly peace and supernatural happiness and thereby know the God of the universe on an intimate level than that superficial level that millions know him by. Your intimate knowledge and relationship with God is exceedingly more important to me than to fit into your shitty-fucky little church club.

Let's make a bet. The statement I just made, the one where I said that unless you speak the 1225 words like I did that sunny summer California afternoon in 1983 the day my green convertible died, then you will *never* feel that supernatural transcendent peace that comes from another world. You'll have only a roommate relationship with God like some of you are only roommates with your spouse. You have only a superficial relationship with your spouse and with God if you don't have a deep emotional intimate connection.

I'll say it again, unless and until you slam his 1225 words into your heart **by the power of your tongue** which thereby *forces* you into his throne room called *The Secret Place of the Most High and* do so with the consistency of Kobe Bryant performing the basics at 4 a.m. at basketball camp, and John Wooden's basketball players putting their socks on correctly, then you cannot, you will not, nor will you ever feel the length, breadth, width, and height of our glorious God. You will never intimately know him. *You can't.* You won't. It's impossible.

Without God's emotions, you and he are simply roommates.

Why can't you know God intimately if you don't have emotions of happiness, joy, and peace and LOVE? **Here's why:** Because those emotions ARE HIM!

Happiness, peace, and joy ARE him!

****

Where There's Fire There's Heat!

God is the fire, and where fire is, there is heat.

YOU CAN'T HAVE FIRE WITHOUT HAVING HEAT

****

Without Emotions You Don't Know God

Whoa Steve, there you go again, sounding like a heretic!

Well, how about you sit down, be quiet and hear me out.

God IS love, God IS happiness, God IS joy, and God IS peace. *Without these emotions of happiness, peace, and joy, how can you know God?*

I'll prove it to you, "If you don't LOVE, you don't KNOW GOD" (1 John 4:8). He said that, not me.

You can know *about* him, you can study *about* him, you can read all the stories of how he delivered Israel from insurmountable enemies like the Pharoah of Egypt…

…you can think he's cool; you can know all the bible stories of Noah, Moses, Isaac, and Jacob, you can listen to thousands of sermons…

…you can ask Jesus into your heart…you can rededicate your life every Sunday to assuage your guilt because you watch porn Mondays, Wednesdays, and Fridays, and you got laid in the back of a Chevy last Friday night…

…you can go through the prayer line and have the preacher lay hands on you until he rubs a bald spot on your head…

…but unless and until you *force-feed* God's peace into your heart by **the power of your VERY OWN tongue**…

…unless and until you pound into your heart HIS peace that is inexplicable, incomprehensible, and unimaginable to the human mind…how? … by **the power of YOUR VERY OWN tongue** and the 1225 words that are TRUTH that **the power of your tongue** converts from TRUTH into SPIRIT with the corresponding FRUIT OF THE SPIRIT like what happened to me that sunny summer California afternoon in 1983 the day my green convertible died…

…until you do…

…then you won't ever know the depth, length, width, and height of him who awaits you with wide-open arms in the deep end of the pool.

You're only roommates.

By the way you can *pray in the spirit* in lieu of the 1225 words and it works just as well and it's way the hell easier, and you'll still dive headlong into the deep end of the pool. More about that in a few minutes.

Remember, "eternal life" is how you know God. What is eternal life? "Eternal life" is to be filled with his spirit, and to be filled with his spirit is to be filled with *the fruit of his spirit* which is…what? What is the *fruit of the spirit* that fills you, and thereby floods you like a river that overflows its banks?

This outpouring of rivers of living water is otherworldly supernatural emotions that spring up from deep inside you and are indisputable evidence that you are intimately immersed in God.

They'll know you by your fruit (Mathew 7:16).

The *fruit of the spirit* draws you so close to God that you can't tell each other apart. These fruit that spring up from deep inside you by **the power of your tongue** are God's emotions of love, joy, peace, patience and all the rest. It is by these emotions that are the FRUITS that are evidence that you are filled, possessed, and dominated by the SPIRIT, who is GOD HIMSELF.

You don't think so? PUT IT TO THE TEST. Go to ShittyToHappy.com and download the 1225 words that are in volume three of this trilogy THE GREAT INVASION. Download them for free, and when you do, then speak the 1225 words with vitriolic sarcasm, anger, frustration, worry, fear, unforgiveness, and whatever other antichrist emotions you feel. Power-pack these sick emotions into your words. Speak the 1225 words three times through. It's a total of 3675 words. It takes 21 minutes. *Do it, but not until the end of the next seven paragraphs. I'll tell you when to speak.*

Don't tell me it doesn't work if you haven't tried it. That's like telling me the bank won't give you $300 if you put the ATM card in the machine, enter the PIN code, and hit the $300 button if you haven't tried it. *"Steve, I'm not so sure about this bank ATM card and PIN number you tell me about."*

My advice to you is STFU and stick the card in the machine, enter the PIN code, and hit the $300 button.

The same is true of the 1225 words and **the power of your tongue**. *"Steve, I'm not so sure about this power of the tongue stuff and 1225 words."* My advice to you is STFU and speak the 1225 words for 21 minutes!

What is STFU? You don't know what STFU is? It's *shuh duh fuh cup.*

After you finish 21 minutes, check your peace levels. What do you feel? It's impossible to not have a change in your emotions, especially if you sling the words like the cocky boy-bitch angry young actor like I did that sunny summer California afternoon in 1983 the day my green convertible died.

"Speak the words...I'm right here."

Go to ShittyToHappy.com and download the words right now for free. As soon as you download the words, speak them through three times OUT LOUD. **Now's the time. Do it now!**

I'll set the clock, and I'll see you back here in 21 minutes.

[TWENTY-ONE MINUTES LATER...]

For those of you that spoke the 1225 words three times through— If you've never known God before, you just met him. If you've never felt God before, you just felt him. If you've never felt close to God, you just did.

When you just now spoke the 1225 words three times through, aloud, and if you shouted them because you're in a gut-wrenching shitshow, or your PTSD has you by the balls, or your business you spent years to build crashed, or you lost your job...

...then you drew a bit closer to him even if was only a taste, even if it was only a hint, but it's the first step of a long journey.

Listen, my friend who hiked Kilimanjaro, she had to take the first step before she could take the second, and the fifth, and the seventeenth, and the fiftieth.

This is just your beginning!

"Speak the words...I'm right here."

By the way, why 21 minutes? You'll learn why 21 minutes in the third volume of this trilogy *THE GREAT INVASION.*

REVIEW

How Do We Know God?

*The **fruit of the spirit** are the **eternal life**, the **kingdom of God emotions** by which you* **KNOW GOD**

It took me forty years to figure out how incredibly simple this is.

"Speak the words...I'm right here."

****

Scene 48

Passionate Spirited Addiction

You're at the base of Mount Kilimanjaro. You're ready to begin your ascent to the top. What drives you to complete a couple hundred thousand steps to get to the top of that glorious mountain?

What are the fruits of the spirit? *What are they?* There are nine of them. Do you remember what the nine fruit of the spirit are?

Love, joy, peace...patience, kindness, goodness...faithfulness, gentleness, and self-control.

All of these are...what? What are all of these?

*They are, all of them, without exception...**EMOTIONS!***

Faithfulness is a unique emotion in that it's also "obedience." *Faithfulness* is consistency. It's an addiction that the fruit of the spirit unleashes. Once you activate the fruit of the spirit, then *faithfulness* steps up to the plate to demand that you feed your heart more and more fruit of the spirit.

Faithfulness has an insatiable appetite that requires more and more fruit to satisfy its unquenchable thirst, like an addiction. In other words, the more fruit of the spirit you produce, the more fruit of the spirit you crave. The more you feed the addiction, the more it craves. That's the addictive power of the fruit of the spirit called "faithfulness."

Curiously the less you feed the addiction, the less it craves. Smokers, druggies, sex addicts, porn addicts...y'all know what I'm talking about. Feed that monster, it wants more. Feed it less, the feeling subsides.

Addictions work for you, or against you.

If you've got a porn addiction, and you look forward to the next time you watch that fake vagina-stuffer charade that looks genuine until you imagine there's a film crew standing around with lights and cameras inside a dank studio, a crew guy straddling the couple with a boom microphone, a random guy off to the side eating a bag of Doritos, and two completely un-horny actors who merely go through the humping motions until the director yells "Cut!" ...it's gross.

Anyway, you'll be excited to read about how the magical 1225 words and **the power of my tongue** conquered my "Lust for Busts" in the third volume of this trilogy *THE GREAT INVASION.*

But I digress.

On the positive side of this scene called "Passionate Spirited Addiction," the more you act out your imaginations, the more you crave. It's like when you go to the gym. The more you work out, the more you want. If you miss a workout you go batshit crazy, but if you skip a few workouts, the less you crave them.

Hence, the more you feed your addictions the more you want. The less you feed your addictions the less you want.

Faithfulness is Your Addiction to the Fruit of the Spirit

Faithfulness is a unique one of the nine fruit of the spirit that is a perpetual motion machine that drives you, induces you, it compels you to speak the 1225 words more consistently so that **the power of your tongue** produces more of the addictive fruit of the spirit...

...which then produces more faithfulness...

...which then drives you to produce more fruit of the spirit...

...which then drives you to ascend to the top of Mount Kilimanjaro.

Thus faithfulness is a perpetual motion machine driven by the other eight fruit of the spirit.

You will never quench the insatiable appetite of faithfulness when you habitually hang out in *The Secret Place of the Most High.*

Thus faithfulness is not limited to an emotion per se, but it is motivated by the other eight fruit of the spirit that are solely emotions.

More about faithfulness later.

****

Scene 49

Nine Spiritual Fruits

The nine fruits are EMOTIONS

When the 1225 words and **the power of your tongue** *force-feeds* you full of these supernatural, otherworldly, transcendent emotions of peace, love, happiness, and joy that spring forth from another dimension, these are the FRUIT of the SPIRIT.

SPIRIT is the WORDS that you SPEAK. Hence, the FRUIT of the words that you speak are EMOTIONS. These emotions are the FRUIT of the SPIRIT that connect you to the lifeblood of the living GOD.

I'm gonna say this quickly so listen quickly: *The fruit of those 1225 words—words that are SPIRIT—are the emotions of peace, joy, and LOVE that are…* [DRUM ROLL PLEASE…] **God himself**.

If you need to read that again, do it because I ain't saying it again.

> Wet is to water…like peace is to God.
> *Where there's water there's wet.*
> ***You can't have water without wet.***

IF YOU DIVE INTO A POOL YOU GET WET, and there's nothing you can do to stop the water from soaking you through and through.

> Heat is to fire…like peace is to God.
> *Where there's heat there's fire.*
> ***You can't have fire without heat.***

IF YOU DIVE INTO A FIRE YOU GET BURNED. There's nothing you can do to stop the feeling of heat from the fire.

> Can you dive into water without getting wet? No, that's impossible.
> Can you dive into fire without feeling heat? No, also impossible.

Can you dive into God without getting peace? Absolutely not! It's unequivocally impossible!

When you're submerged in water there's wet...
When you're submerged in fire there's heat...
Where you're submerged in God there's peace...

IF YOU DIVE INTO GOD…

You get BURNED…and SOAKED…with EMOTIONS—

Happiness, peace, and joy…
Kindness, goodness, tenderness…
Love, patience, humility…soak you.

Just like when you dive into a pool, you get soaking wet…
Just like you dive into a fire; you get flaming hot…
Just like you dive into God; you get soaked with his emotions.

So how do you know beyond a shadow of a doubt that you know God? Examine your kingdom emotions. Do you have inexplicable supernatural incomprehensible peace? That's how you know if you "know God."

Want me to prove it to you?

Alrighty…

"By their fruit is how you know them" (Matthew 7:16). What is *the fruit?* Who's *them?* "Them" is people that know God intimately like a man knows his wife.

What is the fruit by which you "know them"? The fruit by which you know them is "the fruit of the spirit" which are emotions of happiness, peace, and joy. Didn't he say to seek these emotions?

If you don't have these emotions, how do others "know" that you know God?

Good question, huh? You can ask the same question of yourself.

If YOU don't have these emotions, how do YOU "know" if you yourself know God?

ANSWER: Without them, you don't. Intellectually you do. Emotionally you don't.

Emotions Are Your Dipstick to Check Your Intimacy with God

Your KINGDOM OF GOD *EMOTIONS* are how your friends, family, and all those around you recognize that you know God.

Not only that, but your KINGDOM OF GOD *EMOTIONS* are ALSO the dipstick for YOU…to check YOU…to see if YOU…are close to God.

Are we talking about earthly emotions? No, no, a thousand times NO. We're not talking about earthly panty-pie emotions, also known as *comfort*. In fact, *comfort* is a **fake indicator**. It's so close to the genuine that it fools most people. Comfort can deceive you that you're close to God when you're not.

What emotions are we talking about that are a dependable indicator to check your relationship to God? We're talking about peace that transcends this natural world that the human mind cannot comprehend.

We're talking about the spiritual emotions of happiness, peace, and joy that are outside of the confines of this three-dimensional world.

We're talking about God's emotions that are from an otherworldly dimension, submerged deep inside you, so deep that the only way to resurrect them is by 1225 words and **the power of your tongue** like I did that sunny summer California afternoon in 1983 the day my green convertible died.

What is the evidence that you know God? How do you know that you are intimate with him?

The proof…the evidence that you know God is the same evidence by which your friends, loved ones, and those close to you know that you know God.

What's that evidence?

The evidence that you know God is your EMOTIONS of happiness, peace, and joy. They are undeniable evidence that you know God.

By their fruit you recognize them (Mathew 7:16).

These fruit by which your friends see that you know God, and that you are intimate with him are the dipstick for, not only your friends to know how well you know God, but also for YOU *to know how well you know God.*

These fruits are the powerful, otherworldly emotions that rule you, urge you, compel you, and even FORCE you to sit your butt down in *The Secret Place of the Most High.*

These emotions perform a dualistic role. In addition to being the key indicator of your relationship with God, they are also the master key that unlocks the gates to *The Garden of Eden.* God's emotions also known as "The Kingdom of God" are the means by which you get everything you need, want, dream, and desire, plus you must be diligent, persistent, and tenacious in all that your hand finds to do. Oh, and another thing: *You MUST take care of the poor, the fatherless, and the widow.*

Your Emotions are the Proof that You are Tight with God

You can know every bible story from Moses and the Red Sea to Noah and the ark, to Abraham, Isaac, Jacob, the virgin birth, and the resurrection, but until you *fill yourself full to overflowing with the FRUIT OF THE SPIRIT you are merely roommates with God,* like the husband and wife that have no feelings for each other.

I know, I know, this goes contrary to every sermon you've ever heard that says we love God by faith, not by feelings, but hear me out.

Husband and Wife at Dinner on their Tenth Wedding Anniversary

Can you imagine your tenth wedding anniversary, you and your spouse sitting across from each other, candlelight dinner, soft music, a dozen red roses, you gaze into each other's eyes. Your wife gently touches your hand, she gazes into your eyes and whispers, "Tell me how much you love me."

You respond, "Babe, I don't feel anything, but I want you to know I love you by faith."

I'd rather run my dick through a meat grinder than to ride home with her after dinner.

Listen, your emotions open the door to the *Secret Place of the Most High.* That's what happened to me that sunny summer California afternoon in 1983. If you try to enter into *The Secret Place of the Most High* by any other means than *the fruit of the spirit,* he'll say to you, "Why do you call me Lord, Lord, and do not the things I tell you to do? You are an intruder."

Do you wanna know God? *It's this simple.* Are you sure you wanna know God? It's so simple, but you gotta become as a little child or else you'll complicate this so much that you become a drunken fuckaholic, and you conjure up such moronic Pharisaic rationalizations like "Sometimes God tells you "No!" You conjure up shitty antichrist explanations to justify your sorry-ass results because of your empty-headed blundering foolishness to *not follow the basics* that the Jewish rabbi clearly lays out for you.

A distant cousin in this dysfunctional family of asinine rationalizations is the one who says, "I don't feel God, but I love him by faith." ***Happy tenth anniversary Dipshit, when you told your wife you "love her by faith."***

Listen, God's emotions are what the Jewish rabbi who is God in the flesh screams at us over and over again to SEEK FIRST!

Folks, this ain't no Rubik's Cube.

You wanna know what it means to *take up your cross daily?* It means to *daily seek first the kingdom of God emotions of* ***happiness, peace,*** *and* ***joy****.*

You wanna know what it means to *put off the old man?* Who's the "old man"? He's anxiety, stress, worry, fear of failure…he's unforgiveness, he's anger, he's hatred…he's bitterness, he's depression, he's PTSD.

You wanna know what it means to "walk in the spirit"? It means to fill yourself full of *HIS* SPIRIT by **the power of your tongue** with the corresponding *FRUIT* of that SPIRIT, which is love, joy, peace, patience, kindness, goodness, meekness, gentleness, and faithfulness—all of these emotions that crush the "old man," the ogre with boogers in his nose that awaits you under the bridge. The "old man" is the Evil Queen whose sole mission is to steal, kill, and destroy. How do you defeat her demonic forces?

Simple. Seek first the kingdom of God emotions of happiness, peace, and joy. These emotions crush your Evil Queen, they annihilate her, and they thrust you like a rocket ship into *The Secret Place of the Most High* which then opens the doors to the Garden of Eden where everything you need, want, dream, and desire awaits you.

You wanna know what the mission of the Jewish rabbi is? You already know the answer… ***You tell me*** *what his mission is.*

If you need a cheat sheet, re-read the preceding paragraph, the one that starts with the word "Simple." Folks, indeed, this is so simple even a child can get it.

In fact, one can get it ONLY if one becomes as a little child.

Jesus says, "I'm telling you how it is: Unless you become as little children you will never enter the kingdom of God" (Matthew 18:3).

"Speak the words…I'm right here."

****

Scene 50

Incendiary Fiery Oratory

We're almost at the next intermission, one more scene. This scene is a flaming whirlwind of a wrap- up. That's a fancy way of saying SUMMARY of everything you've learned so far.

THIS IS A QUINTESSENTIAL POINT: The words do NOT become SPIRIT until you…what? Until you WHAT? Until you SPEAK them! The words that you SPEAK transform into SPIRIT that generates the EMOTIONS of *peace, happiness, and joy* that mystifyingly appear from deep within you by means of **the power of your tongue**.

I use the word *mystifyingly.* What does "mystify" mean? It means *utterly bewildered* or *perplexed,* an excellent description of how I felt that sunny summer California afternoon in 1983 the day my green convertible died.

The solitary action I initiated that sunny summer California afternoon was to sling angry, vicious, venomous snotty, noxious "biblical cuss words" into the smoggy skies of Los Angeles. These 1225 "biblical cuss words" awakened the God of the Universe who lives in me but had lain dormant from August of 1953 at 7:32 in the morning in a little hospital in Wadsworth, Ohio until that sunny summer California afternoon in 1983 thirty years later, the day my green convertible died.

The 1225 words and **the power of my tongue** awakened God from dormancy deep within. His glory did arise in an unmistakable overwhelming splendor that conquered my heart. This resurrection power did so with an otherworldly indisputable energy that only HIS supreme predominant emotions uniquely perform, a power so great as to conquer my broken heart and restore my life that was splintered into a million pieces from events that had shattered my dreams and desires for a nice life, a prosperous acting career, a girlfriend that loved me, and a green convertible.

The power of our tongue is the preeminent, utmost, supreme power like the rudder of a large ship that *force-feeds* God's otherworldly peace to explode out from within us with a mighty rushing force of a 50-feet high wave off the North Shore of the Banzai Pipeline off the white sands of Oahu.

The preeminent, utmost, supreme power of our tongue is the tiny rudder that powers a huge ship through crashing waves, swirling waters, and mighty winds.

The preeminent, utmost, supreme power of our tongue is what unleashes the spirit of God who then floods every nook and cranny of our heart even though our heart is splintered into a million pieces.

> These *mystifying utterly bewildering, perplexing* energy of emotions that *force-feed* themselves into our heart by **the preeminent, highest, and supreme power of our tongue** are *the fruit of the spirit.* This **fruit of the spirit** is the kingdom of God that is *the kingdom* of *happiness, peace, and joy* that the Jewish rabbi says is our highest priority!

God is Those Otherworldly Transcendent Emotions that Originate From, Not this World, but From the World of Our Innermost Being

Holy shit the sound of that speeding passenger train when the conductor slams on the brakes keeps waking me up out of a drunken stupor that purports to assign God to a lesser degree of who he really is and thus turns him into a more complex complicated twisted byzantine version of our Father. He's not complicated at all, but rather simple—He is THE SPIRIT WITH THE EVIDENCE OF *FRUIT,* also known as *THE **FRUIT** OF THE **SPIRIT**!*

Simple, huh?

What is the SPIRIT that grows the FRUIT? The spirit that produces the fruit is *the words that you speak.* The 1225 words that you SPEAK are HIM who is the SPIRIT that produces FRUIT by THE POWER OF YOUR TONGUE. What fruit? The fruit of love, joy, peace, patience, kindness, and the rest, exactly like what happened to me that sunny summer California afternoon in 1983 the day my green convertible died.

> ***The preeminent, utmost, supreme power of*** **MY TONGUE** *unleashed the emotions of happiness, peace, and joy that sunny summer California afternoon with such a force of fury that I ran smack dab into the face of GOD HIMSELF. Or maybe it was God that ran smack dab into me.*

Do you want to run smack dab into the face of God? Do you? If you want an encounter with the Lord of the Universe, then you speak those 1225 words angrily if you feel angry, hatefully if you feel hatred, worriedly if you feel worried, sadly if you feel sad, powerfully if you feel exuberant—no matter what you feel, whatever you feel, whether you feel bad or whether you feel on top of the world, his mighty 1225 words and *the power of our* tongue—**THE PREEMINENT, UTMOST, SUPREME POWER OF OUR TONGUE** thrusts you higher into the stratosphere of inexplicable emotions than you've ever felt before, even if your life is grand and everything is perfect.

Regardless of how perfect your life is with yachts, Lamborghinis, supersonic jets, trips to exotic locations throughout the world, fine wine, and enough gold to plate the walls of your eight mansions, if you've never felt this supernatural otherworldly inexplicable peace of which I speak, then the peace that you feel up until now is that of a rusty dilapidated tugboat compared to the life of a glistening supersonic ocean liner.

I'm talking about the otherworldly peace that transcends this natural world. It's a blast of peace that only 1225 words and **the power of your tongue** arouse, like what happened to me that summer California afternoon in 1983 the day my green convertible died.

Your God-Emotions are How You Know God, Feel God, Touch God

The explosive emotions of happiness, peace, and joy are steadfast evidence that you and God are so inextricably linked that you can't tell each other apart. In fact, you and he, the one who is the Prince of Peace who is God—and you, his creation made in his image and likeness are so absorbed into each other that nobody can see the difference. Nobody can tell you and him apart. ***You'll know them by their fruit.***

When you *force-feed* yourself full of his emotions you look like him, albeit a mini-me version of the King of the Universe.

The world recognizes you by your fruit. What fruit? EMOTIONS! *The world recognizes you by your EMOTIONS!*

How do you bear fruit, also known as "God-emotions"? **By the preeminent, utmost, supreme power of your tongue** like what happened to me that sunny summer California afternoon, way back in 1983 four decades ago when my green convertible died.

When you *force-feed* yourself full of his transcendent peace, that otherworldly peace that flows up from deep within you, then you can't tell where he stops and you begin, nor can you tell where you stop, and he begins. It is in these moments when you *dwell in the secret place of the Most High* that you "know God," and it's in that throne room my friends, that you experience "eternal life" that knows God according to John 17:3.

Eternal life ain't a mystery. Eternal life is to know God, and to know God is to tap his emotions, emotions that are his kingdom that he says to seek first. Whose emotions? HIS emotions. Which emotions? The "fruit of the spirit," all of which are GOD'S EMOTIONS.

I remind you again that the fruit of the spirit are EMOTIONS. The fruit of the spirit are love, joy, peace, patience, kindness, and the rest. These nine fruits are EMOTIONS, right? And whose emotions are they? They're God's emotions! God's emotions are the KINGDOM that lives inside you that are the KINGDOM he says to SEEK FIRST.

You Contact God, Communicate with God, Know God, Feel God, Experience God, and Hear God's Voice by way of Eternal Life—Eternal Life that is the Emotions of Happiness, Peace, and Joy

God's emotions are the "eternal life" by which you intimately know him

Which EMOTIONS are God's Attributes?

WARNING: You MUST make the distinction between peace that is the mere "comfort" that comes from an extravagant lifestyle, and the "transcendent otherworldly peace" that comes from 1225 words and **the power of your tongue**. Do NOT muddle the two kinds of peace. Don't do it. Don't be a fool. **Don't conflate the two kinds of peace.** This is EXCEEDINGLY IMPORTANT to make that distinction. "Panty-pie peace" that comes from a comfortable lifestyle, even an extravagant luxurious lifestyle, is NOT the peace by which you know God.

The kind of peace by which you know God is the supernatural peace, the otherworldly peace that transcends time, space, and matter, the peace that comes only from 1225 words and **the power of your tongue**. This peace is inexplicable; it's an incomprehensible overwhelming force of emotion that miraculously *force-feeds* itself into your heart like what happened to me that sunny summer California afternoon in 1983 the day my green convertible died.

You tap into God's supernatural otherworldly universe of emotions also known as *The Secret Place of the Most High* by **the power of your tongue**.

If you neglect to penetrate God's emotions, then whose emotions do you by default tap into? Any guesses?

If you refuse to penetrate the depth, length, width, and height of the emotions of the King of kings and the Lord of lords then you, by default, tap into the "Cash" part of your "Johnny" heart, the Mr. Hyde part of your Jekyll and Hyde heart, the part of your heart that is anger, hatred, worry, stress, fear of failure, bitterness, hurt, unforgiveness, mediocrity…

…and *boredom.* That's right, I said BOREDOM. Even though you have tens of millions of dollars in real estate, mansions, jets, and five-star restaurants every night of the week, if you don't have transcendent otherworldly supernatural peace that comes not from this world, but from another dimension, then YOU'RE BORED.

Don't act like you're not, because without peace and joy your luxurious lifestyle is immutably BORING that requires that you jack-off your malaise with drugs and alcohol, or else you massage your BOREDOM with eighteen to twenty-hour workdays because when you sit alone for twenty-one minutes your mind annoys you.

Whiskey Tango Foxtrot Dude, instead of a miserable twenty-one minutes alone in front of a glass of bourbon, spend that twenty-one minutes in between sips to cram yourself full of otherworldly peace by 1225 words and **the power of your tongue** so that *you enjoy your billions of dollars, your twenty-two homes, cars, jets, and yachts and* ***even your glass of bourbon,*** because if you don't, then your emotions control you in spite of your billions of dollars, mansions, jets, and yachts. You are pitiably weak because without workaholic-ism, or drugs, or alcohol, you succumb in spite of your billions like a little boy-bitch to all these unpleasant, uncomfortable, dirty, vile emotions of boredom and mediocrity that come from none other than… [DRUM ROLL, PLEASE…]

THE—EVIL—QUEEN

Stress-Free Extravagant Lifestyle

I asked the two girls, the one on the airplane in Albuquerque and the one in Reno, both who said, "I'm already happy," I said, "If you could have everything you want, need, dream, and desire, and could obtain it stress-free, without worry, without anxiety, and full of peace at all times every day, and have ten times more than you do now, would you be interested?"

Both girls emphatically answered, "Yes!"

These two girls were more interested in goodies than supernatural otherworldly peace, and that's why I emphasize *goodies* as much as I emphasize *supernatural peace that transcends the natural world.*

The GOODIES is what appealed to both girls, and the GOODIES is what appealed to me, and thus my greed for goodies, also known as *the desires of my heart* sucked me into God's vortex of happiness, peace, and joy, and there's a good chance that GOODIES will also be the whirlwind that sucks you into the vortex of God's *happiness, peace, and joy* which are **God's emotions** that are supernatural evidence of THE KINGDOM OF GOD.

I've set a trap for you the same way I set a trap for those two girls, and the same way God set a trap for me, and you're about to fall headlong into it.

I'll see you in seventeen minutes. Oh wait...one more thing before intermission.

JUST A QUICK NOTE TO YOU RICH FOLKS: I know I was hard on you a few paragraphs back, but it's because I need you to get your shit together. We have a world to save, broken hearts everywhere, broken families, misery, heartache, sadness, hunger, starvation, pedophilia, human trafficking...

What's easier: To build a billion-dollar empire, or to follow these simple steps I've outlined for you in *Shitty to Happy in 21 Minutes: THE SECRET KINGDOM?* Which is easier?

The kingdom of God is way the hell easier to build than it is to build a billion-dollar empire. You've already built your earthly empire. NOW YOU MUST UNATTACH YOURSELF FROM YOUR EMPIRE.

HOW?

Seek first the kingdom of God as you *force-feed* peace and happiness into your heart, and when you do, then you'll enjoy your earthly empire a thousand times greater than you do now.

What's more your empire will continue to grow and expand beyond what you can imagine, and it'll be with less effort than what you already expend, and you'll be one of the mighty warriors, a Cyrus that God's called to save this world from their impending implosion.

Cyrus was not a follower of the God of the bible, but instead he was a pagan king used by God to help His people. This pagan king is important in Jewish history because it was under his rule that Jews were first allowed to return to Israel after seventy years of captivity.

I'm begging you; I'm pleading with you oh ye Cyrus's of the world, oh ye Richie Rich's of the world… Join me in this fight to save our world. Richie Rich was the richest kid in the world. He had everything he wanted…

…except love, joy, and peace.

Seek happiness, peace, and joy. Take care of the poor, the fatherless, and the widow, and I promise you that **you'll enjoy your billions of dollars a billion times more than you do now.**

"Speak the words...I'm right here."

INTERMISSION

ACT 11: Problems are Golden

Scene 51

My Potty Mouth

First Comes Peace…Peace FIRST…*FIRST COMES PEACE…*
God Wants You to Get Peace SO THAT You Can Get Your Desires!

It might come as a shock to you how greatly God wants you to have the desires of your heart, but don't take my word for it. Read the gosh dwamn book for yourself! He promises lots of goodies in the Garden of Eden, like when King David says, "Delight yourself in the Lord, and he'll give you the desires of your heart."

What does it mean to "delight yourself in the Lord"?

It's easy to know what it means when he says, "He'll give you the desires of your heart," but what does it mean to "Delight yourself in the Lord"? Can you explain it to me? Probably not, just like you can't explain to me other than in a mumbo-jumbo bunch of insipid religious pablum what it means to "give it all to Jesus."

Let's go to the original language of the bible, Hebrew, to see that *delight* means "pleasure yourself."

What does *that* mean, to "pleasure yourself," and how do I do it?

Three thousand years ago *pleasure yourself* meant something different than it does today. In fact, preachers tell me if I "pleasure myself" it's a naughty no-no, so I quote 1225 biblical cuss words to keep my mind clean while choking the sheriff and waiting for the posse to come. I even scream holy words the moment before the posse arrives, like, "Oh my God…Oh my God…OH…MY…GOD…!!!"

I'm kidding.

No, I'm not. I trash talk like that every so often to keep the churchy people from getting too stick-up-their-ass religious, and the non-churchy people from thinking I'm gonna gobsmack them upside the head with a bible.

Listen, if my salty language offends you…*relax*. I once heard of a guest speaker in a church who said, "There are people starving to death and most of you don't give a shit." There was an audible gasp. "What's more, you're more upset that I said 'shit' in church than you are that people are starving to death."

Incidentally, God used a trash-talking potty-mouth like me, a crass, craven actor to venture into the untapped world of *cussin' blazin' praisin' brazen praise words,* because do you think a Mr. Nice Church Guy would dare cross that line? Hell no, but me? I don't know where the line is until I cross it.

A "nice church guy" isn't ballsy enough or *stupid enough* to lash out at God with "It is written" words of the prophets of old like I did that sunny summer California afternoon in 1983 the day my green convertible died, and I'm *still* grateful he didn't strike me with lightning like what happened to William Cosper, the guy that got struck by lightning four times, but even if God had, there are 250,000 people that survive a lightning strike every year.

For you church folk who scratch your head at my brazen scumminess, bathroom humor, and a few choice words including the F-bomb, I made a conscious decision to do so. Read what Paul said in 1 Corinthians 9:19-23 and you'll understand. You might not agree, but you'll understand. I know you won't look it up in Corinthians, so let me break it down for you.

I sent a letter to folks that might possibly be butthurt and offended at my salty language to enlighten them on why I make my word choices.

Here's the letter.

An Open Letter to Believers Regarding My Potty Mouth

This is a letter I sent to Christians, Jews, and Muslims to explain to them my reasons for the sassy title, a few choice robust off-color words, and a smattering of potty humor. Here's what I wrote.

****

Dear Sir or Madam:

This book is unlike any you've ever read. Please, I beg you…read this book without prejudice at the irreverent title and a few strategically placed F-bombs, some potty humor, and a few sexual innuendos lest you miss out on what I believe is a message to the world for this hour.

Paul interjected a dose of vulgarity in Philippians 3:8, "I consider everything *rubbish* compared to the surpassing greatness of knowing Christ Jesus my Lord." *Rubbish* is the Greek work *skybalon,* also translated as *dung,* also *fecal matter.* You know what "fecal matter" is, right? What's the English word that we consider vulgar for *fecal matter?* If you don't know then ask one of your kids, and if you DO know, then you've heard it before, and probably said it, and if you haven't, then you stick to book titles like "Jesus is My Happy Jam" or "Highway to Happiness" or "Powers of Praise" while the rest of us rascals devour "Shitty to Happy in 21 Minutes."

Paul doesn't use vulgarity often, unlike hip-hop artists who at times use the F-bomb like a comma. I use it less than thirty out of 300,000 words in the entire trilogy. That's one in every 10,000 words.

Why did Paul choose such a vulgar term as *fecal matter?* He chose his words carefully, so he certainly had a reason, would you agree? I presume he purposefully chose a vulgar and offensive term in his letter to grab the attention of his audience and get into their faces, but this is not the only time Paul and other prophets have been known to get up in people's feces…er, faces.

Jeremiah hops aboard the vulgarity choo-choo train when he writes, "Tell them, 'My little finger is thicker than my father's waist.'" Oh, how polite the NIV translation "my father's waste" (1 Kings 12:10) and how quaint the King James version, "…my father's loins." Really, oh ye prudish King James? My father's *loins?!* These bible translators tiptoe around Jeremiah's Hebrew, because this is what he actually said: "Tell these people that your little finger is bigger than your father's pocket rocket also known as a baloney pony, also known as a one-eyed willy, also known as a penis." Jeremiah mocked their small dicks. Yup, even Jeremiah knew *size matters*. [Rim shot "ba dum ching."]

Here's another one. Elijah mocked the prophets of Baal with these words, "Perhaps your god is musing, or he is relieving himself." *Relieve* is the Hebrew word pronounced *siah,* and it means to "go away, step aside" which the Hebrews understood is a euphemism for *defecate.* Elijah says, "Perhaps your gods are taking a dump."

And who can forget in the book of Samuel that six times the author uses the phrase "he that pisseth against a wall" to describe a male. Why?

Well, do females "piss against a wall"? No, they sit when they pee. I was married for twenty-five years, and I never once saw my wife piss against a wall, except for the night she drank a bottle of Cabernet Sauvignon by herself.

Anyway, after you read this book, whip me if you must like Balaam whipped his donkey, but remember, Balaam's donkey had a message for Balaam that saved his life. I stand ready to receive your whippings, your suggestions, and criticisms (and hopefully a compliment or two) which is why I send you this forewarning letter and a copy of the book. I want to hear your thoughts, your opinions, your disagreements—the whole shabangabang, but don't get your panties all up in a bunch that I bray like Balaam's donkey. *Listen to this braying donkey's message Mr. Balaam because I have a message that will save many lives!*

My letter continues for several more paragraphs. Let's forge ahead.

Paul Became All Things to All People

Paul said, "To the Jews I became like a Jew, *to win the Jews.* To those under the law I became like one under the law (though I am not under the law) *to win those under the law."* He continues, "To those without the law I became like one without the law *to win those without the law."* He became like all types of people. Why? So he could *win them!*

"To the weak I became weak, that *I might win the weak"* he says, and then he continues, "I have become all things to all people, that by all means I might save some." The word "save" in this passage includes *to deliver from all the temporary evils of this present world.* Paul communicated in whatever manner necessary to reach whomever in whatever mental condition, belief system, or whatever their culture or background *so that he could win them!*

Here's a few more, just for giggles. Isaiah 36:12, "But the commander replied, "Was it only to your master and you that my master sent me to say these things, and not to the people sitting on the wall—who, like you, will have to *eat their own excrement* and *drink their own urine?"* I can only imagine excrement is the blue plate special. Have you heard of the military dish "shit on a shingle?" And then wash it down with a fresh glass of piping hot urine?! Sounds like what's on the menu the opening day in hell.

And another: Malachi 2:7, "I will rebuke your offspring, and spread **dung** on your faces, the **dung** of your offerings, and I will put you out of my presence." God will spread the dung of their sacrificial bulls on their faces. There's nothing like an Easter Sunday morning service where the pastor smears bull dung all over the faces of those in attendance. I've heard preachers talk bullsh*t, but I've never seen them smear it on people's faces.

And one more: Ezekiel 23:20-21 "There she lusted after her lovers, whose *genitals were like those of donkeys* and whose *emission was like horses."*

Okay Ezekiel, you talk about men hung like donkeys, and semen that squirts like a horse. I'm seventy years old so my semen dribbles more like an old mule.

Ezekiel continues, "So, you longed for the lewdness of your youth, when in Egypt your bosom was caressed, and your young breasts fondled." Yup, just like back in high school when I fondled the cheerleader's breasts behind the gymnasium, but I certainly never learned those verses in Sunday School about when Jeremiah mocked teeny weenies, and Ezekiel taunted Jerusalem for her idolatry, and her lovers with donkey-sized ding-dongs.

To sum it up, the bible is lean, mean, and a bit obscene, and so also is *Shitty to Happy in 21 Minutes: THE SECRET KINGDOM.*

So, whether you agree with my creative panache or not, my irreverent in-your-face style or not, or my potty humor, at least you can understand why I make the irreverent word choices I do, such as the bedrock title of this trilogy: *Shitty to Happy in 21 Minutes*. It's so I, like Paul, can *win the world.* I could've entitled it, "Powerful, Purposeful, Praise" or "Vices to Victory," or "Jesus is My Happy Jam," and those titles succinctly encompass the subject of this trilogy, but I'll let Joel Osteen and other goody two-shoes preachers employ such titles (I *love* Joel Osteen) but there's a likely chance that someone who wouldn't cast a second glance at "Jesus is My Happy Jam" in Barnes and Noble might be drawn to *Shitty to Happy in 21 Minutes: THE SECRET KINGDOM* which ironically *promotes the power of praise* such as do the goody two-shoes authors. I just opt for different word choices. Why? *So I can win the world!*

****

I continued my letter to believers with a final plea for them to jump on the bandwagon to win people that'll never step foot in a church. Let's continue.

****

I began this book during the summer Olympics in Los Angeles. It was 1984, twelve months after I accidentally stumbled upon the secret to peace and happiness on that sunny summer California afternoon in 1983 the day my green convertible died.

The stories are raw. The results are real. The revelations are shocking, but the pathway to peace is undeniable.

I hope you find this book to be enjoyable, powerful, and persuasive, and that you'll see how I skillfully—wise as a serpent, gentle as a dove—lead men, women, and children to tap into the kingdom of God, a kingdom that lives inside each of us so that this kingdom that he said to seek first explodes out from our insides, and spills out into our world, and it *forcefully* leads this broken world into the presence of the King of kings and Lord of lords so that they deeply experience his presence and his love, and they fall head over heels in love with the one whom Isaiah calls *The Prince of Peace.*

I look forward to your thoughts, your opinions, and your critiques.

Steve Hanks

****

So there you have it. This letter explains my reason for my salty language and burlesque stories, so ease up. Don't miss out on what I have to say because your panties are in a bunch.

So, "to pleasure" and "to delight" mean the same in Hebrew. To *pleasure* yourself—to *delight* yourself…is a verb, so if you slept through third-grade English class, let me remind you…a verb is something you *perform.* It's a task you accomplish.

Therefore, to *delight yourself in the Lord* means to *conduct a task.* What task? The number one, most important, highly prized undertaking a human can perform: **To pursue happiness, peace, and joy.**

How do you perform that task? You engage your lethal weapon of **the power of your tongue** to fire off several rounds of the 1225 biblical cuss words like I did that sunny summer California afternoon in 1983 the day my green convertible died, and when you do, **the power of your tongue** kicks into high gear to *forcefully* cram those 1225 words into the depths of your heart to resurrect the kingdom that lives inside you, a kingdom that is already a completed work, and that's how you fill yourself full to overflowing with his otherworldly peace and supernatural happiness like what happened to me that sunny summer California afternoon back in 1983 over forty years ago.

How do you pleasure yourself in the Lord? It's easy: **Force-feed** yourself full of peace with your 1225 words coupled with **the power of your tongue** until you are full of transcendent otherworldly peace that passes all understanding.

That's how to pleasure yourself in the Lord, and when you pleasure yourself in the Lord, then all the desires of your heart come a-runnin' like a river that overflows its banks to flood your Garden of Eden.

******

And here's a word of advice: Pleasure yourself often. Pleasure yourself in the Lord every day, several times a day. It's easy when you have the 1225 words memorized, which is why you'll learn a sure-fire, *simple* method to memorize right before I give you the words in volume three *THE GREAT*

INVASION, but you don't have to wait until then. Go to ShittyToHappy.com and you can download for free the easy memorization method.

It's even *easier* to pleasure yourself in the Lord when you speak in the spirit, which doesn't require *any* memorization.

"Whaaat?! Is that what 'talking in tongues' is? Is that what you're gonna teach me? You're gonna teach me how to talk in tongues?!?"

Yes.

"But Steve, *talkin' in tongues* is weird as shit." Yeah? So were a lot of things when you were a child and didn't know your ass from your elbow.

Do you wanna know what else is weird? Close your eyes for moment…are they closed? Good.

Now picture your mom and dad having sex.

Gross, huh? Ew. Weird, huh? Okay, it's gross and weird, but you wouldn't be here today if they didn't, so just because you think talking in tongues is gross and weird, think of your parents and how grateful you are that they went to pound town even though it's gross and weird.

I'll show you how to speak spiritual words right now if you want. Go to ShittyToHappy.com and download "How to Pray in the Spirit" and I'll have you up and running in five minutes.

And while you're at it, download "How to Memorize." It's the easiest thing in the world to do once you learn how.

Download both of them right now.

Did you download them yet?

If so, good.

Now that you've downloaded "How to Pray in the Spirit" and "How to Memorize," let's wrap this scene up with a short summary.

Keep It Simple

I think we can all agree that the simpler we keep this the better off we'll be, so let's take a pop quiz.

How do you pleasure yourself in the Lord?

Answer: You pursue *his kingdom* of joy, peace, and happiness. *You rest comfortably in his kingdom twenty-four hours a day seven days a week.* You pound his peace into your heart via **the power of your tongue** and 1225 words that are *God himself* so that they escort you into *The Secret Place of the Most High* that King David so eloquently describes in Psalm 91.

That's *how* you *pleasure yourself* in the Lord.

And when you pleasure yourself in the Lord, you fill yourself full of transcendent peace that is the otherworldly kingdom that already lives inside you, and then the byproduct is you get the desires of your heart.

You get your goodies because he promised they get *added* to you.

But first, diligently seek happiness, peace, and joy and THEN your goodies—also known as *the desires of your heart*—PURSUE YOU LIKE A RIVER that overflows its banks!

But seek peace first. **Remember**: *Don't wipe before you poop.*

"Speak the words…I'm right here."

You ask, "Steve, who is it that keeps repeating, 'Speak the words…I'm right here?'"

I'll let the Mystery Man himself tell you: **"It is I, the Prince of Peace that showed up to pound peace into Steve on that sunny summer California afternoon back in 1983 the day his green convertible died who keeps saying, 'Speak the words…I'm right here.'"**

You ask, "Who are you, Mystery Man?" and you follow it up with another question, "*Where* are you, Mystery Man?"

"I live inside you. I've been there since the day you were born, just like I lived inside Steve since the day he was born, and Steve accidentally stumbled upon the secret to stir up my power, and to resurrect a strong tower of transcendent peace that is not of this world."

You respond with a thoughtful question, "So, anytime I feel like it Mystery Man, I can stir up the peace—which is actually you—that already lives inside of me?"

"Yes. All you gotta do is SPEAK THE WORDS…I'M RIGHT HERE!"

You ask, "Does this mean my problems are over, that I'll never have any more problems?"

Oh my, oh my, look up at the big blue sky!

It's much better than that!

Scene 52

Treasures Present Challenges

Can you imagine a life without challenges? Wouldn't it be great to NEVER have any problems? Yeah? That won't happen until you're dead. *Peace does* NOT *mean you won't ever have any more problems.*

Call me a "Debbie Downer" but even when you force-feed joy, peace, and happiness into your heart with your 1225 words and **the power of your tongue** *you'll still have problems*. In fact, the more successful you become, the more problems you'll have, and the bigger they get. Is that a terrible thing? Absolutely NOT. It's a GOOD thing. *Treasures bring challenges!*

For instance, when you marry the man of your dreams, even though you're both ecstatically happy, isn't it true that you inherit a whole new set of problems that you *never* had as a single woman? Are you willing to manage a new set of challenges so that you can be with the man of your dreams?

It's also true that the more successful you become, the bigger challenges that come with those successes.

****

I had my first job when I was eleven. I mowed lawns in my neighborhood in Gainesville, Florida. I charged seventy-five cents to mow a lawn. When I was thirteen, I delivered the afternoon paper the *Gainesville Sun.* I learned how to deal with people, their complaints, their frustrations, and yes, occasionally their compliments. Did I have problems? Yes, but they're tiny compared to making a movie in Hollywood.

When I delivered newspapers, my problems seemed big, but compared to what I deal with today, they're small. Your battles in the little successes in life prepare you for the battles in the bigger successes in life, so get ready for bigger and more complex problems the more successful you become, because the more you sling your 1225 words and **the power of your tongue** like the skilled

Samurai soldier to pierce your heart with peace, PLUS the more **diligent** you are in your daily tasks, and the more you take care of the poor, the fatherless, and the widow then the more natural flow of life you walk in, and the more successes you achieve which then opens the doors to more and bigger challenges.

If I still had that same paper route that I had as a little boy, my problems today would be much smaller, but so would my bank account.

Remember: The bigger your success, the bigger your problems, and *that's a good thing.* Why? Because even though your huge successes bring on bigger problems, your otherworldly peace and transcendent happiness increase your strength and power to make you BIGGER than your problems.

How does this work? How does peace and happiness make you BIGGER than your problems?

Here's how: *Happiness and peace elevate your vantage point.*

****

For instance, if an ant sees a blade of grass, it looks huge to him, but to a giraffe it ain't nothin' but a chicken wing on a string. What others see as a huge insurmountable problem, your transcendent peace that you *force-feed* into your heart by **the power of your very own tongue** makes you see it as small. Insignificant, a chicken wing on a string.

This next truth bomb is monumental.

The size of your reactions
decides the size of your problems

That's a giant-sized revelation, so I'll say it again a little differently.

Big emotional reactions make problems seem big.
Little emotional reactions make the same problems seem little.

When you tap into your 1225 words and **the power of your tongue**, you perceive any problem, any situation, no matter the complexity, the difficulty, the insurmountability as small, no matter how gargantuan the problem, no matter how impossible it seems.

I'll say it once more:

Anger, frustration, worry, stress, and anxiety make problems seem big, huge, gigantic, insurmountable.

On the other hand, happiness, and otherworldly peace that transcends this natural world, coupled with joy unspeakable and full of glory are the emotions that you stir up from deep within you by **the power of your tongue** and 1225 words, and these incontrovertible emotions make all your problems seem small.

****

Here's an example of a difference in the size of your problem as determined by the size of your reaction. Remember as a teenager, the problems that seemed huge to you back then, you barely notice them now, like the weekend you had pimples and no date to the prom. You were devastated. You cried all night and moped around at breakfast the next morning. But now, pimples and no date? You grab a girlfriend, have dinner, drink wine, and laugh the night away.

What's the difference? It's thirty years later and you recall the pimple-faced problem from back in high-school, but today your emotional reaction to pimples and no date back in 1995 are a blip on the radar screen of your heart barely the size of a bead of sweat on the brow of a Cuban Salsa dancer.

Notice that the pimple-face problem is the same today as it was thirty years ago. What's the difference? The difference is *how you felt.* The difference is *how pimples, and no date to the prom affected your emotions*. How does the same problem affect you emotionally today? It doesn't. The pimple-faced problem lost its power when it couldn't control your emotions.

What gave the pimple-faced problem its power? Why did pimples and no date for the prom have power over you back then? EMOTIONS.

Why do pimples and no date to the prom have no power over you today? EMOTIONS.

What gave the pimple-faced problem its power back then? EMOTIONS.

Why does the pimple-faced problem have no power over you today? EMOTIONS.

What Makes a *Problem* a "Problem"

This brings up a probing question: ***What makes a situation become a problem?*** Question: Is it the enormity of the situation that makes it a problem? Or is it the enormity of your *emotional reaction* that makes it a problem?

Anger, fear, and anxiety MAXIMIZE the size of the problem. Well then, since anger, fear, and anxiety maximize the size of the problem, what do you think *minimizes* the size of the problem?

Transcendent peace MINIMIZES the size of the problem.

$100,000 House Deal

I lost $100,000 on a house deal in Los Angeles. When I first heard the news, my sphincter muscle locked up tighter than a skeeter's ass in a nosedive.

I was scared, but I worked to rid my field of the weeds the Evil Queen sowed. I plowed the ground of my heart with the 1225 words and **the power of my tongue** to root out the Evil Queen's weeds that she sowed in my field. By the time I rooted out all her fear, anguish, despair, and anxiety, I had conquered her punk ass self, and I didn't care that I lost $100,000.

When you don't care, you have no problem. The only reason it's a problem is IF YOU CARE.

The only way the Evil Queen controls you is if you refuse to control your emotions. How do you control your emotions? By 1225 words and **the power of your tongue**—*that's how to control your emotions.*

Happiness and peace that burst forth out of your heart when you resurrect them by **the power of your tongue** and the 1225 words—these kingdom emotions *minimize the size* of your hurtful, painful, fearful emotional reactions to any situation, any problem, any circumstance, any devastation including a $100,000 loss in a house deal. You thus shrink, diminish, and limit the size of your reaction which in turn shrinks, diminishes, and limits the size of your problem.

On the other hand if someone has no peace, they react to the situation like it's a gigantic Himalayan rough and rocky mountain. A fearful man thus magnifies and amplifies the size of his situation that turns it into insurmountable difficulty.

Not so for you, Mr. Peace Man and Miss Peace Woman who slam 1225 words by **the power of your tongue** into your heart so that your transcendent otherworldly peace makes you perceive your situation as a chicken wing on a string. It's like during a snowstorm when you're inside a log cabin, fire blazing in the fireplace, you sip hot cocoa in your warm fuzzy slippers, and you're snuggled up, safe and cozy, shielded from the blizzard outside.

****

Remember, if you don't want big problems, don't get married, don't start a business, don't pursue a career, and for God's sake don't have kids because each of these life-changes creates boatloads of problems.

Listen, you'll always have problems. It's imperative to make this important distinction: Transcendent peace is NOT the *absence* of problems. No, transcendent peace is the *presence* of God that lifts you high above your problems.

The power of your tongue causes you to rise above your situation like the eagle soars above the storms.

The Eagle Captures the Power of the Storm

When a storm comes, the eagle spreads his wings until the storm lifts him so high until he busts out high above the storm, and gloriously soars into the blue skies far above the turbulence.

The storm doesn't conquer the eagle. *The eagle captures the storm's power to rise above the power of the storm.*

The storm gives rise to the freedom of the eagle.

The Evil Queen is your storm. Her vile emotions are the energy that you harness, and then infuse that energy into your 1225 words, which intensifies your words and **the power of your tongue**. As you embrace her despicable assholitude like I did that sunny summer California afternoon in 1983 the day my green convertible died, then the Evil Queen's vile power thrusts you high above your shitshow like the eagle soars high above the storm.

The Evil Queen cannot conquer you when you introduce **her evil power** into your 1225 words, because then her powerful thunderstorms lift you high above her swirling emotions like the powerful thunderstorms elevate the eagle high above the turbulence into the blue skies.

It's a brilliant military tactic when you harness **the Evil Queen's demonic power** as her energizing force lifts you high above the storm. She catapults you into the blue skies when you harness her tumultuous winds, her crashing waves, and her raging waters like the eagle harnesses the power of the storm to lift himself high above the torrential winds and rain.

The anger that I harnessed that sunny summer California afternoon in 1983 is the Evil Queen's power. Her power is the force that lifted me high about the storm as I unleashed 1225 angry, frustrated, demonic "biblical cuss words" by **the insurmountable indefatigable power of my tongue**.

It was *her evil, noxious, and demonic power* that launched a robust infusion of energy into my 1225 words, and thus **the power of my tongue** lifted me high above the shitstorm. It was *her vile anger* that gave a boost to **the power of my tongue** to more effectively and quickly demolish that very same anger.

I hijacked the Evil Queen's insidious power. I seized her power to elevate me above her thunderstorms like the eagle seizes the power of the storm to elevate himself above the turbulence.

I seized upon the Evil Queen's anger to crush her very own anger.

The Evil Queen's anger didn't conquer me.

The Evil Queen's anger conquered herself!

This shit gives me cold chills. My goose bumps have goose bumps.

Side note: Do you see how your sincerity is the antithesis to the Evil Queen's power? Sincerity gets in the way of her valuable power! Sincerity and the power of the Evil Queen CANNOT COMINGLE. Pick one, or the other. I pick the Evil Queen's power. If you choose sincerity, do so at your own risk.

****

The good news encapsulated in this scene is you always have problems the more you have successes…BUT…when you seek first the kingdom of God with your enormous 1225 words and **the power of your tongue**, especially when you harness the Evil Queen's anger, and infuse her poisonous emotions into your 1225 words, like I did that sunny summer California afternoon in 1983 the day my green convertible died…

…then your *adverse emotional reactions such as anger, fear of failure, and anxiety* are STORMS that catapult you high above the tumultuous problems the same as the storm thrusts the eagle high into the sky when he spreads his wings as the eagle gloriously harnesses the power of the storm to lift himself higher above the turbulence to soar into the blue skies.

You, like the eagle, spread your wings so that your *nasty emotional reactions* are the tailwinds that thrust you higher and higher into the blue skies, higher and higher until you soar well above your *adverse emotional reactions* like the eagle soars high above the torrential downpour.

When the eagle soars comfortably above the storm, he looks down to see how puny the storm looks. Hence, the higher into the blue skies your problems thrust you, the tinier your problems appear to be, because you soar ever so high in the supernatural otherworldly peace of God's presence called *The Secret Place of the Most High.*

When you're seated in *The Secret Place of the Most High* that is the Lord's presence in the form of *otherworldly transcendent peace that is beyond the ability of your mind to comprehend* then your problems seem like the proverbial chicken wing on a string.

"Speak the words…I'm right here."

****

Scene 53

Our "Fake" Problems

My wife's sister-in-law from her first marriage is the heiress to one of the largest movie franchises in Hollywood. She's worth a couple hundred million dollars, so when she wants a $5 million house she pays cash.

There was a time she owned three homes in Southern California—all within a half hour of each other, all paid in cash, each worth $5 million, all worth twice that in today's dollars.

Her biggest stress on this one day…I know it because I saw her freaking out, so I asked her what was wrong. "I'm sooo stressed," she moaned. I imagined it was something like her boyfriend dumped her, or her son was in a motorcycle accident. She said (I kid you not) with a huge sigh and an even bigger rolling of her eyes, "The gardener is late."

Don't laugh at her. Why? Because *you, oh ye Mr. and Mrs. Douchewipe, are guilty of the same thing.* "Whaaat?" you indignantly exclaim, "How? Her problem is fake. I have *real* problems!"

Listen, no matter what your "real problems," you didn't use **the power of your tongue** and 1225 words to pound peace into your heart to shrink your "real problems" down to the size of her tardy gardener. You failed miserably to force-feed peace into your heart, an otherworldly supernatural peace that in turn *minimizes your butthurt reactions* to your so-called "real problems."

Her tardy gardener problem seems little to you, but to her it was big. Why? Because she had no peace, and therefore had an *overblown emotional reaction.* If you don't have peace, then your reactions too, are *overblown* so as to make your problem that you can't find your cell phone seem HUGE.

She felt **comfort** in her several Malibu mansions, but when her gardener was late she had no peace, just like Eric Clapton, John Lennon, Cameron Diaz, and Jim Carrey prophesy ominously that the same fate awaits us regardless of how much wealth, fame, and fortune we have.

My "Real" Problems

Do you think the movie heiress' problem was small? Do you think your problems are gigantic? Well I have news for you: Regardless of your "gigantic" problem, somebody somewhere sees your "gigantic" problem and laughs at your "gigantic" problem the same as you laugh at the movie heiress's gardener problem.

Listen, there are people that have "bigger" problems than you, and somebody somewhere laughs at their "bigger" problems because they have even "bigger" problems.

John Freund is a Holocaust survivor. The Germans sent him to Auschwitz-Birkenau when he was thirteen.

In early 1945, with Soviet forces approaching, SS troops marched most of the prisoners on death marches toward Germany. John Freund, his brother, and father were among them. In his words, "The death marches just went on and on and on in terrible weather, and my brother fell. My father went back to try to get him up to keep going, and the SS said, 'Get going, get going!' And my father said, 'No,' so they shot them both.

"My mother was too weak, so they put her in the gas chamber."

Do you suppose John Freund would laugh at your "huge" problem the way you laughed at the movie heiress in her million-dollar mansions with her "gardener problem"?

****

I have a friend whose father committed suicide in front of him. His dad put a gun to his own head and pulled the trigger while my friend, who was thirteen at the time, watched in horror. *His father committed suicide in front of his thirteen-year-old son.* To this day the image of his father's bloody brains splattered onto the walls, and onto the living room carpet haunt my friend.

Your problems might be that big, or even bigger. Or they might be smaller, but to you, to me, to any person, ANY problem we face—whether it's a tardy gardener, or whether you watched your father murder himself in front of you, if we don't have peace, we all feel the same horror, shame, guilt, anxiety, fear, anger, and hatred.

Our problems are different from one person to the next, *but our reactions are the same.* Our reactions vary in intensity, but our reactions are all the same. WE ALL WRESTLE WITH THE SAME EVIL QUEEN.

Our Reactions Differ in Intensity, But They're All the Same

Yes, our reactions to lost car keys and misplaced cell phones differ in intensity from one person to the next, but regardless of how big the problem or how small the problem, our reactions as a human race to all problems are the same. We feel anger, hurt, unforgiveness, pain, broken heart, hatred, fear, worry, stress, and anxiety.

The difference between your anger and my anger is the intensity, but it's still anger.

The difference between your worry and mine is the intensity, but it's still worry.

The difference between your stress and mine is the intensity, but it's still stress.

The difference between your depression and mine is the intensity, but it's still depression.

****

Our problems are different in America and in Africa, they are different in Europe and in China…but our emotional reactions are the SAME. The Evil Queen is the same in Americans and Africans, and she's the same in Europeans and the Chinese.

Our problems are different in white families and in black families, different in Asian families and in Indian families…but our emotional reactions are the SAME. The Evil Queen is the same in whites and blacks, and she's the same in Asians and Indians.

Our problems are different in Christian families and in Muslim families, different in Jewish families and in Hindu families…but our emotional reactions are the SAME. The Evil Queen is the same in Christians, Muslims, Hindus, and Jews.

Our problems are different in times of war, different in times of peace, different in times of famine, different in times of prosperity…but our emotional reactions are the SAME.

Our insidious poisonous emotional reactions are anger, hurt, unforgiveness, pain, broken heart, hatred, fear, worry, stress, anxiety, ad nauseum.

Although the problems in all of humanity are wildly different—our emotional reactions are the same.

"There's nothing new under the sun" (Ecclesiastes 1:9).

Worldwide our emotional reactions are the same. The difference between yours and mine is the INTENSITY of our emotional reactions. The degree of your negative emotional reaction is the degree to which your Evil Queen controls you.

The intensity of your emotional reactions is the degree to which the Evil Queen controls you

The size of your Evil Queen defines the size of your problem

If you refuse to shrink the size of your reaction such as I accidentally discovered how to do that sunny summer California afternoon back in 1983, then your reaction—regardless of the size of your problem—is no different than my wife's sister-in-law's reaction to the late gardener.

I gotta say something before I forget. I told you about my wife's sister-in-law and her reaction that the gardener was late. My family will excommunicate me if I don't tell you the beautiful side of my wife's sister-in-law. She has a big heart, a huge heart. She offered scholarships to the family of eleven kids that my wife Tammy and I took in that Christmas Day in Santa Monica. Yes, she had a bad morning with the gardener, but so did you when you couldn't find your car keys.

My daughter Natasha bought a BMW from her. Natasha agreed to make payments of $150 a month, which would take ten years to pay off the car. After five months, my daughter noticed her movie heiress aunt had cashed none of the checks. Natasha asked why, and she said, "Don't pay me for the car. I want to give it to you."

There. I kept my family happy and showed you my wife's sister-in-law's beautiful heart.

The size of the problem is irrelevant—whether the gardener is late, or you broke your leg—the *size of your emotional reaction* is the singular factor that decides the bigness or the smallness of the problem.

This explains why one person has a million-dollar loss in his business but doesn't lose a wink of sleep while another person loses his studio apartment and stresses out for three months.

This explains why one person sleeps in his car and is happy while another person sleeps in a mansion and is miserable.

This explains why one person worries over spilt milk while another person has catastrophic losses in his cornfield and sleeps like a baby.

Your emotional reactions determine the size of your problems.

This is so important I'll say it again in a subtitle:

Your Emotions Determine the Size of Your Problems

Yes, your emotions determine the size of your problems, and you have a trilogy called *Shitty to Happy in 21 Minutes* with three volumes, *THE SECRET KINGDOM, THE EVIL QUEEN,* and *THE GREAT INVASION* that tell story after story, reveal revelations galore, and unveils secrets to happiness that you've never heard before that empower you, strengthen you, and equip you to *control your reactions* to any problem which thus minimizes the size and magnitude of that situation, and you big bonus is the **Game Show Prize**. That is, your emotions open the doors to everything you want, dream, need, and desire that belongs to you in the Garden of Eden.

How does this work? it's simple. It works just like what happened to me that sunny summer California afternoon back in 1983 the day my green convertible died when I slung 1225 of the mightiest words in the universe out into the skies and then watched in amazement as **the power of my tongue** blew open the heavens above, lifted me high above the storm, and crushed my depressed, angry, bitter heart so that I soared above the torrential rains and thunderous lightning like the eagle soars above the storm, and I staggered like a soaking wet drunken sailor into *The Secret Place of the Most High*.

Control Your Emotional Reactions to Control Your Circumstances

You *control* your emotional reactions with the supernatural inexplicable kind of peace—the peace that transcends the natural world—that you *force-feed* into your heart via your 1225 words and **the power of your very own tongue** like I did that sunny summer California afternoon in 1983 the day my green convertible died.

This powerful revelation is not limited to worry, stress, and fear over a tardy gardener, a dead car battery, unemployment, and other first-world problems common to everyone. It works just as powerfully in life and death situations, tragic deaths, and huge financial devastation.

In the third volume of this trilogy *Shitty to Happy in 21 Minutes: THE GREAT INVASION* you'll hear story after story about the times when this miraculous power of words—coupled with **the miraculous power of the tongue**—has delivered me and others from life-threatening situations, horrendous emotional tortures, and devastating financial downfalls, but until you get to volume three *THE GREAT INVASION* then listen once again to the Mystery Man as he encourages you…

"Speak the words...I'm right here."

****

Scene 54

Castrate the Darkness

What robs your problems of their power?

Here comes another zinger, a life-changing zinger for you to help you dissect a problem, and it's simple. The simpler we keep this, the better off we'll be, would you agree? So here comes a simple zinger:

Every nasty emotion, every ounce of loneliness, fear, worry, anxiety, despair, panic, and—fill in your own choice of emotions here—every one of them is really the absence of *the fruit of the spirit,* and in particular, these three—*happiness, peace,* and *joy.*

When happiness, peace, and joy are nowhere to be found, then here come waves of gigantic shitty-fucky emotions to fill the void. Allow me to give you an example to illustrate.

Darkness: A totally black room, a room so dark you can't see your hand in front of your face even though it's three inches from your nose. The darkness of the room is so thick you can cut it with a knife. Got the picture? Okay, good!

Now, light a match. Not a huge match, not a bonfire-sized match—nope, just a match, a tiny little match you pick up free at the restaurant.

My wife used to keep matches in the bathroom for whenever I'd take a dump. Light a match and the smell is gone. It'd piss me off because you know how you like the smell of your own dump.

Okay, back to the darkness example. Light the match. There's a tiny flame. Question for you: Where'd the darkness go? I ask you, where did the darkness go?

My point is that no matter how thick it is, the tiniest light pierces the darkness.

You could have a four-watt nightlight and you could have a lightbulb that emits darkness the size of the world's largest light bulb fourteen feet tall, weighs eight tons located in the Thomas Edison Memorial Tower in the town of Edison, New Jersey, the site of Edison's greatest triumphs,

Now let's say for argument's sake that the world's largest light bulb, instead of producing light it produces darkness.

The nightlight in your kid's bedroom produces only 4 watts of light.

Which light bulb wins?

The four-watt light bulb has more power than the fourteen-foot tall eight-ton light bulb that emits darkness, right? Even the tiniest flicker from the candles on the cute little girl's birthday cake from her party back in 1960 are more powerful than the darkness of any room.

TRUTH BOMB: *Darkness is simply the absence of light.*

Darkness in our three-dimensional world has no power.

Darkness is merely the absence of light.

Darkness has no power over light.

Darkness cannot be present when the tiniest light glimmers.

Even a group of fireflies having a reveal party are brighter, no matter how dark the room.

Darkness is weak, darkness is feeble. It's impossible for darkness to sneak up on a well-lit room. When the room is well-lit there is no darkness in the world powerful enough to make the room dark.

And just like darkness cannot sneak up on a well-lit room, neither can fear nor worry sneak up on a heart full of peace and joy.

Fear and worry CANNOT sneak up on a heart full of peace and joy

Nasty Emotions are Merely the Absence of Peace and Joy

Isn't it true that no matter how devastating the problem, no matter how huge the obstacle, no matter how nasty your situation, your filthy emotions are only the absence of peace and joy!

If you had perfect peace and unspeakable joy, then you wouldn't—in fact, you COULDN'T have nasty emotions. *It'd be impossible!*

Just like nighttime can't sneak up on daytime, neither can depression, worry, and fear sneak up on the joy and otherworldly transcendent peace that you *force-feed* into your heart by 1225 words and **the power of your tongue**. Remember, I'm talking about that level of peace that springs up from a dimension outside of this natural world that your 1225 words and **the power of your tongue** invigorate from the innermost parts of your being.

Darkness only predominates until the sun comes up at which time the darkness flees like a scaredy cat runs from his own shadow.

Nighttime has no power
Daytime has all the power

****

How does this apply to your emotions? *Like this:*

Despair is only the absence of peace. *Despair has no power over peace.*

Worry is only the absence of joy. *Worry has no power over joy.*

Fear is only the absence of love. *Fear has no power over love.*

Any shitty emotion—pick one. Any one of these noxious emotions—pick any one you want—has no power by itself. The Evil Queen is simply the absence of God and his kingdom emotions of happiness, peace, and joy.

****

And here's another one for you: A dark room and a lighted room cannot coexist. Not at the same time.

A dark room and a lighted room cannot be together. A dark room and a lighted room are impossible to be together at the same time in the same room.

Folks, this is not a complex math problem. You can't be **peaceful** and **worried** at the same time.

You can't feel *joyful* and *shitty* at the same time.

You can't feel **happy** and **sad** at the same time.

You can't be *in a good mood* and *a bad mood* at the same time.

You can't go left and go right at the same time.

Got it?

Problems have no power
They are only the absence of peace, happiness, and joy

How do you stir up God's presence as evidenced by supernatural peace, inexplicable joy, and serenity like the deep blue ocean that calms your heart with his glorious emotions that he says to seek first, especially when you're in the middle of a storm when the Evil Queen rages, and she thumps her hairy chest like the weaselly old man in *The Wizard of Oz?*

Everybody shout the answer out loud, "Biblical cuss words!" Shout those 1225 tiny slivers of God by **the power of your tongue** for 21 minutes like I did that sunny summer California afternoon in 1983 the day my green convertible died, and when you do the same as I did—that is, you *force-feed* 1225 of the most powerful words in the universe into your heart by **the power of your very own tongue** for a brief time span of 21 minutes, then your 1225 words, coupled with **the victorious explosive power of your tongue** commandeers your ship through the vicious storms into the calm waters of the safe harbor.

The 1225 words and **the power of your tongue** radiate light into the grotesque darkness as it opens the windows to the sun!

My day was dark when I first heard the news that I lost $100,000 in a house deal, but I quickly turned on the light of the kingdom of God by **the power of my tongue** and 1225 words. What happened to the Evil Queen? She sniveled, whimpered, and crawled her ass back into the dark hole that I reserve for her under the bridge where the rest of the trolls spend time together until judgement day when God, who once and for all time and for all eternity rips that evil bitch out of my heart, but alas, we have to wait until that final day.

I go into extensive detail about this truth bombshell I just dropped on you about "judgement day." *It's fantastic news!* Nothing to be afraid of. In fact, judgement day is a momentous occasion to look forward to because that's the day God once and for all *rips the Evil Queen out of your heart* and **casts her into the Lake of Fire.** She will never again plague you, never again, forever, throughout all of eternity.

I'm excited for you to hear all about it in volume two of this trilogy *THE EVIL QUEEN.*

1225 Words and THE POWER OF MY TONGUE Rule My World

Words—1225 little slivers of God…yes, they are God, like the beer glass size of Pacific Ocean water IS the Pacific Ocean— The 1225 words ARE the God of the universe that eagerly waits for you to call on him.

"Speak the words…I'm right here."

The 1225 words await you. They're like the skilled trackers that incessantly chased Butch and Sundance. They await you in the third volume of this trilogy *Shitty to Happy in 21 Minutes: THE GREAT INVASION* but don't wait one minute longer because you can download them for free right now at ShittyToHappy.com.

As soon as you download them, the rabbi says:

"Speak the words…I'm right here."

The 1225 words are bustling and brimming with excitement. They're ready to cast a floodlight into your dark room. They'll crush the darkness with the power of automobile headlights in a dark garage.

Those 1225 words are the tiny glassful of the oceans of the world. Take a drink from the waters of the fountain of God. You don't need all of him, nor *could* you contain all of him any more than you could contain taking a drink of water from Niagara Falls. *The force of water would sweep you away!*

God's massive forces of transcendent peace would sweep you away just like it would've swept Moses away when he asked God to see all his glory, and God said, "No, not right now. The rush of power would sweep you away with the speed and force of Niagara Falls" (Exodus 33:18-23, paraphrased).

We'll see it and feel all of it one day though, I promise, and even while we live on this earth we will see more of it and feel more of it every day. I have a sneaking suspicion we'll see and feel every ounce of it before we leave this earth to enter the world to come, but don't hold me to it.

Aw heck, go ahead, hold me to it. I boldly proclaim that we will walk in the fullness of God before he splits the skies like lightning that comes from the east and is visible even in the west.

And THAT my friends is the coming of the Son of Man.

God's otherworldly peace that is not of this world increases more and more in direct proportion to the time we spend to fire off those 1225 words by **the power of our very own tongue** that unleashes the kingdom of God forces of happiness, peace, and joy that are buried deep inside each of us—which then transforms us physically and emotionally into the image and likeness of God Almighty who IS the Prince of Peace!

Do you want a massive outpouring of peace?

"Speak the words…I'm right here."

****

Scene 55

God's Staggering Invasion

I'm gonna let you in on a little secret. There are times when I spend lots of hours speaking these words and praying in the spirit, which is talking in tongues, and the enormity of the deluge of peace, joy, and happiness that flood me is more than I can handle, and I must continue to speak the words to increase my heart's capacity to contain the flood.

You heard me right, the immensity of peace and happiness feels like more than my body can contain, so I speak the 1225 words even more, so that **the power of my tongue** enlarges my heart to contain even more of the deluge of peace.

I can handle more than I could yesterday, and the year before, but my heart—and yours must expand to be able to contain all the glory of God, also known as *The Peace of God,* who is of course, THE PRINCE OF PEACE.

Why is this otherworldly peace so incredibly powerful and overwhelming to our puny little bodies of flesh, like God told Moses when he declined to show him all his power?

It's because this peace is God himself and nearly causes our heart to burst.

How Do We Tap This Power?

The power of your tongue bridges the gap between you, who lives in this three-dimensional physical world, and God who is the Prince of Peace who lives outside of our dimensions of time, space, and matter, and yet lives inside of each of us.

The power of your tongue unleashes peace that bridges the gap between you and God...
Peace is the umbilical cord that connects you to God himself

Peace is the umbilical cord that connects you to the life force of God.

Holy shit that's so good I gotta say it again:

PEACE IS THE UMBILICAL CORD THAT CONNECTS YOU TO THE LIFE FORCE OF GOD HIMSELF

He is the Prince of Peace. He is God. He is our creator.

That's why his peace is at times more than I can contain—it's because his peace is HIM.

But I digress. Let's get back to the power of the 1225 words in your mouth and **the power of your very own tongue**.

> *The good news is whatever it is you face today; you only need a tiny mouthful of God. You only need a tiny fraction of the Lord of the universe to force-feed his peace and happiness into your heart.* ***You don't need all of his power to solve your problems any more than you need all the electricity in Los Angeles to run your toaster.***

That tiny sliver of God in your mouth is the explosive atomic energy of…well, a paperclip.

That's right, a paperclip.

If you could harness all the power that's in a paperclip—if you could convert every one of its atoms into pure energy, the paperclip would yield about 18 kilotons of TNT. That's *bigger than the atomic bombs in 1945.*

A paperclip is so small it clasps the pages of this book together. A paperclip is so tiny, and yet there are 18 kilotons of TNT hidden inside that paperclip, just like hidden inside those ever so small 1225 little slivers of God…inside those 1225 tiny words is 18 kilotons of God's massive explosive energy.

"Speak those tiny little slivers of ME" says God, *"because when you do, then* **the power of your very own tongue** *unleashes all my power that resides in those 1225 words, a power with the force of 18 kilotons of TNT* to pound my otherworldly incomprehensible peace into your heart."

Thus saith the Mystery Man, the Prince of Peace who in a powerful show of force showed himself strong to me that sunny summer California afternoon in 1983 the day my green convertible died.

Connect YOUR *emotions…to* GOD'S *emotions… and you'll get all the desires of your heart*

Can you see how over and over I show you how simple this is? I told you in the first few pages of the book how simple this is.

Use your 1225 words and **the power of your tongue** to get happy.

"Happiness is your purpose in life," I told the young girl.

Use your 1225 words and **the power of your tongue** to *force-feed* otherworldly transcendent peace that is not of this world into yourself but be careful. You might burst.

That's why God can't unleash all of his peace into you right now because you'd burst, like the times I've felt that happiness, peace, and joy so fiery and furiously that I feel like I'm gonna burst.

And what other actions do you take to enter the Garden of Eden? Diligence! Be diligent, *be diligent* in your labors, your schoolwork, your business, your career, your goals, dreams, and visions, your family, and your body.

What else? Take care of the poor, the fatherless, and the widow, and then what happens?

You'll get goodies galore! All the desires of your heart! You'll enter the Garden of Eden, the garden of delight where everything you can imagine, think, dream, or feel is yours.

****

Where do you find this knowledge about **the power of your tongue**, and this oddly peculiar idea to harness the Evil Queen's venomous emotions to defeat herself? Will you learn to embrace the Evil Queen's power in seminary, college, or church? Well…did you? No, you didn't.

In fact, seminarians and many preachers poo-poo *Shitty to Happy in 21 Minutes: THE SECRET KINGDOM* and they call me a heretic because I proclaim how I learned to hijack the Evil Queen's powers to fill myself full of happiness, peace, and joy, but I don't care because I woke up this morning with twelve f*cks in my pocket, I'll go to bed tonight with twelve f*cks in my pocket which means I'll go all day long without giving a fuck what religious people think.

The second volume of this trilogy *THE EVIL QUEEN* is even more controversial as Christians embrace their doctrines about the devil like a dying man struggles for a breath of fresh air, but I blow the lid off these silly kindergarten dogmas with the might and power of a tsunami on tiny Foc-Foc Island where it rained six feet in one day.

I've heard thousands of sermons in hundreds of churches, and I've never heard anything like the crazy revelations in *THE SECRET KINGDOM,* and certainly not the "heresies" in *THE EVIL QUEEN,* nor in the third volume *THE GREAT INVASION.* You'll never hear anything of this sort in thousands of sermons on thousands of Sundays.

Did I get a formal education to learn this? Did I get a masters or a PhD in theology? No. In fact I cheated my way through college. I went to college because I had no place else to go. So then where did I learn this information? I learned it through self-study and thousands of hours of prayer, self-education, and a deep dive into Hebrew. No seminary, no formal training, no school, no church, and no university.

To my point on conventional seminaries, and assorted other religious education institutions, a thought popped into my mind. I have a bone to pick with our education system. Not the teachers. The educational system itself. Teachers, I love you teachers.

Now listen to me. Imagine a schoolroom. There are thirty students. The teacher makes them sit in their desks in military order, tells them when to take a break, when to go to recess, and when to go to lunch. They must repeat back to the teacher what they hear. Good recitation gets a good grade, bad recitation gets a bad grade. The afternoon bell rings, the kids go home.

This environment trains students to be factory workers.

John D. Rockefeller founded the General Education Board in 1903. He said, "I don't want a nation of thinkers. I want a nation of workers."

Thus the public education system was born to produce human worker bees for the industrial revolution, factory workers to work eight hours a day, do what you're told, and pick up your paycheck on Friday. The public education system was not designed to create entrepreneurs, business owners, or CEOs. Did you learn how to buy a house, balance a checkbook, start a business, invest in the stock market, or buy real estate in school?

Am I saying there's no value in public education? Put that thought away, but like the old song so aptly expresses, “Readin' and writin' and 'rithmetic, taught to the tune of a hickory stick.” Anything other than “readin’ and writin’ and ‘rithmetic” you can get from the internet.

My daughter Natasha did well in school, but my son Austen did not do so well. So my wife Tammy and I decided to homeschool the kids. I agreed to do the teaching, she agreed to do the administrative work.

On our first day Tammy was so excited, she gave me the first assignment. It was, hell I don't remember what it was, geography or whatever. We finished geography.

I said, “Tammy what's next?”

She said, “Math,” so we proceeded to finish the math assignment.

This continued for an hour and a half. I said to Tammy, “What's next?” She said, “We're done.”

“We're done?!?”

Three days of these ninety-minute days, and the realization hit me: We send our kids to an institution that takes eight hours to teach an hour and a half of knowledge. I understand the reason it takes eight hours is there are thirty kids in the classroom, but that simply gives the reason for the waste of eight hours to perform an hour and a half job. If thirty kids in a classroom ain’t workin’ then change what you’re doin’.

What's more, school doesn’t teach our kids how to solve problems. School teaches them how to recite information, facts, figures, and the students must perform recitations to the teacher’s satisfaction, just like John D. Rockefeller designed. Sorry, not for my kids. You can make your kids memorize the state capitals of all 50 states. I’ll teach my kids how to look it up on the Internet.

I'm gonna say something and I want it to sink into you parents.

Formal education will make you a living
Self-education will make you a fortune

If I may continue my rant, our university system is a crock of shit unless you want to be a doctor, lawyer, architect, engineer or the like, but anything else is a waste of time and money. In fact, what has our society done? We tell kids to get a college degree, then strap them with student debt, they graduate with $60,000 in debt and then get a job as a latte-maker at the coffee shop.

My son Austen did not do well in school at all. So we pulled both kids out and we even stopped homeschooling them. Tammy said, should Austen at least get his high-school equivalent GED? I said, "Why? He wants to be a stunt man."

We trained our kids to be problem-solvers, which brings up another point. When we were home schooling the kids, I had to study the instructions since I had no clue how to teach them the material. One day I get the bright idea to have my two kids study the instructions themselves and figure out the assignment, and then they perform the assignment.

You know how kids are, right? "Daddy that won't work."

I replied with a feigned look of shock, "It won't?!? Well let's try it."

So I had them read the instructions. They quickly skimmed through the instructions so they could prove to me it doesn't work. "See Daddy, it didn't work."

I said with a touch of loving sarcasm, "It didn't work? Well then, do it again."

They did. Same thing. "Daddy, we did it again. It didn't work."

I said, "Let's do it again."

After fifteen times they start to cry. I said, "It's okay to cry, but still work through your tears to figure it out. If you cry so hard that you can't read the page, take a minute, dry your tears, and get back to work."

After fifty times I saw the excitement in their eyes when they figured out how to do the assignment. "Daddy, we did it, we did it!" They figured out on their own how to do the assignment. *They were extremely proud!*

We didn't teach our kids a bunch of facts. We taught them how to solve problems. And isn't that how to succeed in life? Life is problem-solving. Regarding facts we have all the facts at our fingertips with a cell phone and internet, but problem-solving? What school system teaches problem-solving? They don't even teach how to balance a checkbook. I know of a teacher in New York that recently introduced to her class how to balance a checkbook. The school reprimanded her!

Today my beautiful daughter Natasha is married to a great guy, he's a huge success in the movie industry, they have two beautiful children, and my brilliant son Austen is married to a beautiful young girl, they have a young son, and Austen is a stunt coordinator for one of the top television shows in Hollywood.

My daughter never went to college, and my son never got his GED.

Both of them—I'm so proud of both of them. Are they educated? Yes to the double-wide "yes." Did they get educated in public school? No to the double-wide "no."

Is education important? You're darn tootin' it's important, but you do well when you choose self-education over formal education, so I'll say it again:

Formal education will make you a living
***Self-education** will make you a fortune*

Elon Musk says, "There's no need even to have a college degree. At all. Or even high school. If somebody graduated from a great university that may be an indication that they will be capable of great things but it's not necessarily the case."

He continues, "People like Bill Gates, Steve Jobs, Larry Ellison…these guys didn't graduate from college, but if you had a chance to hire them of course that would be a good idea."

One more thing and then I'll get off my soapbox. How can a person who's never built a business teach your kids how to build a business? How can a person who is an employee teach your kids how to be an employer? How can someone who makes $60,000 a year teach your kids how to make a million dollars a year? These are simple, common-sense questions.

I learned at an early age to *QUESTION THE ANSWERS*.

Nobody told me there wasn't a Santa Claus. I was six when I questioned how Santa could visit every home in every country in twenty-four hours. I calculated it takes at least eight minutes per house. We had seventy-two houses on our street in Orlando. If Santa spends eight minutes in each house, plus two minutes to move on to the next one, that's a total of 720 minutes on just our street alone! How many hours is 720 minutes?

Twelve hours. How do you argue with a six-year-old who "questions the answers"? I had a teacher in sixth grade who chastised me for chewing gum in class. I challenged her. I said, "You chew gum in class, but you tell me not to chew gum in class." I pissed her off, so she sent me to the principal's office.

Religious Pharisees, be wary of the crazy young actor who *questions the answers* because he just may blow away your centuries-old religious proclivities with something as simple as an accidental discovery on a sunny summer California afternoon in 1983 the day his green convertible died.

My penchant to "question the answers" is how I stumbled upon this mind-numbing revelation of 1225 words and **the power of my tongue** coupled with an even more wacky innovation to harness the Evil Queen's wicked power that strangely works hand-in-hand with my 1225 words and **the power of my tongue** to *force-feed* otherworldly inexplicable peace into my heart. If I gullibly accepted what preachers and churches taught me like we expect our kids to learn only what schools teach, then I never would've discovered what I did that sunny summer California afternoon back in 1983 the day my green convertible died. *Question the answers!* Okay, I'll get off my soapbox, and return to the subject at hand.

I told you in the first few pages of this book how incredibly simple this kingdom of happiness is: It's 1225 words and **the power of your tongue** to seek first the kingdom of God, the emotions of happiness, peace, and joy, and when you do, then EVERYTHING ELSE WILL BE ADDED TO YOU so long as you're diligent, and you take care of the poor, the fatherless, and the widow.

Listen, if I could complicate this amazingly simple method, I would. If I could complicate this kingdom of God that gives you everything that pertains to life, I would—

But I can't. I've tried to complicate it, but I can't. I've argued with God, "It can't be this simple." But it is…it really IS this simple. *"Speak the words…I'm right here."* Use **the power of your tongue** to speak the all-powerful 1225 words every time you feel like poop, and within 21 minutes **the power of your very own tongue** *forces you* from *Poopy to Peaceful,* the G-rated version of *Shitty to Happy*.

Happiness, peace, and joy is the kingdom of God that he says to pursue first, foremost, and toppermost, and when you make this magnificent kingdom of supernatural emotions your top priority, then *all your dreams, desires, goals, and aspirations overtake you,* and the best part is YOU LIVE IN and ABIDE IN the peaceful paradise called **THE SECRET PLACE OF THE MOST HIGH**! It's so simple that anybody can do this, even if your IQ is negative.

"Speak the words—I'm right here."

INTERMISSION

Scene 56

Queen's Fake Peace

"I know Dad, I *know,"* I whined to him the thousandth time he told me to stay humble, and yet secretly I needed him to remind me. My continual whines of "I know Dad, I *know"* were to shut him up even though I knew he was right.

"I know Steve, I know!" you clamor at me every time I prod you to seek peace and happiness **before** you pursue the desires of your heart. "I know Steve, I *know,"* you implore. Do you? Or do you say that just to shut me up like I did my father?

Why do I drill down on you ad nauseum to pursue otherworldly transcendent supernatural peace? And why FIRST and FOREMOST? Because I know how easy peazy lemon squeezy it is to lose your grip on the kingdom emotions of happiness, peace, and joy, and instead drift aimlessly toward reliance upon the goodies for comfort. I know because I've fallen flat on my face countless times over the years.

When I pursue kingdom emotions, combined with diligence, diligence, and more diligence in my daily tasks, and thereby acquire the desires of my heart, many times I gradually drift away from my foundational strength of otherworldly peace and transcendent happiness that springs up from deep within me from 1225 words and **the power of my tongue**.

It takes persistence to lock into the kingdom of God when your life is comfortable. I've recklessly lost sight of the kingdom, the infinite source that births the desires of my heart. My attention dims as my focus fades away from the glistening ocean liner. I fall overboard into the water, and backstroke over to the tiny, rusty dilapidated tugboat of *panty-pie peace and comfort* that my good fortunes offer.

My comfortable lifestyle lures me into a faux peace that is a counterfeit of the kingdom of God otherworldly peace, until slowly but surely I abandon my dependence on transcendent otherworldly peace, and I shift my attention to my comfortable lifestyle, the "good life," and I get lazy with the 1225 words and **the power of my tongue** to *force-feed* transcendent otherworldly peace and happiness into my heart.

My comfortable lifestyle seduces me. It lures me away from the otherworldly emotions of transcendent peace. It's ironic that it's those kingdom emotions combined with diligence that attracted my good fortunes in the first place!

The deception doesn't happen overnight, but it happens. *It creeps in so subtly that I don't notice.* The deception moves in on me like a stealth bomber. One cannot detect a stealth bomber by radar. The only way to detect a stealth bomber is NEVER. Well, at least not until the pilot drops his payload, but then it's too late.

WARNING! The peace that a comfortable lifestyle offers, and the peace that passes all understanding are so close in how they make us feel that if we're not extremely careful, we conflate the two.

The two kinds of peace look as much alike as IDENTICAL TWINS!

... But in reality, they are as DIFFERENT as identical twins!

BEWARE! This is one of the Evil Queen's most sophisticated traps!

****

I learned this lesson the hard way a few years back when I foolishly gazed upon my fortunes for my peace. The deception stealthily crept in and plopped itself down on the comfortable couch right next to me in *The Secret Place of the Most High.*

My heart noticed, and cried out, "Intruder! Intruder!" but slowly and ever so sneakily the faux peace of this world slowly choked out the inexplicable peace that transcends this natural world.

This panty-pie peace and comfort is an undetectable virus that contaminates like an invasion of black mold in the palace of *The Secret Place of the Most High.*

Even though I had amassed a nice lifestyle that included all the desires of my heart by means of peace, happiness, joy, diligence, and taking care of the poor, the fatherless, and the widow, I took my eyes off the powers of emotions of happiness, peace, and joy, and instead gazed upon my wealth and success for my peace.

Remember: That's not peace; it's *comfort.*

A farmer takes care of the roots of the lemon tree, not the lemons. He knows if he takes care of the roots, the fruits will take care of themselves, but if the farmer spends all his attention on the fruits, and ignores the roots, then what happens to the fruits? That's what many wealthy people, including myself, fall prey to.

I gradually replaced my rock-solid foundation of the kingdom of God emotions of happiness, peace, and joy with one that was made of sand. The stealth bomber silently moved in on me.

When did I know this for sure? I remember one day I asked myself the question, "If I lost everything, would I still be happy?" My answer scared me. I would soon find out.

The stealth bomber dropped its payload on me. It was too late. I had carelessly become dependent upon my beautiful life. Thus, when I lost everything—my home, my family, my business, and my fortunes, I descended into the pit of the deepest depression one could imagine, the worst I've ever felt in sixty-seven years. I never saw the stealth bomber until it dropped its payload on me. *It was too late.*

I had gradually descended into the trap the Evil Queen set for me: *My peace of mind was predicated upon my wealth and success.*

The Evil Queen's Most Devious Trap

When you are wealthy, the Evil Queen's most cunning weapon is that she lures you into a false sense of otherworldly peace

Comfort feels exactly like the peace of God!

I beg that this doesn't happen to you, but if you thoughtlessly ignore your massively powerful kingdom emotions, and instead allow your focus to drift onto the comfort and safety of your material possessions, your status, your family, and your success, she will lure you into her deceptive trap *and you won't even know it.*

If you don't lose your material wealth, you'll lose your internal peace, *and you won't even notice it because* **you'll feel like you have the peace of God.**

If you loosen your grip on the 1225 words, and get lazy with the power of your tongue, the comfortable lifestyle feels EXACTLY like the peace of God!

When that happens, the desires of your heart slowly lose their glitz. The thermostat of your happiness set point drops lower. You take your wealth for granted like the backwoods villager takes the light switch and the toilet for granted. Like the four celebrities Eric Clapton, Cameron Diaz, John Lennon, Jim Carrey and J. Paul Getty all warned how futile it is to look to your wealth for your peace of mind. John Lennon's infamous quote, "We had it all, and there was no joy."

Who else can we learn from, this concept that when we look to material wealth, fame, and fortune for our peace, they cannot give you supernatural abundant otherworldly transcendent peace that is the kingdom of God—

How about Marilyn Monroe, Philip Seymour Hoffman, Jim Morrison, Jimi Hendrix, and Janice Joplin, amazing talents all, as were John Belushi, George Michael, Prince, and Michael Jackson, all of whom died of drug overdoses; and suicides by Kurt Cobain, Robin Williams, Ernest Hemingway, and Vincent van Gogh whose last words ring hollow, "The sadness will last forever," and Freddie Prinze Sr. who left a suicide note, "I must end it. There's no hope left. I'll be at peace…"

You need not experience the hopeless heartache of these famous celebrities nor of mine. You can learn from their lives, and you can learn from mine.

If we look to the goodies as our source of peace instead of the kingdom of God's *transcendent peace and supernatural happiness,* the kind that spring up from the 1225 words and **the power of your tongue**, then it's a grind to pursue the desires of your heart. You are "toiling and spinning," and even if you achieve all the desires of your heart, it's a temporary high. As the four celebrities said, it's futile to try and derive lasting peace and enjoyment when you build your foundation on goodies, fame, and fortune.

Remember the hedonic adaptation experiment with the lottery winners? Remember how they sank down to their "happiness set point" shortly after they won the lottery?

Another thing: If you lose hold of your transcendent otherworldly peace whilst you pursue the desires of your heart, then you'll stress out like a tightly wound crackhead, and the sick part is even if we gain everything we need, want, dream, and desire, but drift away from the kingdom of God emotions, then the desires of our heart taste like gravel in our mouth that we wash down with a glassful of piping hot vinegar.

Remember the four celebrities tell you that material things, fame, and fortune don't make you happy, and yet God promises you that these goodies *are a colossal part of the kingdom.* **They flow naturally from it.** You cannot stop the desires of your heart from flowing any more than you can stop the waves from crashing.

Therefore my dad's warning to me is my warning to you: *Stay humble.*

What's humility? Humility is that you diligently pursue the kingdom of God which is the emotions of happiness, peace, and joy.

Wherever you are on your journey to acquire all the desires of your heart, and to build your empire, whether you just today got the idea, like I did that day in the church around the corner from my life insurance office in Orlando, or whether you're far along and have amassed millions of dollars in real estate, assets, a thriving career, booming business, strong family, spouse, and kids…when you maintain these emotions first and foremost on the throne of your heart, they protect you from collapsing into the laziness that creates weak men by way of "the good life."

Humility is to stay strong and to *force-feed* yourself full of the otherworldly transcendent emotions of happiness, peace, and joy not only when times are bad, but also when times are good.

Good Times Create Weak Men

G. Michael Hopf summed up man's circle of life from weakness to strength back to weakness; from poverty to wealth back to poverty in his apocalyptic novel called "Those Who Remain."

Listen to these prophetic words:

****

Hard times create strong men…

Strong men create good times…

*Good times create **weak** men…*

***Weak** men create **hard** times.*

****

That's my circle of life for the last forty years: Weak, strong, weak again, and back to strength.

If you fall off the horse, get back in the saddle. "A good man falls seven times yet rises again" (Proverbs 24:16).

"Stay humble, Steve."

"I will, Dad. I love you."

****

"Speak the words…I'm right here."

Scene 57

Dreams Chase You

If you promise me you'll work harder than a Walmart cashier on Black Friday the day after Thanksgiving to pursue the kingdom of God, especially after you get all your goodies, then I'll let you in on the next secret.

I mentioned that when you inundate yourself with peace and joy, that's the perfect time to go after your dreams, and not before, but it gets even better.

Do Things the Correct, Right, and Godly Way so that the Desires of Your Heart *Forcibly* Come Onto You and OVERTAKE You

After you *pursue and conquer your emotions*... in other words *after* you *FORCE-FEED* peace and happiness into your heart so that they dominate you like they dominated me on that sunny summer California afternoon in 1983 the day my green convertible died, and you do this continuously day after day, that's *when* and that's *how* your career, your employment, your apartment, your car, your family, and your health *naturally unfold.*

When you, the man, woman, or child *force-feed* yourself full of inexplicable happiness and incomprehensible peace, and you diligently tackle your everyday tasks, your errands, your business ventures, your trade, your craft, your schoolwork, your farm, your manufacturing company, your family, a fit body, and your desire to wisely raise your kids, then YOUR DREAMS INEVITABLY CHASE YOU DOWN AND OVERTAKE YOU.

Your dreams effortlessly chase you and overtake you when your transcendent peace jacks your talents to the max.

Your peace unleashes supernatural wisdom that enhances your skills and abilities.

Your jacked up skills and abilities thrust you into the stratospheric success by the power of the kingdom of God's supernatural emotions of happiness, peace, and joy.

These are the kingdom of God emotions that you unfurl by **the power of your very own tongue** just like what happened to me that sunny summer California afternoon in 1983 the day my green convertible died.

Therefore, as you pursue the kingdom which is peace, joy, and happiness, and you're **diligent in your duties, tasks, errands, and efforts**, and you *take care of the poor, the fatherless, and the widow*, then you'd better *prepare yourself for the outpouring of God's massive goodies.*

Moses says in Deuteronomy 28:2, "If you'll do what I command you—if you'll *diligently* pursue happiness, peace, joy, and love—and as you *diligently* work toward your goals, dreams, wishes, and desires, and as you diligently take care of the poor, the fatherless, and the widow then all these good, awesome, and wonderful things will come on you and OVERTAKE you."

"Steve, you're telling me that I need not chase my dreams, but my dreams will *chase me?!?*

Yes, that's the way the kingdom works.

Your dreams OVERTAKE you

How would you like your dreams to chase you, tackle you, and wrestle you to the ground? The girl I met on the airplane from Albuquerque to Los Angeles certainly loved the idea, and so did the girl I met at the seminar in Reno.

Here's what it looks like.

It's a beautiful summer afternoon in August in New York City. Imagine you go for a jog in Central Park. You glance over your shoulder to see the world's fastest human Usain Bolt sprint toward you at full speed. Where'd he come from? You didn't notice him before, but the world's fastest man *overtakes* your slowpoke, slogger, jogger self.

In like manner your dreams sneak up on you and *overtake* you as you feverishly and continuously pursue these three things:

ONE: Take care of the poor, the fatherless, and the widow—

TWO: Force-feed yourself full of supernatural peace and happiness with your 1225 words and **the power of your tongue**— and—

THREE: Meticulously and diligently walk tiny step by tiny step toward your dreams and goals. **Be diligent!**

****

Talking about diligence, many successful people say that when they first set out on a quest for their dreams, they had no idea how big their success would become.

I've played keyboard my whole life. I earned my living in music at various times throughout the years. I quit my football scholarship at Florida State to segue into rock n roll. I put together a band in Tallahassee, and we played like rock stars at fraternity parties and bars. One of the guys was so talented that he relocated to New York to play the lead role of the phantom in *Phantom of the Opera* on Broadway.

I practiced the keyboard 20-40 hours a week. My wife Tammy would beg me to get off the piano to have dinner with the family.

I set up my keyboard in the walk-in closet because even though I wore headphones, I banged the keys for hours on end hard enough to keep her awake at night.

Here's my point: One evening, after tens of thousands of piano scales and thousands of hours of practice, I riffed on a jam session so fluidly that I watched in amazement as my fingers took on a life of their own. Yes, it was me, and yes, it was my mind and body, but the music that flowed out of my hands and fingers blew me away.

My point is, thousands and thousands of scales, finger exercises, and thousands of hours of practice that at the time seemed like, "Wax on, wax off"—Remember that from the movie *Karate Kid?* After thousands of "wax on, wax offs" I could rip my keyboard to shreds.

My talent started small but overwhelmed me.

****

Your dreams start small as you take tiny steps. Your dream grows bigger, your achievements grow larger until one day you notice your dreams sneaked up on you, chased you down, and overtook you like Usain Bolt overtakes you in Central Park.

You started out unskilled, but now you're a master. You started out unqualified, but now you're a teacher. You started out illiterate, but now you're an expert. You started out a lousy tennis player, and you're still a lousy tennis player. Oh wait…that's me at my first and only semi-pro tennis tournament in Memphis.

What else? Your circumstances seem to miraculously fix themselves.

What else? Everything you *do* prospers, and on top of that, God supernaturally intervenes to influence people, your family, situations, and circumstances beyond your efforts. He even changes the hearts of those in power to help you. You reach a point where you create effortless solutions to insurmountable obstacles.

Divine Invasions

A friend of mine was a super-successful hairstylist. She retired from hairstyling at twenty-seven to start a fashion business but ran into some financial difficulties, couldn't make payments on her car, and so she returned it to the loan company to avoid a repo like what happened to my green convertible. She didn't have a car for several months.

Rabbit trail: Many if not all successful people tell you they went through lean times on their way to the good times. They slept in their cars, showered at the gym, and ate beans and rice. Steve Harvey and Les Brown come to mind. Steve slept in his car. Les slept in an office. Why'd they live in squalor? I've done the same. Why'd we do it? So we are unencumbered by the daily grind that ensnares so many, and therefore we're free to go balls to the wall in our dreams, hopes, and visions.

I'm back from the rabbit trail. I was talking about "divine invasions."

One day, a client for whom my hairstylist friend cut hair for many years called her out of the blue and said, "I'm gonna buy you a camper van." I hear you want one to travel the country to pursue your dream as a fashion designer." Next thing you know he flies down to Los Angeles, takes her van shopping, buys her a fully equipped camper van, he pays cash for it and signs it over to her. That's the supernatural hand of God *over and above* her human efforts.

She labored in sustained diligence for ten years, blood, sweat, and tears to become a top-level hair stylist, met this client who, without provocation, turned out to be a huge financial blessing. *Her dream to travel the country in pursuit of her vision as a fashion designer chased her down like Usain Bolt overtakes you in Central Park.*

When you unleash the power of 1225 words by **the power of your very own tongue**, you not only get happy, peaceful, and joyful, but you set in motion the supernatural divine intervention of God Almighty to move mountains on your behalf.

****

Are you fretting about **a place to live**? If you are, then jam-pack your 1225 words full of that poisonous worry like I packed mine full of poisonous anger that sunny summer California afternoon in 1983 the day my green convertible died, because in doing so, you throttle the Evil Queen's throat with her very own noxious anger, fear, worry, stress, and that dreadful feeling of anxiety.

Pound the 1225 words like a dagger into the heart of your Evil Queen, her anger, fear, anxiety, and her despair. Do it for 21 minutes until **the power of your tongue** causes peace to arise from the depths of your heart like the Son of Man arose from the depths of the earth.

As you daily use your 1225 worry-filled, anger-laden biblical cuss words and **the unbeatable power of your very own tongue** to *force-feed* peace and happiness into your heart like I did that sunny summer California afternoon in 1983 the day my green convertible died, then you simultaneously open the doors for **a place to live**.

Do you want a better job? Speak the 1225 words. Say them through three times. It's 3675 words. It takes 21 minutes. Do it every day, even several times a day. The more the better. You'll see!

The power of your very own tongue *force-feeds* peace, happiness, and joy into your heart which then intensifies your abilities to unlock the "good life" supernaturally, yet naturally.

Fortify your emotions. **They are your superpower!** Then add massive amounts of diligence in your daily tasks, plus a healthy dose of taking care of the poor, the fatherless, and the widow, and then watch the windows of heaven open wide as your emotions and your diligence march you into the Garden of Eden, the garden of luxury and delight with its host of blessings that provide you the life you greatly desire. You'll meet the right people; it could be something as simple as running into an old friend on social media.

One day as I perused social media, I saw a friend was looking for a seminar speaker for his new company. Why didn't he think of me before he posted? Anyway, I contacted him. He asked how long it would take me to learn the two-hour seminar. I told him "Tomorrow," and I told him about the earpiece.

He exclaimed, "Whaaat?!? You can do a two-hour seminar by tomorrow on an earpiece?!?" I said, "Yes." He said, "Get to New York right away." The next day I flew to New York, and over the next year and a half made a small fortune with his company.

My point is your impulse could be *anything. Follow your impulse!*

****

What do you want? Do you want a better marriage? Then use your 1225 words and **the power of your tongue** to fill your heart full of happiness, peace, and joy.

Do you want your husband to help you with the dishes? Then speak the 1225 words and watch **the power of your tongue** kick into high gear to fill your heart full of happiness, peace, and joy, and then watch how your happiness, peace, and joy affect your husband.

What happens to you when you're full of that supernatural force? —You get stronger, wiser, and more patient, *and you'll melt his heart with your beauty!* And believe me when I say this girls, you will transform your man into Prince Charming when you walk around the house with a heart full of peace, happiness, tenderness, and a sense of calm. You'll make him change, but even if he doesn't…well, I'll go into greater detail how this works in your marriage and relationships in the third book of this trilogy *THE GREAT INVASION.*

Anyway, here's something else that happens when you *force-feed* happiness and peace into your heart by your 1225 words and **the power of your tongue**: There are those times that you need supernatural divine intervention over and above your human efforts, whether it's your marriage, your work, or your family, your business, your career, or your home, and in those times that you need that supernatural divine intervention, then your transcendent peace and supernatural happiness that you pound into your heart via **the power of your tongue** and the 1225 words *open the doors for God to intervene in your circumstances,* and **he catapults you to heights over and above your human limitations**.

How do you activate him?

How do you ignite his power?

How do you unearth the wisdom of the ages?

How do you wake up the sleeping giant called "The Lord of the Universe?"

How do you unearth the glorious emotions that the Jewish rabbi said lives inside you that he said to SEEK FIRST?

How? HOW? **HOW?**

"Speak the words…I'm right here."

Scene 58

Holy Street Fighter

During your long and arduous journey from where you are now to your promised land called *The Garden of Eden* where your dreams chase you down and overtake you, the Evil Queen fights you every step of the way. She persists, she fights you, she knocks you down, but God and you together kick her scrawny little ass every single time, whenever you want.

But how?

God's fought Israel's battles throughout the centuries, but how does he fight their battles, and how does he fight yours?

All throughout history, neighboring nations have tried to wipe Israel off the face of the earth.

So here's what God told Israel (Judah, actually) during one of these attempts by three surrounding armies that teamed up together to attack the Jews.

The year was around B.C. 898, and the Lord said to the king whose name is Jehoshaphat when several hostile armies surrounded him and the men of Judah, all of them poised for an attack: "Don't be afraid! Don't be paralyzed by this mighty army, for the battle is not yours, but God's!"

The main point here: *The battle is not yours.* If the battle is not yours, then whose is it? ***The battle is God's.***

The battle against your strong-willed impervious cancerous emotions is not yours because you're a wimp, a candy-assed sniveling limpdick wimp, but here's how you, Kippy the candy-ass limpdick wimp wins the fight:

You're little Kippy that gets bullied at school and then goes home and tells his big brother, and then big brother follows you back to school and kicks the bully's ass. You didn't fight the bullies. Your big brother did.

It's the same with God. It's God's battle. You're Kippy the little kid, God is your big brother, and you tell God about Billy the Bully that picks on you, so he follows you back to school and kicks Billy's ass. And since God fights Billy, then you have a 100% guarantee that you win. That's good odds, would you say? That's what makes this fight a hell-stomping good show because you know you win. God never loses. He wins every battle when you do your part. *What's your part?*

"Speak the words...I'm right here."

Speak the 1225 words by **the power of your tongue** like I did that sunny summer California afternoon in 1983 the day my green convertible died. When you speak the 1225 words then God shows up. *Like a flood* HE SHOWS UP; and when God shows up, he never loses—NEVER. God wins every time.

"Speak the words...I'm right here."

If your high-school football team is undefeated, you're 10-0 for the season, and your opponent lost every game this year, chances are good you'll kick their butts this Friday night.

You look forward to the final game of the season this Friday because you know most certainly your team will win, right? The two teams are unevenly matched. Your team is heavily favored to decisively win the game.

On that sunny summer California afternoon in 1983 the day my green convertible died it was a great game, because the two teams were unevenly matched. My team was heavily favored to win the game.

You Rest, God Fights, You Win

On that sunny summer California afternoon in 1983 the battle didn't belong to me. I didn't fight. No, no, Cheerio, who did the fight? Who fought the battle?

The power of my tongue and 1225 words fought my battle.

Therefore is it fair to say that God fought my battle since he is those 1225 words?

"Speak the words...I'm right here."

Today I'm so ultra-confident in **the power of my tongue** and 1225 words to fight my battles for me that it's a fun and exciting game to sit back and watch the 1225 words and **the power of my tongue** score a knockout blow every time I'm pissed...

...every time I'm angry...

...every time I have unforgiveness...

...every time I worry, stress, or get anxious.

My undefeated team of 1225 words and ***the power of my tongue*** *is heavily favored to win the football game Friday night!*

I win every fight and yet it's **not my fight** because I'm the spectator at a Las Vegas MMA event who watches from a distance up in the grandstands as my 1225 words and **the power of my tongue** kick the butt of my bloated out-of-shape overweight opponent who is the Evil Queen.

Yes, I do the fight and yet I don't. I'm merely a spectator who sits in the stands and watches the incredible rescue operation the Lord performs. I'm the fan who sits in the VIP section as I watch my 1225 words and **the power of my tongue** open up a can of whup-ass in a mighty flurry of action that does serious damage to the Evil Queen.

The odds are overwhelmingly in my favor that my 1225 words and THE POWER OF MY TONGUE win the fight.

What is required of me? Nothing. Not a damn thing.

I do nothing, except speak the 1225 words loudly enough for myself to hear, and thereby unleash the rudder of the ship—**the power of my tongue**—which then skillfully fights the Evil Queen.

"Speak the words...I'm right here."

Your chances of victory are as good as if the mighty military of the United States attacked the islanders of Foc-Foc Island where it rained six feet in one day. The islanders don't stand a "Fock-ing" chance against the might and power of the armed forces of the United States.

Thus I compare my thoughts and emotions to the islanders. The United States military is the 1225 words unleashed by **the phenomenal power of my devastatingly potent tongue**.

My sissified emotions haughtily parade about as if they're Superman, but my 1225 words and **the power of my tongue** are Superman's kryptonite.

My 1225 words and **the power of my tongue** are the Mighty Warrior that crushes my Evil Queen's emotions of worry, fear, doubt, and stress, and when the Prince of Peace hears those words, he fervently explodes in a flurry of wrath to leave the ninety-nine to come rescue me from the deathtrap of the Evil Queen.

"Speak the words…I'm right here."

****

My King, my Conqueror, my Prince of Peace gives me the victory every time as he kicks Billy the Bully's ass. The Las Vegas odds are 100% in my favor because of the supreme might of the 1225 words and **the vast power of my tongue**.

If I could place a bet on **the power of my tongue**, I'd take 100 to one odds that I win.

Life—victory—peace of mind—joy and happiness—all these are in **the power of your tongue**.

"Speak the words…I'm right here."

****

God continues his instructions to King Jehoshaphat. "Tomorrow, go down and attack them, but you will not need to fight. Take your places; stand and see the incredible rescue operation God will perform for you!" The story is found in 2 Chronicles 20:15-17, but you won't look it up.

How would you like for God to perform an incredible rescue operation for you?

God performs incredible rescue operations when his 1225 words and **the power of your tongue** *delivers you from your anger, pain, heartache, worry, stress, jealousy, and frustration.*

This victory is the secret map that leads you to everything you need, want, dream, and desire, including all the desires of your heart that he promised you.

Notice God tells Jehoshaphat and the army of Judah to attack, and then he adds, "But you will not need to fight."

That's an interesting juxtaposition, wouldn't you agree? You attack but ***you don't need to fight***.

In the next few minutes, you'll read about who won the battle but suffice it to say that God opened up a can of whup-ass on Judah's enemies, so even though you can already guess who won, what's remarkable—and it'll come as a shocking surprise to you is HOW it happened.

When God fights your battles, he tells you to attack but you need not fight. You attack with the audible written 1225 words and **the power of your tongue**, and twenty-one minutes later the 1225 words and **the power of your tongue** whips the Evil Queen's ass and wins the fight for you.

"Speak the words...I'm right here."

And then he describes your victory as "an incredible rescue operation." God performs an incredible rescue operation to save your ass from the Evil Queen's vices of anger, worry, stress, and those grudges against people that have hurt you.

It's remarkable that HE GIVES YOU THE CREDIT. Why does he give you the credit even though he fights your battles? Because YOU unleashed his power by **the power of YOUR tongue**.

YOU DID IT.

Yes, it is his 1225 words, but it is **the power of YOUR tongue** that teams up together *with the words* to release the Lord of the Universe so that God your creator fights your battles for you.

It's interesting that God gives YOU the credit because even though he is the 1225 words, he can't do anything without **the power of YOUR tongue!**

YOU! SIR! MA'AM! *"SPEAK THE WORDS! I'M RIGHT HERE!"*

Then what happens? You as a spectator sit mesmerized in the grandstands as you watch the two warriors duke it out in the Octagon on the floor of the arena. It's a contest between the Evil Queen versus your 1225 words and **the power of your tongue.** You cheer wildly as you sit in the stands, and drink in the refreshments of **the power of your tongue** and 1225 words, the twin armaments which then beat the shit out of the Evil Queen as you continually *force-feed* yourself full of peace—otherworldly transcendent supernatural peace that comes only from God himself in the form of 1225 words that you unleash by **the power of your tongue**—and isn't that the kingdom of God the Jewish rabbi says to seek first? And what happens next?

ALL THE DESIRES OF YOUR HEART GET ADDED TO YOU!

Whew, there goes the screeching sound of the speeding passenger train as the conductor slams on the brakes!

Don't Be a Lazy Ass

Now that you've learned that the blessings come on you and OVERTAKE you, does that mean you slack? Does that mean you don't work? Does that mean you nap on the couch all day? No, no, no, a thousand times no.

If I catch you sleeping on the couch all day because you think God magically drops blessings out of the sky, then I'm gonna slap you to sleep and then slap you for sleeping. If you don't *do something,* how can he multiply *nothing?* One hundred times zero is still zero. You must DO something. You must perform tasks. You must be diligent. "The hand of the diligent makes you rich."

Why do I warn you so sternly against slothful behavior that surreptitiously thinks God magically drops blessings out of the sky even if you're not diligent? Because in the beginning of my journey I was guilty of the same thing. Everything a man can do wrong in his quest for the kingdom of God, I did them all.

Laziness leads to poverty, but *diligence makes you rich* (Proverbs 10:4). F.M. Alexander put it this way, **"People do not decide their future, they decide their habits and their habits decide their futures."**

Diligence, combined with peace and happiness, is the mastery of the ages. Running a business requires diligence. Authoring a book takes diligence. A successful career requires diligence. Unleashing 1225 words by the power of your tongue takes diligence. Praying in the spirit requires diligence. Being a hairstylist takes diligence. A successful happy family requires diligence. Whatever you want in life demands diligence. You want a fit body…takes diligence.

Your future hides inside your *diligence.* Your daily routine is your diligence, which is to say your small steps that lead to big results.

It's easier to hold back the dawn than it is to hold back a man's success when he's diligent in his labors AND when he force-feeds peace and happiness into his heart AND when he takes care of the poor, the fatherless, and the widow

****

Let's finish that story about Jehoshaphat. You already know who wins, but what's fascinating is HOW he wins. Remember God said to attack but you will not need to fight, for the battle is the Lord's.

God says, "Tomorrow march down against them. They will be climbing up by the Pass of Ziz, and you will find them at the end of the gorge in the Desert of Jeruel."

And then he tells them, "You ***will not have to fight this battle***. Take up your positions; stand firm and see the deliverance the Lord will give you, Judah and Jerusalem. Do not be afraid; do not be discouraged. Go out to face them tomorrow, and the Lord will be with you."

Jehoshaphat bowed down with his face to the ground, and all the people of Judah and Jerusalem fell down in worshipped before the Lord. Then some Levites from the Kohathites and Korahites stood up and praised the Lord, the God of Israel, with a very loud voice." Notice they praised God with a very loud voice. Why? *Because praise stills the avenger.* Who's the avenger? THE EVIL QUEEN! Who's the Evil Queen? Your ratchet heart!!

They had to crush their ratchet hearts to win the battle!

"SPEAK THE WORDS…I'M RIGHT HERE."

Isn't that what I've drilled into your brain for the last three hundred and fifty pages?!? The power of your 1225 words and **the power of your tongue** *stills the avenger.* Who's the avenger?

You are! YOU are the avenger. YOU are the enemy. It's YOUR *ratchet heart of cantankerous emotions* that blocks the power of God that's buried deep inside you like David was buried deep inside the seventeen-foot-high block of marble.

When you crush your ratchet heart's emotions, then the power of God rises like a mighty warrior to crush the Evil Queen and opens wide the doors to the desires of your heart!

Anything else?

Yes. *A man has joy by the answer of his mouth.* Your 1225 words and **the power of your tongue** are "*the answer of your mouth*" that fights your battles.

"Speak the words…I'm right here."

And one more since we're on the topic of joy… Why is joy important?

BECAUSE: *The joy of the Lord is your strength.* For what reason do you need strength? TO OVERCOME YOUR PISSY LITTLE RATCHET SELF!

When you overcome your pissy self you UNBLOCK the kingdom of God, and when you unblock the kingdom of God, then he rises from dormancy where he's lain inactive inside you.

He then fights your battles for you, and when the 1225 words and **the power of your tongue** unleash the glory of God to destroy the Evil Queen, then ALL THE DESIRES OF YOUR HEART COME A-RUNNIN'.

Your first and foremost duty, obligation, and line of attack is to *force-feed* yourself full of inexplicable peace and unsurpassable joy and happiness like I did that sunny summer California afternoon in 1983 the day my green convertible died, and when you do, this is the kingdom of God the Jewish rabbi says to seek first, and when you seek, pursue, and attain the kingdom then *all these things will be added to you which includes, but is not limited to* **all the desires of your heart**.

You accomplish all of this by your almighty powerful 1225 words that you unleash by **the power of your tongue** like I did that sunny summer California afternoon in 1983 the day my green convertible died, and that's how you unleash the kingdom of God which is joy and peace, and that's when THE PRINCE OF PEACE fights your battles.

I'll say it again: Use your 1225 words and **the power of your tongue** to uncover that which has lain dormant in you for decades, and it's this mighty force of peace that passes all understanding that lives in you that arises from dormancy to fight your battles for you!

"Speak the words…I'm right here."

****

Back to the story. Early in the morning they left for the Desert of Tekoa. As they set out, Jehoshaphat stood and said, "Listen to me, Judah and people of Jerusalem! Have faith in the Lord your God and you will be upheld; have faith in his prophets and you will be successful."

I gotta take another rabbit trail here. Notice Jehoshaphat said to have faith in the Lord your God AND to have faith in his prophets. Is "faith in his prophets" the same as "have faith in God"? In this scripture, yes, it's a parallelism. Look it up, parallelism, but I don't have the space to write about it here, although I cover parallelisms in detail in the next volume of this trilogy *Shitty to Happy in 21 Minutes: THE EVIL QUEEN.*

What is faith in God? The English dictionary defines "faith" as **the assent of the mind to the truth of a proposition or statement for which there is not complete evidence.**

May I submit to you that the English meaning of the word "faith" is NOT what the word means in Hebrew!

Whaaat Steve?!? Every preacher says that's what faith is. Every book ever written about FAITH says that's what faith is. Now you're telling me that's NOT what faith is?

I hate to burst your religious bubble, but no, that's not what the word means. If that's what the word means, then this entire trilogy is a fraud, it's a fake, it's heretical, and you need to have a book-burning party in your back yard.

Why? Because what have I said ad nauseum about sincerity? That you don't need it, right? Isn't "sincerity" faith? In other words, "You gotta believe what you're saying is true or else the 1225 words don't work. If you don't believe what you're saying is true, then you're a cackling cockatoo."

I told a white lie when I said, "I hate to burst your religious bubble." I LOVE bursting religious bubbles, can you tell?

So anyway, WHAT IS FAITH? Get ready Pretty Lady and Mr. Humble Man, because y'all are about to hear something wickedly cool you ain't NEVER heard before!

****

Scene 59

What Is Faith?

Ladies and Gentlemen, may I introduce you to the greatest power known to man: The gift that God gives us to overcome our fears, our doubts, our unbelief, and *our lack of faith.*

I'll show you how God helps us to annihilate our despairing pleas as we cry out in desperation, "I TRY SO HARD to believe your amazing promises, but no matter how hard I try *I just can't believe them!"*

In other words, "I don't have faith to believe God because his promises are so huge, beyond mind-blowing, and they're phenomenal, they're life-changing, *and because they're so big, I can't wrap my mind around them. I can't comprehend them. I try to, I try to believe him and his promises, I really do, but no matter how hard I try, I can't."*

Have you ever been there? If you can fog a mirror, then yes, you've been there.

So what's the solution?

God gives us a flawless energy and immutable force that empowers us to believe every word he says. It's an energy that overrides our doubt-filled scrawny little mind. This flawless force and energy that God gives us to overrule our doubt-filled selves is [DRUM ROLL PLEASE] the **power of our tongue** and 1225 words.

Did you expect me to give you another answer other than the basics like UCLA Coach John Wooden, Kobe Bryant, and the Jewish rabbi proclaim? Would you rather hear an assemblage of deep revelations because you're "bored with the basics"? If so, you go right ahead and download another "Three Steps to Believe God" seven-week series where the preacher gums you to death, but I prefer to stick with the basics of "Seek first, the kingdom of God, with his incredible emotions of happiness, peace, and joy, and all these things will be added to me."

But I digress. Do you want to know what faith is? **Put your 1225 words and the power of your tongue into action.** *That's faith.*

What is faith? **The power of your tongue** and 1225 words overrides every faulty thought, every doubt, every unbelief. *That's faith.*

What is faith? **The power of your tongue** and 1225 words crushes your anger at God. *That's faith.*

What is faith? **The power of your tongue** and 1225 words overcomes every worry, every fear, every anxiety, every DOUBT, and EVERY UNBELIEF that goes contrary to the words of King David in Psalm 37:4 where he says, "Delight yourself in the Lord and HE WILL GIVE YOU THE DESIRES OF YOUR HEART." Do you have a hard time believing that God will give you all the desires of your heart? *Well, I have good news!* **The power of your tongue** and 1225 words jam-packs you full of confidence to believe God's amazing promise to give you all the desires of your heart! *That's faith.*

The English definition of the word "faith" places stupid amounts of undue pressure on you to "perform," undue pressure *to assent with the mind the truth of a proposition or statement for which there is not complete evidence.*

Fuck that shit.

God makes "faith" so easy that you argue with him, and you argue with me that "it can't be this simple," just like I've argued with God countless times over the last forty years, "It can't be this simple," and isn't it what I said in the first few pages of this book how simple God's plan for happiness, peace, and joy is?

What is faith in biblical Hebrew? It's an ACTION. It's a verb. It's NOT a state of mind. This is the subject for another book, but suffice it to say that faith is:

ONE: Speak the 1225 words out loud, and thus **the power of your tongue** kicks into high gear to *force-feed* peace that is not of this world into your heart, and when you do, then this otherworldly peace gives you the confidence that ALL THESE THINGS THE RABBI PROMISES, which includes all the desires of your heart, **WILL BE ADDED TO YOU**.

That's REAL faith, and certainly not the kind of religious gobbledygook that your preacher heard from another preacher who heard it from another preacher who heard his grandma say what faith is.

It's like your mom cuts off both ends of the ham. You, the inquisitive student who "questions the answers" asks "Why?"

"Because my mother did it." You ask your mom's mom, "Grandma why'd you cut off both sides of the ham?" *Because your great grandma did it,* so you ask great grandma, "Why'd you cut off both sides of the ham?"

Great grandma says, "Because the ham was too big to fit in my oven."

That's why I question the answers, and when we **question the answers**, we might very well discover a biblical definition of faith that astounds the pharisaical mind, because what "faith" did you conjure up to speak 1225 words with **the power of your tongue**?

What role did you play in having extraordinary faith?

NOTHING you simpleton (of which I am chiefest) …not a cotton-pickin' thing.

Your only act of faith for which you can take credit is that you unleashed **THE GOD-GIVEN POWER OF YOUR TONGUE**, the tiny, miniscule lifeless rudder that in turn controls your great big mighty ship, a ship that's tossed by fierce winds and crashing waves of doubt, fear of failure, and unbelief. I ask you: *Other than* ***the power of your tongue****, what did you do?* YOU DID NOTHING! Did you hear me? **YOU DID NOTHING!**

Your God-built, God-ordained rudder that you discharge as in a military action as you unleash the 1225 words removes all obstacles so that, like greased lightning, you easily comprehend God's promises. How? By the mighty power of 1225 words and **the unassailable undeniable victorious power of your tongue**.

THAT'S TRUE FAITH!

Did you *mentally assent to the truth of a proposition or statement for which there is not complete evidence?*

No silly boy, you didn't!

You didn't engage your mind at all except to speak the 1225 words out loud so that **the power of your tongue** kicks into high gear to slam-dunk the peace of God that passes all understanding into your heart like a mighty rushing wind.

Did you create the 1225 words? No you didn't.

Did you create **the power of your tongue**? No, not that either.

Did you create the *peace that passes all understanding* by which you can believe all things? No, you didn't do that, either.

You didn't do jack shit! ***Except SPEAK.*** *That's ALL you did!*

God created the words AND the rudder. *You simply OBEYED the Jewish rabbi to "seek first the kingdom of God" by your 1225 words and* ***the power of your tongue,*** and thereby you release from the caverns of your heart the *peace that passes all understanding.* Now that you've unleashed the kingdom, it's HIS PEACE that gives you the ability to believe all things. *When you dwell in The Secret Place of the Most High you can believe darn near anything!* ANYTHING!

God's Dual Creations Fight Your Battles for You

The power of your tongue is the rudder of the ship.

THE RUDDER—the **RUDDER**—*THE* ***RUDDER*** does EVERY BIT OF THE WORK. You do none of the work. You're rudder does the work.

ALL THE WORK!

That's faith.

So what is faith? Let's keep moving along.

ONE: *"Speak the words…I'm right here."* **That's faith.**

TWO: Be diligent in your labors, in your study, in your business, in your family, in your body, and in all your hand finds to do, because "the hand of the diligent makes you rich." *That's faith.*

THREE: Take care of the poor, the fatherless, and the widow. *That's faith.*

How do I know these are faith? Look at the fruit, that's how. What's the fruit? What do you see? Do you see fruit? If so, what fruit do you see?

Let's look at the fruit.

The *fruit of the spirit* is love, joy, peace, patience, kindness and the rest, all of which are EMOTIONS.

That's right, the end result of these 1225 words and **the power of your tongue** are the fruits of happiness, peace, and joy—EMOTIONS!

I challenge you to prove that these feelings are anything other than EMOTIONS.

EMOTIONS are one of the inevitable result of the 1225 words and ***the power of your tongue****.*

Therefore, when you *force-feed* yourself full of these supernatural otherworldly kingdom of God EMOTIONS then you are *possessed with, controlled by, and compelled by* the **fruit of the spirit**—*SUPERNATURAL OTHERWORLDLY EMOTIONS*—

...Kingdom of God emotions that you *force-feed* into your heart by the power of 1225 words and **the power of your tongue**—

...Emotions that are the pearl of great value—

...It is these supernatural otherworldly EMOTIONS that assure that **you WILL, you WILL, you WILL get everything you need, hope for, dream, wish for, and desire**. *THAT'S FAITH!*

These EMOTIONS are the dipstick that gives you confidence that your engine is full of clean oil. *That's faith.*

These EMOTIONS are the sure sign that you're on the right track and the result is that ALL THE THINGS YOU WANT WILL BE ADDED TO YOU. *That's faith.*

These otherworldly transcendent incontrovertible EMOTIONS are **the Kingdom of God**.

That's faith!

Faith is Actions, also Known as Behavior

Faith is "actions." It's *behavior.* What actions? What behavior? Three ACTIONS, three BEHAVIORS. **ONE**: Diligence in all that your hand finds to do. **TWO**: Take care of the poor, the fatherless, and the widow. **THREE**: 1225 words and **the power of your tongue** to *force-feed* the mighty powers of happiness, peace, and joy into your heart like I did that sunny summer California afternoon in 1983 the day my green convertible died.

These three actions, these three behaviors are the "substance" of things hoped for, the "evidence" of things not seen.

How do I know you'll achieve your heart's desires whatever they are, even though I can't SEE them?

FAITH.

BEHAVIOR.

What is faith? Faith is your behavior. Faith is your actions. What actions? What behavior?

ONE: Diligence to pursue the desires of your heart.

TWO: Take care of the poor, the fatherless, and the widow.

THREE: 1225 words and **the power of your tongue** to slam dunk the kingdom of God EMOTIONS of happiness, peace, and joy into your heart, to kick the Evil Queen off of your throne, and to exalt the kingdom of God to take its rightful place in your life, which is to say, to propel you into the throne room of the Most High God, the reverential palatial estate known as *The Secret Place of the Most High.*

I Ask You: What is the Kingdom of God?

What's the kingdom of God that opens doors for you? It's the EMOTIONS of happiness, peace, and joy, all of them supernatural, all of them otherworldly, all of them from another dimension outside of our three-dimensional world, and yet reside on the inside of us, like David was buried inside the seventeen-foot-high block of marble.

I know your FUTURE RESULTS when I see your PRESENT BEHAVIOR.

That's faith!

That's so good I'm gonna say it again: ***I know your future results when I see your present behavior.***

That's faith.

Your *present actions,* your *immediate behaviors* are the **substance** of things hoped for, your *present actions,* your *immediate behavior* is the **evidence** of things not yet seen (Hebrews 11:1).

I'll eventually see your RESULTS when I see your PRESENT BEHAVIOR.

That's faith!

"Speak the words...I'm right here."

****

Shall we continue on our quest to "Question the Answers"?

LET'S KEEP MOVING!

Scene 60

See Your Future

How do I see your future? How do I know you'll be a successful lawyer? I watch your behavior; I watch your habits. Like Mr. Alexander said, "You don't decide your future. You decide your habits. Your habits decide your future."

I Watch Your Habits

As a future lawyer, what are your habits? You sign up for LSAT, you enroll in law school, you study, you studiously tackle your books, you argue cases, you get clients, and you'd damn well better be sure a lawyer is what you want because "lawyer" is what you'll get, as long as you **ONE**: Seek first happiness, peace, and joy **TWO**: Be diligent in all your hand finds to do, and **THREE**: Take care of the poor, the fatherless, and the widow. *That's how I know your future.*

I must add number **FOUR**: Make sure whatever you pursue is a desire of your heart, because if "lawyer" is what you desire, then "lawyer" is what you'll get, so carefully examine your desires.

These LAWYER HABITS, ACTIONS, and ACTIVITIES are the biblical definition of faith and it's *your lawyer actions, habits, and actions* that are the substance of things hoped for, *your lawyer actions, habits, and activities* that are the evidence of things not seen. *Your lawyer actions, habits, and activities* show me, your friends, yourself, and your family, and anyone else who's curious that *you'll be a lawyer.*

I see your habits. ***That's lawyer faith!***

I'm gonna say something that'll rock a lot of boats, but I'll say it anyway. If you're a Christian that ascribes to the English meaning of the word "faith" as *the ascent of the mind to the truth of a proposition or statement for which there is not complete evidence* then it'll take more than a library of books to convince you otherwise, and even then many will remain riveted to a concept taught to them since childhood about what faith is; like you mom adheres to the belief that she should cut off both ends of the ham. However, as you can see this book is not written for Christians. Yes, many Christians will grasp these principles, but many won't. *Many will reject them.*

So to all of the closed-minded church folk, you just sit tight in the front row of your shitty fucky little church club that never gets shit done for the kingdom of God, and sit back and watch from inside the four walls of *The First Church of the Frozen Chosen,* and watch these young lions take ahold of the gospel of peace, and spread the message of transcendent otherworldly supernatural peace that is the kingdom of God far and wide because they acknowledge the song we all learned as a little kid, "Jesus loves me this I know, for the bible tells me so, little ones to him belong, *they are weak* BUT HE IS STRONG."

Who are THEY that are weak? Me. You. Everybody. Your aunt, your granddaddy, your kids. Your wife. Your husband. Your cows.

Who's HE that is strong? **HE that is strong is the 1225 words** that you resurrect from death to life from deep within your innermost being by **the mighty God-given glorious supernatural power of your tongue**.

Who's the HE that is strong? **HE** that is strong is the 1225 words that created the universe (John 1:3). **HE THAT IS STRONG** is the 1225 words loaded with 18 kilotons of TNT packed inside the words—*words* that are GOD HIMSELF.

Speeding passenger train...!!!

Excuse me while I SHOUT IT FROM THE MOUNTAINTOPS—

"Speak the words...He's right here!"

If you insist that "faith" is your human ability to *mentally agree with the truth of a proposition or statement*—a statement for which there is *not complete evidence,* then muthafucka you can count me out.

There's not an ice cube's chance in hell that I can do that. I find it impossible to work up a "belief" such as that! It puts undue pressure on ME to perform.

I can't perform. I can't work up a belief.

However, if faith is ACTION that overrides my repugnant weakness of unbelief...

If faith is an action that taps into HIS and ONLY his strength which is the 1225 words and **the power of my tongue**…

If faith is the power of **HIS** 1225 words and **the power of MY tongue** that HE gives ME to open up the doors to the kingdom of God which then opens the doors to the Garden of Eden…

If it's HE who lives inside me that does these incredible mountain-moving operations in spite of my feeble ability to comprehend that he does such feats in spite of my fears, doubts, anger, worry, and stress…

Then **good God Almighty with a dash of mighty alrighty** I CAN DO THAT!

Sing it boys and girls, "**We are weak,** but HE IS STRONG."

I don't fight. HE does!

How does he fight?

"Speak the words…I'm right here."

But I digress. I have more to tell you about the story of Jehoshaphat.

After consulting the people, Jehoshaphat appointed men to sing to the Lord and to praise him for the splendor of his holiness as they went out ahead of the army, saying: "Give thanks to the Lord, for his love endures forever."

Let's park here for a moment. What did the Lord tell Jehoshaphat to do? He told him to appoint men to sing to the Lord and to praise him for the splendor of his holiness as they went out ahead of the army and shouted, "Give thanks to the Lord, for his love endures forever."

Now stop and think about this. Let's say the United States is under attack, and the president says, "Let the praise guys go out first in front of the infantry and the tanks." Can you imagine if you're one of the praisers that's assigned to go into battle in front of the tanks, the military, the missiles, and the soldiers, and the president commands you to gather a couple hundred of your buddies, your rabble-rousing fraternity brothers, and instead of drunkenly stealing bags of business exams from the dumpster outside the business building of Florida State, or instead of 150 freshmen at Florida Southern College pushing the fire engine into Lake Hollingsworth at the bottom of the hill, you guys corporately shout at the top of your lungs, "Give thanks to the Lord, for his love endures forever!" I'd have to serve my guys lots of vodka before they'd do that, and yet that's exactly what King Jehoshaphat told his gang of rabble-rousing praisers to do, minus the vodka.

****

How does this apply to you and me today, right now, in the 21st century? The praisers were the tribe of Judah, and they always led first in battle. God told Jehoshaphat, “Send Judah out in front of the armies” (Judges 20:18).

Even so, when you have a fight on your hands, send your praises up first.

And isn’t that what I’ve been preaching for over three hundred and fifty pages? Seek FIRST the kingdom of God—happiness, peace, and joy. How? By the PRAISES of your mouth, which is the 1225 words and **the power of your tongue** that you sling out into the skies, and like a boomerang they turn right around and attack your vile heart to fill it with immense otherworldly peace and indescribable happiness, that when you do, God rises from slumber from deep inside you to fight your battles, and when God fights your battles, YOU WIN!

Well hallelujah, spit the onions out of your mouth because you’re a champion. Take a victory lap. THE CONQUEST IS YOURS!

That’s faith.

From now on when you’re in a hellhole and your life is a shitshow, then your first and foremost line of attack is to shout the 1225 words by **the power of your tongue**. Why? Because these 1225 words and **the power of your tongue** LEAD YOU INTO BATTLE as they *force-feed* HIS happiness, HIS peace, and HIS joy into your heart, just like what happened to me that sunny summer California afternoon in 1983 the day my green convertible died, and when you dethrone the Evil Queen, and thus YOU take your rightful place on the throne in the palatial estate of *The Secret Place of the Most High*, then ALL THE DESIRES OF YOUR HEART WILL BE ADDED TO YOU! *That’s faith.*

“Speak the words…I’m right here.” That’s faith.

Let these mighty forces of the 1225 words and **the power of your tongue** fight your battles for you. *That’s faith.*

Who’s the battle against? Who’s your enemy?

Your enemy is your pissy, bitchy, whiney, complainer self who is depressed, anxiety-ridden, worried, stressed, pissed off, and angry. Every one of these is an EVIL QUEEN EMOTION, ever so venomous so as to paralyze God’s kingdom power like the poisonous venom of a viper paralyzes its prey; like kryptonite paralyzes Superman’s power. Is that you, Mr. Kryptonite Man? Maybe not today, but yesterday or last week?

We ALL have our Evil Queen, and she's a formidable foe; that is, until you pull back the curtain like Toto pulled back the curtain to reveal a decrepit old geezer whose wife is nowhere to be found, he lives on social security, he's gotta pee every twenty minutes, and he can't get a boner.

****

Let's continue with the story. As they began to sing and praise, the Lord set ambushments against the men of Ammon and Moab and Mount Seir who were invading Judah, and they were defeated.

Did you catch that? THEY WERE DEFEATED. But how? *How were they defeated?*

Oh Ladies and Gentlemen, this is where this gets juicy goosy Lucy good.

The three armies that sought to annihilate the men from Judah, they were the Ammonites, the Moabites, and the men from Mount Seir, all of them filled with profound rage at the men of Judah. They hated the Jews back then just like Israel's neighboring countries hate them today. In fact, only the names of the countries have changed. Israel's modern-day enemies are the same regions from which the Moabites, the Ammonites, and the men from Mount Seir lived several thousand years ago.

Back to the story, and it's quite strange how it went down.

Jehoshaphat's enemies, the Ammonites and Moabites turned against the men from Mount Seir to destroy and annihilate them. That's a bit odd, don't you think, that two of the three armies annihilated the third army? *They're on the same team!*

What if the Dallas Cowboys offensive line turned around and tackled their own quarterback? Or the Lakers dunked baskets on their side of the court? *That's what these armies did!*

But it gets even better. After the Ammonites and the Moabites finished slaughtering the men from Mount Seir, there's only two armies left. The two armies looked at each other with confused looks on their faces, and shouted, "KILL 'EM!" and proceeded to **slaughter each other**.

Notice that Jehoshaphat and the men of Judah haven't even arrived yet. Meanwhile the Ammonites and the Moabites who just finished their killing spree against the men from Mount Seir, are now in a killing spree against each other. Remember, they're all on the same team. Fucking idiots.

Where were Jehoshaphat and the men of Judah who *haven't even shown up yet?* They're still in the hot desert out there somewhere praising God like a pack of wild hyenas like I did that sunny summer California afternoon in 1983 the day my green convertible died, and like that time I sat in the back of a stinky bus in LA, two hours late for my interview for the Detroit auto show, stuck in the cold rain, praising God to protect my heart with the ferocity of a momma bear who guards her cubs.

****

So anyway, in a nutshell here's what happened: Armies one and two—the Ammonites and the Moabites—slaughtered army number three, the men from Mount Seir. After armies one and two slaughtered army number three, then armies number one and two slaughtered each other until no man was left standing.

In other words, Judah's enemies got confused, and in their state of bumbling foolhardiness they turned their swords against one another. They pulled out their weapons and massacred each other until no man was left standing. Well except I guess for one lone guy, and I wouldn't be surprised if he freaked out over all the dead soldiers that killed each other and said, "Fuck it," and stabbed his own damn self.

Jehoshaphat and the men from Judah STILL haven't shown up yet. They're still out in the blistering desert praising God. I guess they went longer than 21 minutes.

****

The moral of the story is that all three armies, all the neighboring countries that were the enemies of Israel that exist even today in the modern-day Middle East confusingly turned on themselves to kill one another just like the Evil Queen turns on herself and in her state of flabbergasted stupidity stabs her own damn self in the heart. What the Evil Queen means for evil, you turn her power around to work for your good.

YOU INCITE HER FURY TO TURN AGAINST HERSELF SO THAT SHE STABS HERSELF IN THE HEART JUST LIKE JUDAH'S ENEMIES MERCILESSLY ANNIHILATED EACH OTHER.

How did Jerusalem, Judah, and Jehoshaphat defeat their enemies?

THE RABBLE-ROUSING KICK-ASS PRAISERS WENT FIRST.

That's faith.

PLOT TWIST!

Incidentally, if you remember the English meaning of the word "faith," it's *the assent of the mind to the truth of a proposition or statement for which there is not complete evidence.* Wouldn't it be nice to have that mental and heartfelt conviction that your life is in God's hands, that your career is a certainty, and wouldn't it be nice to reach that level of nirvana to have that heartfelt conviction of the English meaning of the word "faith!"

Well guess what? When you *force-feed* your heart, mind, and soul full of the transcendent otherworldly peace that passes all understanding by the 1225 words and **the power of your tongue,** then lo and behold your mind easily latches onto the promises of God so that you wholeheartedly expect them just as naturally as you expect the sun to come up in the morning.

In other words *you* EASILY *mentally assent to the truth of a proposition or statement for which there is not complete evidence!*

You had it backward this whole time. You tried to *mentally assent to the truth of a proposition or statement for which there is not complete evidence* **so that you could have peace!**

No fool! Your ability to comprehend God's promises comes **AFTER** you *force-feed* yourself full of transcendent otherworldly peace. Got it? Seek FIRST the transcendent incomprehensible peace that is the mysterious kingdom, also known as THE SECRET PLACE OF THE MOST HIGH. When you're in *The Secret Place of the Most High* then IT'S EASY to believe God's promises.

That's right dingleberry, you tried to mentally assent to God's promises **BEFORE** you pursued the kingdom of God of happiness, peace, and joy.

You had it backward.

Well guess what, when you fill yourself full of transcendent otherworldly peace by **the power of your tongue** and 1225 words like I did that sunny summer California afternoon in 1983 the day my green convertible died, then it is easy to *mentally assent to the truth of a proposition or statement for which there is not complete evidence!*

****

Nice plot twist, huh?

What's faith?

"Speak the words…I'm right here."

That's faith. It's simple.

INTERMISSION

Scene 61

God Polishes Turds

Let's revisit Paul's letter where he says it's impossible for him to be a good man when all hell breaks loose in his noggin, yet there's a part of him that wants to do what is right but there's also that dominant part of him that wants to do bad. Also remember the bad part of him is stronger than the good part of him, like Johnny Cash quips, "Sometimes I'm two people. Johnny is the nice one. Cash causes all the trouble. They fight."

Paul you see, like you and me, and Johnny Cash…we all have our pissy little selves.

God created all things, even that "pissy little self" part of you called the Evil Queen. So if God created that part of you that wants to be bad, do you think maybe there's a useful aspect of that evil part of you that works for your good? And if so, how?

If anybody can polish a turd, God can. That's a Baby Boomer sage-ism. Here's the Gen Z version: If anybody can turn shit to bling, God can.

If he turns a lump of coal, a smelly, dirty, ugly piece of coal into a sparkling diamond that princes and kings pay millions to adorn their women and themselves and does so with tons of the earth's heat and bone-crushing weight of the planet onto an ugly piece of coal, carbon actually, then certainly he can turn your smelly, dirty, ugly piece of anger into a sparkling diamond by the Evil Queen's very own flaming fires and bone-crushing pressure. Her heat and pressure intensify the 1225 words and **the power of your tongue** to cause an explosive eruption of peace and joy!

Coal, plus heat, plus pressure equals diamonds. Start with the coal, add tons of pressure and intense heat, and out pops the diamond. *Thank you God.*

"You're welcome."

A diamond is actually carbon similar to coal. What would you think if a wife on her tenth wedding anniversary opens her husband's gift, she looks into the box and says, "What the hell?!? You bought me a piece of coal?!?" She looks at it again. *"You bought me coal?!?"*

He retorts, "Sweetheart, it's a diamond."

She argues, "I studied geology. It's a piece of coal. Take me home, you ain't gettin' any tonight."

The husband says, "Babe, I'd rather stare at National Geographic photos of Sub-Sahara baboons multi-colored butts than look at your face right now. Let's go, and you pay for dinner."

However they both assiduously studied "How to Have a Happy Marriage" in volume three in this trilogy called *Shitty to Happy in 21 Minutes: THE GREAT INVASION* and they rush to the car and have stupendous make-up sex in the parking lot before they go back inside and order dessert—a double-chocolate cake smothered in ice cream, even bigger than the cute little girl's birthday cake at her party back in 1960.

Coal is black and nasty, it's greasy and causes lung cancer. It's dirty, filthy, and smelly, but when you add thousands of pounds of pressure plus the intense fires of the earth's blazing inferno to the coal, then what happens? Out pops a beautiful, sparkly, elegant chick magnet—a gorgeous diamond.

Compare that piece of coal to your anger. Anger is black and nasty, it's greasy, and causes lung cancer. It's dirty. It's filthy. Now add thousands of pounds of the Evil Queen's pressure plus the intense fires of her blazing inferno to the anger and what happens? Out pops joy that like a diamond is a beautiful, sparkly, elegant chick magnet.

Here's another piece of advice to you guys: Do you wanna look hot for your girl? When someone is rude to you, or they cut you off on the freeway, or your food server is slow and incompetent, and you want to act like a bad ass to impress your girl, nope, that is not the way to do it. It turns her off worse than smelly balls.

But when you return kindness for rudeness, sweetness for incompetence, she feels a strong yet gentle man. *Girls get hot for a strong man.* A strong man is a chick magnet. Guys, when you're tempted to go macho anger in front of your girl, instead crush your anger, *force-feed* peace into your heart, treat rudeness with kindness, and she sees you as a hottie and wants to drop her pants.

Hey Christians, the ones on the front row of the church pews, does that make you squeamish when I say girls wanna drop their pants for a man that walks in the peace of God? Flip through your bible to Song of Solomon, and then tell me how you get offended when I say girls wanna drop their pants for a man who walks in supernatural, otherworldly transcendent peace that's beyond the ability of the human mind to comprehend. Girls and guys, does this make you want to read the Bible?

Let's get back to the diamonds, the coal, and your anger.

The pressure and the heat that squeeze your anger is that forceful pressure of the Evil Queen's noxious emotions that you fuse with the 1225 words and **the power of your tongue**.

The Evil Queen's anger runs headlong into a brick wall. She does a radical turnabout when she massacres herself with her own anger as she thirstily drinks the anti-poison of the 1225 words that you ignite by **the power of your tongue.**

You feel an odd stirring deep inside of you as **the power of your tongue** crushes the Evil Queen's anger and *force-feeds* otherworldly peace and unspeakable happiness into your heart like what happened to me the day when I stumbled upon this magnificent revelation that sunny summer California afternoon in 1983 the day my green convertible died.

The intense heat and pressure of your Evil Queen's plethora of noxious emotions that you infuse into the 1225 words, plus **the power of your tongue** produce the diamond-like qualities of joy unspeakable and full of glory as they transform your anger into peace. The inescapable flood of peace and happiness that originates from another world, a world deep inside the human heart swells within you like a river overflows its banks.

Start with your wickedly vile anger, fuse your vile anger into your 1225 words, ignite them with **the power of your tongue** to spark a fantabulous nuclear explosion, and BOOM.

Out from the anger pops joy! *Thank you, God!*

"You're welcome."

****

Scene 62

Two Splendiferous Mindfuckifications

More coal equals more diamonds

If you start with enough coal to fill three football stadiums, you'll have more diamonds than you know what to do with. What does that have to do with anger?

If you start with enough anger to fill three football stadiums, you'll have more than enough happiness to get you all the desires of your heart.

Follow my logic and I'll prove it to you. The next time you're obsessed with anger, or worry, or fear and doubt that your dreams are dead, your life feels hopeless, and you're ready to give up, then by golly speak the 1225 words WITH THE ANGER, FEAR, AND HOPELESSNESS that you feel.

Speak them *with the worry* that you feel.

Speak the words *with the discouragement* and *fear of failure* that you feel.

Speak the words *with the frustration* that you feel.

Your 1225 words and **the power of your tongue** work more quickly and efficiently when you fill them full to overflowing with your noxious emotions, your vile, and wicked emotions like what I did that sunny summer California afternoon in 1983 the day my green convertible died, and like what I did in 2018 on the treadmill when I was worried, fretful, and jealous over my new girlfriend.

In other words, take advantage of the immense heat and pressure of the Evil Queen's noxious emotions.

The Evil Queen unwittingly intensifies **the power of your tongue** like the earth's heat and pressure intensifies the transformation of the coal into a diamond. Thus THE MORE ANGER YOU HAVE, the more powerfully you *force-feed* elegant joy unspeakable and full of glory into your heart, the otherworldly emotions that adorn you with the jewels of transcendent peace that is not of this world, a supernatural peace that is buried way down deep inside you like the coal is buried way down deep inside the earth.

Start with the Evil Queen's anger, doubt, and fear of failure, then apply the massive pressure of those toxic emotions onto the 1225 words and **the power of your tongue**. This infuses her wicked forces into your words like the earth's intense heat and pressure exerts force onto the coal, which then transforms that piece of coal into a sparkling diamond. So therefore:

The more coal you start with...
the more diamonds you end with.

The more anger you start with...
the more peace you end with!

When you pour the Evil Queen's white-hot burning phosphorous of fear of failure, anger, worry, and stress into your 1225 words, the Evil Queen's noxious fumes accelerate the fires of **the power of your tongue** to convert those nauseating emotions into peace and joy, just like the heat and pressure of the earth convert the foul smelly coal into a sparkling diamond so elegant and beautiful.

This defies human logic. It also irritates the brain-dead Pharisees, those bumfuzzled religious leaders who don't know baby shit from butterscotch. "You must feel sincere," they pontificate, which is why nobody listens to them.

The diamond starts out an ugly piece of coal, but the intense heat and pressure inside the earth turns it into a sparkling, elegant, beautiful piece of jewelry that woman adorn their necks, their ears, their nose, and their bodies.

Even so your anger starts out an ugly, vile, and noxious emotion, but the intense heat and pressure of your anger fused with the 1225 words and **the power of your tongue** converts the ugly, vile, putrid anger into a sparkling diamond of beautiful transcendent peace that is not of this world, a peace that originates from another dimension, yet lives inside of us.

Just as miraculous as the earth's heat and pressure convert coal from deep in the earth into diamonds for the harvesters to gather, even so your 1225 "biblical cuss words" and **the power of your tongue** mysteriously unearth the treasures of peace and joy from deep within you for the harvesters to gather.

Can you see why it took me so many years to recognize this? This is some crazy shit. The last few paragraphs go contrary to every sermon, every book, and every internet article on happiness I ever read.

No preacher ever taught me this radical approach to use the Evil Queen's anger to your advantage. I've never read a book or an article that told me to corral the Evil Queen's nefarious power so that it supercharges your 1225 words and **the power of your tongue** to rapidly *force-feed* peace into your heart so that you live prosperously every day, all day, and every moment of every day in *The Secret Place of the Most High* also known as his world of transcendent peace, that place of rest that is the heart of God's own priceless emotions, emotions that are the pearl of great value called "My peace that I leave with you."

Do you think this revelation to corral the Evil Queen's power to make her work for you is well-known? If you do, then ask your local preacher to explain how "biblical cuss words" which are the word of God that you speak with your vitriol and vile anger *work for you* in your pursuit of the kingdom of God. Chances are he'll scoff, and the church board will ban you from the potluck dinner this Sunday afternoon in the church social hall. That's okay. Tell them they can take their shitty fucky little church club and stick it up their ass.

Story of Demon-Possessed Homeless Guy

I was in Santa Barbara in the final weeks of finishing this book. One morning while feverishly editing such as only a perfectionist does, I heard violent screaming that sounded like a man holding his hand in a bonfire. It was painful to listen to. This went on for an hour and a half until I approached the man, offered to make him a cup of coffee, and he accepted.

Then I deviously unveiled my plan. I asked him what he was screaming about, and he said, "Voices in my head."

None of that shit intimidates me because I know **the power of this man's tongue** to dominate **the thoughts in his head.**

I challenged him to replace the sick words in his head with the 1225 words. I told him the ONLY way these 1225 words calm his mind is **if he screams them WITH THE SAME VIOLENT ANGER** as I heard him scream for the last hour and a half. He agreed. I went my way, he went his.

I saw this guy again five hours later. He walked up to me with a smile on his face and thanked me. He told me that today was the first time in eleven years that he had peace of mind.

***The power of his tongue** and 1225 words, infused with eleven years of this man's relentless anger, fear, and mental torment converted his ugly lump of coal into a sparkling diamond.*

If you'd like to see this man after his remarkable transformation, go to ShittyToHapppy.com and download the video labeled "The Santa Barbara Demoniac."

Religious alert!! Most fervent, yet illiterate religious people would've tried to cast a devil out of this man. 99.99% of the time when silly preachers cast out devils, it's nothing more than a person who is enslaved to their vile thoughts, noxious feelings, and tormented emotions. The surefire way to cure them is to encourage them to scream the 1225 words **by the power of their tongue**.

Instruct the person to fill their 1225 words to overflowing with their tormented feelings, their intense anxiety, and their putrid thoughts, and voila! The power of THEIR VERY OWN TONGUE delivers them, not your comical circus of casting out devils.

QUESTION: Did the kingdom of God reside in this man, deep down inside him, but hidden, buried, covered over by eleven years of torment, blind rage, and a merciless Evil Queen that spares no mercy, has no compassion, and has one mission: To kill, steal, and destroy her host, in this case, a broken-down man in Santa Barbara? The answer is YES! The kingdom of God had lain in wait for however old this guy was, maybe forty years old. Why hadn't God delivered him? Why did God allow him to suffer? If God is all-powerful, why didn't he send me sooner?

The answers to these questions, and many others like them are found in the second volume of this three-part trilogy *THE EVIL QUEEN.*

Nevertheless, this man's **power of his tongue** and 1225 words delivered him from eleven years of mental torment.

Speak the Words With the Torment That You Feel!

Folks, if you want the 1225 words and **the power of your tongue** to work more quickly, don't we all? —Then speak the words *with the anger* that you feel. Pack your audible words with the vitriol, anger, and self-loathing that you feel. Cram your words full of your *discouragement* and *fear of failure* that you feel.

Like the song lyrics say, "We are weak, but he is strong." In other words, HE fights. NOT US. He fights for us. We rest. God says, "SPEAK THE

WORDS because YOU ARE WEAK, but by your 1225 words and **the power of your tongue** I AM STRONG."

He fights for us so that we don't have to, just like what I accidentally discovered that sunny summer California afternoon in 1983 the day my green convertible died. I was weak, but he was strong from the moment I *accidentally* and *unintentionally* corralled the Evil Queen's noxious emotions of anger, bitterness, and resentment to join me in my fight against that vile wicked Evil Queen.

Yes I was weak, but I accidentally unearthed HIM WHO IS **STRONG**, which thereby transforms my weak, decrepit self-loathing feelings of bitterness, resentment, despair, worry, and stress into a sparkling diamond of peace that is indestructible, indescribable, a peace that is from another dimension, a peace that transcends this natural world—a peace that only bursts forth from the *Prince of Peace* who is God himself. *I am weak but HE IS STRONG.*

That which starts out ugly, smelly, and dirty…**a piece of coal**…transforms into a precious stone that's exquisite, lovely, and expensive…**a sparkling diamond**.

*That which starts out ugly, smelly, and dirty…your anger, your bitterness, and your resentment…**the mighty power of your tongue** transforms these noxious emotions into a beautiful gemstone made in the image and likeness of God*

We're weak, oh so very weak. We're ugly coal, but God is the majesty that seizes upon the Evil Queen's tempestuous power, her incendiary heat, and her raging fire and thus converts the Evil Queen's anger, fear, and loathing into a sparkling diamond by **the power of our very own tongue**.

"Speak the words…I'm right here."

One more eye-popping, intriguing, mind-blowing factoid, so please listen carefully: My anger is **the same anger** whether I said, "My green convertible is a piece of crap," or whether I said, "My green convertible is a well-oiled machine."

The anger was the same. **The words were different.**

The difference was not the anger. *The difference was* THE WORDS.

Whoa, that's so good I'm gonna say it again—

The difference was not the anger…the difference was THE WORDS.

The anger was THE SAME—**the words were different.**

That's why the demoniac in Santa Barbara could speak nasty, tormented "biblical cuss words," yet unleash waves of peace that he'd not felt in eleven years.

"Go to Heaven" Words With a "Go to Hell" Attitude

That sunny summer California afternoon in 1983 I unleashed prophetic, biblical, King Davidic "go to heaven" words with an Evil Queenish demonic "go to hell" anger. The results surpassed my mental capacity to understand how such a thing could happen. I could easily have fueled my anger with these words, "Hey you green convertible, you are a son of a bitch, you're an asshole, a wacko fuck job, and I wish you'd die." If I speak these unsavory, spirit of antichrist words about my green convertible, then it pisses me off more than ever. Well, that's not the kingdom of God he says to seek first, is it? That's not the peace and joy that he says is the pearl of great value, is it? What then happens?

What happens is we lose out on his promise that "all the good things, dreams, visions, goals, and desires of our heart get added to us," because they don't. Sadly, **the power of our tongue** unleashes our antichrist words that harden the anger, worry, and stress, which then prolongs entrance into the Garden of Eden, or even worse, prevents it altogether.

But what did I do instead on that sunny summer California afternoon in 1983 the day my green convertible died? I grabbed ahold of my anger by its throat; I tightened the grip, and as much as I tried to grasp onto the wicked anger to enjoy it, savor it, and bathe in it, I CHANGED MY ANGRY WORDS, and MY ANGRY WORDS CHANGED ME!

The result: ***The power of my tongue*** *unleashed a whirlwind of peace, a massive 100-year flood of the kingdom of God that invaded my heart and OVERRULED my vicious rebellion.*

That's what happened to me that sunny summer California afternoon in 1983 the day my green convertible died, and that's what happened to the demoniac in Santa Barbara, and that's how God turns coal into a diamond, and that's how God polishes a turd.

I changed the words, and the words changed me

"Speak the words…I'm right here."

Scene 63

Words Revolutionize Emotions

The power of your tongue cares NOTHING about your feelings. **The power of your tongue** cares ONLY about your words. **The power of your tongue** cares NOTHING about your bitchy whiney, pipsqueak insincerity because your insincerity has zero influence over the rudder. Insincerity has no power to stop your rudder from pile-driving your mighty ship tossed by fierce winds and crashing waves through the storm into the calm waters called "The Secret Place of the Most High."

OMG I gotta say that again: THE POWER OF YOUR TONGUE DOESN'T CARE A WHIT ABOUT YOUR EMOTIONS whether they're nasty or beautiful. This is a powerful nugget, a new item on the fast-food menu, the McFuckIt McNugget made with the ingredients of your bitchy anger, petulant worry, agonizing stress, anxiety, and heart-wrenching depression, none of which refrain the power of your tongue from breaking through the blood-brain barrier to give you the gifts of everlasting, inexplicable, otherworldly peace and happiness. Not only can these disastrous emotions not stop **the power of your tongue**—*they accelerate it.*

I'll say it again: **The POWER of your tongue** *doesn't give a crap about your cantankerous emotions.* **The POWER of your tongue** doesn't care about your sincerity. **The POWER of your tongue** doesn't give a fuck whether you're sincere or insincere.

That's why on that sunny summer California afternoon in 1983 it didn't matter that I poisonously spewed the 1225 words that were diametrically opposite of the words I wanted to say, because the Evil Queen's cantankerous emotions had no power over me to force a sustained grip on my anger in the face of "biblical cuss words" that I spoke so viciously and venomously.

Furthermore the 1225 words exploded inside me into a quick and forceful violent execution of the Evil Queen as **the power of my tongue** slayed with such a shocking transformation. The entire transformation from a dirty piece of coal into an exquisite diamond took about twenty minutes.

The power of my tongue FOUGHT and WON the battle IN SPITE OF my whiney, bitchy, rebellious, argumentative, disbelieving, angry, pissed-off self.

In 1983 **the power of my tongue** cared nothing about my emotions.

In 1983 **the power of my tongue** cared nothing about my insincerity.

In 1983 **the power of my tongue** cared only about MY WORDS.

This is a profound proclamation that separates this book from every other you've ever read, so I want to make sure you hear it:

****

The power of your tongue doesn't give a shit about your funky emotions

****

The power of your tongue cares nothing about your whiney insincerity

****

The power of your tongue cares ONLY about your 1225 words

****

NOTHING stops the power of your tongue

****

"Speak the words… I'm right here"

Scene 64

Does Anger Dematerialize?

Here's an interesting shit-disturber: When the coal converts into a diamond, where does the coal go? Does it disappear? Does it cease to exist? Or does the coal still exist?

The coal is still carbon just like the wife accused her husband on their anniversary, but the coal transforms into a different, almost incomprehensible glistening diamond, a remarkable transformation.

The dirty nasty coal transforms into a beautiful sparkling diamond.

Does the coal vaporize into nothingness? Does the coal disappear? Does the coal cease to exist?

The coal still exists! It just changes form.

Coal and diamonds are carbon, and yet coal and diamonds are worlds apart in beauty, style, and elegance even though they revolutionize outward from the same raw material.

*You ask, "Steve, are you telling me that **anger**...**worry**...**stress**...as well as **happiness**...**peace**...**joy** COME FROM THE SAME RAW MATERIAL?"*

Well let me ask you, when your anger converts into happiness, peace, and joy, does your anger vaporize into nothingness? Where does your anger go? Does it still exist? *Yes it still exists*. It's still emotion, but the **emotion** transforms. Anger doesn't dissolve into nothingness. It changes form. Now it's a diamond.

Coal doesn't cease to exist: It changes form

*Anger doesn't cease to exist: **It changes form***

****

Anger and peace, although diametrically opposite in appearance are PASSION.

Sadness and happiness are diametric opposites yet are both PASSION.

Coal and diamonds are as different as night and day, yet they are both carbon.

Hatred and love are as different as east and west, yet they are both **PASSION**.

All emotions, good and bad, ugly and pretty, strong and weak come from the *same raw material* found inside the deepest core of the innermost parts of your being: PASSION.

What is the Power that Decides Your Passion?

When you fuel your passion with idiotic words like "I hate you" and "I'm so pissed I could punch your fat face if I could tell it apart from your fat ass," then **the power of your tongue** distorts your passion, and turns it into a deformed, rogue, greasy, dirty, and smelly piece of coal.

But on the other hand when you fuel your passion with 1225 words that are God himself, even though you speak them vitriolically and grotesquely with the same attitude as "I hate you and your ass is fat," it doesn't stop their power because the 1225 words and **the power of your tongue** renovates your unruly passion into a beautiful, sparkling, elegant, majestic diamond.

"Go to heaven" words with a "go to hell" attitude

The POWER OF YOUR TONGUE—that tiny rudder turns your passion from wild and wooly to calm and peaceful.

The power of your tongue is the rudder of your ship that forces your passion through the rough seas to return safely home.

The power of your tongue converts your passion from a dirty lump of coal into a sparkling, beautiful, robust, diamond…a sparkling gem that's filled to the brim with vigorous explosive emotions that empower you far beyond your wildest imagination to kick open the doors that lead into the Garden of Eden.

Does your passion of anger disappear? No, your passion doesn't dissolve into obscurity when you transform it from anger to peace. Your passion doesn't go away on a rainy day. No, your passion converts from a lump of dirty coal into a sparkling elegant diamond.

****

You can fuel your passion with *poisonous words* that preserve your passion as a lump of greasy coal, but right on the other hand you can fuel your passion with *1225 words* that are the Lord God Almighty that converts your passion of anger into a sparkling diamond fit for a king.

The power of your tongue enhances your passion in whatever direction you want it to go.

The power of your tongue commands your passion to produce ugly, greasy, smelly coal.

The power of your tongue commands your passion to produce elegant, sparkling diamonds.

The power of your tongue creates whatever the hell you tell your passion to create.

Your passion creates whatever **the power of your tongue** dictates.

The power of your tongue is the decisive force that rules your passion.

YOUR PASSION IS THE RAW MATERIAL THAT GENERATES EMOTIONS

Passion is a neutral raw material that **the power of your tongue** transforms into happiness…or anger—

Passion is a neutral raw material that **the power of your tongue** converts into peace…or fear—

Passion is a neutral raw material that **the power of your tongue** converts into unforgiveness…or forgiveness.

Passion is raw material that produces ANGER…
The same raw material produces HAPPINESS!

Passion is raw material that unbridles the Evil Queen…
The same raw material unbridles the Kingdom of God!

Passion *transforms into whatever* **the power of your tongue** *commands it to transform into,* like anger, hatred, anxiety, worry, stress, and fear of failure, passions that are **strong and barely controllable emotions** that you unwisely pervert into an ugly, nasty, greasy piece of coal by **the power of your tongue** with such vile words that complain, moan, bawl, and squall about how shitty your life is, what a bitch your wife is, what a lousy quarter it's been because sales are in the toilet, what a boneheaded doofus you are for your decision to become an actor because *it's taking sooo damn long!*

I repeat: *Passion mysteriously transforms into whatever* **the power of your tongue** *tells it to transform into.* Like happiness, peace, and joy. Happiness, peace, and joy are **strong and barely controllable emotions** that you wisely unshackle by **the power of your tongue** and 1225 "biblical cuss words," two mighty soldierly forces that force your passion to erupt into a flurry of sparkling, elegant, flawless diamonds, precious jewels and treasures untold.

Happiness, peace, and joy are **strong and barely controllable emotions** that **the power of your tongue** transforms from the Evil Queen into the kingdom of God, a mighty force of power and strength, a vibrant source of otherworldly supremacy that strengthens you, and fills you full of transcendent otherworldly peace, and forces wide open the doors that lead into the Garden of Eden.

Passion is raw material. **Passion is the building block of your emotions.** *Passion assiduously obeys the* **power of your tongue**.

If you use **the power of your tongue** to turn your passion ugly you are a blockheaded moron when instead you should SEEK FIRST THE KINGDOM OF GOD—HAPPINESS, JOY, AND PEACE.

The power of your tongue turns your passion happy and peaceful which kicks open the doors to the Garden of Eden, but **the power of your** tongue also turns your passion cancerous, and makes you sick physically, emotionally, and mentally and slams shut the doors to the Garden of Eden.

Passion is Your BEAUTIFUL SERVANT
...AND...
Passion is Your WICKED TASKMASTER

You either use **the power of your tongue** to master your passion so that it serves you or you use **the power of your tongue** to give free rein to the roaring lion who evilly devours you.

Passion is like cells in your body in that they are designed to benefit you, to conduct your vital functions, and to give life to you, but you can screw up your cells with a shit diet, no exercise, stress, and you can Google the rest of the deadly ramifications. It's people's dumbass decisions that turn their cells from healthy into rogue cancerous perversions. There are exceptions like a baby born with a debilitating disease, but mostly it's the man himself who contaminates his body when he eats shit for food and exercises with no more than a walk from his couch to the kitchen, and even worse is he unleashes the Evil Queen's death hormones into his body via his evil emotions of stress, worry, anger, fear, and unforgiveness.

Man's vile emotions are a body-killer. Remember earlier I talked about how anger, worry, fear, and stress leaks cortisol into your body, and cortisol is known as the "death hormone"? *Stop leaching death into your body!*

In like manner, passion is akin to your body's cells in that your passion is God's gift to benefit you. However, just like you can corrupt your cells into rogue renegades that rise up in rebellion, turn violently against you, and make you sick, diseased, and ultimately turn into a bloody monster that sucks the life out of you…

…even so, you can pervert your beneficial passion to go rogue, it rises up against you, and turns into a bloody monster that crushes your dreams, goals, visions, and the desires of your heart. If you allow your perverted passion to run its course, it causes your dreams to abort, turns your life to shit, and sucks the energy out of you.

Remember: PASSION IS STRONG and BARELY CONTROLLABLE EMOTION whether anger, hatred, worry… Or happiness, peace, and joy—

It's one or the other. Your passion is either **dastardly devious, and an evil taskmaster**, or it is **exceedingly constructive, a life-giving servant**.

What is the power that determines between passion that is a vitally healthy servant, and passion that turns killer?

The power that decides the course of your passion is THE POWER OF YOUR TONGUE.

> **THE POWER OF YOUR TONGUE unleashes healthy passion that benefits you, but THE POWER OF YOUR TONGUE turns your passion rogue and cancerous, a horrific force that ultimately destroys you.**

Passion either empowers you and opens wide the doors that lead into the Garden of Eden, or passion goes rogue and opens wide the gates that lead into the flames of hell. When you fuel your passion with "I hate you" words, then **the power of your tongue** unleashes destructive passion that ravages your soul and devastates your body. Ain't that fun, boys and girls?

Rogue passion destroys your dreams, goals, visions, and the desires of your heart. Rogue passion makes you sick; even unleashes cancer, heart disease, and makes your life miserable.

The passion that God intended to benefit you turns violently ugly, and destroys you, just like the cells God gives you to benefit you turn ugly and cause your body to rot.

I go into gruesome detail about the horrific devastation a perverted rogue passion causes in the second volume of this trilogy *Shitty to Happy in 21 Minutes: THE EVIL QUEEN*. It's beyond anything you can imagine. Everything you learn in volume two of this trilogy called *THE EVIL QUEEN* goes against everything, and I do mean EVERYTHING you've ever heard about the evil in this world, the spirit world, and the world to come. I'm excited for you to finish this first volume so you can get to the next one, but until then—

Passion Works FOR You or AGAINST You

When passion floods out from your body in the form of joy and peace, the passion affects you mightily, and it's powerful, it stimulates your mind, heart, and soul, and it's otherworldly amazing. It makes you live a long and prosperous life and adds to you ALL THE DESIRES OF YOUR HEART in THE GARDEN OF EDEN.

However, if you choose to speak words of revenge and hate in response to your vile anger, then **the power of your tongue** unleashes the might and fury of the Evil Queen's poisonous emotions that attack you like a dark demon.

Your passion possesses you with your own perverted emotions of anger, fear of failure, worry, stress, unforgiveness, anxiety, depression…need I go on? Your anger forces you to behave in ways that harm you, and slams shut the gates to the Garden of Eden.

The good news is anger can't burn all by itself, nor can any of the Evil Queen's emotions. You must provide fuel to energize them. Without the fuel of vile words, the fire of anger goes out.

Fire Needs Fuel to Burn

Fire can't burn alone. It needs fuel.

Fire doesn't magically appear out of nowhere with no spark or fuel. Fire needs a spark, some kindling, and logs to stay alive. If you start a fire, but remove the logs, the fire goes out.

Neither can anger burn by itself. It must have a spark, kindling, and fuel.

The spark, the kindling, and the fuel for your damning anger is **the power of your tongue** that hurls poisonous words like "woe is me, my green convertible is dead, my life is shitty, my wife is a bitch, my dreams will never happen."

Fire only burns with fuel; anger only burns with infernal words. On the other hand, happiness, peace, and joy must also have fuel. *What's the fuel?*

"Speak the words…I'm right here."

Trick the Evil Queen with the Fuel of Your "Biblical Cuss Words"

Here's a fantabulous plot twist. When you speak the 1225 "biblical cuss words," words that go opposite the sicko anger words that you want to say when you're angry and frustrated, what happens? Well, this converts the Evil Queen's noxious anger into an advantageous, beneficial fuel that adds explosive energy to **the power of your tongue**. Her anger adds enormous amounts of energy to your 1225 "biblical cuss words" like the intense heat and pressure of the earth as it squeezes the coal that transforms it into a diamond.

So not only does the Evil Queen enhance your "biblical cuss words," but simultaneously she quenches her own scorching flames, which causes her fires to subside, and thus produces a glistening diamond.

You're welcome. Love, your Creator.

"Biblical cuss words" and **the power of your tongue** perform a tremendous feat you've never felt ever before in your life, a feat so radical it astounds. Your 1225 words and **the power of your tongue** transforms your rogue passion from death power into resurrection power, the kingdom of God's magnificent power that even IF YOU TRY TO BLOCK ITS MAGNIFICENT FORCE **YOU CAN'T!**

I'd never felt anything in my life like what happened that infamous day in 1983.

The power of your tongue overrules your rogue passion and transforms you into a happy and peaceful and joyful person EVEN IF YOU TRY TO STAY ANGRY like I tried to that sunny summer California afternoon in 1983 the day my green convertible died.

The power of your tongue extinguishes your anger like a firehose extinguishes the birthday candles on the cute little girl's birthday cake the day I was such an embarrassed seven-year-old with the ugliest gift at her party.

Not only does **the power of your tongue** extinguish your anger, but it also extinguishes fear of failure, frustration, unforgiveness, lust, drug addiction, alcoholism, infidelity, but it doesn't stop there. It crushes worry, stress, anxiety, depression, and a lonely heart.

The power of your tongue and 1225 "biblical cuss words" annihilate the wily deceptions of the enemy who is the notoriously wicked EVIL QUEEN.

"Speak the words…I'm right here."

****

Scene 65

Feed the Beast

What I'm about to say I said earlier in the book, and it is a world-renowned logic bomb. Here it is once again. When you feel angry and hateful toward another person for what they did to you, give your anger what it wants. It wants to eat. It wants to go viciously crazy, like a frenzied animal at feeding time, snarling fangs, ferocious deep-throated guttural growls, and spittle dripping down its chin. It cries out "Feed me, feed me muthafucka, *feed me*."

So do it! FEED YOUR ANGER! *Feed your anger all the food it wants.*

What food does it want?

WORDS.

It wants to eat *words*, **words**, and more **WORDS. Your anger doesn't give a flying fuck-a-rooney what words you feed it** AS LONG AS YOU SAY THEM ANGRILY!

If you feed your anger typical self-destructive "anger food" like you have for the last thirty years, then your anger has an abundance of fuel it needs to burn like a raging fire, like when you feed it words such as "I hate you and your ass has pimples."

Your anger arises like a roaring lion as it devours you with misery, sickness, and disease.

You foolishly fuel your anger with words that incite the fires of hell when you scream a slew of profanity-saddled insults when you're pissed at your spouse, or at the red Ferrari that cut you off on the freeway, or at your neighbor that just this morning ripped you a new asshole because your dog pooped in his yard.

BUT HERE'S THE TRICK OF THE AGES: Give your anger the food it wants—WORDS, but instead of your previous habitual "I hate you, my life sucks," words…and "I'm worried, I'm fat, I'm afraid, I'm frustrated" words… instead feed your anger the 1225 "biblical cuss words."

The beauty of this revelation is the more nastily you speak the words, words that you fill with the Evil Queen's vicious gut-busting anger that courses through your veins, well then the faster and more effectively the words perform their miraculous transformation like what I unintentionally ran headlong into that sunny summer California afternoon in 1983 the day my green convertible died, and just like what happened to the demoniac homeless guy in Santa Barbara.

Your anger does not know the difference, nor does it care, nor can it distinguish between "I hate you" words and "I love you" words AS LONG AS YOU SPEAK THE WORDS **ANGRILY**.

Did you catch that?

AS LONG AS YOU SPEAK YOUR 1225 WORDS ANGRILY—anger that turns your 1225 words into "BIBLICAL CUSS WORDS," YOUR ANGER DOESN'T CARE *what words you feed it.*

Listen, the Evil Queen cannot distinguish between "I hate you" and "I love you" when you speak "I love you" words with "I hate you" anger.

Remember when I said in the first few pages of this book, "Go to heaven" words with a "Go to hell" anger?

LOVE words with a THUG attitude

The power of your tongue combines with 1225 "biblical cuss words" that you fill with a mega-boatload of the Evil Queen's anger, and thereby **the power of your tongue** kicks the shit out of your wickedly unforgiving bitchy anger while you stand amazed as your ravenous hate-filled angry heart devours your 1225 "biblical cuss words" that, unbeknownst to your wicked Evil Queen are the Lord God Almighty that slays her.

YOUR HEART IS BLIND; IT CAN'T MAKE THE DISTINCTION.

Your heart gobbles down angry 1225 "biblical cuss words" that are the Lord God Almighty. Your angry heart unknowingly and unwittingly devours God like a feeding frenzy, like a lion tears into a wallaby.

Your anger wants to devour WORDS, and so your anger foolishly devours 1225 "biblical cuss words" that are GOD HIMSELF that you disguise with a beautiful "coat of many colors."

Your anger cannot discern that the words are God himself, and thus she devours your 1225 God-filled glorious, majestic words that are the SPIRIT that sets the captives free.

Surprise, *surprise,* SURPRISE, oh ye doltish Evil Queen! You are as fooled as the rat who devours rat poison. You foolishly devour words that are THE LORD GOD ALMIGHTY that are as deadly to you as the rat poison is to the rat. They taste as good to you as the rat poison does to the rat, but unbeknownst to both of you, your gluttony seals your fate.

You greedily gobble 1225 angrily spoken "biblical cuss words" that are a Trojan Horse that suckers you to swallow every morsel of the words who are the Lord God himself, the ruler of heaven and earth, oh ye dimwitted and foolhardy, stupid and moronic Evil Queen!

What a cloddish loser you are!

Imagine the headlines all over the world when mankind wakes up to who the enemy is, and how easily we defeat her:

THE EVIL QUEEN DEFEATS HERSELF!

WE ARE VICTORIOUS OVER THE EVIL QUEEN!

The Power of Your Tongue Pours Hot Molten Lava Down the Throat of Your Evil Queen

The power of your tongue pours the living waters of God Almighty down her gullet that sears her throat like hot molten lava.

The power of your tongue crams the 1225 words of the living God down the throat of your vile, vicious, vitriolic Evil Queen, and *she voraciously guzzles every drop!*

YOUR ANGRY EVIL QUEEN FOOLISHLY DEVOURS 1225 "BIBLICAL CUSS WORDS." She becomes intoxicatedly delirious, stupefied, and so confuckingfused that she turns cross-eyed and stumbles, and passes out like the town drunk at a fish fry at the town square.

And then the most glorious cinematic plot-twist unfolds for the world to see. They sit spellbound on the edge of their seats in the movie theater with their eyes glued to the silver screen. The Evil Queen violently projectile vomits huge meat-chunks with intense heaves and gut-churning convulsions as the Lord God of the Ages storms through the Evil Queen's impenetrable fortress to storm the beaches of her stronghold like the Navy SEALs sneaked up on me that sunny summer California afternoon in 1983 the day my green convertible died. That was the day my 1225 words and **the power of my tongue** mercilessly strangulated my anger and FLOODED MY HEART WITH EVERLASTING INCOMPREHENSIBLE SUPERNATURAL OTHERWORLDLY PEACE that to this day forty years later I cannot comprehend how such a thing happens.

Those 1225 "biblical cuss words" and **the power of your tongue** THOROUGHLY CONFUSE YOUR ANGER so that your befuddled anger hankers to wolf down MORE WORDS, and in her muddled state she voraciously devours THE LORD GOD ALMIGHTY, and from that moment forward the Evil Queen, that perennial bitch who spews vicious diabolic anger brutally turns AGAINST HERSELF as she CANNIBALISTICALLY DEVOURS HER OWN SELF like the enemies of Jehoshaphat and Judah cannibalized each other and devoured themselves.

****

I took a long rabbit trail, but let's finish the story of Jehoshaphat and the army of Judah.

When the men of Judah came to the place that overlooks the desert and looked out over the vast army, they saw only dead bodies lying on the ground; no one had escaped. Judah's enemies got confused, turned on one another, and in their bewildered state of confusion slaughtered one another *just like your "biblical cuss words" confuse the Evil Queen who then turns on herself and slaughters herself.*

After no man was left standing, Jehoshaphat and his men went to carry off their plunder, and they found a great amount of equipment, clothing, and loads of articles of value—more than they could take away. Is this the "all these things will be added to you" that the Jewish rabbi promises? **There was so much plunder that it took three days to collect it!**

What's the takeaway here? Remember I've told you over and over to seek the kingdom of God FIRST?

When? **FIRST**, before anything else, and then what happens?

All these **things** *will be added to you.* What **things** will be added to you?

When Jehoshaphat's army of praisers led the armies of Judah, their enemies got so befuddled and confused that they turned on themselves and slaughtered each other, and meanwhile left behind gold, silver, great amounts of equipment and clothing and articles of value—*more than Jehoshaphat and his men could carry away.*

These are the **things**, the **plunder** that gets added to you.

And this my friends is *The Greatest Story Ever Told,* a story of the magnificent **power of your tongue** that raises God from dormancy where he has patiently waited for years for you to get your shit together. He's been buried deep inside your heart since birth, your heart that is the permanent residence of the Lord God Almighty, the creator of heaven and earth, our Father, the Master Builder who created us.

The power of your tongue unfurls Him—Him who is **the 1225 words** as you assemble a mighty victorious military action by which you pursue the kingdom of God like a lion pursues his prey.

You are the lion, your *enemy* is the wicked Evil Queen, and your reward is the pearl of great value of happiness, peace, and joy that unlocks all the wonderful things that you hope for, dream about, envision, all the desires of your heart that he says are yours when you—

ONE: Seek first his kingdom.
TWO: Be diligent in all your hand finds to do.
THREE: Take care of the poor, the fatherless, and the widow.

IN SUMMARY: *Seek first the kingdom of God*—**peace, joy, and happiness**—and thereby you and Jehoshaphat's army confuse your enemy as she pulls out her sword to attack you, but instead she brutally massacres herself. The Evil Queen falls flat on her face like a drunken sorority girl at spring rush, and then you easily and effortlessly step over her lifeless drunken body to enter the Garden of Eden where ALL THESE THINGS *get added to you.*

"Speak the words…I'm right here…"

…like I did that sunny summer California afternoon in 1983 the day my green convertible died.

****

It's break time! Take another seventeen minutes before we dive into the next glorious thought-provoking scenes of *Shitty to Happy in 21 Minutes: THE SECRET KINGDOM.*

This first volume in the trilogy *THE SECRET KINGDOM* sets the stage for the upcoming two volumes *THE EVIL QUEEN* and *THE GREAT INVASION.*

Oh the things I have in store for you! I'll see you in seventeen minutes.

INTERMISSION

Scene 66

The Final Frontier

Let's hop aboard a crazy ride with more twists and turns than Elvis Presley the night he angered millions with his show-stopping hip gyrations with his iconic performance of "Hound Dog" on The Ed Sullivan Show in 1956.

My journey began in 1983 on a sunny summer California afternoon the day my green convertible died, and I've pissed off lots of people like Elvis did but for different reasons, but here we are, nearly atop the first summit forty years later, so let's continue to explore where very few dare venture into the faraway land called "The Final Frontier." Are you ready? Hop aboard, let's ride!

How to Be Led by the Spirit of God

As you cruise through life how many times have you encountered a situation when you don't know what to do? If you're like me it's a million thousand times. What do you do when you don't know what your next step is? I've had many times when I'm clueless what to do next.

If you're at a place in your life, or your business, your family, your nutrition, your kids, your whatever, and you're in the valley of indecision, then dive headlong into the kingdom emotions of transcendent otherworldly peace by the twin forces of 1225 words and **the power of your tongue**.

After you slam-dunk your heart full of transcendent peace—in other words, after you *force-feed* the incomprehensible peace into your soul like what I did that sunny summer California afternoon in 1983, then you'll get your answer, maybe in five minutes, maybe tomorrow, maybe next week, it might come immediately, but *your answer comes as certain as the river flows.* You'll *know* with maximum clarity what your next step is.

It might be something as simple as a phone call. It might be a quick text. It might be someone you randomly meet. It might happen as you peruse social media like what happened to me when I answered my friend's clarion call, and he flew me to New York the next day. It could be *anything.*

What Do You Do When You Don't Know What to Do?

In 1975 I was twenty-two, had just graduated from Florida State, and relocated to Orlando to sell life insurance. It's not easy to sell death certificates when you're twenty-two years old. *I hated it.* I'd rather beat off with sandpaper, but I didn't know what else to do with my life. I felt hopeless and demoralized. I was lost.

One morning in utter desperation I wandered into an empty church around the corner from my office, and I defiantly announced to God, "I'm not leaving here until you tell me what to do with the rest of my life." I sat there. For an hour. Then another hour. Then several hours.

"God?" No answer.

Five hours later I get an idea. What would I do if anything were possible? That's a profound question!

What would *you* do if anything were possible, if you would succeed at anything you choose, and whatever you pick, it's impossible for you to fail? What would you decide to do?

I gave every profession a fair shot: astronaut, lawyer, gardener, garbage man, electrician, plumber, professor, preacher…my list was both eccentric and extensive, but I settled on four possibilities: preacher, professor, politician, and performer. Can you see the similarities other than they all start with a P? Do you notice they all speak to crowds of people? I didn't know this at the time, but I had given myself a personality assessment that uncovers my interests, strengths, dreams, and goals.

I tossed out politician and professor because I needed more school. I'd rather have a botched colonoscopy than sit through another university class.

Preacher seemed easy because my dad was one, but performer…it intrigued me, but I thought, "Nah, impossible." I quickly reminded myself of the rule: "Whatever you choose, you cannot fail. You WILL succeed."

That was the day I made the decision to become an actor.

The point is I stood my ground until an answer came. Do you have to sit for five hours? Do you have to pursue the answer over several days? Who knows? Who cares? *Your answer will come like the cavalry.*

If you don't know what to do with your life, I encourage you to do the same as I did that day I wandered into the church around the corner from the Lincoln National Life insurance office in Orlando. If you don't know what to do with your life, or even if you know what you want but you don't know what your next step is, then your plan of action is to pursue peace *first*.

When? Later on today? Tomorrow? No. NOW! *Do it now, brown cow!*

When you slam 1225 words into the blue skies like I did that sunny summer California afternoon in 1983, then you'll get an idea what to do. If you don't get an idea right away, then continue 21-minute joy rides that whisk you away into the land of otherworldly peace that transcends this natural world.

Tap into these supernatural powers by **the power of your tongue**. Observe **the power of your tongue** as it detonates the 1225 words. Watch how your words and **the power of your tongue** release Thor's hammer that chisels away the excess marble that unveils the Ark of the Covenant, the hidden treasure inside you, that otherworldly peace that perplexingly surpasses the human ability of your mind to comprehend, a mysterious peace that knows all things, sees all things, even the future.

Do it until you get the thought, or an idea what to do.

It might be the smallest, tiniest, minuscule idea, like when I perused social media and stumbled upon my friend's clarion call. I wasn't looking for anything in particular that day, just scrolling, and BAM! A huge financial opportunity hit me. Other times, something small, other times, nothing at all.

Whatever you do throughout the day, trust that it is your peace that is full to overflowing that leads you and guides you where you should go, what you should do, what you should say.

It's that simple.

Don't do what we as humans do, and that is we overcomplicate life.

Let me ask you a question: How complicated is it to go to the store if you need fruit, veggies, and a loaf of bread? Not complicated at all, is it? *That's how simple it is to be led by the spirit of God.*

How complicated is it to invite your wife to dinner? Not complicated at all, right? Unless y'all just got in an argument, and then it's like chopping a frozen lake with an ice pick. But other than that, it's simple. *I can't stress this enough how simple it is to get ideas from your spirit when you've tapped into the supernatural peace of God via your 1225 words and* ***the power of your tongue****.*

"Speak the words...I'm right here."

Your idea will most certainly be a tiny idea, a quick text, a walk around the block, a trip to the coffee shop. It'll be a thought so natural that you think it's your own. It doesn't matter if nothing substantial happens. Just follow your thoughts, just like you do now, but the difference is, when you're full to overflowing with peace, then your peace guides your thoughts, and your thoughts lead you to where you are supposed to be. Your thoughts feel like your own thoughts, but they're not! *The more you walk in otherworldly peace the more fruitful your thoughts become.*

Your thoughts become a compass that lead you and guide you into success, prosperity, and abundance, also known as *the desires of your heart!*

How much simpler can God make this for you!!! To hell with all those sermons that blather on for a seven-week series on "How to be Led by the Spirit of God." It's so simple to be led by the spirit that anything longer than a five-minute sermon complicates the process, confuses people, and nobody understands.

Here's my five-minute sermon on "How to be Led by the Spirit."

Ready?

ONE: Seek peace and pursue it. Do so until you *force-feed* yourself full to where you feel like you'll pop, like what happened to me that sunny summer California afternoon in 1983 the day my green convertible died.

TWO: When you're full of peace you can trust your thoughts, because the Prince of Peace rules your heart. Henceforth, trust your thoughts as whispers from God. End of sermon.

THREE: Pass the offering plate.

FOUR: Meet your buddies after church at the restaurant.

It didn't even take five minutes for you to learn *How to be Led by the Spirit of God.* It took thirty-three seconds.

See how simple this is?

Trust your thoughts as whispers from God

My thought to peruse social media turned into a gold mine when my friend flew me to New York, and I made a small fortune with his company.

I trust my thoughts as whispers from God.

When you cram yourself full of the *peace that passes all understanding* such as I did that sunny summer California afternoon in 1983 when my green convertible died, then you can ***trust your thoughts*** *as whispers from God.*

Your tiny thoughts are God's subtle whispers that grow into large trees when you act on them. That's how simply his kingdom works.

Force-feed peace and happiness into your heart by **the power of your tongue** that speaks the 1225 words like I did that sunny summer California afternoon in 1983, and when an idea hits you, do it.

Be diligent to trust your thoughts because ***your thoughts are whispers from God.***

WARNING: Don't depend upon your thoughts as *whispers from God* if you're not filled with the transcendent, otherworldly peace that defies explanation! *They can deceive you!* Those same thoughts that lead you, and guide you, and show you the way also lead you down the path of destruction that includes failure, stupid business decisions, clumsy family decisions, and all-around blundering dumbass decisions.

For thoughts to be trustworthy you must have transcendent, otherworldly peace

The difference between untrustworthy thoughts and trustworthy thoughts is your emotions. What emotions? Peace, joy, and happiness versus worry, fear, doubt, anger, and unforgiveness. When you're diligent to fill yourself full of peace, then trust your thoughts, trust your tiny whispers because you can rely on them when you have *force-fed* yourself full of his kingdom, his happiness, peace, and joy.

And on top of that you take care of the poor, the fatherless, and the widow.

See how simple this is, that your tiny impromptu cues turn into big and surprising results!

This leads us to our next hugely important step to your peace, happiness, joy, and success.

****

Scene 67

Eighth Wonder: DILIGENCE

The eighth wonder of the world is DILIGENCE.

I have a friend that hiked up Mount Kilimanjaro in Africa, one of the highest mountains in the world. It's an eight-day journey of thirty-seven miles. She didn't get to the top of the mountain by sipping coffee and thinking about the trek. She didn't get to the top of the mountain by dreaming and visualizing. Those are important, but she never got to the top of Mount Kilimanjaro until she took her first step. She must take the first step; otherwise, she never gets to the second.

After the first and second steps, she takes the third. And the fourth, and the thirty-seventh, and the fiftieth. *She took thousands of small steps.* That's diligence, *diligence,* and **more diligence**.

It's a steep uphill trek, so each of her steps she moved forward a meager 12 to 14 inches. Thirty-seven miles took her 195,360 tiny steps to trek Kilimanjaro, but she conquered one of the highest mountains in the world *one step at a time.*

Tiny Steps Yield Big Results

Now, imagine every step you take up Kilimanjaro you move forward, not twelve inches, but *three feet.* Every step you move forward not one foot, but one *yard.* That's what happens when your *peace and happiness* pump steroids into your tiny yet diligent, humble yet persistent human efforts.

Supernatural, inexplicable, otherworldly peace that is not of this world that you pile drive into your heart by **the power of your tongue** and 1225 words magically boosts your humble efforts to unleash supernatural results.

Diligent efforts whilst full of happiness, peace, and joy is how your dreams sprint up from behind you, chase you down, and *overtake* you like Usain Bolt in Central Park and like what happened to me when my music skills spilled over onto the keyboard after thousands of hours of "wax on, wax off" piano scales and finger exercises.

This Trilogy is the Culmination of Tens of Thousands of Small Steps Spanning Over 50,000 Hours Over Forty Years

This trilogy is the most daunting undertaking of my life, more than any other of my endeavors including acting in television and film, public speaking on stages around the United States and Canada, music performance in Florida State University night clubs, bars, and fraternities, to music and acting performances in a 10,000-member mega church in Los Angeles…more so than the beautiful marriage God gave me as a gift that I destroyed because of my wild dick, more so than raising two beautiful successful Godly kids…more than *anything*.

I began this journey forty years ago on a sunny summer California afternoon in 1983 that day my green convertible died, and it was one year later that I began this colossal magnum opus when I first sat down to write on a yellow note pad at a friend's condominium in Marina del Rey during the Los Angeles Olympics in the summer of 1984, and every day since then I've trudged through pitfalls, scaled mountains and valleys, and forged rivers as I labored to unfold this gargantuan magnum opus one step at a time.

During these forty years, I have traversed uncharted territory, stumbled headlong into accidental discoveries, shocking encounters, and discovered more revelation, and unveiled deeper and more intimate layers of God than I ever imagined possible.

Why a yellow notepad? Because I didn't have a computer in 1984.

I've traversed many pitfalls, obstacles, and raging waters during this arduous forty-year journey. I averaged ten hours a day to write for the first five years. After I got married in 1989 I cut back to four to five hours a day.

When I became a seminar speaker, I wrote only two to three hours a day, but for the last seven years I've been a man on a mission with an average of eight to nine hours a day for seven years. At times I'd hit twelve hours a day, many times fifteen.

The total time I put into this trilogy over the last four decades is around 50,000 hours, maybe more, maybe less, and that doesn't include the thousands of hours of research, the study, and the innumerable hours to slam peace into my heart to squash the Evil Queen, and thusly purify my mind to keep it open to innovative ideas, fresh revelations, and deep yet simple insights.

It includes the time I spent refining my verbal swordplay to thoroughly entertain and engage you, the reader.

It includes the time I spent streamlining these revolutionary spiritual encounters so as to preserve the simplicity of this message of the kingdom lest I foolishly complicate what even a child should be able to understand.

It doesn't include the many hours I slept on my computer when I passed out from utter exhaustion.

One night I was so exhausted that I fell asleep in a sitting position on the barstool in my kitchen as I sat at my computer. Somebody sneaked up from behind me and smacked me in the face so hard it felt like they broke my nose and cracked a tooth. I turned to see who it was but realized I had fallen off the barstool and face-planted headfirst onto the hardwood floor.

Tens of thousands of hours of dedicated ***diligence*** for forty years until the day I looked over my shoulder to see Usain Bolt overtake my slowpoke slogger jogger self.

Diligence is the eighth wonder of the world.

Why did this trilogy take me so long? Because nobody taught me this revelation. Nobody I'd ever heard of knew this. I was alone, in uncharted waters.

To this day I've never heard anything like this from anybody, any preacher, any book, and I've perused hundreds of books, and listened to thousands of sermons over thousands of days, and I've never heard or read anything like this ever before in my whole life, and I'm seventy.

That's why it took me so long to garner this simple idea.

How long will it take you?

You decide.

Start with 21 minutes.

"Speak the words…I'm right here."

The Hand of the Diligent Makes You Rich (Proverbs 12:24)

When you diligently pursue your dreams and goals, when you persistently *force-feed* yourself full of happiness, peace, and joy like I did that sunny summer California afternoon in 1983 the day my green convertible died, then your dreams and goals are the skilled trackers who pursued Butch and

Sundance. They relentlessly hunt you down and pursue you until they overtake you like Usain Bolt overtakes your slowpoke slogger jogger self in Central Park.

But like my friend, you gotta take the *first TINY STEP* up the trails of the ginormous Mount Kilimanjaro.

How Does God Multiply Your Tiny Steps? *Via Your Peace and Happiness That Flood Up from the Inside of You* by 1225 Words and THE POWER OF YOUR TONGUE!

How do you thrust the supernatural power of God into motion so that your dreams chase you instead of you chase your dreams?

Take your happy pills, men, women, boys, and girls. Get happy *first, force-feed* peace into your heart FIRST with your 1225 words and **the power of your tongue**.

When?!?

FIRST!

"Before I do anything else?!?" you ask, astonished that Coach John Wooden and Kobe Bryant's commitment to the basics pops up over and over again. *Yes, pursue the kingdom of God emotions of happiness, peace, and joy before you do anything else.* ***Those are the BASICS.***

Next, be **diligent** in all that your hand finds to do.

Finally, **take care of the poor, the fatherless, and the widow**.

When you pursue these three plans of action, the three work together, each one draws upon the other to *force your dreams to sneak up on you and overtake you.*

Even though all three tasks are equally important, you must **seek peace and happiness FIRST**.

That's why I told the young girl, "Happiness is your purpose in life."

Is it the only thing?

No, but it's the FIRST thing.

"First" implies there's a second, and a third, and a seventeenth, and a fiftieth like my friend as she hiked the thirty-seven-mile trek up Mount Kilimanjaro.

When you seek peace, and pursue happiness FIRST before anything else, then **the power of your tongue** kicks into overdrive to *force-feed* you full of unspeakable energies that coalesce with your diligence, which increases the magnitude of your efforts, tasks, and errands, and it multiplies the distance each of your painstaking persistent steps thrusts you forward in life, your work, your family, your health, and your fitness.

This otherworldly transcendent peace that is not from this world propels your progress forward more effortlessly, more easily than you can imagine, and it's these forces that enhance your diligent efforts to work together seamlessly, all in sync to ensure that the desires of your heart come true.

Remember: This otherworldly peace of which I speak is not *the comfort that comes from a nice life.* It's not the peace that comes from a pleasant lifestyle, a nice home, a car in the garage, and fine food. Those are nice, and if you don't have them yet, you will in this earthly Garden of Eden, and when you get them like he promises you will, then you will enjoy them, and you'll never take them for granted.

However the peace that opens doors to the fourth dimension and beyond, including the Garden of Eden is not *comfort,* but rather is the transcendent otherworldly peace that comes ONLY from 1225 words and **the power of your tongue** that supernaturally slams peace, and mysteriously *force-feeds* happiness into your heart like what happened to me that sunny summer California afternoon in 1983 the day my green convertible died.

It's a standalone peace that is worlds apart from the peace that comes from a comfortable lifestyle.

This otherworldly supernatural happiness and inexplicable peace that transcends this natural world rips open the veil into the fourth dimension and beyond as you thirstily drink from the deep well of God's emotions so that he intervenes in your life to thrust you far above and beyond the success of your modest human yet diligent efforts.

This is why the Jewish rabbi tells us to make God's peace and happiness our TOPPER MOST, UTMOST, and FOREMOST priority

Why? Because PEACE taps you into God's power

****

Folks, this is not religion.

It's *happiness.*

Supernatural happiness.

It's *peace.*

Transcendent peace that passes all understanding…

…peace that's outside this earthly natural realm…

…peace that is *The Secret Place of the Most High.*

It's not the comfort from a nice lifestyle.

It's peace, transcendent otherworldly peace.

It's happiness, supernatural inexplicable happiness.

And how do you get supernaturally inexplicably happy? At this point if you can't answer, I'm gonna smack you so hard you'll starve to death before you stop sliding.

How do you get happy? How do you *force-feed* peace into your heart? How do you slam dunk the kingdom of God so that it explodes up from deep within you like an underwater blast of the atomic bomb at Bikini Atoll that caused a 94-foot-high tsunami and a 2,000-foot-wide crater in the surface of the sea floor.

Here's how you force-feed peace into your heart: Ramrod those 1225 words down the Evil Queen's throat for 21 minutes several times each day by **the power of your tongue**.

Choke her, strangle her, suffocate her noxious emotions with your 1225 words and **the power of your tongue** daily, 21 minutes at a time like I did that sunny summer California afternoon in 1983 the day my green convertible died.

I've laid out the 1225 words for you in volume three *THE GREAT INVASION* but download them now for free at ShittyToHappy.com.

These 1225 words are God himself that when you unleash into the skies by **the power of your tongue** they *force-feed* happiness and peace to spring up from deep within your heart like they did for me forty years ago when these same words and **the power of my tongue** unchained supercharged mighty forces that invaded my heart like the Navy SEAL team storms the beaches of enemy territory in the middle of the night.

The 1225 words and **the power of my tongue** resurrected the kingdom of God and *force-fed* his emotions into my angry heart that sunny summer California afternoon the day I screamed bloody murder at him that infamous afternoon when my green convertible died.

Go to ShittyToHappy.com to download them for free.

Download them now, I'll wait a few minutes.

Grab Ahold of the Rudder!

Have you downloaded them yet? Good. Now, use **the power of your rudder and those 1225 words** to set your ship on course in the direction you want it to go, especially when it's tossed by fierce winds and waves, and mountains of water that crash against the sides of the ship.

How?

Grab ahold of the rudder!

How do you get ahold of the rudder?

SPEAK.

Speak what?

Speak the words, the 1225 words *that you just downloaded.* **Speak them aloud, loudly enough for yourself to hear**.

The 1225 words firmly lock the rudder of your ship in the path you want your ship to go. Don't let go of the 1225 words until **the power of your rudder** drives your ship safely into the harbor.

You'll feel it begin to work long before you complete twenty-one minutes, usually in the first five. It's different for everybody, but what all men have in common is IT WORKS!

Peace overwhelms, safety comes, contentment abounds. **That's how you ask, seek, and knock, and thereby the doors open for you, doors that escort you into** *The Secret Place of the Most High.*

Nothing in the world stops your 1225 words and **the power of your tongue** *as they escort you into* ***The Secret Kingdom*** *where peace fills your heart.*

Nothing can stop these twin armaments of 1225 words and ***the power of your tongue*** *from slamming peace into your heart, mind, soul, and body.*

NOT EVEN YOU!

You can't, I can't, the Evil Queen can't, nobody can.

I absolutely could NOT **break the back of the power of my tongue** that sunny summer California afternoon in 1983 the day my green convertible died, even though I tried. *God knows I tried. But I couldn't.*

No matter how hard I tried to block the Navy SEAL team from storming the beaches of my heart *I couldn't!*

The power of my tongue was impenetrable even though I was a stubborn whiney imbecilic minion boy-bitch, a complainer, a whiner, a sarcastic unemployed actor.

Was it even remotely possible that I could rustle up enough opposing energy to intercept the nuclear power of 1225 words and **the power of my tongue**?

NO!

Try it.

Speak the 1225 words that you just downloaded a few minutes ago. Did you download them yet? If not, do it now. Go to ShittyToHappy.com, download them, and then…what?

Speak…*speak*…***speak***…SPEAK!

Now.

You'll see you can't stop their power.

YOU CAN'T STOP THE POWER!

****

It's easier to stick a wet noodle up a bobcat's ass.

"Speak the words...I'm right here."

Scene 68

God's Umbilical Cord

When you spoke the 1225 words that you downloaded, did you try to stop their power? **Try to stop their power!** YOU CAN'T! It's the wackiest feeling, but you can't stop their power from pounding peace into your heart, just like in the experiment when you counted from one to fifty, remember?

I surely tried to stop **the power of my tongue** *and the 1225 words from ramrodding peace into me but couldn't!* The 1225 words and **the power of my tongue** overruled my bitchy self and my cantankerous pissy attitude that sunny summer California afternoon in 1983 the day my green convertible died. My dark humanity was toothless against the forces of the 1225 words and **the power of my tongue** as these two field generals *force-fed* me full of otherworldly transcendent peace that originates from another dimension: an otherworldly realm outside of this three-dimensional world yet lives deep inside me, and inside you, and inside the young girl, even the evening she asked me with sadness in her eyes, "What is my purpose in life?"

What is it that connects you, and me too, to these deeper dimensions that Dr. Hugh Ross talked about earlier, these infinitesimally small deeper dimensions that live inside us? What's your umbilical cord that connects you to the forces of life? Do you know the answer? I've given you the answer four hundred and sixty-five thousand two-hundred and twenty-three times since page one—

The Power of Your Tongue and 1225 Words Is the Umbilical Cord

You wanna know why I couldn't sever the umbilical cord that connects me to God that sunny summer California afternoon no matter how hard I tried, and neither can you no matter how hard you try? I haven't read all the scientific journals, but I've never heard of an infant inside the womb that chewed through his own umbilical cord.

You can't chew through the umbilical cord of the 1225 words and ***the power of your tongue!*** Not when you tap into these otherworldly dimensions that transcend space, time, and matter. **The power of our tongues and 1225 words** are the inexplicable forces that open the doors that transport us into the incomprehensible world of transcendent otherworldly peace who is God himself, who is the Prince of Peace.

The power of your tongue and 1225 words is the formidable umbilical cord that connects you to the fourth dimension and beyond, these otherworldly dimensions that reside inside you. They're so tiny that they are imperceptible to the human mind, the nanotechnology microscope, the doctor, the scientist, the preacher, your friends, even you.

But not to God. He sees them perfectly, and wants you to tap into them which is why he implores you again and again to…what? What does he tell you to do again, and again, and again…?

Ignite the 1225 words by **the explosive power of your tongue** to thereby *seek and pursue the kingdom of God.*

He divulges unto you the most sought-after secrets of the universe, these deeper dimensions, these other worlds that live inside you.

How do you open their doors that lead into these otherworldly dimensions of victory, might, and power? How do you tap their otherworldly powers? SHOUT IT OUT LOUD, "**By the power of your tongue and 1225 words** that FORCE-FEED peace and happiness into your heart." *There goes the sound of the screeching wheels on the speeding passenger train when the conductor slams on the brakes.*

Peace is your lifeline, the umbilical cord that connects you to the supernatural world that lives inside you. **The power of your tongue** unleashes supernatural peace that hooks you up to the God of the universe who is the Prince of Peace who is joy unspeakable and full of glory, and who is the mighty force of love.

All these emotions are none other than *the fruit of the spirit.*

Where Are the Fourth through the Tenth Dimensions?

Where are these fourth through the tenth dimensions? They're inside you.

How'd they get there? God did it. He put them inside you!

Why can't you see them? Because they're infinitesimally smaller than a nanoparticle. Why can't you tap into them? YOU CAN. How? By **the power of**

your tongue and 1225 of the mightiest words in existence who are GOD HIMSELF.

Remember when the astrophysicist Hugh Ross held his hand a centimeter above the cutouts of Mr. and Mrs. Flat? His hand was closer to Mr. and Mrs. Flat than they were to each other, closer than even their next breath, but they couldn't feel his hand, they couldn't sense it, they were oblivious to it. That's the distance God is from us.

How do you sense, feel, and be aware of the God of the universe who is closer to you than your next breath?

"Speak the words... I'm right here."

WANNA FEEL GOD?!

How badly do you wanna feel God's presence? How badly do you want to be more aware of him than you are your next thought? How can you, Mr. and Mrs. Flat, contact Hugh Ross's hand that floats a nanoparticle above you?

Listen to the wisdom of the ages from the Prince of Peace, the mystery man who appeared to me that sunny summer California afternoon in 1983 the day my green convertible died, "**My peace I leave with you, not as the world gives do I give you**."

What kind of peace do you leave with us, Mr. Prince, and I don't mean the rockstar Prince.

He answers, "The kind of peace I leave with you is not comfort. It's not *panty-pie* peace. It's not peace that comes from a luxurious lifestyle. That's not the kind of peace I leave with you."

He continues to explain, "Even though those kinds of peace are wonderful, and my promises fulfilled give you all the desires of your heart that does indeed unleash this kind of peace in superabundance, but this kind of peace is mere *comfort."*

He concludes with this thought, "Comfort is not the kind of peace that passes all understanding, it's not the peace that I'm talking about that I leave with you, and neither is comfort the peace that transcends this three-dimensional world of time, space, and matter." (John 14:27).

God's Peace

HE is the Prince of Peace. **HIS peace** is how you feel God, **HIS peace** is how you are aware of God, **HIS peace** is how you close the nanoparticle gap between the second dimension of Mr. and Mrs. Flat and the third dimension of Hugh Ross's hand that floats just above them.

Dr. Ross's example holds true whether it's the gap between the second and third dimension, or whether it's the gap between the third dimension of our brick-and-mortar world, and the fourth, fifth, sixth, seventh, eighth, ninth, and tenth dimensions inside us where God lives.

Peace is the umbilical cord that connects us to all these deeper dimensions. The Prince of Peace concludes, "It's *my peace that I leave with you* that guards your heart and mind" (Philippians 4:7). If it was Song of Solomon talking about sex, you'd look up these scriptures.

I have supreme confidence in the unrelenting power of my 1225 words and **the power of my tongue** to *force-feed* the Prince of Peace into my heart as evidenced by this promise in Proverbs 12:6, "The mouth of the upright delivers him."

Yep, my mouth—**the power of my tongue**—clearly delivered me from anger on that sunny summer California afternoon in 1983 the day my green convertible died when the Prince of Peace invaded my heart.

And then there's this one: "He who guards his mouth preserves his life" (Proverbs 13:3).

Yep, that afternoon I guarded my mouth and thereby **the power of my tongue** preserved my life, my peace, and my sanity.

And here's another one: "The lips of the wise preserve him" (Proverbs 14:3).

Yep, my lips—**the power of my tongue**—preserved the good part of me with happiness, peace, and joy and supplanted the evil part of me that is anger, frustration, worry, stress, and unforgiveness, the Evil Queen's netherworld that also lives inside me.

Remember, your warfare is not external. We don't wrestle against flesh and blood, like people, or places or things, but against principalities, powers, and rulers of the darkness in high places.

Where are these "high places"?

These "high places" are the highest place of all, but they're not "high places" as in a long way off, or way off in the distance, or *way up in the sky,* or somewhere out in the universe, or even in the ethereal spirit world.

That's not where the "high places" are.

No silly, the "high places" refer to AUTHORITY, not location.

There's no higher authority than the power of your very own heart.

There's no authority higher in all the universe, in all of heaven and earth, and under the earth…than… [DRUM ROLL PLEASE]

The throne room of YOUR heart

THAT'S WHY GOD CHOOSES YOUR HEART AS HIS TEMPLE!

I know, I know, I can hear pharisaical minds explode all over the world as their shit for brains splashes onto the sidewalk.

Regardless of what preachers say, your warfare is against the Evil Queen, the ruler of the darkness who lives inside you.

Just like God lives inside you.

So if the Evil Queen lives inside you, and God lives inside you, GUESS WHERE THE BATTLEFIELD IS!

See how simple this is?

Anyway, you conquer the Evil Queen's formidable forces, and thereby overthrow her kingdom, and you dethrone her from the supremacy of your heart, and you install new leadership when you exalt the God of the heavens, his kingdom of happiness, peace, and joy. You replace her kingdom with God's kingdom to reign over your life from the throne room of your heart.

How do you do this?

By the 1225 words and **the power of your tongue**, two mighty military armaments that resurrect from dormancy the kingdom of God *who lives inside you in the fourth through the tenth dimensions.*

The Evil Queen lives inside you.

God lives inside you.

The kingdom of God lives inside you.

Your warfare is not external.

YOUR WARFARE IS INSIDE YOU.

****

That's some pretty heavy shit we just covered, so let's lighten it up with a little story about the grand master of revelators regarding **the power of your tongue** Solomon, his peccadillo father David, and a hot young chick named Bathsheba.

Scene 69

David Bangs Bathsheba

It's no coincidence that this is the 69th chapter, so sit back, relax, and enjoy this torrid tale of an R-rated romance.

For those of you unfamiliar with Solomon, he's the author of Proverbs from which these verses about **the power of your tongue** and many other **power of your tongue** scriptures originate.

His father is David, the shepherd boy who was the king of Israel, who is the same David that Michelangelo sculpted out of the seventeen-foot-high block of marble in Florence in 1501.

David's son Solomon was the wisest man who ever lived, so it stands to reason he taught more about **the power of the tongue** than any other before or after except for James, the guy who teaches the tongue is like the rudder of an exceptionally large ship that turns it wherever the captain decides.

The bible is not a single book. It's a compilation of sixty-six books written by forty separate authors on three different continents over a period of 1500 years. When one of the forty authors, deemed the wisest man who ever lived continually harangues, browbeats, and cajoles about **the power of your tongue** *then I listen*. By the way if you think the bible is sixty-six books of fairy tales, then enjoy the following fairy tale.

Here's the story. Solomon was born from an illicit relationship between his father, David, and the wife of an elite soldier in David's army, Uriah. David got down and dirty with Uriah's wife while Uriah fought loyally for his king on the battlefield. David, that scoundrel, got Uriah's wife pregnant. The wife's name was Bathsheba, and she was Victoria Secret model hot.

One night she was bathing naked on the rooftop, David looks across the way, sees her, and thinks, "What a fine piece of ass." So he sends for her, stuffs his boloney pony into her cream pie, and gets her pregnant. I have no idea why she would bathe naked on the rooftop right across from the king's palace in plain sight of the king, but I have my suspicions that she was not Mother Teresa and wouldn't mind a roll in the hay with the hot-looking and enormously powerful king of Israel.

When David learns one of his sperms deep-dove into Bathsheba's egg, he initiates a cover-up. So he calls Uriah her husband back from the battlefield, invites him into his palace, feeds him a nice meal, gets him drunk, and says, "Uriah, take a little time off from the battle and go sleep with your wife." Uriah stumbles out of David's palace and into the night, and David figures his cover-up will work perfectly. Uriah will have sex with his wife (and hopefully not have whiskey dick) and David can claim Uriah's the baby-daddy.

Only one small problem…when David wakes up the next morning to get the morning newspaper, he opens the front door, and who should be there asleep on the front porch? Uriah!

David exclaims, "What the hell man, why didn't you sleep with your wife?" To which Uriah replies, "I refuse to take time off from the battle and sleep with my wife while my men are still at war." Uriah you see, was very loyal to his soldiers, and to David.

So David thinks to himself, "This is bad. This will be all over CNN and Fox News. My social media followers will go on a rampage. The Jerusalem Post will run a hit piece on me."

So David proceeds with plan B. "I know what I'll do. I'll send Uriah and his battalion and several others into enemy territory, and then command all the other battalions to retreat except Uriah's, and then we'll see what happens," and he laughs wickedly to himself like the wicked witch of the west in Wizard of Oz.

And sure enough, when David commands a retreat by the other battalions, it leaves Uriah and his men defenseless without backup, and the enemy slaughters many soldiers, including Uriah. David thinks he's home free, but not so fast oh ye gossip lovers, the story ain't over yet.

So there's a prophet named Nathan that pays a visit to David. Nathan lays out a scenario for David. Nathan says to David, "There was a wealthy man with thousands of sheep, and there was another poor man who had nothing except one little ewe lamb he had bought. He raised it, and it grew up with him and his children. The little lamb shared his food, drank from his cup, and even slept in his arms. It was like a daughter to him."

Nathan continues with his story. "A visitor comes to town. The wealthy man wanted to prepare a sheep for a feast with the visitor. So rather than kill one of his own sheep, the wealthy man stole the one little beloved lamb from the poor man and his family, killed it, dressed it for the feast, and partied for the night. Tell me King of Israel, what should be done with this man?"

David rises up off his throne in fury and shouts, "That man must die because he had no pity."

Nathan points his finger at David and scolds him, "You Sir, are that man!"

BUSTED!!

This story is told in 2 Samuel Chapters 11 and 12, and I want you to hear it for a couple of reasons. One is to let you know that God's people are a funcken bunch of rabblerousers, but even in the midst of their fuckups, many of them run back to God.

I'm guilty too. I hurt my wife with untold pain because of my bad behavior with young women. I hate that I did that to her and my kids. I've apologized to her many times over the years we've been apart.

Anyway, as I point out the peccadillos of King David I refuse to hide my own. The bible is the only holy book that hangs out all the dirty laundry of all the men from Moses to Noah, to David and Solomon. The litany of bad deeds these men did is a laundry list that could fill the pages of the New York Times, and their photos would be plastered in every post office across the country from California to New York in the Ten Most Wanted category. Murder, sex, lies, and all sorts of criminal behavior permeate their lives.

No other religious book exposes the faults, the weaknesses, and the wickedness of its leaders like the bible does. Do you know any that do? It seems that all the holy books protect the reputation of their founders and leaders and covers up their dirty deeds; all of them except for one. The bible.

The bible exposes the murder, deceit, illicit sex, weaknesses, and lies of its leaders. The bible exposes these men and rips them new assholes.

Now that we're on the subject, King James who oversaw the translation of the King James version of the bible in the early 1600s loved men's assholes. He was gay. Yep, King James parked his cooch cork in male poop shoots, so in fact he was "Queen James."

Does that upset your religious apple cart? Too bad. God used this flaming homosexual to oversee the translation of the Queen James…er, the *King* James version of the bible (Freudian slip) so get over it oh ye judgmental hate-ologists.

David and Bathsheba got married by the way. After all, Uriah is dead. And of course David is the king, so the Department of Justice refuses to press charges just like today when men with power and money get off without consequences.

But only for a while.

They still have God to deal with, because God tells David that his actions will cause heartache for him and his family for the rest of his life.

Several of his kids killed one another, one of his sons raped his half-sister. That's right. Amnon, David's son, rapes Tamar, his half-sister. Those kids played too many video games.

Can you imagine your son raping your daughter?

Another of David's sons had sex with all of his wives, not in private, but in public for the whole city to see, because God warned David after Nathan the prophet confronted him, "What you did to Bathsheba in private, your son will do to you in public." Since David had three hundred wives, his son was busier than a cucumber in a women's prison.

God didn't cause the bad stuff to happen to David.

David caused the bad stuff to happen to himself.

It's like men in power today that do bad things and get off scot-free, or so they think, but the noose tightens. Shit's about to get real very soon for these corporate leaders, government leaders, religious leaders, leaders in entertainment, health, and education that love power and money more than people.

God's wheels of justice grind ever so slowly but ever so finely, and it's not God who destroys them. God doesn't destroy people. They destroy themselves from within when they self-implode by their own actions, actions driven, urged on, and motivated by that dastardly Evil Queen.

I'll go into juicy detail about how the wicked destroy themselves in volume two of this trilogy called *Shitty to Happy in 21 Minutes: THE EVIL QUEEN.* It's quite sobering, and hideously shocking.

Here's another reason I tell you this story of David and Bathsheba. After Nathan the prophet confronts David on his dumbass decisions, David runs to God and pours his heart out to him. It didn't bring Uriah back from the dead, but what're you going to do? You can't unscramble an egg.

And now that Bathsheba is David's wife, remember she's still pregnant, but the baby dies; too bad.

Bathsheba was distraught over the death of her child. The bible says that David, to console her, has sex with her again. *Hey Dave, have you ever heard of a simple hug and some flowers when you're wife feels down?*

Anyway, David's roll in the hay to comfort Bathsheba gets her pregnant again, and this time the baby lives, and the baby is Solomon—the wisest man who ever lived.

I think we can all agree from this story, as well as all the other stories I cited earlier when Ezekiel talks about men whose genitals were like those of donkeys and whose emission was like horses, and Ezekiel, who says "Perhaps your gods are taking a shit," and Malachi talks about "spreading dung on your faces" that the bible ain't for pussies and namby-pamby Christians.

Anyway, the baby grows up to become the king of Israel like his dad. King Solomon authored Proverbs from whence I get the wisdom about **the power of the tongue** to control your body, your emotions, your soul, and your businesses, your wealth, your family, your health, and every other facet of your life. Solomon's father David mentored his son Solomon, and also authored the book of Psalms from whence I get the 1225 words.

The world's wisest men know more about **the power of the tongue** *than any others before or after.* ***Until now.***

So you see God uses anybody no matter what a shitty life they've lived, no matter their sexual peccadillos: The gay man King James, the father-son fuckboys David and Solomon, and an angry pissed off young actor who slung snot words into God's face on a sunny summer California afternoon in 1983 who twenty years later cheated on his God-given treasure of a precious and beautiful wife not once, but many times with many young women over many years.

God's love is unconditional, it's forever, and no matter what you've done, you can't kick God in the shins so hard that he stops loving you.

****

Another point regarding God's mercy: I find it interesting that when Jesus told the twelve he was gonna get crucified, Peter said, "No way, ain't gonna happen!" Jesus said, "Get behind me **Satan**," and yet when Judas kissed him on the cheek to betray him to the Roman soldiers, Jesus addressed him as "**Friend**, do what you came for."

It wasn't "friend" like, "Hey buddy." No, "friend" is a covenant word.

I don't have all the answers, but I have all the questions, such as why did Jesus address the loyal disciple Peter as "Satan" and why did he address the scumbag traitor Judas as "Friend"?

I'll answer these questions and many more in the next two volumes in this trilogy: *THE EVIL QUEEN* and *THE GREAT INVASION.*

****

My personal gratitude to God even though I was a whore-boy to my family is, "Thank you Lord, that even though I broke my beautiful family, and crushed my beautiful wife's heart and broke my kids' hearts, even so you still use me to get this message of love, joy, and peace to the world, and my wife has an amazing new husband who adores her, and my son Austen and daughter Natasha are happy, successful, and thriving in their lives, their careers, and their families."

If you've messed up your life so stinking badly like I did, or David did, or Solomon did, then run to him and let him love you like no one ever has.

"Speak the words…I'm right here."

And because of his amazing love, there's no room for anyone to point the finger of judgement at any other person for anything they've done. This will come into play in later scenes as you continue your journey through this three-part trilogy *Shitty to Happy in 21 Minutes*, especially in the third volume *Shitty to Happy in 21 Minutes: THE GREAT INVASION.*

INTERMISSION

Scene 70

Pursue Peace Passionately

Peace is a perpetual motion machine.
It feeds on itself. It draws boundless energy from itself.

Force-feed transcendent otherworldly peace into your heart. Do it often, do it consistently, do it diligently. Do it daily.

The feeling of peace that floods you is beyond what I can describe in earthly words. How do you describe the feeling of having your first baby? You can't. It's inexplicable. It's surreal.

How do you describe the feeling of being in love? You can't. You can try but words fail you. "It feels *GREAT*" doesn't come close to the deep intimate feeling of love.

How do you describe this otherworldly feeling of peace that transcends this natural world? You can try but words fail you. *"It feels GREAT"* doesn't cut it.

This otherworldly peace is intangible, yet you feel it. It's supernatural yet it's simple. It's beyond the ability of the human mind to express, primarily because this peace transcends this natural world.

The wind blows wherever it pleases. You hear its sound, but you cannot tell where it comes from or where it is going. So it is with everyone who is born of the Spirit with the corresponding fruit of love, joy, peace, happiness, patience, goodness, kindness, and faithfulness.

This invisible peace *forcefully invades you;* it *force-feeds* itself into you **even if you buck against it** like I defiantly fought against it with grandiose intensity that sunny summer California afternoon in 1983. My inability to resist this peace is one of the many reasons *the wind* of *this supernatural peace that blows wherever it pleases* **defies all explanation**.

It's weird that the 1225 words and **the power of your tongue** overwhelms your whiney, cantankerous self, but the two armaments of 1225 words and **the power of your tongue** are impenetrable, unshakable, unstoppable. *I cannot describe the unfathomable feeling.* The only way you will experience the feeling of this transcendent otherworldly peace is YOU POUND IT INTO YOURSELF by **the power of your very own tongue**.

I can't speak the 1225 words for you. Only you can. Your next-door neighbor can't speak the words for you. Only you can.

Your pastor can't speak the 1225 words for you. Only you can.

Even God can't speak the 1225 words for you. *Only you can,* and hence the repetitive instructions, *"Speak the words...I'm right here."*

You can ask God for peace, you can beg God to give you peace, you can pray to God a thousand times to ask him to give you peace, but ain't shit gonna happen until YOU—I say nothing happens until YOU—YOU—**YOU** *unleash **the power of your VERY OWN tongue** and 1225 of the mightiest words in the universe!*

Nothing happens until you... *"Speak the words...I'm right here."*

Ain't no winds of peace gonna happen until YOU ramrod the 1225 words into your heart by **the power of your VERY OWN TONGUE**, but glory to God, when YOU SPEAK the 1225 words, then **the power of your tongue** *forcefully resurrects* this invisible supernatural force of peace that lies deep within you where it's lain dormant for years, even decades.

"Speak the words...I'm right here."

Nobody else can do it for you.

"Speak the words...I'm right here."

Nobody including God can speak the 1225 words for you.

"Speak the words...I'm right here."

You're the only person on the earth, in the heavens, and under the earth that can *force-feed* supernatural otherworldly peace into your heart.

Why's that, Steve?

Because it requires **the power of YOUR TONGUE**.

Not your wife's tongue, not your pastor's tongue, not your neighbor's tongue, not your prayer group's tongue, not God's tongue.

No, it requires **YOUR** TONGUE, and if you don't use **the power of your very own tongue** to get peace, and instead you expect God to fill you with peace, well, God can no more give you peace than he can give you muscles if you don't pick up the dumbbells.

"Ohhh Dear God, puh-leeze, I'm begging you, please give me muscles." How long are you gonna pray that prayer?

If you don't lift weights God ain't gonna give you muscles any more than he'll make you thinner if you refuse to quit soda and other shit-for-food items like my friend refused.

By the same token, neither will God give you peace if you don't **perform open heart surgery with the power of your tongue**.

If a preacher tells you that you can pray to God for peace without exercising **the power of your tongue**, then you tell that preacher he needs to wipe his mouth because there's still a tiny bit of bullshit around his lips.

*I give you this stern warning that **you must exercise the power of YOUR VERY OWN tongue** so that you avoid the bone-crushing disappointment of unanswered prayer.*

****

Don't pray for God to give you peace. It won't happen.

Don't ask preachers to pray for your peace. It won't happen.

Don't ask your prayer group or call the prayer hotlines to pray for your peace. It won't happen.

There is Only ONE WAY to Get Peace

It sounds super holy and highly reverent to ask God for peace and to ask people to pray for your peace, but it's frivolous and sanctimonious bullshit because there is ONLY ONE WAY to supernaturally *force-feed* otherworldly peace into your heart—*ONLY ONE WAY*—and that is the overwhelming force of *the Word of God,* THE 1225 WORDS, and **the power of YOUR VERY OWN TONGUE**.

"Speak the words…I'm right here" to unleash the wind that blows wherever it pleases, the wind of the spirit that is unfazed by your Evil Queen's pissy

emotions, unfazed by your pesky insincerity, unfazed by any force, except for one: **THE POWER OF YOUR TONGUE**!

It is these dual armaments of 1225 words and **the power of your tongue** that team up to *force-feed peace into your heart* like what happened to me that sunny summer California afternoon in 1983 the day my green convertible died.

Ewww Steve, why are you so narrow-minded?

Because Pendejo*: **Straight is the way, and narrow is the gate that leads into life, and *few there be* that find it!** (*Spanish for "stupid.")

That's why I'm so fricking narrow-minded!

THERE'S ONLY **ONE WAY** TO GET PEACE, and it's God's way, the one way, the way that is straight and narrow, the way that "Very few be that find it," and that is: *"Speak the words…I'm right here."*

I told you in the beginning, "If your way works, keep doing what you're doing," but I was bullshitting you. I tiptoed on eggshells to not alienate you by reason of exclusivity of how to get peace, but no longer.

Now I rip the band-aid off.

THERE'S ONLY **ONE SUREFIRE WAY** TO GET PEACE, but remember, I'm NOT talking about comfort. I'm NOT talking about "panty-pie" peace.

Neither am I talking about the kind of peace that comes from trivial meditation exercises that at best keep you calm when the shower water runs cold, or you burned the dinner, or your kids are late for school. There are many ways to get that kind of peace.

However, the peace that I'm talking about is the supernatural, otherworldly, transcendent peace that *does not even exist* in our three-dimensional world, and since it does not exist in this three-dimensional world, it is impossible to achieve this sophisticated otherworldly *fruit of the spirit* by any means other than THE SPIRIT, which is 1225 words, coupled with the mightiest power God gives to his highest creation that gives life to those 1225 words, **the power of man's very own tongue**.

"Speak the words…I'm right here."

****

Scene 71

Why 1225 Words?

The 1225 words aren't the only ones that slam peace into your heart. Psalms has around 20,000 words, all of them *powerful happy bombs*.

I merely chose 1225 of them to keep it simple, like the small number of paint colors I'd show my clients to make their decision easy.

When I used to paint houses, I'd bring the homeowner thousands of paint choices, but they could never make up their mind until I limited their choice to five colors. Then they easily chose which color they wanted. From then on I never brought thousands of paint choices. *I brought five.*

It's the same with 1225 words. You can choose any of the 20,000 words in the book of Psalms, they all work just as well as the 1225 words that I chose, and then there's Proverbs with tens of thousands of words, and Isaiah, and Jeremiah with their tens of thousands of words, and so on. All the words are just as effective as the 1225 words that I selected.

I merely chose 1225 words like I selected five paint colors for the homeowner, and they happen to be the same 1225 words I personally have used for the last forty years. There are thousands of words just like there are thousands of paint colors, but I only brought five paint colors, and I only bring 1225 words.

I have a friend that chose her own words out of Psalms and Proverbs. All the words in Psalms, Proverbs, and the rest of the sixty-six books of the bible work just as well to slam peace into your heart by **the power of your very own tongue**.

"Speak the words...I'm right here."

****

Scene 72

Coolest Turnabout Ever

The crux of this three-volume trilogy is to *force-feed* this **supernatural peace** into your heart like I did that sunny summer California afternoon the day my green convertible died when I had no acting jobs, my girlfriend broke my heart, I had no money, and I slept neatly curled up in the fetal position under a friend's piano on a skanky throw rug in a one-bedroom apartment in West Los Angeles in 1983.

And listen, I'm not talking about just **any old kind of "panty-pie" peace**.

No, I'm talking about the otherworldly incomprehensible peace that Jesus promised to us when he said, "**My peace** I leave with you, the kind that is supernatural…otherworldly…the kind that transcends this natural three-dimensional world."

I'm not talking about the kind of well-deserved peace and comfort that comes from your beautiful lifestyle— No, no, no, I'm talking about the kind of peace that forcibly floods your soul like the Navy SEAL team stormed the beaches of my heart that day in 1983 the day my green convertible died. Forty years later it's still incomprehensible to me that we have the gift of 1225 words that are the most authoritative in the universe, words that are a tiny sliver of God himself like the sixteen-ounce glass of Pacific Ocean water is a tiny sliver of the Seven Seas, and how amazing it is that God gives us **the power of our tongue** to hammer this tiny sliver of HIM into our hearts which *force-feeds* transcendent otherworldly peace—which is also HIM—into our hearts, a supernatural peace, an incomprehensible unexplainable peace that the human mind cannot understand; a peace that piledrives us into the fourth dimension and the other nanosized dimensions that live deep inside us like the Ark of the Covenant lived deep inside the caverns of the lost city of Tanis.

These 1225 words and **the power of our tongue** uncover this mighty kingdom to pound peace into our brains. They *force-feed* peace into our hearts with the same forceful rush as taking a drink of water out of a tidal wave. And the craziest and most insane part of all is the words and **the power of our tongue** work best when we harness the power of our enemy, like the Aikido martial artist who harnesses the energy of his attacker to defeat his attacker.

Even so we harness the energy of the Evil Queen to defeat the Evil Queen.

It's the coolest turnabout EVER.

However, nothing happens until you employ the 1225 words by **the power of your very own tongue**.

"Speak the words...I'm right here."

Until then they're just 1225 words on a page, clasped together by a tiny paperclip, and yet both the paperclip with its hidden 18 kilotons of TNT and the 1225 words with their unseen powers that create solar systems lie dormant for as long as you turn a blind eye to them.

In *Beauty and the Beast* each of the characters in the movie is dormant, frozen in time: The clock, the teapot, the feather duster, the footstool, and the wardrobe. They're lifeless and inanimate until Belle arrives. When she arrives at the castle they come to life in song and dance.

Your 1225 words lie dormant, frozen in time, lifeless, and inanimate until **the power of your tongue** arrives at the castle to bring them to life, and when you do, then you unleash the massive pent-up thunderous energy that hides inside the 1225 words like the 18 kilotons of TNT hides inside the tiny paperclip.

"Speak the words...I'm right here."

Cut loose the mighty rushing wind of THE SPIRIT with the corresponding fruit of love, joy, peace, happiness, kindness, goodness, patience, and faithfulness.

How? *How?* HOW?!?

"Speak the words...I'm right here."

****

Scene 73

The Easy Way

"My way is sooo easy" says the Jewish rabbi

Everybody wants the magic wand, the easy way. Is that you?

Well…*I have some oddly interesting and captivating news.*

The Man of Mystery with the Hebrew name *Yeshua* who is the Prince of Peace says, "Come to me all you who are full of anxiety, stress, worry, and frustration, and I'll give you rest **because my way is *easy*.**

"Learn my way, the *effortless way*, the EASY way, and you will find rest for your weary souls" (Matthew 11:28-30).

He claims his way is easy. Effortless. Not hard. Not difficult, not insurmountable, nope, he said his way is EASY.

What's his way that he says is "The easy way"?

The easy way is *"Speak the words…I'm right here"* like I did that sunny summer California afternoon in 1983 the day my green convertible died.

The power of your tongue is the EASY WAY. How frickin' hard is it to speak 1225 words three times through?!? It takes 21 minutes. It's a mere 3675 words.

Have you downloaded the words yet? Go to ShittyToHappy.com and download them *now.*

"Speak the words…I'm right here."

That's HIS way, the EASY way.

Sing it Mr. Sinatra, "I did it HIS way!" Well, Frank sang, "I did it MY way," but I altered the lyrics.

When you do things GOD'S way, which is to say you forcefully enter God's rest by way of his peace and happiness by the power of his 1225 words and **the power of your tongue** like I did that sunny summer California afternoon in 1983, then his way is the easy way.

We Are Weak but He is Strong
His Burden is Easy, and His Yoke is Light

His way is easy because even though we are weak, he is strong, and it is *his strength* that is the incredible life-giving force that pours out of your mouth by **the power of your tongue** that *forces* rest to explode up from deep inside of you.

What does he require of you? **Nothing**.

What does he do? *Everything*.

That's why his way is easy because it is HE, *it is HE,* **it is HE** that forces you, drives you, and propels you into the secret place of the Most High where you *rest under the shadow of the Almighty.*

It is **the magnificent incomprehensible power of the beautiful gift he gave you called THE POWER OF YOUR TONGUE** that forces you to be seated in that place of rest where everything falls beautifully into place, which includes your work, your family, your physical body, and everything else you could possibly want and more, all that is yours in The Garden of Eden.

And when I say "everything else" falls beautifully into place, I mean *everything!*

Jobs, careers, family, kids, material needs, business deals, study, new career, your first job, your first apartment, your dream home, your future husband, or if you're already married your present husband, your wife, your girlfriend, and everything else you can imagine.

It's all yours in the Garden of Eden.

"SPEAK THE WORDS, PENDEJO...I'M RIGHT HERE."

****

Scene 74

Peace is Addictive

And another thing…when you feel his peace—this peace that *forcefully awakens* to rise to the surface from deep within your soul, the Prince of Peace hooks you like a drug addict who can't break free from addiction. Transcendent peace is more addictive than you can imagine. It will hook you so fancifully that you'll never want to let it go.

But you will.

Remember your first boyfriend, how hooked you were? But you let your love slip, didn't you? You took him for granted, didn't you?

Many of you have let your love in your marriage slip, am I right? *You're darn right I'm right!* But don't fret. When you finish the first two volumes of this trilogy, you'll dive into volume three *THE GREAT INVASION* where you'll learn everything you need to know to have *The Greatest Love Story Ever Told.*

Oh the things I have in store for you! But I digress.

Back to my point. Yes, you'll let this otherworldly transcendent peace slip like you let the feelings for your first boyfriend slip. It's a struggle to overcome lethargy.

It's tough for the salmon to swim upstream for days on end to reach the spawning ground where they lay eggs. If she stops flapping her salmon flippers the current sweeps her backward.

Even though transcendent otherworldly peace feels great, if you relax like the salmon, you'll let peace slip and you'll take it for granted, and the Evil Queen sweeps you away in the currents of anger, frustration, worry, stress, fear of failure, and unforgiveness, back to where you started.

How do I know? I know, because I've walked in this supernatural peace for forty years and listen to me: Absence from this transcendent peace does NOT make the heart grow fonder. Absence makes your heart grow weaker. It's very strange, but when you let happiness and peace slip away like a greased pig at the country fair like I have countless times, you forget how amazing and liberating it feels, and before you know it the Evil Queen shoves her boot up your ass and tightens the vice grip on your cojones.

The Wizard Regains His Strength

Imagine if Toto closes the curtain to the Wizard of Oz. The wizard goes back into hiding behind the curtain, and consequently Dorothy and the others forget that Mr. Oz is a weaselly old geezer who's all brag with a limp dick. He has nothing to back up his blustery threats, but when Dorothy and the others lose focus, the wizard regains power, and they become frightened of him once again, but NOT because he gained power—but because Dorothy loses focus.

Have you ever lived through a hurricane? When I lived in Florida I lived through several. For a few days, the city is in the grips of a monstrous storm. Nobody thinks about the good times of last week's blue skies and sunny days. They lose sight of pleasant weather. All they can see is the storm.

The same happens when you lose focus on how weak and anemic the Evil Queen is. When you lose sight of her weakness like you lose sight of blue skies and sunny days, then all you can see is her power, and hence she regains control.

The Evil Queen's only chance to control you is if you take your eyes off the blue skies and sunny days of your inexplicable transcendent supernatural peace

The good news is that for as long as you speak the 1225 words with **the power of your tongue** then she remains pitiably weak, and you continue to swim upstream, but she remains weak only for as long as you unleash 1225 words by **the power of your tongue**.

Listen carefully, if you neglect the 1225 words and **the power of your tongue** for too long, then Will Smith and Tommy Lee Jones in *Men in Black* zap you with the memory zapper that wipes out your remembrance of what a little pissant the Evil Queen is, and you forget she's a puny little twatgoblin, and thus she regains strength over you with a fierceness that is worse than ever as she explodes with hideous strength. She slithers like a serpent up the walls of your heart as she crawls back onto your throne. She exalts herself as the ruler of darkness in heavenly places. She regains rulership over you from the highest position of authority in the universe—you're very own heart. *Your world of pain* *and sorrow becomes more real than your world of peace and joy* like in the Florida hurricane where you forget all about last week's blue skies and sunny days.

When that happens, you tumble off the throne of your exalted position. You spiral downward as if suctioned into a vortex, into the grip of the raging monster who is the wicked Evil Queen who waits for you below. She's the horrible ogre with boogers in her nose that lives under a bridge that controls illiterate minions who naively scream out to God, "Help me God, please help me!" when God clearly tells them what they must do to get his help.

How Does God Help You?

How does God help you? You must "Seek FIRST the kingdom of God so that ALL THESE THINGS will be added to you."

That's how God helps you! Anything else is wasted breath and bloviated pablum.

"Straight is the way and narrow the gate that leads into life, and few there be that find it" (Mathew 7:14).

Like a Dog Returns to His Vomit

Solomon, whom you met in the story of David and Bathsheba, said in his many wise sayings, "As a dog returns to his vomit, so a fool repeats his foolishness" (Proverbs 26:11).

Even so we are vomit-lapping dogs when we forget how good is the taste of the good life of supernatural happiness and otherworldly peace that comes solely from 1225 words and **the power of our tongue**.

Like a fool, I've returned to my vomit many times over the last forty years. It starts small. It does not happen overnight. Do you want to know how easily it overtakes you? One little worry thought, one little thought of impatience, one little thought of anger at the driver on the freeway in front of you, and before you know it you've stepped out of the warm jacuzzi into icy torrential rains and crashing waves of a vicious cyclone.

If that happens to you, don't fret. What's the answer? The answer is the 1225 words and **the power of your tongue** that I stumbled upon that sunny summer California afternoon in 1983 the day my green convertible died. Don't stray too far away from the jacuzzi though. Come a-runnin' back to the warm waters!

"Speak the words…I'm right here."

Scene 75

Trap Your Thoughts

You must…I repeat, you *must*…I'll say it one more time, YOU MUST take captive *every thought* that exalts itself against your peace and joy lest a looming catastrophe ever so subtly sneaks up on you, and that is your peaceless state of mind becomes the norm, *especially if your life is comfortable, filled with nice homes, cars, and lots of money* like what happened to me.

I've strongly and sternly warned you against this.

Don't settle for comfort! Don't let a comfortable lifestyle lie to you. Indeed, enjoy your comfortable lifestyle, but comfort will LIE to you that you're living your best life.

I repeat: *Don't let* ***comfort LIE TO YOU*** *that you're living your best life!*

Don't you dare return to the meager "comfort" of a rusty dilapidated covered wagon. Why settle for the comfort of a covered wagon when you can live in the ecstasy of a supersonic jet! However, you must diligently speak the 1225 words by **the power of your tongue** to renounce the temptation of the shallow faux comfort of the covered wagon.

Remember, if you rest in the peace that comes from the covered wagon, then your houses, cars, businesses, and careers lose their glitz and glamor. You take them for granted. You don't enjoy them as much as you did at first, and eventually you resent them because they no longer meet your expectations to make you happy. Neither do you enjoy your family and kids as much as when you're full of transcendent otherworldly peace and happiness.

Remember the four celebrities warned of impending doom if you look to material things, fame, fortune, and success to make you happy.

Remember the study of the lottery winners and their happiness set point? No matter how happy the lottery winnings made them feel, they returned to their previous happiness set point. It doesn't matter how many homes you have, fine cars, fast jets, vacation homes all over the world. The ecstasy of those blessings is temporary. You will fall back to a predetermined happiness level, a set point, like a thermostat sets the temperature in your home, like gravity pulls Michael Jordan right back down to the court.

You can only increase the temperature of your thermostat by 1225 words and **the power of your tongue**—NOT by material things.

You must persevere to continue in the ecstasy of the supersonic jet of supernatural otherworldly happiness, peace, and joy because the Evil Queen persists. *If you let down on your perseverance, she slowly seduces you with comfort.*

Resist the soft and lazy lifestyle of comfort. It's *Mediocre-Ville* compared to the ecstatic hyper-energetic life of transcendent peace and joy unspeakable and full of glory.

Be vigilant to gobsmack that weaselly, low-down scumbag girl-dog who, if she cannot conquer you with fear, worry, and anger, then she conquers you with mediocrity. Yeah, that's right—I called her a female dog, otherwise known as a buh—buh—*bitch.*

Don't let a comfortable lifestyle entice you to topple down off your throne, and thus allow the Evil Queen to switch places with you..

Indeed God wants you to take pleasure in a lavish life, and to enjoy your lifestyle in the Garden of Eden that you built by 1) happiness, peace, and joy, 2) *diligence in all your hand finds to do,* and 3) taking care of the poor, the fatherless, and the widow.

Indeed enjoy your homes, your cars, your vacations in the Caribbean, Bora Bora, and wherever else your heart desires; and don't forget your fine restaurants, your wonderful family and great kids, your jets, cars, and three vacation homes, and whatever else you want in the Garden of Eden.

BUT—*here's the stern warning:*

DON'T GET LAZY! Maintain vigilance to "seek peace and pursue it," or else your Garden of Eden becomes a faux peace with a weak foundation that turns to quicksand when the earth shakes like what happened in the Northridge earthquake in 1994, and *great is the fall* of your paper-thin empire. It happened to me. BE DILIGENT. Be diligent…be very DILIGENT to pursue transcendent peace with your 1225 words and **the power of your tongue**. "I wish I hadn't gone to the gym to get that workout," said no one *ever*. The post-workout feels great. It's the pre-workout that takes diligence.

Be diligent. Make peace and happiness a habit. Continually pursue peace.

The theme of this trilogy is *to pursue peace that transcends this natural world.* Pursue it every day. Don't let it slip. It's sooo easy to let it slip, but DON'T.

What's the protective force, the shield of faith, the breastplate of righteousness, the helmet of salvation, your feet covered with the gospel of peace? For those of you familiar with that scripture, you'll notice that every one of those metaphors are literally a man who speaks the word.

"Speak the words…I'm right here."

…like I did that sunny summer California afternoon in 1983 the day my green convertible died.

REVIEW

1) Words that you speak, especially angrily, overpower your cantankerous out-of-control bitchy self.

2) Harness the power of the Evil Queen's anger, fear of failure, worry, stress, depression, and unforgiveness. It'll magnify and enhance **the power of your tongue**.

3) Your tongue is like the rudder of a large ship, tossed about by fierce winds and crashing waves. Yes, **your tongue** has THAT MUCH POWER.

4) Seek first the keys to the kingdom. They're the PIN number that opens the door to your rich granddaddy's safe. The keys are the supernatural EMOTIONS that open the doors to the Garden of Eden, God's garden of luxury and delight. What're the supernatural emotions that are the keys that open the doors to the Garden of Eden? **Happiness**, **peace**, and **joy**.

5) These EMOTIONS are *the kingdom of God* that the Jewish rabbi says live inside you, and for you to exalt onto the throne of your heart.

6) Be diligent in all your hand finds to do.

7) Take care of the poor, the fatherless, and the widow.

Are you having fun? Get ready because I have more good news, simple news, so pack your bags, your guns, your hair dryer, a change of underwear, and pack a brown bag lunch. Get a good night's sleep. We're going on an adventure.

We ride at dawn.

INTERMISSION

Scene 76

Lipstick or Dipstick

Only two intermissions between here and the finish line.
We're on the home stretch, so let's ROCK!

How do you know if you have enough oil in your car? Check the dipstick. That's the foolproof way to ensure there's enough oil in the engine, and thus is the preemptive method to protect your engine from damage, because if there's not enough oil, your car engine dies, and it costs you a few paychecks to rebuild the engine.

If you neglect to check the engine's dipstick, and instead rely on how well your car runs to determine whether you need oil, by the time your engine runs low on oil it's too late. If you wait for smoke to billow out from under the hood, you waited too long.

Check your dipstick regularly!

Here's another salient point: Your car drives perfectly fine without oil…for a while, for days, possibly weeks. Your car feels like it runs fine, no problems, and then—BAM. You blow your engine.

Your heart also has a dipstick, a gauge to discern if you cruise with an engine full of clean oil to protect you so you don't blow your engine.

What's that dipstick? I'll tell you in a short minute.

****

How many times have you wondered if you are on the right path in life?

Check your dipstick.

And even better, how would you like to foresee your future with 100% certainty and accuracy?

Check your dipstick.

And best of all, how would you like to feel closer to God than you ever imagined, as close as if the two of you sit together at the kitchen table, he pours you a glass of two-thousand-year-old Cabernet from the wedding feast when he turned water into wine, and he tells you what his plans are for you? What a feeling of indescribable confidence that you know that he protects you, guides you, and cares for you as only the Lord of the universe can do…!!! ...and how would THAT make you feel?

Alright, we're getting into some heady stuff here, but it's really good, so let's proceed.

I asked you a moment ago, "What's your dipstick?"

So, what is it? What is your dipstick?

The **dipstick** to gauge whether you're on the right track in life is your EMOTIONS.

The **dipstick** to gauge your future success is your EMOTIONS.

The **kingdom of God's emotions** are your DIPSTICK.

Your **KINGDOM EMOTIONS** lead you and guides you into all the truth.

The **kingdom of God** is your EMOTIONS that are the DIPSTICK to examine if you're on the right path.

See how simple this is?

The dipstick to predict your future, your relationship with God, and how well you know God is YOUR EMOTIONS *of* ***happiness, peace,*** *and* ***joy****!*

Emotions are the Dipstick to Check Your Spiritual Levels

I know. It's simple…almost *too* simple, but God is incredibly simple, which is why he says you gotta be like a little child to enter into his kingdom.

Preachers, priests, shamans, gurus, and psychotherapists who prance about onstage with their complex doctrines and perplexing revelations annoy me more than the first time I peed on an electric fence. They foolishly prattle on about such nonsense that needlessly complicates the simple truths; truths so simple that you must become like a little child to understand them.

One Who Rejects the Simple Truth Holds to the Complex Lie

When one rejects the simple truth, he will embrace a complicated lie.

What is the simple truth the modern-day Pharisees reject? They ignore Jesus' simple instructions to ***seek first the kingdom of God,*** and not only do they ignore how simple it is to *force-feed* peace into men's hearts like I did that sunny summer California afternoon in 1983, but they go so far as to cry "Heretic! Heretic!" when I encourage people to embrace the Evil Queen, and to corral her evil power to magnify the power of the tongue and the 1225 words and fire away with "biblical cuss words" like a Gatling gun until she stabs her own damn self in the heart.

Hence they miss out on the simplicity of the 1225 words and **the power of their tongue**, and so they blather on with such endless mind-numbing drivel so as to convince you how to get $300 out of the ATM machine without the PIN number, and when it doesn't work, they make up stupid shit that God never said, like "Sometimes God answers 'No.'"

They've assiduously ignored God's instructions for so long they'd have to get smarter just to get stupid.

"You honor me with your lips, but your heart is far from me, because your worship is a bunch of man-made rules" (Isaiah 29:13) and now we have tens of thousands of man-made rules that parade as Sunday morning sermons that are nothing more than soggy word salad because they completely abandon the basics like Kobe Bryant and Coach Wooden emphasize, the number one most basic commandment that Jesus said, which is "Seek first **the kingdom of God** of *otherworldly, transcendent peace,"* the peace that he promised to us, the peace that is, "**My peace** I leave with you."

That's the kind of peace that exists nowhere in our third dimension *and yet it's the basics!* UCLA Coach John Wooden and the great Kobe Bryant emphasized over and over again, "EXECUTE THE BASICS!"

Anyway, my goal for you is *you don't need preachers, shamans, gurus, psychotherapist, or ME anymore*. LEARN THIS FOR YOURSELF so that you don't need me or anybody else to suckle from, and then like I told the young girl, when you achieve your purpose in life—to be happy, then you expand your purpose to teach others so that they too can be happy.

YOU BECOME THE TEACHER for all the world to hear…*and then THE END SHALL COME.*

The harvest is great, but the laborers are few. Demand the Lord of the harvest that he send more laborers into his field (Luke 10:2).

****

Scene 77

The End Cometh

Preach the kingdom, then the end shall come

"This good news of the kingdom shall be preached to all the world, and then the end shall come" (Mathew 24:14)

What means 'the end shall come'? What the heck is "the end"?

And what's more, what is the "good news"?

And what's the kingdom?

These are all great questions.

Here are the answers.

The kingdom is *supernatural happiness* and *otherworldly peace*…peace that transcends this three-dimensional world, coupled with joy unspeakable and full of glory. It's this otherworldly peace that transcends this natural world that the Prince of Peace promises to us when he says, "MY peace I leave with you."

He continues, "Not as the world gives, such as comfort, also known as 'panty-pie peace,' but the peace I leave with you is 'the peace that passes all understanding' that does not exist in your third dimension." He concludes, "That's the kind of peace I leave with you."

And that my friends, in all its simplicity, is the kingdom of God that shall be preached to all the world, and then the end shall come.

That's the kingdom of peace and happiness that I shared with the young girl that evening when I told her, "Your purpose in life is to be happy"

And when she reaches that pinnacle of happiness, peace, and joy, then she too, shall join this army of preachers who proclaim this gospel of peace to all the world, and so will you, and so will I, and when the whole world hears the simple message of WHAT the kingdom of God is, and HOW to seek the kingdom of God, and TO MAKE IT YOUR TOP PRIORITY—

THEN THE END SHALL COME!

What's "the end"?

It's the completion, the fulfillment, the end of the age.

When you fill yourself full to overflowing with *the fruit of the spirit,* also known as otherworldly peace, supernatural happiness, and joy unspeakable and full of glory twenty-four hours a day seven days a week, then you've arrived! You enter the gates of the Garden of Eden, God's garden of delight where everything you can think, dream, or imagine is yours!

Adam and Eve began in the Garden of Eden. You and I, and the young girl return to the Garden of Eden, *and that's when we'll have that big party I promised to her.*

Listen, if I hadn't held fast to the simplicity of this book for the last forty years with the determination of a bull and the innocence of a child, I wouldn't tell you to do it, but I've held fast to the purity and the uncomplicatedness of his simple command to "Seek first the kingdom of God, and everything else will be added to you."

I staunchly avoided the complex "deep revelations" for forty years. I refused to get caught up in seven-week sermon series on whatever the hell they preach about for seven weeks, because if it's not the kingdom of God, I don't give a whit what it is they preach. **The amazing simple message of the gospel of the kingdom has never let me down for four decades.**

Why complicate the simplicity of the gospel!

Years ago, when I first began to look to my emotions of joy and peace as my dipstick to gauge if I was on the right path and if my future would turn out okay, I questioned its authenticity many times like a five-year-old who asks his mom and dad on a trip to the river, "Are we there yet?"

Could life be this incredibly simple?

It seems not, but I kept God's command on the forefront of my mind, mainly **seek first the kingdom.**

That written command was the sole evidence I had because no preacher, priest, or religious person ever acknowledged, or taught me that life was as incredibly simple as I outline for you in this three-part trilogy about the power of 1225 words and **the power of my tongue** such as I stumbled upon that sunny summer California afternoon in 1983 the day my green convertible died.

And as if that wasn't the only outlandish discovery I made that day, then you add my zany idea to corral the Evil Queen's wicked emotions.

It's too much for many religious people to wrap their heads around, and their sphincter muscles stiffen up so tight that you couldn't pound a wet watermelon seed up their ass with a sledgehammer.

If you remember scene six entitled *World's Hoariest Cockblock* I warned you that the biggest enemy to this revelation is church people. Religious people. Pharisees.

They were also the rabbi's biggest cock blocks, and they'll certainly be yours too, but tell them they can take their shitty fucky little church club and stick it up their ass, which might prove to be an insurmountable challenge if you can't even hammer a watermelon seed up there.

When you know how to *forever-feed* yourself full of indescribable peace, you don't give a fuck what the Pharisees think.

****

Although God's kingdom is simple you must *be vigilant because the Evil Queen lurks in the shadows. She waits to pounce on you,* but all you gotta do is speak the 1225 words. Do it for 21 minutes. Do it daily. *Do it every day, and then SHE CAN'T TOUCH YOU.*

"Speak the words...I'm right here."

Speak the 1225 words three times through like I did that sunny summer California afternoon in 1983 the day my green convertible died.

SHE CAN'T TOUCH YOU.

It's 3675 words.

SHE CAN'T TOUCH YOU.

Takes 21 minutes.

SHE CAN'T TOUCH YOU.

The 1225 words and THE POWER OF YOUR TONGUE *force-feed* peace onto the throne of your heart so that she can't touch you!

Do it more than once. Do it every day. The more you engage in 21-minutes sessions, the more power you bring to the surface, power that has been buried deep within you, power that arises from the depths where the Prince of Peace has lain idle, covered over by the sludge, the muck, and the mire of the decades-long rulership of the Evil Queen over your heart.

But NOT ANYMORE!

The power of your tongue and his 1225 words *force-feed* peace and happiness into your heart which then mightily arises like a powerful warrior to fight your battles for you.

"Guard your heart with all diligence, make it the highest of your priorities, for out of your heart—the headquarters of your emotions—flow the mighty forces of life. Everything you do in life flows out from your heart. It is this heart of emotions that determines the course of your life. Your emotions are the forces that supercharge your life, your success, your family, and your health. They are all the things you need that pertain to life and godliness" (Proverbs 4:23, paraphrased and amplified). What does all this mean?

"Speak the words…I'm right here."

When you unleash the 1225 words by **the power of your tongue**, and add forty pounds of diligence, and you compassionately take care of the poor like when my wife Tammy and I took care of the family with eleven kids, then your potatoes au gratin turn out just as good as Chef Ima Good Cook.

That's when your dreams sneak up on you and overtake you like Usain Bolt overtakes your slowpoke slogger jogger self in Central Park.

****

"But Steve, how do I know with an absolute guarantee, and with complete certainty if I'm on the right path? Huh? Tell me…*How do I know?"*

I'm so glad you asked that question. I've asked the same question thousands of times myself, as have thousands of others, so listen…

How many times have you questioned if you're on the right path in life? Have you ever wondered if "he's the man" that you should marry? Have you ever wondered "What the hell am I gonna do, I've gotten myself into a hot-ass mess and I don't know how to get out," like what happened to me when I copied the other company's seminar script in San Francisco.

One of the most pressing questions of the ages is, "How do I hear the voice of God?"

Scene 78

Hear God's Voice

How do I hear God's directions for me?

Hundreds of times over the years I've wondered, "Are my dreams and desires trustworthy? Are they a pipe dream? Are they wishful thinking? How do I know they'll happen? Should I continue on this path? Should I change course? Should I choose something else?"

In my quest to pursue my destiny I found the simple solution, but before I tell you, I must ask: What is your first priority before you seek the answers to these questions? *What's your* FIRST *undertaking?*

Pursue the kingdom. *Pursue the kingdom.* PURSUE THE KINGDOM. When? **First, *first,* FIRST!**

How do you pursue the kingdom?

"Speak the words...I'm right here." **That's how.**

Force-feed yourself until you're full of the happiness that's been buried inside you, the suppressed peace that's buried deep inside each of us that he gifted us the day he ascended into heaven when he promised, "**MY PEACE I give to you. Not as the world gives, but MY PEACE I give to you. Therefore, don't let your heart be troubled, and do not let it be afraid**" (John 14:27).

Resurrect his happiness and his peace that's been buried deep inside you since the day you were born. Use your weapons of 1225 words and **the power of your tongue** like Clint Eastwood in *Dirty Harry* like I did that sunny summer California afternoon in 1983 the day my green convertible died to unearth this mighty kingdom.

Resurrect a megadose of peace and happiness from inside you, do it first thing before you do anything else, then check your dipstick to make sure you're filled to the brim with plenty of clean oil, and then ask yourself like I did in the empty church around the corner from my life insurance office that day in Orlando, "What do I want? Do I want a booming business? What kind of a business? Do I want a thriving career? What kind of a career? Do I want a bustling family? Do I want to lose weight? Do I want a puppy?"

What are YOUR *desires?*

Remember Psalm 37:4 that we talked about earlier, where he says *he'll give you the desires of your heart.*

"Give" is a double meaning. Think back to the husband and wife on their tenth wedding anniversary. First, the husband "gives" her the idea of a gift as he kisses her on the cheek in the kitchen at breakfast. Second, at dinner he "gives" her the gift. I was kidding that his wife haughtily bristled that her diamond was a piece of coal, but in moviemaking we call that "artistic creativity," also known as a joke.

But God's not joking when he "gives" you the idea for your desires, and then he "gives" you those desires.

Where are they?

They're in the Garden of Eden.

How do you tap into your Garden of Eden's desires so that you transfer them from the inside of you to outside of you, into your three-dimensional brick and mortar world?

How do you get your Garden of Eden from the inside of you to the outside of you so that you can walk through the door of the three-dimensional gates?

Don't faint, you've heard me say this before, but here's the key: Pursue the SUPERNATURAL EMOTIONS of happiness, peace, and joy FIRST, then be **DILIGENT** in all your hand finds to do, then TAKE CARE OF THE POOR, THE FATHERLESS, AND THE WIDOW. These all three unlock the doors to the earthly Garden of Eden, God's garden of luxury and delight.

Dayum this is curiously simple, is it not?

****

But how do you know for certain those dreams in your heart are legitimate, and therefore you can confidently rest assured they'll come to pass? Listen to this: "Let the peace of God rule like an umpire in your heart" (Colossians 3:15).

Let peace rule and make your decisions for you.

In other words when you have his supernatural abundant transcendent peace that floods you from the inside out thanks to the incredible 1225 words and **the overwhelming power of your tongue**, ask yourself these questions: "Is my dream strong? How badly do I want it? Does my dream excite me? Do I absolutely want it? I know I'll succeed, so is this what I really want?"

…and then quietly listen, like I did that day in the church around the corner from the life insurance office right down the road from Disney World in Orlando.

If your answer is "yes" to all these questions, then your dream is real, and God gave it to you, but if your dream is short-lived and you lose the excitement, then it's not, and he didn't.

It's that simple folks, *it's that simple*.

God is not so much concerned with WHAT you want, but he's intensely adamant with *HOW you get it.*

Let peace guide you and determine what direction you should go.

Now, don't be a doltish chowderhead and say to me, "God said I can have *anything* I want, right?"

Yes, that's right.

"Well then I want to be the world's greatest jewel thief."

If that's you then grab your ears firmly and pull your head out of your ass.

Listen, when you're filled with happiness and peace you can trust your desires. So again, he doesn't care what your desires are because he trusts them as real and genuine, and so should you.

Why? *Because God gave them to you.*

How can you distrust what God gives you?

He cares deeply that you achieve your dreams and desires, and that's why I've shown you over the last four hundred and fifty pages *how he says to get them.*

He wants you to achieve your dreams and desires so much more than you can imagine. Hence he gave you these emotions of happiness, peace, and joy, and gifted you the twin armaments of 1225 words and **the power of your tongue** to force-feed your heart full to overflowing with these incredible life-changing emotions who's inexplicable power and incomprehensible valor transports you away from the ills of this world like a rushing mighty wind and catapults you into *The Secret Place of the Most High.*

The Life of God Pours Out From Your Heart Into the World When You Reside in that Exalted Position of Authority

Now that you're seated together with him in heavenly places, then he smartly instructs you, "Be diligent in all that your hand finds to do," and in addition to your diligence, he says, "Take care of the poor, the fatherless, and the widow"—

Well glory be, follow these three instructions, and thereby you force yourself into the perfect position for God Almighty **to step in to supernaturally boost your efforts over and above your hopes and expectations**.

He wants badly for you to accomplish your hopes, dreams, and desires, so much so that when you seek his kingdom he intervenes to give you supercharged boosts of inexplicable interventions along the way.

Why, and how? Because when you tap into his kingdom powers of emotions, this moves your punk-ass self out of God's way, and when you remove yourself out of God's way THEN HE STEPS IN to move abundantly in your life.

Do you remember the words of the Jewish rabbi, "Whoever says to this mountain, be thou removed and cast into the sea, it shall be removed, and nothing shall be impossible to you"?

WARNING: *Do NOT assume what the mountain is until you hear what I have to say!*

Everybody I've ever heard preaches these are mountains of problems, financially dire straits, failing marriage, wayward kids, etc. etc. etc. and these are the mountains you speak to.

Bullshit. Those aren't the mountains you speak to.

Oh for Pete's sake Steve, where the hell are you taking us now?!?

Hang tight Pendejo, you'll see!

Scene 79

Move That Mountain!

You have as many as thirty-five mountains in your life that you need to move out of the way. So you've been running around like a trained seal, yelling at your mountains, "Mountain of debt, be thou removed and be thou cast into the sea."

And then you've had sickness, so you scream, "Sickness and disease, I speak to you mountains, be thou removed, and be thou cast into the sea."

And then you've had problems in your marriage, so you're shouting at the problems in your marriage, "Mountain of marriage problems, be thou removed, and be thou cast into the sea."

I'll bet nothing happened, and not because you spoke to your mountains in King James English with its infamous "thou" instead of "you." Weeks and months passed, nothing happened, so you got discouraged, threw your hands up in the air and hissed, "Fuck this faith shit!"

Then you went to church on Sunday morning, and the preacher sermonized that the reason your mountains didn't move is because sometimes God says 'No.'"

I swear if stupid was a jet he could fly, and you too, for listening to his clownish insights and childish reasonings that are weak and fleshly explanations for your stupid foolhardiness and moronic ineptitudes that senselessly disregard what God TOLD YOU TO DO, and that is, "Seek first the emotions of happiness, peace, and joy."

I'm not insulting you. I'm describing you.

Listen, it's as naïve to speak to the mountain of debt as it is to speak to the mountain of obesity. "I command you, obesity, to be thou removed and be thou cast into the sea!"

Your commitment to a low IQ is impressive.

What's the Mountain You Speak To? The Mountain is YOU!

The mountain you speak to is the mountain of your "blessing blockers" of anger, worry, fear, stress, anxiety, bitterness, and unforgiveness because these are the mountains that block your access to the promise that ALL THESE THINGS WILL BE ADDED TO YOU.

How do you get rid of that mountain? How do you speak to that mountain?

You speak to your mountain the same way I did that sunny summer California afternoon in 1983 the day my green convertible died when I screamed "biblical cuss words" into the smoggy skies of Los Angeles, and those 1225 words and **the power of my tongue** obliterated the Evil Queen's mountain, and thus resurrected the life of God who lives on the inside of me. That's how I remove the mountain and cast it into the sea.

When you rid yourself of the mountain of emotional anger, pain, bitterness, stress, worry, anxiety, and depression, then everything else takes care of itself.

How many more times must I tell you how simple this is!

Remove the mountain of YOU
so that the DESIRES OF YOUR HEART burst forth

The 1225 words and **the power of your tongue** blasts away at the mountain of your bitchy whiney self as you resurrect **God's peace that he gave to each and every one of us** that day he ascended into heaven, that day he said, "My peace I leave with you."

The two armaments of 1225 words and **the power of my tongue** brings to life the One whom Isaiah calls "The Prince of Peace," the mighty warrior who fights my battles, yet had lain strangely dormant, inactive, asleep inside me for three decades.

I blasted away the mountain that had covered my kingdom, and who should arise in power and might but THE PRINCE OF PEACE!

The power of my tongue and 1225 "biblical cuss words" aroused the peace from the innermost depths of my heart that live deep down inside of me that was covered by the mountain.

Once the mountain was removed, then the Prince rose from slumber, fought my battles, won the war, and brought home the victory.

Did I scream like a wild football fanatic at my mountain of anger to "Be thou removed and be thou cast into the sea"? Did I yell and scream, and blow snot, and scream until I'm hoarse, "Mountain of anger, be thou removed and be thou cast into the sea!" No. That's equivalented to screaming at the mountain of obesity.

What did I do? I screamed "biblical cuss words," and those 1225 words who are God himself that I unleashed into the smoggy skies of Los Angeles by **the power of my tongue** did ALL the work to blast away the mountain of ME that blocks the mighty kingdom of God.

I AM THE MOUNTAIN!!!

Yes, it's you...YOU are the mountain that blocks the manifestation of everything that you need in this life to live prosperously, abundantly, happily, in every facet of your life, from your marriage to your kids, to your pets to your business to your career to your profession, to your dreams and your goals, and your visions.

Listen to me, when you cast the mountain of YOU into the sea, then you unleash the forces of *the fruit of the spirit* that have been locked inside you since the day you were born. Those forces that are commandeered by the Prince of Peace are your mighty warriors that tackle the other thirty-five mountains.

Don't speak to the individual thirty-five mountains, unless of course you listen to dumbass preachers who tell you to.

Did Jesus speak to the mountain of debt, and cast the mountain of debt into the sea? No, he told Peter to cast a hook into the sea, and the first fish he catches there's a gold coin in his mouth. Voila! **Mountain of debt gone!**

When he told his disciples, let's go to the other side, and then a typhoon arose, did Jesus cast a typhoon into the sea? No. What did Jesus say? He said, "Peace!" Voila! Mountain of typhoon GONE.

The reason Jesus had such authority over this three-dimensional world is because he walked in the supernatural realm of peace so much so that everything he said came to pass. *Anybody care to join this kingdom?*

I am guilty in years past of screaming at mountains, casting them into the sea to the point of exhaustion, but that's like I step into the ring with Muhammad Ali when he was in his prime, and expect to kick his ass. It's like a kindergartner who tries to design a rocket ship to fly to the moon. Whether it's Muhammad Ali, or flying to the moon, you need preparation, strength, endurance, and specifically a heart full of indescribable incomprehensible peace that empowers you to, not speak to the mountain of debt, but to tell your business partner to go cast a hook into the sea, the first fish he catches, there's a gold coin in his mouth.

That's precisely why he tells you to seek first the kingdom of God, which is the same kingdom he operated in to walk in such power, might, and authority in this three-dimensional world. He tells you to seek the same kingdom that gave him power and authority over whatever stood in his way!

Speak to the ONE mountain that's blocking you from victory over the other thirty-five. *That mountain is the Evil Queen; the Evil Queen is YOU.*

When you cast that one mountain into the sea, all that remains is the real you, the prosperous you, and the powerful you that springs up out of your innermost being and thrusts you into *The Secret Place of the Most High* which then opens the doors to the Garden of Eden, and lo and behold, you look around, and all thirty-five mountains have been leveled *because you pulverized the ONE mountain.*

You can yell and scream at the mountain that blocks your ATM machine. You can fight with the ATM machine, you can kick and scream at the ATM machine, you can spit at the ATM machine, and you can yell at the ATM machine to "Be thou removed and be thou cast into the sea" as you foolishly scream, "I command you to give me $300!"

Fucker ain't moving an inch into the sea and sure as hell ain't giving you $300 until you follow the instructions to punch in the PIN code.

The same is true of all the desires of your heart.

When you punch in the PIN code of P.E.A.C.E. then you cast out the mountain, you enter the garden, you rule your world, and you are the master over your circumstances.

What the Hell Are You Waiting For?

These kingdom of emotional forces have waited patiently for thirty years for you to unlock them so they can rush onto the scene and crush your other thirty-five mountains, and thus open the doors to the desires of your heart that God promises you when he says, "Seek first my kingdom, and *all these things will be added to you."*

All these blessings are waiting patiently for you to remove the mountain of YOU—that's right, the mountain of YOU that blocks them like rust covers over an automobile. When you remove the rust all that remains is a shiny automotive machine.

When you remove the rust of the Evil Queen that is her anger, fear, worry, stress, unforgiveness, then all that remains is the wide-open spaces of the promised land, also known as *The Garden of Eden.*

Everything you hope for, dream about, and desire waits patiently for you to unleash the cords that bind them so that they can spring up, and sprint forward to overtake you like Usain Bolt overtakes you in Central Park.

God says, *"Speak the words…I'm right here."*

In other words God says, "Get the heck out of my way. *Let me do my thing.* You speak to the ONE BIG MOUNTAIN of YOU. I'll take care of the other thirty-five!"

And isn't that exactly what he implores when he says, "Seek first the kingdom of God, and all these things that the village idiots seek after—clothing, cars, homes, businesses, wives, husbands, children, farm animals—will be added to you."

Why foolishly speak to thirty-five mountains?

Annihilate the one mountain that blocks the other thirty-five.

It's YOU Dude, or Dudette if you're female … YOU are the mountain that blocks your blessings

YOU have been blocking your blessings. Yes, I said YOU have been blocking your blessings!

Get the hell out of God's way.

Happiness, peace and joy annihilate the real enemy that blocks God's power so he can unleash a flood of blessings to pour down on you like the six feet of rain on Foc-Foc Island. Who's the real enemy? YOU.

God waits patiently for you to move the mountain of yourself out of his way.

Quit with your sorry-ass explanations, your sickly reasonings, and your childish explanations for why God didn't answer your prayers when it's your own damn fault because you didn't do what Jesus told you to do. That is, make peace and happiness your first and highest priority.

And then comes the sorriest, lame-ass excuse for your disobedience, "Sometimes God tells me 'No.'"

Anybody who says "God sometimes tells me 'No'" doesn't know God except at a kindergarten level.

For instance, if you foolishly cast the mountain of obesity into the sea, God doesn't tell you, "No."

He doesn't say anything, except, "What a dumbass!" and then does a face-plant, and calls you, "Pendejo!"

The fact is, not only does God never tell you "No," but God chomps at the bit like a racehorse to say "Yes!" to intervene to help you in your life of impossibilities so he can unleash the desires of your heart.

Cut him loose and GET THE HELL OUT OF HIS WAY!

How do you remove yourself out of his way?

What are his primary instructions?

Instruction number **ONE**: Seek FIRST the kingdom of God—happiness, peace, and joy.

Where is this kingdom? INSIDE YOU. Where's he? INSIDE YOU.

Where are all your dreams, desires, wants, and wishes? INSIDE YOU.

What blocks them, and covers over them with twenty-two tons of rubble? YOUR MOUNTAIN OF THE EVIL QUEEN.

Who's the mountain of the Evil Queen? YOU ARE.

Where is the mountain of the Evil Queen? INSIDE YOU.

How do you blast through the mountain of the Evil Queen with her anger, pain, heartache, jealousy, bitterness, unforgiveness, worry, stress, and frustration? How do you bypass her? How do you dig deep inside yourself where the desires of your heart reside, and how do you get them from inside you to outside you? ARE YOU READY? *You chisel away the superfluous stone as did Michelangelo to reveal the completed version of David that only Michelangelo could see.*

ONE: *"Speak the words...I'm right here."*
TWO: *Be diligent* in all your hand finds to do.
THREE: Take care of the poor, the fatherless, and the widow.

The Completed Statue of David Awaits Inside You So Cast the Mountain of YOU into the Sea

When you arise in supernatural otherworldly peace that transcends this natural world then you hose away the mountains of mud, the muck, and the mire that covers your perfect kingdom, a kingdom that is a glistening lighthouse, an exact image of God.

When you cast the mountain of YOU into the sea, you unveil the man of power and confidence, the one who calmly states, "Cast a hook into the sea. The first fish you catch there is a gold coin in his mouth."

You arise in the power of your sparkling glistening kingdom that blasts open the doors to your dreams, your wishes, your wants, and your desires.

When you speak to the mountain with its megatons of dirt and rocks that cover your kingdom, the kingdom that is perfectly complete although buried deep down inside you so far down that very few ever find it, then you unleash the mighty you, the powerful you, the prosperous you, the abundant you, the successful you, the COMPLETED YOU that *God created in his image and likeness.*

The power of your tongue and 1225 words is the pressure washer that washes away the mountains of sludge, the swamp, and the slime that covers your beautiful kingdom that he says "is inside you."

It's like you run your four-wheeler jeep through the car wash. It's covered with mud and slime from the Colorado mountain dirt trails, but after the car wash, it comes out the other side a glistening four-wheeler that sparkles in the afternoon sun.

That's how you UNVEIL HIS CLEAN, SHINY, GLISTENING KINGDOM OF EMOTIONS.

That's how you arouse these kingdom emotions from dormancy where this kingdom has lain idle in your heart for decades.

That's how you exalt this mighty kingdom onto its rightful throne!

That's how you thrust his kingdom to take its preeminent place in the highest realm of authority known to God and man, the highest place of all, the highest of the heavenlies, that is, the authority and dominance of your very own heart, God's creation that he made in his image and likeness!

That's the God-ordained mission of the twin armaments of 1225 words and **the power of your tongue**. These two mighty forces strip away the superfluous marble like Michelangelo stripped away the marble that covered the biblical David to reveal the treasure that was hidden inside the seventeen-foot-high chunk of stone.

Michelangelo cast the mountain of the superfluous stone into the sea. You do the same. Cast the mountain of the Evil Queen with her anger, bitterness, unforgiveness, fear of failure, and the impatient cries of "When are my dreams going to happen?!?"—Cast these mountains into the sea because they're what block your blessings, and when you remove these mountains, then nothing shall be impossible to you.

Your 1225 words and **the power of your tongue** chisel away the Evil Queen's mountain of sludge that *ENTOMBS* your buried kingdom, a kingdom that is the Ark of the Covenant, the hidden treasure.

The power of your tongue is Thor's hammer that smashes away all the cement blocks of cantankerous pissy emotions, pain, suffering, depression, worry, anxiety, and stress that *cover all the jewels buried INSIDE you* to unleash the inexplicable emotions of happiness, peace, and joy that are the pearls of great value that the Evil Queen suffocates with her serpentine emotions.

These *fruit of the spirit* are the emotions that are the pearl of great value that the Jewish rabbi says sell everything, so that you can buy.

The Evil Queen's vile demons of putrid emotions are the mountain that blocks the emergence of God's kingdom from blasting forth from hidden dormancy inside you to supreme dominion outside you.

God your father, your creator implanted a complete version of himself inside you, but that treasure lies dormant, asleep, inactive, covered over by thirty tons of the Evil Queen's mountain of rubble. *How do you resurrect this impressive, commandeering, authoritative, powerful kingdom?*

Move that mountain. How do you move the mountain?

ONE: *"Speak the words…I'm right here."*
TWO: Be diligent in all your hand finds to do.
THREE: Take care of the poor, the fatherless, and the widow.

Then…LOOK OUT! Your life catapults into the upper stratospheres of glory. When you consistently carry out these three instructions then *trust your desires Mister and Missus, because your success is inescapable,* **so you damn well better make certain those are the desires you want!**

****

But once again I clearly hear your question, “But Steve, can I truly trust my desires?”

Let’s settle this question once and for all.

When my wife and I were engaged, we were bowling with some friends. She was cold, so I went to the car to get a jacket for her. On the way back inside, there was a beautiful sunset. I stopped in the parking lot, looked up into the gorgeous sky, and asked God to give me a sign to show me for sure if she was the girl I should marry, like the burning bush God gave to Moses. He didn’t give me a burning bush, but instead I heard this thought, “What do *you* want? She wants to marry you. Do you want to marry her? Then marry her. You don’t? Then don’t.”

I married her and we had twenty-five fantastic years together.

When you *force-feed* yourself full of transcendent otherworldly peace then wholeheartedly *embrace your desires and your decisions.* In other words, the *peace in your heart* accurately dictates the decisions you make, and therefore you can trust them.

Without peace, you CANNOT *100% trust your desires,* neither can you *100% trust your decisions.* However, when you *force-feed* yourself full of transcendent peace that passes all understanding that flows up from deep within you by the 1225 words and **the power of your tongue**, then your desires are as trustworthy as a morning sunrise.

When we were still married and our kids were little, my wife Tammy would lay out their clothes for them to wear. Otherwise, our son Austen would come dressed in a tennis shoe and a boot and a raincoat on a sunny day, and our daughter Natasha would come dressed in a pink tutu turned inside out. Now they’re adults. They can wear whatever they want, even a tennis shoe and a boot, and a pink tutu turned inside out.

But they don’t.

Can you trust your desires? Can you trust yourself to choose the right dreams? Yes you can, but ONLY *when you* FORCE-FEED *peace, happiness, and joy into your heart.* It’s then, and only then that you can **trust your desires** and *choose your dreams* as easily as my adult kids choose their clothes.

The peace that you *force-feed* into your heart makes you adult enough to choose good and right dreams, and adult enough that you can trust your desires, and it's as easy as picking out your clothes to wear for the day, except for some of you girls, "Babe, what should I wear? *I don't have a thing to wear."* Pick anything. You'll look great.

"Should I wear the pink tutu?"

INTERMISSION

Scene 80

God's Fiery Desires

We're on the home stretch, the final intermission!

Listen, God has two fires of desires ablaze in his belly:

One is for you to be full of *his peace*, and full of *his joy*, and full of *his happiness*. These comprise his mighty kingdom, his everlasting kingdom that is the eternal life that we preach to all the world and then the end shall come. That's his fire of desire number **ONE**.

His fire of desire number **TWO** is that God wants you to have all the *desires of your heart.* He wants you to have *all* your goodies. *He wants you to have the desires of your heart more than you want them for yourself.*

Some of you can't grasp what I just said, so I'll prove it to you.

Is it true that you want the best for your kids? You want them to be happy both now and when they become adults, right? You want them to be financially secure. You want them to have a happy marriage and a beautiful family so that you can have adorable grandchildren that you dote over, and then hand them back when it's time to change their diaper.

Not only do you want good and wonderful blessings for your kids, but how much does your heart ache when you see your children struggle under the immense burden of poverty and lack, or drugs, or sickness, and disease?

Listen to the heart of God, "If you that are evil know how to give good gifts to your children, how the heck much more will your father in heaven give good gifts to you!" That's a tweaked paraphrase of Matthew 7:11.

Think about how much *you* want to give good gifts to your children. Got it? Alright, God wants to give good gifts to you more than even you want to give good gifts to your kids. In fact, his desire to give good gifts to you is far beyond your wildest imagination.

What are his good gifts he has in store for you?

His FIRST and FOREMOST good gift is a gloriously happy heart, a transcendent peaceful heart that surpasses the ability of your mind to understand. These inexplicable emotions of transcendent peace and otherworldly happiness are what he calls "eternal life." *They are God's highest priority.* They're the kingdom of God, the eternal life that David cries out in Psalm 145:13, "Your kingdom is an everlasting kingdom!" It's this eternal kingdom of happiness, peace, and joy that is **THE PIN NUMBER** that opens the doors to unlimited access to the ATM machine.

When you resurrect this eternal life that is God's kingdom of emotions—happiness, peace, and joy—and you thrust them into their rightful position of authority to take their place as the sovereign ruler that sits upon the throne of your heart— then his pressing desire is *to lavish you with all the things you need, want, dream, and desire* in direct proportion to the supernatural kingdom forces of emotions that you awaken from within.

These fantasies are the *desires of your heart,* the long-awaited dream of "all these things will be added to you." It's the $300 the ATM spits out at you when you punch in the PIN code. **What's the PIN code?** The PIN code is the indescribable kingdom of happiness, peace, and joy. It's the hidden treasure that's buried deep within you, the secret kingdom that opens the door to the ATM machine where ALL THESE THINGS GET ADDED TO YOU, all the things that you need, want, dream, and desire.

YOUR desires and HIS kingdom are so interconnected that they are INSEPARABLE. *They are ONE.* He connects himself to your dreams via the umbilical cord of *himself. That's how generously and benevolently he desires for you to be HAPPY and for you to have ALL THE DESIRES OF YOUR HEART.*

How happy is God when you are happy? Well let me ask you, how happy are *you* when your kids are happy?

And how deeply does God feel our pain?

I ask you the same question: How deeply do you feel your child's pain when he hurts? Does your heart ache even more than your child's? Remember the times your child was sick, and how much it pained you? As for God, it's *immeasurable* and *incalculable* how horrifically he feels our pain AND happily feels our joy.

He's a good father who wants you to be happy and have good fortune. God wants the desires of your heart more than you want them for yourself.

God wants his happiness for you more than you want happiness for yourself.

God wants his transcendent otherworldly peace for you more than you want it for yourself.

God wants his SPLENDERIFIC EMOTIONS *and his* GARGANTUAN DREAMS *for you more than you want them for yourself. He wants them* so badly for you, which is why he gives you his three-step instructions so that worlds inexplicable open their doors wide for you to enter his throne room where you sit together with him in heavenly places, and it's from that position of exalted authority that you conquer all that your hand finds to do.

Here's his three-step plan of instructions for your success, happiness, and prosperity, all of which are included in the Hebrew word "peace" pronounced *shalom.*

ONE: Pursue peace by the force of your 1225 words that you unleash into the skies by **the power of your tongue**.

TWO: Take care of the poor, the fatherless, and the widow.

THREE: Be diligent in your labors, your efforts, your plans, your pursuits, your family, your fitness, your garden, your business, your farm, your manufacturing company, your acting career, your writing career, your music career, your astronaut career, your gardening career, your teaching position, your truck-driving job, your fashion business, your dog-catcher job, your cashier job at Walmart— *Whatever* your hand finds to do, do it with all your strength, and when you follow God's three-steps in his instruction manual, God promises YOU WILL PROSPER IN WHATEVER YOU DO.

I'd better quote that one for you. Here it is, and it's a quote from King David, the guy Michelangelo unearthed from deep inside the block of marble. He says, "Happy, prosperous, and wildly successful is the man who DELIGHTS himself in, immerses himself in, and bathes himself in God's instructions."

What instructions?

"Seek first the kingdom of God."

Those instructions.

And then what?

"ALL THESE THINGS that you need, want, dream, and desire WILL BE ADDED TO YOU."

Are there additional instructions? Yes, two more. "The hand of the DILIGENT makes you rich." And one more… "Take care of the poor, the fatherless, and the widow."

All these comprise the meaning of the word "delight" as in, "Delight yourself in the Lord and he'll give you THE DESIRES OF YOUR HEART."

Remember we talked about the meaning of the word "delight"?

David says, in addition to the wild success of the man who delights himself in the Lord, "He not only *delights,* but he *meditates* day and night."

That's good to hear David, but what's in store for me when I *delight* and *meditate?*

Here's what's in store for you:

You are happy, prosperous, and wildly successful in everything your hand finds to do, which leads to the inevitable promise that ALL THESE THINGS WILL BE ADDED TO YOU!

I know you won't look it up, but to those that do, you see I did an amplified version. I'm familiar with Hebrew but not proficient, but I can Google Hebrew words, and this translation is one that I concocted.

One point I want to make: The word "meditate."

The meaning of meditate nowadays compared to the meaning in Hebrew is like stale bread. The modern-day definition is "to ponder."

Not so in Hebrew. In Hebrew, "meditate" means *to mutter to oneself under one's breath loudly enough for self to hear.*

"Meditate" in English is **silent**.

"Meditate" in Hebrew is **audible**.

Well hello Sunshine, isn't that what I've blasted into your ears for the last several hundred pages? …

…speak the 1225 words…

...**speak the 1225 words**...

*"Speak the 1225 words...**I'm right here**!"*

And when you SPEAK THE 1225 WORDS loudly enough for yourself to hear, such as what means *meditate* in Hebrew "to mutter the words to yourself under your breath loudly enough for yourself to hear," then **the power of your tongue** kicks into high gear to unearth the kingdom that's buried deep inside you, and thusly *force-feeds* peace and happiness to take its rightful place on the throne of your heart like what happened to me that sunny summer California afternoon in 1983 the day my green convertible died.

When you resurrect this dramatic mighty kingdom from deep within, and thus force-feed its vast emotional powers of peace and happiness onto the throne of your heart by **the power of your tongue**, that's the kingdom of God, and it's this kingdom that opens the doors wide for you to walk through that leads straight into the Garden of Eden where ALL THESE THINGS WILL BE ADDED TO YOU.

Peace doesn't force-feed itself into you by way of the modern-day definition of "meditate" as in *to think about.* Even though "thinking" is good it's not the definition of the Hebrew word "meditate."

By the way most of the time if not all the time I quietly mutter the words under my breath, yet loudly enough for myself to hear, which is what it means "to meditate." The only time I scream them is when I'm in a raging emotional fire, or when circumstances have a death-grip on me, or I'm so frustrated that I want to blow up the world. THEN I SHOUT THEM LIKE A WILD MAN ON A MISSION. Otherwise I mutter them under my breath loudly enough for myself to hear, and they quietly perform surgery on my heart to keep my engine running in tiptop shape, filled with clean oil, firing on all 12 cylinders.

There was this one day when I was deeply tormented, my guts churned, my heart ripped wide open with sorrow, pain, and anxiety. I had no other choice but to scream the 1225 words with such a painful wretched cry that I can barely watch the video of me. I'm embarrassed for you to see this video, but I have no other choice. Many of you are going through this very same gut-wrenching pain in your life, and I'd rather be embarrassed than to allow you to go one more minute in your extreme high-level pain that few can comprehend. I can barely write about it without crying as I relive the wretched pain from that horrible day.

You can download the video of my vicious praises that I screamed with gut-wrenching violence and heart-wrenching despair that day when my heart was ripped wide open by an overwhelming flood of anguish. Go to ShittyToHappy.com to download this video that's a perfect example of our warfare, and thereby you can see how I fought with every ounce of my being when my life was hell, and I couldn't see any way out.

I must warn you though, it's gut-wrenching. It's even hard for me to watch, but it's real, it's raw, and it's where every person finds themselves at one time or another. Go to ShittyToHappy.com to **download the video** called "Gut-wrenching *Biblical Cuss Words* Video."

"Speak the words…I'm right here."

****

Scene 81

God Metamorphoses You

So we see that King David, King Solomon, and the King of kings who is the Jewish rabbi agree how you have good success. Listen, I'm no genius, but when three of the mightiest prophets in history instruct me how to succeed, I pay attention.

Just a side note, the Jewish rabbi is more than a prophet. *Much more!* He is *the Word made flesh.* Who's the Word? God is the Word. So can we conclude that the Jewish rabbi who is *the Word* made flesh is *God made flesh?*

What I'm about to say calls for a worldwide celebration. Doesn't it stand to reason that when God's highest creation—who is *you*—speaks the 1225 words, words that are the substance of the very God himself, then **the power of your tongue** kicks into high gear to convert God's words into a living, breathing, version of God Almighty inside you?

In other words, YOU are the temple wherein *the word becomes flesh* just like the Jewish rabbi is *the word made flesh.*

This might be cause for the big party I promised the young girl. Is it possible that your body assimilates the 1225 words the same as your body assimilates the wild-caught salmon? Is it possible your body turns the 1225 words into you, exactly like your body converts the wild-caught salmon into you? It's utterly and miraculously fantastic that your body alters the physical and genetic makeup of the salmon so that *the salmon becomes you,* but hold on, I'm not through, because when you speak these 1225 words, then **the power of your tongue** converts the physical and genetic makeup of the words so that *the words become you!*

Steve my head is about to explode! Yeah, tell me about it. I've been marinating on this for forty years. My head has exploded a time or two over the last four decades.

By the way, where'd the salmon go? Did it disappear into nothingness?

No, the salmon TURNED INTO YOU.

Oh. So where'd the 1225 words go? Did they disappear into nothingness? Did they fade into the skies of Los Angeles?

No, the 1225 words TURNED INTO YOU.

Steve, Steve, Steve, my head is like a pumpkin dropped from thirty feet.

Keep it together hombre, let's keep it moving.

The power of your tongue converts the 1225 words—who are God—into a living, breathing, likeness of him that is the image he created you to be, which is…what?

A duplicate of him!

[MILLIONS CHEER WILDLY WITH RECKLESS ABANDON]

Cheer people, cheer! The 1225 words that are the living God **transform into you** the same as the piece of wild-caught salmon **transforms into you.** Thus **the power of your tongue** conforms you into an exact duplicate of God your Father, who lives on the inside of you.

The Salmon and the 1225 Words Transform into YOU

Remember: When you swallow the salmon, your body goes into overdrive to change the physical and genetic makeup of the salmon to *turn it into you.*

Well holy moly sweet sassy molassy, when you swallow the 1225 words, your body absorbs the words, and then your body goes into overdrive to change the physical and genetic makeup of the words to *turn them into you.*

The 1225 words become YOU like the salmon becomes YOU.

The 1225 words become your soul, your heart, and your emotions like the salmon becomes your cells, your blood, your skin, and your bones.

Another way to say it: *The WORD becomes flesh just like THE SALMON becomes flesh.*

Albert Einstein: "Energy Can Neither Be Created nor Destroyed"

The salmon cannot be destroyed. The salmon converts into you; it transforms into your blood, cells, bones, and marrow—

Neither can the 1225 words ever be destroyed. They convert into you; they transform into your heart, soul, mind, and heart—

The 1225 words transform into your soul, your heart, your body, your brain, your mind, and your emotions so that you are the Word—who is God—made flesh.

***The power of our tongue** causes THE WORD to BECOME FLESH!*

The Word Becomes YOU Just Like the WORD Became Flesh

Wait, wait, wait Steve...are you saying that WE become THE WORD MADE FLESH?!? Nope. I didn't say it. HE did.

Listen carefully…

How did the Word become flesh, the man who walked the dusty highways of Israel two thousand years ago? By way of the womb. That's how God became a man. How did God become this man? *He spoke it into existence.* Mary said, "Be it unto me *according to your word."*

How do YOU become the Word made flesh? How does the Word become YOUR flesh? Certainly not by the way of the womb. God only needs to do that once.

So then, how does God, who is the Word, become YOUR flesh?

YOU speak it into existence. How?

By the power of your tongue—

By the power of your tongue—

BY **THE POWER OF YOUR TONGUE**!

***The power of your tongue** is God's gift to transform his 1225 words, which are him, into you so that you become a duplicate of him*

****

Follow me here because this is gonna get deeper than the deep blue sea.

Your body is the building…

…the home…the temple…

…the apartment complex that provides the residence for the 1225 words to have a place to live.

Your body is the temple in which God takes up residence in since he doesn't have a body.

God, who is the 1225 words, possesses you so that HE has a body to move about freely in your three-dimensional world.

I can already hear your question, and it's a brilliant one: *Why doesn't he just create a body for himself if he wants to walk the earth?*

Listen to me carefully: I just said HE ALREADY DID.

Whoa Steve, are you telling me that God already created a body for himself to live in so that he could walk this earth in a three-dimensional body?!?

YES!

When did he do that?

Have you been listening? He birthed himself to become the body of a man through the womb of a woman two thousand years ago. That's who the lonesome Jewish rabbi is, the man who walked the dusty highways of Israel so long ago.

He's the Good Shepherd who leaves the ninety-nine to come rescue the lost lamb, remember him?

He's the Prince of Peace who stormed the scene of my broken heart four decades ago back in 1983 on that sunny summer California afternoon the day my green convertible died, remember him?

He's the Jewish rabbi, the Good Shepherd, the Prince of Peace, the mystery man who walked the dusty highways of Israel 2000 years ago.

He's God the creator of heaven and earth, the great I AM, the One who is, was, and forever shall be...yes, he's all those attributes WITH A BODY!

There goes the sound of the screeching wheels of the speeding passenger train!

But wait…there's more to come.

How does the infinite all-knowing, all-powerful, omnipresent God live in you, possess you, and BECOME you, so that you become him with a body? *How is he you?*

How does the God of all creation transform from 1225 written words that are letters and consonants on the smudged and jelly-stained pages of a dusty bible that you picked up in a second-hand store in downtown LA into a supernatural human version of "God in the flesh," as is the Jewish rabbi?

How does God duplicate himself in your body?

How does he become you, you who is a feeble human with a frail body of flesh?

HOW DOES GOD DO THAT?!?

Sing it loud like the rockstars thunder under the stars on a beautiful summer evening in Yankee Stadium in the Bronx…

> ***THE POWER OF MY TONGUE*** *transforms the 1225 written words from the pages of the bible into my body, heart, my soul, and my mind so that I become an exact duplicate of God!*

Wait a minute Steve, did you say "We are God"?

No dumbass, I didn't say we are God. I said, "The Word who is God becomes us."

He's forever the One and Only Almighty, the Great I Am, the Alpha and the Omega, the Creator of heaven and earth and the Creator of every man, woman, and child, and yet he, the Creator, created us to look like and ACT JUST LIKE HIM!

WE'RE not him.

HE'S him.

HE becomes US.

Did I confuse you?

It doesn't matter. Speak the words. Let him do the work.

"Speak the words…I'm right here."

Wait…God…are you telling me that all I have to do is—??

"Yes, speak the words…I'm right here."

What is the power that God gives us that authorizes this transformation from a seventeen-foot-high block of marble into an exquisite, picturesque statue at the hands of Michelangelo's hammer and chisel?

The power that transforms us into the image of God is the HAMMER *of **the power of your tongue** and the* CHISEL *of his 1225 words*

In other words **the power of your tongue** transforms the 1225 words into your body and into your heart so that it births a brand-new creature called *"The Word made flesh."*

Wowsers, the sound of the screeching wheels on that speeding passenger train is deafening, but I'm getting way ahead of myself. We'll go into extensive detail in this trilogy about how God becomes YOU IN THE FLESH in the sequel. We'll dig deep into how God becomes you in the next volume of this trilogy *Shitty to Happy in 21 Minutes: THE EVIL QUEEN.*

It's simple, yet profound. It's not complex, it's easy, and it's doable, but you'll have to wait for volume two entitled *Shitty to Happy in 21 Minutes: THE EVIL QUEEN* for all the nitty gritty details.

Anyway, seek FIRST the kingdom of God by your 1225 words and **the power of your tongue** like what I did when I *force-fed* peace into my heart that sunny summer California afternoon in 1983 the day my green convertible died, and when you do then those words convert you—they *transform* you and they *transfigure* you into a formidable force that is a super-powerful magnet that pulls in from the north, the south, the east, and the west all the blessings, success, wisdom, health, and happiness in your family, your work, your business, your body, and your world.

These are the profound benefits that await you in **The Garden of Eden** *when you pursue otherworldly transcendent peace that comes from another dimension that is buried deep inside you, exactly like the Jewish rabbi told us.*

"Speak the words...I'm right here."

...like I did that sunny summer California afternoon in 1983 the day my green convertible died.

****

Scene 82

God's Gigantic Visions

This is the [DRUM ROLL, PLEASE] … this is the final scene, the grand finale in the first volume of this trilogy *Shitty to Happy in 21 Minutes: THE SECRET KINGDOM,* so let's finish up strong with God's dreams and desires that he has for you, and then take a rest before you dive into volume two of this trilogy *Shitty to Happy in 21 Minutes: THE EVIL QUEEN.*

How big are God's dreams for you? They're way bigger than you can imagine.

I'll give you an example. When your child was two years old, did she have dreams for more than a clean diaper and a drink of breast milk? Not likely. Although your baby's desires were only for a booby and a clean diaper, did you, her loving mother have bigger dreams than that for her? Yes, of course you did! A business? A rewarding career? An amazing husband? A big beautiful bustling family? A golden retriever and a Siamese cat? Three grandkids?

Even though your baby could see no further than the tip of her nose, YOU could! You could see dreams, goals, and opportunities for her that are impossible for a two-year-old to see.

It's the same with God. God sees BIG PLANS for you that *you can't see* for yourself.

He sees our big and exciting future that we cannot see.

"I know the end from the beginning" he says in Isaiah 46:10.

Can you see into your daughter's future what she cannot? Yes, you can see into her future, but not through a magical "Mirror, mirror, on the wall, what's her future, tell me all," but by your own life experiences. How often does a son or a daughter take on the business acumen of their parents? Hence, the parents can see possibilities for their kids that their kids cannot yet see for themselves.

However, God sees into *your* future way more accurately than "Mirror, mirror, on the wall." He sees your future in the multi dimensions in which he operates. He operates outside of time and space, and therefore he sees our future as easily as we see our past. If you remember, that's the seventh dimension, the one where you travel back and forth from the future into the past and can exist in all three eons AT THE SAME TIME.

God "knows your end from the beginning," and he urgently wants to show you things to come, but how? How does he show you things in your future that only he knows?

Oh my golly the answer is so astounding yet simple it'll warp your brain cells into a twisted pretzel the size of the largest one in the world ever baked by Industrias La Constancia in El Salvador on October 25, 2015. The pretzel weighed 1,728 pounds and measured 29 by 13 feet.

I Googled it.

I repeat the question: *How does God convey his big plans to you for your future that only he knows?*

I'm about to give you the easiest, yet most profound and simple answer you'd ever expect, and it can only come from a God who is complex yet simple, everywhere at all times, yet inside your mouth, all-powerful yet gives you all power.

HOW DOES GOD TELL YOU HIS PLANS THAT YOU DON'T KNOW?

Through YOUR *wishes...*

Through YOUR *desires...*

Through YOUR *ideas...*

Through YOUR *thoughts...*

YOUR *thoughts are God's whispers.* YOUR *wishes are God as he whispers in your ear.*

The desires of your heart are God's voice as he whispers to you.

YOUR ideas feel like your own thoughts, but they are *God as he softly breathes into your ear.*

When I stood in the parking lot of the bowling alley with my fiancé's jacket under my arm as I gazed at the beautiful sunset, and asked God if she's the girl I should marry, he didn't speak to me in an audible voice. He spoke to me *through my thoughts and through my desires.*

What an amazing God, a God so simple that he communicates his plans for our lives through OUR thoughts, OUR *very own desires,* OUR wants, and OUR wishes.

If what I'm saying is true, how incredibly easy is it to hear God's voice!

Pssst…it's true, and it's this easy.

If you ask a hundred people what their desires are, they'll give you a hundred different answers. How does God communicate his desires to each and every individual?

God communicates his desires through the individual's desires.

How does God tell you his desires and plans for your future?

He communicates his desires and plans for your future through YOUR VERY OWN DESIRES!

TRUST THEM.

Trust your desires! They're from God.

God tells you HIS *plans,* HIS *wishes, and* HIS *desires for you by way of YOUR wishes, YOUR wants, YOUR dreams, and YOUR desires*

Would you agree that if this is true, then God is a heckuva good God?

I'm telling you…it's true!

God communicates HIS *desires for you through* YOUR *desires!*

Listen, he's not a religion. He's not a boring church service. He's not a grumpy old man who's gonna sucker punch you whenever you f*ck up.

Yeah I know, I spelled it that way this time, and Jesus still knows what I'm saying, and he thinks I'm a pussy, but I limit myself to a handful of F-bombs, like a PG-13 movie, so this book is still PG-13.

But I digress.

He's a God that loves you. He wants the best for you. He's like a good father and mother—he wants you to be happy, because when you're happy, he's happy.

And when everybody on planet earth is happy…

…and when everyone sees how phantasmorgastically *good* God is…

…and when everyone sees how he's a good father who wants you and me, and every person on earth to be happy and enjoy life…

…and how forty years ago he tricked an unemployed, pissed-off actor to stumble headlong into an accidental discovery on a sunny summer California afternoon in 1983, a discovery that in 21 minutes we can go from *Shitty to Happy* when we use angry, cynical, vicious sarcastic praise words to rip through our broken heart like Denzel Washington in *Man on Fire* to activate God's kingdom of happiness, peace, and joy, and to *force-feed* our heart overabundantly full to overflowing, and to make our broken life whole again…

…and when we've done all this, then he invades our circumstances to give us "all these things added to us" to where life becomes fun, almost effortless, even easy, and every day is a joy to be alive. When that happens, that's when we have that big party I promised to the young girl!

****

This journey began in 1983 on a sunny summer California afternoon with a dead car battery in my green convertible. That afternoon I accidentally stumbled upon the supernatural power of 1225 words that, when you speak them with anger, they eradicate anger.

When you speak them with lust, they eradicate lust.

When you speak them with unforgiveness, they eradicate unforgiveness.

I have tested these 1225 words and **the power of my tongue** in every conceivable manner, in every way imaginable over the last forty years, all the while dodging bolts of lightning…not from God, but from my own self-loathing and self-doubt that "it can't possibly be this easy."

But it is. It *is* this easy.

I present you the best gift I could ever give you: The gift of 1225 "biblical cuss words" that are the ugly gift I brought to the cute little girl's birthday party so long ago; words that you speak by **the power of your very own tongue**, and when you do, **the power of your tongue** *forces* you to feel a transcendent peace that passes all understanding, it *forces* you into a treasure trove of joy unspeakable and full of glory, a peace and happiness that's independent of your lousy circumstances, a peace and happiness that is far beyond what you ever dreamed possible.

It is from that exalted position of authority that you rule your world, that your thirty-five mountains crumble in the most improbable ways possible, that sickness and disease dissolves out of your body, and that joy unspeakable floods your marriage, your family, your city, your church, and your world.

Seek Peace to Solve *Every Single One* of Your Problems

It is when you are seated with him in heavenly places in *The Secret Place of the Most High* that you have all the answers, all the solutions, all of the miracle working power that any human needs to conquer every problem, every situation, every pitfall, every missing piece…

…and it flows out from you like an avalanche to cover the globe and everyone you come in contact with. It is the glory of God. They feel his presence; they wonder aloud, "What just hit me?" and you tell them simply, "The kingdom of God is here."

IN CONCLUSION…

The young girl asked me, "What is my purpose in life?"

I answered her, "Your purpose in life is to be happy."

I wrote *Shitty to Happy in 21 Minutes: THE SECRET KINGDOM* so that she, and you my dear friend, could live happy, peaceful, and at rest beyond your wildest dreams in *The Secret Place of the Most High,* and thereby achieve all your dreams, desires, and wishes that are yours in *The Garden of Eden.*

****

Now that you're pumped, excited, and ready to enjoy life to the fullest…and now that you know God's *on your side*…let me insert a word of caution. I do not mean to imply that your life is effortless from here on out. Not at all. You gotta fight. You gotta fight hundreds and thousands of 21-minute battles so that you continuously lodge in *The Secret Place of the Most High* lest you spiral down hundreds of flights of stairs into the Evil Queen's dungeon. However, your fight is no longer against circumstances, people, bad situations, can't pay your bills, hate your boss at work, business is floundering…*not anymore!*

YOUR FIGHT IS AGAINST YOURSELF!

Yes you fight, but not like you have in the past.

In the past you fought to survive.

In the past you fought to keep your head above water.

In the past you fought against your boss and your coworkers.

In the past you fought against your husband, and you've argued with your kids. In the past you've fought against your backbiting friends.

In the past you've fought against sickness and disease…and drugs, and a horrible childhood, and PTSD…the list goes on forever.

But now you fight to *force yourself full* of happiness, peace, and joy so that you sit in *The Secret Place of the Most High* with the Prince of Peace, sipping a glass of Cabernet with him (or lemonade if you prefer) as you bask in his glory that is the peace that transcends this natural world.

THAT'S YOUR FIGHT!

…and then…

ALL THESE OTHER THINGS WILL BE ADDED TO YOU.

Got it? Simple.

****

But there's a thief that lurks in the shadows who plots to steal all your treasures from you. Who is this vile creature that would do such a dastardly deed? The answer is coming up faster than a speeding ticket.

Get ready for the second volume in this trilogy called…

Shitty to Happy in 21 Minutes: THE EVIL QUEEN

The road ahead is rough and rocky, so get ready!

Oh…and one more thing…

"Speak the words…I'm right here." …like I did that sunny summer California afternoon in 1983 the day my green convertible died.

I'll see you in the sequel.

ROLL END CREDITS

About The Author

This trilogy is the most daunting undertaking of my life, more than any other of my endeavors including acting in television and film, public speaking on stages around the United States and Canada, music performance in Florida State University night clubs, bars, and fraternities, to music and acting performances in a 10,000-member mega church in Los Angeles…more so than the beautiful marriage God gave me as a gift that I destroyed because of my wild dick, more so than raising two beautiful successful Godly kids…more than anything.

Over the last forty-five years my acting roles include starring in a television series with Michelle Pfeiffer called B.A.D. Cats. I played Daisy Duke's boyfriend on Dukes of Hazzard. I've spoken on stages all over the United States, and now, after an accidental discovery smacked me hard in the face back in 1983—*the secret how to be happy*—I have completed this three-part "Shitty to Happy in 21 Minutes" trilogy. Volume one is THE SECRET KINGDOM, volume two is THE EVIL QUEEN, volume three is THE GREAT INVASION.

I will take you on a journey unlike any other. When you finish these three volumes you'll discover for yourself how easy it is to force-feed peace and happiness into your heart. This method is so powerfully overwhelming that even if for some strange reason you didn't want to be happy, it matters not. When you employ this ridiculously simple method, your body and heart have no other choice but to follow you on the path to happiness.

I invite you to ride along with me on this journey. Find out for yourself. You'll come out the other side with an incomprehensible secret weapon that works every time, without fail, and lest I forget…this method procures for you *all the desires of your heart.*

Are you ready for an escapade like no other? Grab a brown bag lunch, a change of clothes, and a bottle of wine. We're going on an adventure.

We ride at dawn.

****

Also by Steve Hanks

CONGRATULATIONS! You completed volume one of the three-part *Shitty to Happy in 21 Minutes* trilogy, THE SECRET KINGDOM.

I'm excited for you to dive headlong into volume two of this three-part trilogy *Shitty to Happy in 21 Minutes:* THE EVIL QUEEN.

The third volume *Shitty to Happy in 21 Minutes:* THE GREAT INVASION is the greatest climax of love, joy, and peace you could ever imagine. It is the infestation of God's kingdom on this earth.

Both volumes will be released soon. I'll notify you when they're available.

You can visit me at ShittyToHappy.com

I'll see you there!

To contact the author, send an email to:

info@ShittyToHappy.com

www.ingramcontent.com/pod-product-compliance
Lightning Source LLC
Chambersburg PA
CBHW062354090426
42740CB00010B/1276

9798987899939